THE OXFORD HISTORY OF LIFE-WRITING

Volume 1

The Middle Ages

THE OXFORD HISTORY OF LIFE-WRITING

General Editor: Zachary Leader

THE OXFORD HISTORY OF LIFE-WRITING

Volume 1

The Middle Ages

KAREN A. WINSTEAD

OXFORD
UNIVERSITY PRESS

OXFORD
UNIVERSITY PRESS

Great Clarendon Street, Oxford, OX2 6DP,
United Kingdom

Oxford University Press is a department of the University of Oxford.
It furthers the University's objective of excellence in research, scholarship,
and education by publishing worldwide. Oxford is a registered trade mark of
Oxford University Press in the UK and in certain other countries

First Edition published in 2018
Impression: 1

Published in the United States of America by Oxford University Press
198 Madison Avenue, New York, NY 10016, United States of America

British Library Cataloguing in Publication Data
Data available

Library of Congress Control Number: 2017912235

ISBN 978-0-19-870703-5

Printed and bound by
CPI Group (UK) Ltd, Croydon, CR0 4YY

For Paul Strohm
Teacher, Advisor, Mentor
With thanks

Acknowledgements

I am deeply grateful to the people and institutions that assisted me in writing this volume. Zachary Leader, a most patient editor, supplied valuable feedback on the manuscript as a whole. I thank him and Jacqueline Norton of Oxford University Press for their advice and encouragement. The project also benefited greatly from the comments and suggestions of the anonymous readers of my proposal and manuscript.

Some of my ideas on Margery Kempe were developed during the 2014 Project Narrative Summer Institute led by Robyn Warhol and Amy Shuman; I am grateful to them as well as to my fellow seminarians for their feedback. A Professional Development Leave from The Ohio State University in 2014-15 allowed me time for writing. I have drawn strength from inhabiting the rich community of medievalists within the English Department at The Ohio State University, including Richard Green, Drew Jones, Lisa Kiser, Ethan Knapp, and Leslie Lockett. My husband, Carl Winstead, has, as ever, been a perspicacious reader; I could not have written this book without him.

Portions of the Margery Kempe section of Chapter Two first appeared in *On-Life Writing*, ed. Zachary Leader (Oxford University Press, 2015), and are reprinted by permission of Oxford University Press.

The writing of this book has renewed my acquaintance with many texts that I first met while a graduate student at Indiana University during the 1980s and thereby reminded me how fortunate I was to be at Indiana then, not least because of the presence of Paul Strohm. I dedicate this book to Paul, who has taught me so much not only about the Middle Ages but about being a scholar, a teacher, an advisor, a professional.

General Editor's Preface

'Life-writing' is a generic term meant to encompass a range of writings about lives or parts of lives, or which provide materials out of which lives or parts of lives are composed. These writings include not only memoir, autobiography, biography, diaries, autobiographical fiction, and biographical fiction, but letters, writs, wills, written anecdotes, depositions, court proceedings (*narratio* first existed not as a literary but as a legal term), marginalia, lyric poems, scientific and historical writings, and digital forms (including blogs, tweets, and Facebook entries). Some theoreticians and historians of life-writing distinguish between shorter forms, conceived of as source material, and 'life-writing proper' or 'extended life narratives' or 'formal biography and autobiography'; others distinguish between life-writing that is exemplary or formulaic, often associated with older periods, and the sort that seems or seeks to express qualities thought of as modern: authenticity, sincerity, interiority, individuality. More commonly, at least since the 1970s, theoreticians and historians of life-writing fuse or meld sub-genres, as in the neologisms 'auto/biography', 'biofiction', 'biografiction', 'autonarration', and 'autobiografiction' (this last, surprisingly, the most venerable as well as the most ungainly of coinages, having first appeared in print in 1906). The blurring of distinctions may help to account for life-writing's growing acceptance as a field of study, conforming to a wider academic distrust of fixed forms, simple or single truths or meanings, narrative transparency, objectivity, 'literature' as opposed to writing.

The larger aim of *The Oxford History of Life-Writing* is to focus and consolidate recent academic research and debate, providing a multi-volume history of this newly recognized genre. Constituent volumes will often focus on the lives of writers, but they will also consider the lives of non-writers, especially in cases when these lives have altered or influenced literary life-writing, or when they are *by* literary figures. Some attention may also be given to works about forms of life-writing, or about topics obviously related to life-writing, such as Hume's *Treatise of Human Nature* or Carlyle's *On Heroes, Hero-Worship and the Heroic in History*, or to novels and plays about real-life figures, or fictional writers, including memoirists, letter writers, and biographers.

The constituent volumes of the *History* provide selective surveys of the range of life-writing in a period, giving extended attention to the most important or influential authors and works within the genre. The advantages of contextualizing influential works through a broad survey should be clear, but individual authors will carve out their own narrative accounts of the field, in the process producing discoveries, obscure or unjustly neglected works and authors, themselves worthy of extended treatment. Although the primary focus of the *History* will be on life-writing in English, when relevant, influential works in other languages will be discussed.

Inevitably there will be variation in structure and approach from volume to volume (as well as over particulars, including decisions about old spelling or versions quoted). But all volumes will contain some discussion of the following topics: the range of life-writing in the period, in terms of different schools, traditions, types, themes, forms, and functions; detailed accounts of those writers or writings deemed most important or influential or innovative in the period, either by contemporaries, or by literary history, or by the authors of the individual volumes themselves; the production and consumption of life-writing in the period, including discussion of the nature of the audience, the rewards of authorship, and the standing of the genre; the genre's debt to the wider culture of its period, for example to dominant notions of personal identity, nationhood, political and religious authority, authorship, creativity, literary criticism, and literary value; some reference, where relevant, to developments in life-writing in contemporaneous non-English-speaking cultures and to national distinctions within the English-speaking world; and the accuracy or usefulness of influential characterizations of life-writing in the period.

Individual volumes will take clear or distinctive lines and approaches, but the *History* as a whole will not, thus avoiding both predictability and authorial constraint. Not all volumes will be structured chronologically, but all will make clear the importance of a historical understanding of the genre. All authors will be encouraged to consider the needs of a general as well as an academic audience, in keeping with the comparatively broad-based readership of the most prominent types of the genre (biography, autobiography, memoir). For similar reasons, strong narrative will be encouraged, as will the avoidance of abstruse terminology. The seven volumes in the series are divided along roughly traditional literary-historical lines, though there may be some overlap between adjacent volumes and some innovation both in nomenclature and in beginning and ending dates, particularly in the case of later volumes.

Zachary Leader

Contents

Introduction

Historians of biography and autobiography have long treated medieval life-writing as peripheral. Those who have considered medieval life stories at all have tended to view them as mostly exemplary, plucking their subjects down to bare types of good or bad conduct rather than fleshing them out into individuals. In that view, the formulas and conventions that dictate the narration of lives allow little room for creativity or experimentation. Thus, in 1930, Donald Stauffer conceded a single thirty-two-page chapter of his *English Biography Before 1700* to the eight centuries from 700 to 1500, declaring that

Biography as an art was static in the Middle Ages. The Latin models for the chroniclers and hagiographers were fixed, and developments or modifications in the practice of writing lives were rare. Mediaeval English biography...will here be described as something comparatively solid, permanent, and unchanging, as a background for the diversity and richness of the biographies written in England after the Renaissance.[1]

To Stauffer, medieval biographies are 'impressive' only for 'their mass and their uniform cast and purpose', while 'their relation to modern life-writing is slight'. Recent studies are less hostile but hardly more expansive. The entry on 'Biography and Autobiography' for the Oxford Bibliographies includes not a single work of scholarship on medieval authors or texts, even though 'biography' is described liberally as 'the writing of another's life story' and 'the interpretation of another's life'.[2] Under the heading 'Major Life Writers and Narratives', the sole representative of medieval Europe is the *Book of Margery Kempe*. In the Modern Language Association's *Teaching Life Writing Texts*, Kempe is likewise the only medieval author who rates a mention.[3]

Both medievalists and non-medievalists have tended to the view that medieval forms of life-writing were too alien from the modern genres of biography and autobiography to bear useful comparison; indeed, many aver that the very sense of self that undergirds those genres was absent or at least incomprehensibly Otherwise. To be sure, 'the medieval "self" is not the modern "self"',[4] but then again the postmodern self is not the modern self, either. Indeed, to many in the twenty-first century, the nature or even the existence of 'selfhood' is far from clear. Today scholars are expanding the study of life-writing beyond narrow definitions of 'biography' and 'autobiography' to accommodate the forms—from blogs to YouTube videos to biopics—that express the selves of the present. 'There are no rules for biography', Hermione Lee writes.[5] In the same spirit, it is appropriate to look backwards and reconsider the forms that expressed the selves of the medieval past, when boundaries between fiction and nonfiction were fluid and authors both entertained multiple realities—spiritual, bodily, virtual, visionary, imagined—and creatively negotiated the relationships among them. To do so is neither to argue that medieval people were 'just like us' nor to argue that medieval life-writing is, as Stauffer thought, valuable only as 'background' to more interesting and more modern texts. It is only to assert—as I think is true—that recent thinking about life-writing and the cultural ideas implicit in it can be applied usefully to medieval texts, and conversely that consideration of medieval texts can enrich and extend our thinking about life-writing.

Medieval authors were fecund writers and theorizers of lives. They reflected on the stages of lives and considered whether body, soul, or some collaboration of the two is most responsible for how people act. They experimented with ways of telling life stories, either their own or others'. Some medieval life stories proceed chronologically, while others disregard temporal sequence or even coherence. Lives unfold in dialogues, in debates, and in visions. Many claim to be factual, even those that are patently fictional or polemical. Some are amply documented with letters or other texts written to, by, or about their subjects. To be sure, the Middle Ages yielded nothing resembling the hefty tomes suffused with footnotes and photographs that fill the 'Biography' sections of bookstores today. Nonetheless, during the medieval period, we encounter the distant ancestors of many of our own diverse biographical forms: tabloid lives, literary lives, brief lives, revisionist lives, lives of political and religious heroes, memoirs, fictional lives, and psychologically-oriented lives that register the 'virtual realities' experienced by their subjects.

In the following pages, I shall survey important prototypes in late antique sources, including passions of the martyrs and lives of the desert fathers, Augustine's *Confessions*, and Boethius's *Consolation of Philosophy*. Subsequent chapters will explore the variety of life-writing that blossomed in the Middle Ages: Anglo-Latin lives of missionaries, prelates, and princes; high medieval lives of scholars and visionaries; late medieval lives of authors and laypeople; and much more. Though my focus is England, I shall consider Continental authors and texts—Boccaccio, Petrarch, Christine de Pizan, the *vidas* of the troubadours, the letters of Abelard and Heloise— both to demonstrate the range of medieval life-writing and to indicate important prototypes of later forms. Along with recognized classics of medieval life-writing, I shall consider a few works—for example, *Beowulf*—that most readers today do not think of as life-writings. The quantity of medieval materials is staggering, and I in no way claim to be comprehensive. My own expertise and interests inform this book, which focuses on life *stories*, that is, works that narrate all or a large portion of their subjects' lives and thus are most nearly related to modern autobiography and biography.[6] To maintain a close parallel with modern biography and autobiography, I focus on writings about historical persons, but I am less interested in whether their lives are 'accurately' reported than with *how* they were reported. To make this study more accessible to scholars outside medieval studies, I shall quote primary texts in modern English; where available, I cite translations that include the originals on facing pages.

Imitation was the cornerstone of the principal medieval genre of biography, the form of religious biography known as hagiography.[7] Christian martyrs imitated Jesus Christ by professing his message and dying for it; non-martyred saints, or confessors, likewise imitated him by professing (or 'confessing', hence the term) that message, but also imitated Christ's suffering by enduring illness and practising asceticism. Incidents from saints' lives echoed incidents from Christ's life. In the first surviving martyr legend, dating from the second century, the martyred bishop Polycarp of Smyrna was 'a sharer with Christ' who was betrayed by a member of his own household and brought before an official named Herod, and who rode a donkey into Smyrna on the Sabbath, recalling Christ's entry into Jerusalem.[8] Hagiographers routinely claimed that their subjects prophesied, walked on water, calmed storms, fed the hungry, healed the sick and disabled, exorcized demons, excoriated hypocrites, and even performed resurrections. No matter if they had to invent the parallels. As Gregory of Tours theorized in the sixth century, it is more accurate to speak of the *life* of the saints, or *vita sanctorum*, than the *lives* of the saints (*vitae sanctorum*) because the lives of the blessed all manifest Christ's life.[9] Borrowing incidents from the Gospels and from other saints' lives merely drove home that fundamental truth. Only in this sense, for this sub-species of medieval biography, were lives 'fixed'.

Athanasius of Alexandria, in his life of the fourth-century desert father Anthony, established a prototype for telling lives of the confessors that would persist throughout the Middle Ages and be adapted to many classes of holy people, from recluses to bishops, abbots, and missionaries.[10] An 'Antonian' life relates its subject's virtuous childhood, entrance into religious life, performance of miracles, struggles against demonic and human enemies, and holy death. Influential examples include Sulpicius Severus's life of Martin, Bishop of Tours (d. 397), and Gregory the Great's life of Benedict of Nursia (d. *c.*547), founder of the monastic order that bears his name. Although the Antonian model remained highly popular, as did the tendency to conform the lives of both martyrs and confessors to a universal *vita sanctorum*, other approaches that laid less stress on miracles and more on individualizing detail also arose. Paulinus's life of Ambrose of Milan (d. 397) and Possidius's life of Augustine of Hippo (d. 430) focus on specifics of their subjects' accomplishments and experiences in the way that modern readers expect of biographies.[11] Miracles, though present, are less important than the bishops' participation in church councils and their campaigns against heretics. Holiness was indicated through their effectiveness as preachers, writers, debaters, and politicians—in short, through their achievements on behalf of the institutional Church.

Just as we can broadly divide the modes of relating saints' lives into universalizing and particularizing, we can, in broad terms, divide the subjects of medieval hagiography into two kinds of saint: historical figures whose lives are more or less well documented and figures who are either wholly fictional or attested only by an inscription on a monument or a passing reference in a chronicle, and whose life stories are therefore unknown.[12] Saints of all kinds were invented or elaborated out of nothing more than a name in a list, including martyrs, bishops, popes, abbots, missionaries, and royals. Some categories—virgin martyrs, for example—were so well populated that they constitute recognizable subgenres of hagiography.[13] In addition to borrowing from the Bible to construct lives for fictive saints, hagiographers borrowed liberally from each other—and not only incidents and passages. The corpus of hagiography includes lives that are identical in all but the name of the protagonist! Lives were concocted for various purposes—for example, to entertain and edify, to advance a political agenda, or to provide a suitable background for newly discovered relics.

As we shall see in later chapters, medieval writers and audiences express an awareness of the distinction between fiction and documentable fact, between ahistorical and historical, but in the practice of producing and consuming hagiography, they rarely observe these binaries. Fictional and historically attested saints commingle in the liturgical calendar and in the popular anthologies. Moreover, though it is usually true that the lives of invented saints tend to be 'generic' in plot and content, and that the greatest reliance on witnesses and documentation is found in the lives of historical figures, exceptions abound. The lives of some historical figures who are solidly documented—Thomas Becket, for example, or Edward the Confessor—have also been reinvented in narratives that are nearer to what we now call historical fiction than to biography, and that conform more nearly to generic expectations than their actual careers did. On the other hand, fictional saints such as Katherine of Alexandria were, especially in the later Middle Ages, sometimes provided biographies that are long, circumstantial, and abundantly documented through the simple expedient of inventing both 'facts' and the sources for them.

Hagiography influenced other forms of biography in the Middle Ages, especially royal biography. Indeed, some sovereigns, such as Oswald and Edward the Confessor, were venerated as saints. But it was also common for royal biographers to use hagiographical conventions simply to underscore a ruler's goodness, as Asser did in his *Life of Alfred* (893). The royal biographer had to borrow judiciously, though, for the secular responsibilities of a sovereign were at odds with the otherworldliness that was laudable—even expected—in a saint. Some royal biographers, indeed, used hagiographical conventions obliquely to disparage their subjects, couching criticism of their ineptitude in praise for their piety.

The ancient world furnished congenial models for royal biographers in Plutarch's *Parallel Lives* and Suetonius's *Lives of the Caesars*. Elements of these classical texts combined with appropriate hagiographical elements to form the secular equivalent of the *vita sanctorum*, a 'life of the kings' that covered a ruler's background, public career, virtues, habits, and death. A paradigm of kingly virtue is readily discernible in most royal biographies, one that emphasized mercy, justice, chastity, and prudence. The good king loved peace even if he had to make war; he took counsel before taking action. Like sacred biographers, certain royal biographers were strongly conventional, borrowing heavily from pre-existing sources to transform headstrong conquerors into peace-loving purveyors of justice and mercy. Others, however, chose historical accuracy over convention. Rulers, like saints, were invented—and very convincingly. In narrating his biography of King Arthur, Geoffrey of Monmouth mimicked the style and tone of scrupulously researched royal biographies composed by his contemporaries, so much so that both those contemporaries and subsequent generations could scarcely credit the scale of his fabrication.

Medieval autobiography was relatively rare—before the twelfth century, we find no more than autobiographical moments within larger works, as in Bede's *Ecclesiastical History* (731). Augustine's *Confessions* (c.400) and Boethius's *Consolation of Philosophy* (c.525) were important influences. Guibert of Nogent explicitly models his *Monodies* (1115) on the *Confessions*, while Petrarch's *Secret* (c.1350) takes the form of a dialogue between himself and Augustine that emphasizes the parallels between their lives. In his *Testament* (c.1449), John Lydgate alludes to incidents in the *Confessions* and presents himself as an Augustinian figure. The *Consolation*, a dialogue between Boethius and Lady Philosophy that takes place on the eve of Boethius's execution, only briefly relays the events leading up to his condemnation; mostly it deals not with the particulars of his life but with how he ought to think about it. When Boethius complains that he has been the victim of an amoral Lady Fortune, who makes people prosper or fail regardless of merit, Philosophy replies that, if Boethius learns indifference to the 'gifts' Fortune bestows—fame, wealth, status, etc—she cannot harm him. As we shall see in Chapter Four, medieval literati frequently relayed their lives, or portions of their lives, through Boethian dialogue. Petrarch, as I noted earlier, conversed with Augustine, Christine de Pizan with Lady

Philosophy, and Thomas Hoccleve with an unnamed old man. These authors, it seems, longed to tell their stories—but without wholly revealing themselves. Dialogue allowed them to create a disclaimable 'self' that, as a literary character, could not be equated with the writer, along with the interlocutor as a second self who challenges the first self's interpretation of life.

I have already mentioned that the focus of this book will be life narratives written in England; however, it will not attempt to be an exhaustive survey of even medieval English life narratives. Instead, it will examine in turn what I see as the most essential and/or the most interesting facets of that topic. Thus, Chapter One addresses the most prolific class of medieval biographers, career religious, as they wrote about themselves and each other. Chapter Two treats three important lives of religious English women—important not because women's lives such as these, intimate and circumstantial, were common, but because they were rare. Chapter Three treats the major form of secular biography, the king's life, while Chapter Four examines the medieval antecedents of literary biography and autobiography. Chapter Five looks at anthologies of brief lives, one of the commonest forms of medieval life-writing, and at how such anthologies used life-writing to express themes and points of view. Finally, Chapter Six deals with four fictional lives that show medieval authors experimenting with, adapting, and expanding the conventions of life-writing.

1

Career Religious

By far the most common subjects of medieval biographies were men and (to a significantly lesser degree) women in religious vocations. The preponderance of religious is hardly surprising: most medieval biographers were also career religious, and hence more likely to have the resources, the training, and the time to record the lives of late colleagues than any others. Bishops and abbots often commissioned these lives, usually from somebody who knew the subject personally or had experience as a biographer, but the motives for producing them varied. Monasteries used life stories to publish the deeds and virtues of deceased denizens whose reputation for holiness might enhance the prestige of their institutions and so draw patronage, pilgrims, and new members. Lives were also meant to instruct and inspire other religious, while some were commissioned in response to 'popular' demand. For example, the ambush and slaying of Boniface while on a mission to Frisia in 754 shocked friends and admirers in England, who clamoured to know more about their fallen compatriot;[1] similarly, a sensational death combined with a controversial career appears to have inspired the unprecedented flurry of biographical activity that followed Thomas Becket's death in 1170: fourteen lives published within twenty years of the archbishop's murder in Canterbury Cathedral.[2] Yet another motive for producing biographies, from the thirteenth century onwards, was for inclusion in the official dossier that the papacy required for any candidate being put forward for canonization.[3]

Many medieval biographers knew their subjects personally as colleagues, friends, disciples, or family members. Many others were associated with their subjects' religious institutions and thus knew people who knew them. An ability to write from experience was naturally a desideratum in the eyes of those who solicited biographies. Bishop Eadfrith commissioned the earliest biography of an Englishman, that of Cuthbert of Lindisfarne (d. 687), from one of Cuthbert's fellow monks. Bishop Wilfrid's first biographer was a colleague, Bishop Æthelwold's a former student, and Archbishop Dunstan's a member of his staff. Five of Becket's earliest biographers knew him; two witnessed his death, and one of those two tried to shield him from the assassins' blows. Where an appropriate biographer could not be found among the deceased's acquaintances, a reputable professional might be recruited. During the eleventh century, for example, numerous English abbeys enlisted Flemish expatriates to write, or rewrite, the life stories of holy men and women associated with their institutions.[4] Beginning around 1100, many religious wrote what might be described as memoirs of late colleagues, that is, lives that are about the authors as well as about their subjects.

It is no surprise that the overwhelming majority of biographies about historical persons, religious or otherwise, written by (near) contemporaries were written in Latin, the lingua franca of medieval Europe and the language of learning. Two authors of Latin lives do claim to have translated Old English originals that have not come down to us,[5] and a handful of lives written in French survive.[6] However, no surviving lives about near-contemporary holy people were originally composed in Middle English, though many Latin lives of early religious were translated into English, particularly during the fifteenth century.

This chapter will examine the rich and varied approaches that early biographers took to writing the lives of their contemporaries or near-contemporaries, then turn to explore the demands for greater accuracy and intimacy that induced a major shift in biography writing during the eleventh and twelfth centuries, when authors and their readers were demanding both a more rigorous adherence to 'fact' and a more probing study of the subjects' character, emotions, and spirituality. In the final section of this chapter, I will turn to the Continent, where in the twelfth century the earliest medieval experiments in autobiography were being produced, to examine the stories that two abbots and two abbesses told about themselves.

Pre-Conquest Biography: Methodologies

From the inception of biography in England in the late seventh century, English biographers asserted their commitment to accuracy, laying out their methodologies in terms that seem startlingly modern.[7] The anonymous Lindisfarne monk who wrote Cuthbert's biography entreats his readers 'not to think that I have written anything except what has been received on good authority and tested'.[8] When the Venerable Bede rewrote and elaborated the anonymous *Life of Cuthbert*, he also elaborated his predecessor's claims of accuracy: 'I have not presumed to write down anything concerning so great a man without the most rigorous investigation of facts' and 'the scrupulous examination of credible witnesses'.[9] He goes on to explain that, in researching every stage of Cuthbert's life, he consulted the bishop's colleagues and acquaintances and took notes on everything they said. After sharing a draft of Cuthbert's life with those who had known him, Bede says, he amended the text 'in accordance with their judgment' before submitting it to the Lindisfarne elders and teachers for their approval.[10] In the same vein, the eighth-century writer Felix asserts that he 'would not presume to write something about so great a man' as the hermit Guthlac 'without an exact inquiry into the facts', while Felix's contemporary Willibald assures readers that he 'learned the facts' about the missionary Boniface 'from holy men who lived in daily contact with him and who, therefore, knew his manner of life and were in a position to recall those details which they have heard or witnessed'.[11] Also writing in the eighth century, Huneberc of Heidenheim claims to report about her kinsman Willibald, Bishop of Eichstatt (not to be confused with Boniface's biographer), only 'facts which have been ascertained and thoroughly investigated'; her chief source, she says, was Willibald himself, who relayed his experiences to her in the presence of two deacons who can vouch for the accuracy of her reporting.[12] She even remembers the date she met with Willibald and the deacons: 20 June, the day before the summer solstice. Though most of her narrative is in the third person, occasional lapses into the first person suggest that she reported at least some—and perhaps most—of the material just as she heard it.

Rudolph of Fulda recounts at length his frustrating pursuit of reliable information about Leoba, Abbess of Bischofsheim. Writing in the 830s, some decades after Leoba's death in 779, he drew chiefly on records left by 'venerable men' of their conversations with four of Leoba's pupils.[13] But making sense of those records was a nightmare. Rudolph describes wrestling with the detritus of one of his sources:

A holy priest and monk named Mago, who died about five years ago, was on friendly terms with these women [i.e. the late Leoba's pupils] and during his frequent visits to them … he was able to learn a great deal about her life. He was careful to make short notes of everything he heard, but, unfortunately, what he left was almost unintelligible, because, whilst he was trying to be brief and succinct, he expressed things in such a way as to leave the facts open to misunderstanding and provide no basis for certainty. This happened, in my opinion, because in his eagerness to take down every detail before it escaped his memory he wrote the facts down in a kind of shorthand and hoped that during his leisure he could put them in order and make the book more easy for readers to understand. The reason why he left everything in such disorder, jotted down on odd pieces of parchment, was that he died quite suddenly and had no time to carry out his purpose.[14]

Rudolph was left to sift through 'scattered notes and papers' to reconstruct the events of Leoba's life, combining the facts he garnered from written sources with the verbal testimony of those who knew, or at least knew *of*, her to produce what he claims is a trustworthy life.[15]

Assurances such as these, which can be found in almost all lives written about historical persons by their (near) contemporaries, suggest that medieval readers expected biographies to be factual and carefully researched, much as we do. Medieval biographers, for their part, would seem to have been in the habit of conducting interviews, gathering documentary evidence, and, where feasible, cross-checking the information they obtained against other sources. And many—perhaps most—of them probably did. Yet we cannot take their truth-claims entirely at face value. The anonymous Lindisfarne monk who composed the earliest *Life of Saint Cuthbert* copied his preface word for word from Sulpicius Severus's *Life of Saint Martin*, including the fervent wish that readers not think 'that I have written anything except what has been received on good authority and tested' and the declaration that 'I would rather hold my peace than state what is false'.[16] When, about a decade later, Stephen of Ripon composed his *Life of Saint Wilfrid*, he recycled Cuthbert's recycled preface, truth-claims and all. These authors and others routinely copied descriptions of their subjects' deeds and virtues directly from other lives. Guarantees of diligent inquiry and scrupulous veracity were themselves tropes, to be used as needed along with other conventions. Even authors who fabricated almost all of their information availed themselves of those tropes. Commissioned *circa* 1016 to write the life of Ecgwine, the eighth-century bishop of Worcester and founder of Evesham Abbey, who survived only as a name in some charters, Byrhtferth of Ramsey declares, 'I shall not insert my own writings here, but rather things I found in ancient charters, or which I heard from reliable witnesses; for it is clear that it is a sin to speak and to tell a lie.'[17]

Historical veracity, after all, was not the only thing—or even necessarily the main thing—that medieval readers demanded. Because most of the abbots, abbesses, bishops, missionaries, and other clerics whose lives were recorded were being represented as saints, readers would expect them to adhere to the universal *vita sanctorum* discussed in the Introduction to this book: they would expect a saint to display certain virtues; they would expect his or her life to commence with a pious childhood and conclude with a holy death; and they would expect plenty of miracles, especially miracles with biblical precedents such as healings, exorcisms, and prophecies, perhaps even a resurrection or two. Authors and their patrons were also interested in purveying moral lessons and spiritual truths and in advancing political, social, or religious agendas. To serve those ends—or perhaps simply to relay a more compelling story—biographers were willing to alter, elide, and even invent 'facts'. Even the most scrupulously researched medieval biographies inhabit the nebulous border between what we call 'fiction' and 'nonfiction'.

Tradition and Innovation

Perhaps not surprisingly, the earliest life of an Englishman, the anonymous *Life of St. Cuthbert*, adheres most rigorously to hagiographical convention and borrows most liberally from prior lives. In commissioning Cuthbert's biography, Bishop Eadfrith hoped to promote for England a saint on a par with widely venerated Continental saints such as Martin of Tours (d. 397).[18] Drawing copious parallels between Cuthbert and his would-be peers was an obvious means to that end. Following prestigious Continental models, the anonymous English biographer organized Cuthbert's life into four books, each devoted to a stage of his life—his life before becoming a monk, his life as a monk, his life as a recluse, and his life as a bishop.[19] To show Cuthbert as Saint Martin's peer, the author presents him, *literally*, as a Martinian bishop. In a passage copied almost verbatim from Chapter Ten of Sulpicius Severus's *Life of Saint Martin*, he avers that, after becoming a bishop, Cuthbert 'continued with the utmost constancy to be what he had been before; he showed the same humility of heart, the same poverty of dress, and, being full of authority and grace, he maintained the dignity of a bishop without abandoning the ideal of the monk'.[20] Isidore of Seville's description of a good bishop furnished the author's elaboration of Cuthbert's qualities.[21] Passages describing the ascetic practices of Saint Anthony and the virtues of Saint Silvester were applied, word for word, to Cuthbert.[22] Who could doubt that such a man deserved a place of honour among the blessed?

Following Sulpicius Severus's approach to writing his *Life of Saint Martin*, Cuthbert's anonymous biographer offers few specifics about his religious career and many accounts of his miracles. Most of these are drawn from hagiography's stock of standard cures, though the author occasionally adds local colour by specifying where they occurred—'on the hills near the river which is called the Leader', at 'a place called Chester-le-Street', etc.[23] In the tradition forged by Athanasius and Sulpicius Severus, the author compares Cuthbert to biblical predecessors, even in incidents he declines to narrate: 'I omit...how when dwelling in camp with the army...he yet lived abundantly all the time and was strengthened by divine aid, just as Daniel and the three children.'[24]

The eighth-century *Life of Saint Guthlac* by an author known only as 'Felix' is another strongly conventional biography. Just as the anonymous Lindisfarne monk (and later Bede) aimed to create in Cuthbert England's equivalent to Saint Martin of Tours, the archetypal bishop, Felix sought to shape Guthlac into England's Saint Anthony of Egypt, the archetypal desert father. He did so by borrowing heavily from Athanasius's *Life of Saint Anthony*. Guthlac had an Antonian childhood, youth, and adulthood. He followed an Antonian diet, performed Antonian miracles, and, like

Anthony, fled the cities to do battle with the devils inhabiting the wilderness. Guthlac's 'desert', the isle of Crowland in the Midland fens, though moister than Anthony's, is populated by the same kinds of raucous demons who once badgered, bullied, beat, tortured, and tempted the desert father.

Yet Felix veers from his model in his development of Guthlac's character by supplying details of Guthlac's comportment and even his inner life. Where Athanasius merely states that Anthony is loved by all, Felix enumerates the qualities and deeds that inspired the devotion of others, recounting specific incidents that show Guthlac being a good friend, a fond brother, a loving protector of animals, a dedicated teacher, and a compassionate healer of bodies and souls. He also describes Guthlac's failings. As a young man, Guthlac abandoned his childhood ambition to become a monk and instead became a soldier. In that role, he 'devastated the towns and residences of his foes, their villages and fortresses with fire and sword', and 'amassed immense booty'.[25] But military success brings inner turmoil: after nine years of fighting, Guthlac finds himself 'storm-tossed amid the uncertain events of passing years, amid the gloomy clouds of life's darkness, and amid the whirling waves of the world'.[26] An epiphany comes as he is lying in bed after a hard day of soldiering, where his 'wandering thoughts were…as usual anxiously contemplating mortal affairs in earnest meditation'. In the spirit of the Old English elegies, he reflects upon the meaning of life—or, more accurately, the *meaninglessness* of the life he has been living:

When, with wakeful mind, he contemplated the wretched deaths and the shameful ends of the ancient kings of his race in the course of the past ages, and also the fleeting riches of this world and the contemptible glory of this present life, then in imagination the form of his own death revealed itself to him; and, trembling with anxiety at the inevitable finish of this brief life, he perceived that its course daily moved to that end. He further remembered that he had heard the words: 'Let not your flight be in the winter neither on the sabbath day.' As he thought over these and similar things, suddenly by the prompting of the divine majesty, he vowed that, if he lived until the next day, he himself would become a servant of Christ.[27]

This is, to my knowledge, the most extended passage of soul-searching in early Anglo-Latin biography. Felix reveals Guthlac's state of mind in similar detail when he later describes him as a young hermit on the verge of losing confidence in the vocation he is pursuing:

He began to despair about what he had undertaken, and turning things over in his troubled mind he knew not in what place to rest. For when he remembered that the sins he had committed in the past were of immense weight, it seemed to him that he could not be cleansed from them. He began indeed to despair so utterly that he thought he had undertaken an infinite and insupportable labour.[28]

Thus, as he moves Anthony's desert to the fens of Mercia, he transforms Athanasius's ascetic into an introspective and fallible man of God.

Felix, like Bede and Cuthbert's anonymous biographer, apparently has no scruples about filling with stock miracles a work for whose accuracy he strenuously vouches. Another early biographer, however, an anonymous monk at Whitby Abbey writing a life of Pope Gregory the Great (d. 604), expresses more ambivalence. At the beginning of his life, the Whitby monk confesses that his research has uncovered 'few miracles'.[29] Lest their absence diminish the pope's stature in the eyes of readers, he notes that some of the greatest saints—John the Baptist, for example—were never known to have performed them. Yet these saints are by no means inferior to the wonder-workers, he argues: had they *needed* miracles to carry out the tasks God assigned them, they could doubtless have performed many. He concludes that Gregory's sanctity was proven through his teachings rather than through marvels: 'Christ avails us more as He speaks through St. Gregory than when He made the apostle Peter walk on the waves.'[30]

After such an impassioned apology, readers may be surprised to find that the author ends up relating quite a few miracles. In fact, the final third of his biography (Chapters 20–29) is a pastiche of wonders. Gregory's prayers transform a Eucharistic wafer into a bleeding finger, and his tears baptize a deceased pre-Christian emperor. Gregory certifies the authenticity of some relics by causing them to bleed. Magicians intending to harm him are struck blind. A servant sees a white dove resting on Gregory as he is composing his homilies on Ezekiel. The author anticipates that readers may recognize the miracles he has attributed to Gregory from lives they may have read of other saints and therefore suspect a swindle. They should not be 'disturbed', though, because

all saints have everything in common through the love of Christ of whose body they are members. Hence if anything we have written did not concern this man—and, remember, we did not learn about them directly from those who saw and heard them but only by common report—yet in his case we have little doubt on the whole that they were true of him, too.[31]

There is a certain irony in the Whitby monk's angst. Pope Gregory himself had composed his influential *Life of Saint Benedict* from wondrous incidents that were originally attributed to biblical patriarchs and apostles. Yet even as he followed Gregory's recipe for writing the life of a holy man, he obviously worried that what was appropriate in writing the life of a long-dead saint such as Benedict

(d. 547) would not do in writing the life of Pope Gregory, whose life was well documented and whose deeds the diligent biographer could and should uncover through research.

Those composing the lives of Anglo-Saxon missionaries frequently glossed over their subjects' miracles, declaring that there were too many to recount.[32] 'The ministry of preaching the Gospel is to be preferred to the working of miracles and the showing of signs', the English expatriate Alcuin declared in his life of Willibrord (d. 739), the earliest surviving life of an English missionary to Germany.[33] Alcuin and later biographers of missionaries wrote in part to inspire other missionaries and may have worried that saints who succeed by divine fiat would dishearten rather than hearten those who might not feel themselves quite so favoured in God's eyes. Willibald celebrates Boniface for soldiering on in the face of setbacks and disappointments:

A strange thing in the sanctity of the saints is that when they perceive that their labours are frustrated for a time and bear no spiritual fruit they betake themselves to other places where the results are more palpable, for there is nothing to be gained if one stays in a place without reaping a harvest of souls.[34]

God does not quell the storms that hinder missionaries' journeys; nor does he blind their enemies or wow crowds with exorcisms, bleeding relics, or resurrections. Boniface and his colleagues prevail through intelligence and hard work. Inspired teachers and savvy politicians, they preach, negotiate, lobby, and argue their way to victory. When necessary, they resort to force and bribes.

On the whole, early medieval biographers seem perfectly comfortable borrowing or departing from tradition as it suits them. Towards the beginning of his *Life of Saint Wilfrid*, Stephen attributes to Wilfrid the very virtues that the anonymous Lindisfarne monk attributed to Cuthbert.[35] But he proceeds to tell the story of a bishop wholly unlike the reclusive Cuthbert. Where the *Life of Cuthbert* reads like a collection of miracle stories, the *Life of Wilfrid* narrates Wilfrid's ecclesiastical career, with an emphasis on his achievements and his tribulations. Stephen details the building projects Bishop Wilfrid undertook and the luxury manuscripts he commissioned. He describes Wilfrid's ventures abroad and his triumphs as a preacher. He also offers a detailed, and intensely partisan, account of the ecclesiastical politics that consumed Wilfrid practically from the moment he became bishop of Northumbria—disputed sees, contentious council meetings, transgressions against canon law, misguided colleagues, wrong-headed kings, a spiteful queen, extended exile, and ultimate vindication. He documents his account with transcriptions of letters, petitions, and other relevant materials.

In her preface, Huneberc promises a conventional cradle-to-grave life story of the missionary Willibald with an emphasis on how he 'followed the examples of the saints and how he imitated and observed their way of life'.[36] What she delivers is a 'life' that focuses so intensively on the pilgrimage to the Holy Land and Constantinople that Willibald undertook during the 720s that it has been called 'the earliest travel-book from an English pen'.[37] Huneberc's anecdotal account of this pilgrimage is full of colourful descriptions of adventures and misadventures, including a brush with the plague, two months of blindness, dangerous sea journeys, and an encounter with an angry lion. She records strange people and customs, among them the 'stylites' of Miletus, religious zealots who lived atop high stone columns. She describes how Willibald and his travelling companions were arrested as spies en route to Jerusalem and rescued by a savvy merchant with political connections. She reports how the wily Willibald risked his life to sneak contraband balsam past inspectors in Tyre. She provides minute descriptions of the saints' shrines and the biblical sites that Willibald visited. She also describes natural wonders, from mountain peaks 'covered with snow and wreathed in banks of cloud', to a live volcano, belching flames and rumbling ominously.[38]

Huneberc's hybrid narrative—part travelogue, part biography—is truly a masterpiece of early life-writing. As startling as her focus on tourism is her deft portrayal of Willibald's idiosyncratic personality, with all its contradictions—his piety and his reckless curiosity, his yearning for adventure and his devotion to monasticism, his impulsive wanderlust and his steely self-control. Above all, his magnetic self-confidence shines through. Willibald is a man who lives very much on his own terms. But those terms are not constant. The youth who bullied his father into accompanying him on his pilgrimage mellows into a kindly teacher and mentor whom Huneberc likens to a hen clucking over her chicks.

Bede's Embedded Lives

Though I have focused thus far on free-standing lives of career religious, many lives were embedded within histories. Bede produced some of the most influential examples. Advertising his *Ecclesiastical History* (731) as an account of 'the sayings and doings of the men of old, and more especially the famous men of our own race', he tells abbreviated lives of Bishops Wilfrid and Cuthbert, Pope Gregory the Great, Abbesses Hilda of Whitby (d. 680) and Etheldreda of Ely (also known as Æthelthryth and Audrey, d. 679), and many more.[39] Life stories, Bede claims, give history its moral and didactic value by allowing readers to learn both from the good deeds of its heroes and from the iniquities of its villains. These stories he relays in many ways.

Some bishops, popes, and missionaries appear and reappear as he unfolds his overarching tale of Britain's conversion to Christianity and of the triumph of Roman Catholic over Celtic Christian practices. Through narrative interlacing, readers learn much about these individuals, particularly about their ecclesiastical careers. But Bede also recounts a variety of discrete life stories. In some of these, he focuses on matters immediately relevant to ecclesiastical history; in others, he digresses from his stated subject. Sometimes he covers the entire life of an individual, while at other times he focuses on a particular stage of life. Some lives are encapsulated in a selected incident or two. Perhaps because they treat the more recent past, a period more familiar to Bede, the concluding two books of the *Ecclesiastical History* are especially rich in inscribed biographies. These brief lives provided a major source of information for later authors wishing to honour saints such as Etheldreda with their own lives, either in Latin or in the vernacular. Several of Bede's embedded lives were extracted from the *Ecclesiastical History* by later medieval compilers and circulated in anthologies of saints' lives or as free-standing stories.[40]

Commemorating men he knew and the monastery he loved, Bede's *Lives of the Abbots of Wearmouth and Jarrow* is his most personal work, even though he never mentions himself.[41] The book is dominated by two abbots: Benedict, the founder, and Ceolfrith, his right-hand man, who shared his values and his vision. Within the story of these partners and friends, Bede recounts the stories of Eosterwine, whom Benedict appointed as what we might call the 'acting abbot' of Wearmouth because Benedict himself was so often absent on abbey business, Sigfrid, who succeeded Eosterwine when the latter succumbed to the plague, and Hwaetberht, who succeeded Ceolfrith.

Bede introduces Benedict Biscop with a hagiographical flourish, declaring that what Gregory the Great said of the Benedict who founded Benedictine monasticism holds true for the Benedict who founded Wearmouth and Jarrow: like his famous namesake, Benedict Biscop was a man of exceptional holiness from youth who rejected family, marriage, and material advancement for God's sake. Though we might expect from such a beginning the kind of conventional life Bede provided for Cuthbert, long on miracles and short on individualizing details, Bede delivers something altogether different: the particular life of a devout, talented, and ambitious individual pursuing his dream to found a great Roman-style monastery.

Each of Bede's abbots is a finely wrought individual. Benedict is a bibliophile and a connoisseur of fine art, a cosmopolitan with an eye for the latest trends. Above all, he is a Romophile, so smitten spiritually and aesthetically on his first visit to the Holy City that when he returned to England 'he devoted himself wholeheartedly and unceasingly to making known as widely as possible the forms of church life which he had seen in Rome and had come to love and cherish'.[42] As a monk and later an abbot, he took every opportunity to visit his beloved city, returning from each trip full of new ideas and laden with books, relics, vestments, and other treasures. Bede plays up those facets of Benedict's personality that made him a successful founder, showcasing his *modus operandi*. With Ceolfrith he focuses upon the practices of an expert administrator—his negotiations with the King, the Pope, and a wealthy patron for land, privilege, and wealth; his building projects; and his acquisition of fine ecclesiastical vestments, vessels, and books. Whereas Bede focuses on actions and events in the lives of Benedict and Ceolfrith, he dwells on Eosterwine's character, habits, and virtues, particularly his humility. Even after he became abbot, Eosterwine continued to sleep and eat with his fellow monks, and he was always ready to help his brothers with their work, whether ploughing, metalworking, or winnowing. Bede's account of Sigfrid deals mostly with his patient endurance of a debilitating illness; his life of Hwaetberht stresses the abbot's continuance of a tradition of culture and learning established by Ceolfrith and Benedict. Together the lives of these five abbots form a life or biography of Wearmouth and Jarrow itself: its conception, birth, growth, character, appearance, ideals, privileges, and activities.

Diverse Forms, Continuing Ideals

As these examples attest, early medieval biography was diverse in its subjects—recluses, ascetics, administrators, politicians, proselytes, reformers, and pilgrims—and in its approaches. Most biographers idealized their subjects, but others show them giving way (at least temporarily) to temptation. The balance between individualizing detail and convention also varied—even, as we have seen with Bede's treatment of the lives of Cuthbert and of the abbots of Wearmouth and Jarrow, within the *oeuvre* of a single author. Incidents borrowed from other biographies commingle with anecdotes that have the appearance, at least, of authenticity.

Just as they varied in subject and approach, pre-Conquest lives varied in form. Most focus on the saint himself or herself and unfold in chronological order, but the *Life of Gregory the Great* by the anonymous Whitby author is anecdotal, non-linear, and digressive, full of history but supplying only a few vividly rendered incidents from Gregory's life. Similarly, much of Byrhtferth's *Life of Saint Oswald* has little, if anything, to do with Archbishop Oswald. The first of its five books is essentially a life of Oswald's uncle Oda, a Benedictine monk who became Archbishop of Canterbury, while its lengthy report of the 978 assassination of King Edward amounts to an inscribed martyr story. Byrhtferth recounts Viking attacks and the ill-fated expedition led by Byrhtnoth in 991 to repel them.[43] In addition to his accounts of political figures and events, Byrhtferth recounts offbeat incidents that occurred at monasteries under

Oswald's jurisdiction. For example, he provides a touching account of a friendship between monks that survives the grave and a hilarious recounting of the mayhem that ensues when a cantankerous abbot seems to rise from the dead. Byrhtferth even indulges in literary criticism: he prefaces a long extract from a poem that Abbo of Fleury composed in Archbishop Dunstan's honour with an analysis of Abbo's metre. Not surprisingly, he describes the building of his own Ramsey Abbey at particular length. As the *Life*'s modern editor and translator points out, the many 'digressions' dealing with Benedictines, their establishments, and their supporters suggest that the *Life of Saint Oswald* is less a tribute to a particular man than to the monasticism he championed.[44]

Though most early biographies were written in prose, a number were composed in verse, and a few in both. Bede wrote a life of Cuthbert in verse and another in prose, which he later conjoined to form an *opus geminatum* ('twinned work').[45] Alcuin's *Life of Saint Willibrord*, composed some decades later, was intended from the outset as an *opus geminatum*. The prose portion, Alcuin explained, was meant for public reading and the verse for private study.[46] Byrhtferth's *Life of Saint Oswald* epitomizes a trend in the late tenth century towards highly stylized prose, rife with classical and biblical allusions, convoluted syntax, polysyllabic words, and graecisms.[47] Illustrative of this manner of writing is this passage, wherein Byrhtferth recounts Oswald coming to the attention of Archbishop Dunstan:

When no great number of months from the days of a solar year had passed by, Dunstan, the reverend servant of Christ, directed his clear gaze on to Oswald's face—not like that petulant woman who gazed at Joseph, who is said to have been stronger than the besieger of cities, but rather (as it is pleasing to record in humble words) like Christ, who gazed with kindly vision upon the Disciple [Peter] who was denying Him: thus did the great bishop gaze upon the humble Oswald.[48]

While recognizing their diversity, I also want to stress that early biographies have commonalities that attest to the shared values of the authors, their subjects, and their communities. The most ubiquitous of these is an attention to scholarship and to excellence in teaching. All of the historical figures celebrated in early medieval biography were avid scholars, and their biographers routinely provide details about the disciplines they studied and the books they read. The *Life of Leoba* is a prime example. Despite her busy schedule, Leoba makes time to deepen her learning by studying not only the Old and New Testaments but also 'the writings of the church Fathers, the decrees of the Councils and the whole of ecclesiastical law'.[49] 'Because of her wide knowledge of the Scriptures and her prudence in counsel', princes, nobles, and bishops 'often discussed spiritual matters and ecclesiastical discipline with her'.[50]

The subjects of early biography model pedagogy as well as scholarship. Boniface labours to make abstruse material accessible to average pupils by 'shrewdly spicing' his explanations 'with parables'.[51] The pragmatic Leoba, realizing that her nuns must be able to concentrate in order to learn, insists on afternoon naps and will not allow them to stay up late or to wear themselves out with rigorous ascetic practices; the women she trains become respected abbesses at other institutions. Effective instructors, like Leoba, apply passion and *compassion*. Willibald is 'a hen that cherishes her offspring beneath her wings'; his students, protected 'with the shield of his kindliness' and trained 'with gentleness and sympathy', themselves mature into distinguished teachers.[52] Enthusiasm and positive reinforcement are powerful weapons in an instructor's arsenal, as Wulfstan shows in his *Life of Saint Æthelwold*:

It was always agreeable to him to teach young men and the more mature students, translating Latin texts into English for them, passing on the rules of grammar and metric, and encouraging them to do better by cheerful words. Many of his pupils accordingly became priests, abbots, and notable bishops, some even archbishops, in England.[53]

Studiousness and effective teaching are two of the many imitable virtues that early biographers praise in their subjects. Others include humility, persistence, patience, compassion, generosity, and tolerance. Biographers rarely fail to point out that their subjects became holy by studying and imitating the holiness in others—not only in saints of old but in their colleagues and their students. Moderation is another virtue routinely praised, and one encouraged by the Benedictine rule which most early religious followed. Though biographers may indicate that their subjects engage in ascetic practices such as fasting and vigils, they do not describe those practices in detail, and they give no indication that their subjects engaged in the grisly bodily punishment and self-deprivation that became common from about the twelfth century. Nor do they attribute to their subjects the strident commitment to virginity or the deep suspicion of members of the opposite sex that would characterize biographies of religious composed later in the Middle Ages, when new trends in spirituality emerged along with new approaches to the composition of sacred biography.

New Directions

Walter Daniel, a twelfth-century monk of the abbey of Rievaulx in Yorkshire, was incensed to receive a letter from a colleague at another religious house—a certain Maurice—informing him that his life of the late Aelred (d. 1167), his abbot and close friend for seventeen years, was under attack. According to Maurice, certain readers were frankly sceptical of the miracles Daniel attributed to Aelred, of his claim that Aelred lived like a monk during the years he spent as a youth at the court of King David of Scotland, and that his corpse 'shone like a carbuncle' as it was prepared for burial.[54] Maurice suggested that Daniel rewrite his life to specify the sources for his assertions.

Daniel retorted that he would do nothing of the sort. As he already stated in the life, everything he had written about Aelred he had either witnessed himself or learned from reliable men. In fact, his account of the abbot's miracles was conservative, omitting 'very many fine things...confirmed by the verbal testimony of saintly monks'.[55] Why should he be expected to name witnesses when few other biographers did? Nevertheless, to please Maurice, he would in his letter provide the documentation his critics demanded. Daniel proceeded to name witnesses for each and every miracle he had attributed to the deceased. In one case, he admitted that he might have identified as a miracle something that in retrospect only *seemed* miraculous; but he also added several miracles not in the original life. Justifying his praise for young Aelred's monk-like behaviour was trickier. Conceding that Aelred 'occasionally deflowered his chastity', he explained that what he meant by 'lived like a monk' was that Aelred was humble, not celibate.[56] As for Aelred's corpse, Daniel had been present when the body was prepared for burial, and it had certainly seemed to glow. If his obtuse critics had any understanding of rhetoric, they would not take him to task for the 'permissible hyperbole' of comparing it to a carbuncle.[57]

The criticism of Daniel's *Life* may have been politically motivated. Aelred was a controversial figure in his lifetime, and it is hardly surprising that some would have objected to his representation as a saint.[58] But Daniel was being somewhat disingenuous in claiming that few of his contemporaries bothered documenting their claims. As Thomas Head puts it, 'attitudes toward the past and toward the writing of history were changing in twelfth-century Europe.'[59] Gone were the times when biographers could freely supplement reports of what their subjects were known to have done with fancies of what they might have done, often lifted verbatim from the lives of other holy people. By the time Daniel was writing during the 1160s, writers of sacred biography had for some decades been confining themselves more closely to what they could plausibly claim to have verified. As early as the first decade of the twelfth century, Eadmer had devoted an entire chapter to the sources for his life of Anselm, Archbishop of Canterbury. [60] Eadmer's contemporary Coleman named those who were present at incidents—particularly miraculous incidents—that he described in his *Life of Wulfstan*. Perhaps put off by demands for documentation, perhaps genuinely less impressed by wonders than their predecessors, some biographers declined to report miracles at all, claiming that there are better indicators of holiness. Writing *circa* 1100, Margaret of Scotland's confessor and biographer, Turgot, declared that he was restricting himself to the virtues that made Margaret a saint in the eyes of God–her charity, piety, righteousness, and mercy.[61] Miracles, he said, merely make a person saintly in the eyes of men.

To deflect the kind of criticism that Walter Daniel met, Adam of Eynsham expresses his outright scepticism of wonders reported to him about Hugh, Bishop of Lincoln (d. 1200). When 'certain people' relay that the recently deceased bishop's cheeks were 'red as roses', Adam protests that they must be mistaken. Indeed, as he describes the scene in his *Life of Hugh*, he and his companion, the dean of Lincoln Cathedral, are dragged ('somewhat against our will') to the bishop's bier, where they wonder at 'the fresh and ruddy hue of his face'.[62] Later, when 'several people' announce that a blind woman regained her sight after touching Hugh's body, he urges caution on the grounds that 'it was essential carefully to ascertain the truth about this and other miracles…and not have any proclaimed or published unless they were confirmed'.[63] In the case of the blind woman, he points out, 'the woman was a stranger and had perhaps pretended to be blind and lied about recovering her sight, which, in spite of being old, she had never lost'.[64] It turned out, Adam writes, that the woman's recovery was as genuine as Hugh's ruddy cheeks, but advertising his scepticism in this manner was bound to boost readers' confidence that everything in his book has been subject to equally scrupulous fact checking. Similarly, as he draws comparisons between Hugh and Saint Martin of Tours, Adam writes, 'I should perhaps beware of making Hugh resemble Martin in everything.'[65] He does not want his readers to suppose that he is following the convention of inventing parallels between a modern holy man and an established saint: if Hugh seems Martinesque, it's because he really *was* like the venerated bishop of Tours!

William of Malmesbury was the most vehement champion of a strictly fact-oriented approach to sacred biography during the first half of the twelfth century.[66] In his *Deeds of the English Bishops* as well as in his free-standing biographies, we see him grappling with his sources, vociferously contesting their methodologies, and demanding more rigour in the writing of sacred biography. Attributing to saints deeds performed by other saints is to 'retail falsehoods' about them; what is more, it shows 'contempt' for them by implying that their lives need padding.[67] William criticizes biographers for putting words in their subjects' mouths that could not have been accurately transmitted, for relying too much on 'personal authority', and for failing to corroborate their claims.[68] Where possible, he compares versions of the same incidents in different texts to remove the 'lees of untruth' and strain out 'a purified version of the facts'.[69]

Though authors commonly allowed themselves licence when writing about holy people who lived long ago, William insists that writing of those long dead requires more, not less, vigilance.[70] In the long life of Aldhelm (d. 709) that concludes his *Deeds of the Bishops*, he follows a practice akin to modern footnoting. After recounting details of Aldhelm's early life—that his father sent him to study under Hadrian, Abbot of Saint Augustine's in Canterbury; that in time he returned home to Wessex and joined Malmesbury (formerly *Meldunum*) Monastery; that he spent time as a hermit; that he took on pupils to support himself; and that, desiring to be a better teacher, he returned to Canterbury to further his education in the liberal arts— William declares, 'evidence must follow my assertions, in case my hearers doubt what I say':

That Hadrian taught him in childhood he says himself in a letter to his old master: 'To the most revered father, the respected teacher of my unformed inarticulacy, Hadrian, Aldhelm, servant of Christ's household, and suppliant foster-child of your piety, greetings,' and so forth. That he was from childhood brought up and taught in the monastery of *Meldunum* is intimated by Bishop Leuthere in the privilege by which he granted the abbey to Aldhelm: 'I Leuthere, bishop by God's grace, have been asked by the abbots that I should deign to give and grant the land called *Maldulfesbirg* to Aldhelm the priest, to live a regular life there. It is here that he was raised in liberal studies from his earliest infancy and the start of his education, and nourished in the bosom of holy mother church, and here that he has led his life.'[71]

William continues in this fashion to document the incidents he narrates. His readers, forewarned, could skip the 'evidence', just as readers today can ignore a biography's footnotes and focus on the story. The *availability* of the documentation, here as in modern biographies, may have meant more to readers than its actual content insofar as it attests to the author's scholarship.

Though William expresses scepticism of direct speech, several twelfth-century biographers purport to have scrupulously transcribed conversations and reminiscences. Eadmer, Robert Southern writes, pioneered this new use of direct speech in his *Life of Anselm*, Archbishop of Canterbury: 'Eadmer's chief claim to fame as a biographer lies in his mastery of the art of recording the spoken word in a vivid and natural way....The words he reports give the impression, and were intended to give the impression, that it is Anselm who speaks. This was more than a technique of writing. It was the stirring of a new sense of personality.'[72] Eadmer's Anselm reflects on the importance of past events in shaping the man he is now. He elaborates the psychological principles that underlie his approach to teaching, he expatiates about friendship, and he explains how he prioritizes his time. He describes his writing process and recounts his intellectual development. He acknowledges his pangs of conscience, dilemmas, and regrets. He even jokes. Adam of Eynsham's biography of Hugh is likewise full of material he claims to have transcribed verbatim from the bishop's memories of his first assignment as a parish priest to his speeches, teachings, and conversations. He relays what Hugh said about others and what others said about Hugh. He tells us that instead of swearing, Hugh would exclaim, 'By the holy nut!'[73] Lest readers mistake the direct speech he reports for the invented speech William of Malmesbury denounced, Adam constantly interjects that he is reporting what he heard himself.

Aiming for intimacy and accuracy inspired formal experimentation. Writing in the eleventh century, Bede's earliest biographer was careful not to invent anything, even though he had little information to work with.[74] Instead, this anonymous author pioneered an approach similar to the 'life-and-times' model favoured by modern biographers of authors about whom little is known beyond their own writings. Thus his narrative is rich in the history and geography of Bede's Northumbria and in facts about Bede's monastery of Wearmouth and Jarrow. The biographer uses his reading of Bede's writings as a basis for meditations on what it must have been like to be Bede—for example, to have studied at an institution with a magnificent library or to have learned to read and sing from the former arch-chanter of St. Peter's in Rome. From a description of Bede's death written by one of his disciples, he embroiders a richly textured scene of weeping monks ranged around their master's bed, putting final questions to him in sob-choked voices. Instead of inventing, then, he extrapolates. At the time of his writing, Bede's body lay in a tomb beside Cuthbert's in Durham Cathedral, attracting pilgrims 'almost equally with St. Cuthbert'.[75] But the life he wrote for Bede is nothing like the life that Bede wrote for Cuthbert. Though his enthusiasm for Bede's holiness was as great as Bede's for Cuthbert's, he expresses it without resorting to hagiographical boilerplate.

Saturated with first-person reflections and reminiscences, the biographies written by Eadmer and Adam are quite unlike anything composed before the twelfth century. Adam's narration is especially rich and textured. He conveys not just what Hugh said but what he thought and felt, as in this passage describing Hugh's first sight of Chartreuse Monastery:

He gazed with awe at this place, situated almost in the clouds, with nothing between it and the sky, and so far removed from the turmoil of the world. He realized the great opportunity it offered of living alone with God....The whole place seemed to be planned just for this. He observed the physical austerities of the inhabitants, their untroubled spirit, their freedom of mind, their cheerful countenances and the simplicity of their words. Their rule encouraged solitude, not isolation. They had separate cells but their hearts were united....He noticed these things there and also the security caused by obedience, of which many hermits are frequently deprived and so are exposed to great peril. Hugh was delighted and attracted by all this, in fact it carried him away and completely captivated him.[76]

We 'overhear' Hugh reflecting about himself in an address to God that reads like a passage from Augustine's *Confessions*: 'I marvelled at what I had been, and what I had now become. Such struggles against me, nay within me, made me often forget myself, but I remembered you.'[77] At one point, describing Hugh struggling with a difficult dilemma, Adam exclaims, 'What should he do?'; he then addresses himself directly to Hugh in a long passage that begins, 'Let us now see what you did.'[78]

These varied modes of narration may stem from Adam's sense of the magnitude—indeed, hopelessness—of his project. Though he had been Hugh's confidant and constant companion for over a decade, he admits that he did not, and could not, truly know him.[79] Nor could he presume to write Hugh's biography; it would take a life to write a life, he reflects.[80] Indeed, he concludes, he cannot hope to capture even the memory of the man that was Hugh: 'What the author has set down in writing about this astounding personality bears the same resemblance to the memories treasured in his heart as a bundle of light faggots does to the magnificent branches of a fir or cedar reaching almost to the sky.'[81]

Private Lives and Relationships

As these examples suggest, biographers of the high Middle Ages were increasingly eager to convey not just the deeds, habits, and virtues of their subjects but also their personalities and private lives.[82] To this end, they described their subjects' relationships with those closest to them, including their colleagues, disciples, friends, and family members. Wulfstan used to favour 'boys of elegant appearance' by 'fondling them with his holy hands and kissing them'; he would tell them, 'with a pleasant twinkle', about how God saved him from temptation and wet dreams.[83] Anselm helped his friend Lanfranc adjust to English customs after the Norman prelate assumed the archbishopric of Canterbury.[84] Hugh, when his father became infirm, 'used to lead him and carry him about, dress him and undress him, wash him, dry him and make his bed, and when he grew feebler and weaker, prepare his food and even feed him'.[85] Edmund of Abingdon (d. 1240) was especially close to his mother and his two sisters; indeed, were it not for his mother, he would not have pursued a career in the Church.[86]

Friendship was a subject of great interest during the twelfth century, and one of the period's chief theorists of friendship was Aelred of Rievaulx.[87] It is not surprising, then, that in writing Aelred's biography, Walter Daniel should pay particular attention to his friendships. More surprising is that he should devote a great deal of attention to one of Aelred's messier friendships: his mentorship of a wayward brother at Rievaulx. According to Daniel, this (unnamed) brother knew he was unsuited for religious life from the time he entered Aelred's monastery as a secular clerk. Aelred, however, talked him into taking vows.[88] When Daniel next mentions him, the brother, desperately unhappy, is petitioning Aelred to be released from his vows. He hates the long vigils, bad food, and rough clothing. Manual labour exhausts him. Indeed, everything about monastic life disgusts him, and he longs for the pleasures of the world. Aelred offers to relax the rule, promising better food, softer clothing, and 'every indulgence allowable to a monk' if only he will agree to 'live with me in the monastery'.[89] The man remains obdurate. All the wealth of the monastery could not entice him to remain, he replies. Yet Aelred prevails, thwarting every effort the younger man makes to abandon religious life, until the brother at last sickens and dies in Aelred's arms. Aelred has compelled him to remain a monk, but he has not convinced him to see monastic life as anything other than 'death without end'.[90] Daniel offers no suggestion that Aelred's attachment to the monk is requited; to the contrary, he allows readers to see the self-delusion and fixation that let Aelred view his friend's dying a monk as a great victory. The episode characterizes rather than idealizes Aelred.

Because post-Conquest biographers were more inclined than their predecessors to expatiate on their personal relationships with their subjects, their lives read somewhat more like memoirs than do the lives of prior centuries, where even biographers who knew their subjects—Stephen of Ripon, for example, and Bede— were disinclined to intrude into the narrative.[91] Adam of Eynsham avers that the value of his book is not as a biography of Hugh—others, after all, have written his life and done so better—but rather in its record of his first-hand observations as Hugh's confidant and constant companion for over twelve years.[92] He was, his modern editor observes, something of a 'medieval Boswell', an 'excellent raconteur' who evinced his devotion to Hugh by 'recording many authentic facts and sayings which would otherwise have been lost'.[93]

Eadmer, another proto-Boswell, presents his *Life of Anselm* as both a collaboration and a struggle with the archbishop. He explains that he began compiling his notes on Anselm's frequent reminiscences into a biography during Anselm's lifetime. Anselm read his work-in-progress, confirming and correcting the material, reordering some passages and deleting others. Then, in an apparent change of heart, he ordered Eadmer to destroy the manuscript. Eadmer complied—but not without first making a copy. He confesses to mixed feelings: on the one hand, he regretted defying the spirit of his master's command, but on the other hand, 'I was not willing to lose altogether a work which I had put together with much labour'.[94] The cause of his disobedience was more than a disinterested desire to preserve Anselm's reputation for posterity. Eadmer, like many biographers of his generation, was *personally* invested in his project; his subject's story was also his.

Occasionally biographers displace their subjects. Coleman describes the frustration he experienced on occasions when Wulfstan designated him to preach in his stead. The parishioners paid little heed to their substitute preacher, and they walked out when he broached matters that offended them. One of them, a plasterer by the name of Earnmaer,

flattered himself with the cheering reflection that it was not the bishop speaking, and that what a monk said could safely be ignored. God thought otherwise. Not much later, this same workman was standing on a contraption he used when plastering a wall; it broke, and he sustained an injury that aroused the pity of others and brought him lasting distress, for he damaged both legs. That year he spent in bed, and never afterwards did he lose the pain in his feet.[95]

This episode is all about Coleman. Wulfstan is not even present. It illustrates what Jay Rubenstein calls 'the autobiographical urge' in twelfth-century biography, the urge 'to make the story of others' lives into the story of the writer's own life.'[96]

The personal quality of narration is not confined to free-standing biographies, as evinced in Jocelin of Brakelond's *Chronicle of the Abbey of Bury St. Edmunds*. Jocelin began reporting the events that took place at his abbey in 1173, just after he became a monk there. Emphasizing that he writes from 'personal experience', he tells stories about himself and freely offers his opinions of incidents and persons.[97] One of those persons, Samson of Tottington, abbot from 1182 to 1211, figures so prominently that the *Chronicle* might almost be read as Samson's biography.[98] But it might also be read, as Brian Patrick McGuire has done, as the chronicle of a friendship, with Jocelin revealing 'his own development as a person while tracing Samson's'.[99]

The intimacy and immediacy of Jocelin's narration can be illustrated with an incident he recounts early in his *Chronicle*. The year is 1181. Abbot Hugh is dead and his successor not yet determined. Jocelin and a few friends are gathered together during 'blood-letting time', debating who would make the best abbot.[100] Jocelin judges unsuitable a monk who had in the past been generous to him and voices his support for somebody he likes less but thinks would make a better abbot. His words get back to his benefactor, who will have nothing further to do with him. Appalled that expressing his honest opinion should get him into such trouble, he commits his frustration to writing:

It remains for me to be careful in future, and if I live long enough to see the abbacy vacant again, I shall watch what I say on the subject, and to whom and when I speak, so as to avoid offence either to God by telling lies or to man by speaking out of turn.[101]

It is no wonder that this brash idealist should be drawn to Samson, then forty-six years old and serving as subsacrist. Samson practises the restraint that Jocelin knows he needs to cultivate: while Jocelin and his friends blurt out their opinions, the older monk observes, listens, and remembers. Samson also appears to share Jocelin's values, including the integrity that got him into trouble with his benefactor. When Samson becomes abbot, he refrains from appointing his best friends to high offices 'on the strength of their old association, unless they were also right for the job'.[102] Jocelin writes admiringly of Samson's seriousness of purpose, his sense of duty, his abstemiousness, and his habit of wearing shirts and breeches of haircloth rather than of wool and linen. He got to know Samson well, he says, from being his chaplain and constant companion for years.

But Samson changes—or at least Jocelin *perceives* him to change—as he settles into his abbacy. He befriends the flatterers he once disdained. He overlooks his servants' misbehaviour and does things that strike Jocelin as ill judged, if not corrupt. Jocelin is hurt by Samson's curtness and nonplussed when Samson calls him a fool for questioning his conduct in private ('That certainly silenced me, and in future I watched what I said').[103] At first, he tries to excuse or rationalize the behaviour that upsets him, but over the years he becomes disenchanted and disillusioned.[104] In his disillusionment, he delivers a searing exposé, as Daniel Gerrard put it, of 'a strategist who schemed, manipulated, terrified, bribed, and lied his way through a shifting and largely hostile political environment'.[105]

Jocelin's *Chronicle* ends abruptly in 1202. It's not clear whether Jocelin stopped writing or whether the sole surviving 'complete' manuscript was copied from a damaged exemplar.[106] In any case, the final sentence of the *Chronicle* as it has come down to us perfectly captures the cynicism of the older Jocelin and his changed attitude towards the hero of his youth. About to depart on business abroad, Samson meets with his monks, promising

that on his return he would administer everything with our advice, arrange matters justly, and restore to each man what was his due. After this discussion there was calm, but not a great calm, because 'in promises anyone may be rich'.[107]

Jocelin's portrait of Samson may not be a fair and accurate portrait of the historical abbot.[108] Jocelin does, however, offer a provocative interpretation of his friend and of their friendship and in the process draws a fascinating self-portrait. In his attempt to provide an intimate account of his abbot's character, he resembles Daniel, Eadmer, and Adam.[109] Had he not fallen out with his friend, he might have produced a narrative more like theirs, playing up Samson's piety and asceticism. As it is, he maintains a critical distance from his subject that they do not; Samson most emphatically could not be mistaken for a saint. Jocelin's documentation of changes in Samson's personality, in his own attitudes, and in their relationship resembles, to my knowledge, no other biography of the period. However, his portrait, filtered through the mixed and intense emotions of love, hurt, confusion, and resentment, is akin to Goscelin of St. Bertin's portrait of his friend Eve of Wilton, which we will be examining in Chapter Two.

Garnier's *Life of Thomas Becket*: A Literary Approach

A very different approach to life-writing is seen in the *Life of Thomas Becket* com-posed *circa* 1175 by the itinerant poet Garnier of Pont-Sainte-Maxence. Garnier combines the current zeal for accurate narration and intimate detail with a self-consciously literary approach to his material to produce a narrative that reads something like the romances popular in his native France. He boasts of having the credentials of a scholar, and he writes with the flamboyance of a performer.

Garnier claims that he began researching his life of Becket shortly after the arch-bishop's murder in 1170. He spent almost four years on the project, travelling, check-ing his facts, and interviewing those who had known Becket from as far back as his childhood, including the martyr's sister. In the spirit of William of Malmesbury, Garnier names his sources for statements that readers might doubt, and he embeds large extracts from letters and other corroborating documents. Prior narratives about Becket–'by clerks or laymen, monks or a lady'–are 'neither accurate nor complete'; as he launches into his account, he promises, 'here you can listen to the truth, the complete truth; I will not stray from the truth, not if I were to die for it.'[110]

Garnier painstakingly charts the conflict between king and archbishop–the strategies, alliances, moves and countermoves, miscalculations, misunderstandings, and betrayals–that culminated in Becket's murder. Dialogue and descriptive detail vivify his story. His audience listens in as Becket argues with first the king and later with the barons. The harrowing scene of Becket's murder is almost cinematic: we see the Canterbury monks hauling Becket from his quarters to the protection of the cathedral, certain that even the royal assassins would not violate that sacred space, while Becket shouts, 'Leave me alone!' (p. 145); the ensuing chaos as Henry's henchmen break into the church–Becket trading insults with his assailants while castigating both the monks trying to save him and the barons trying to kill him; the knights vainly trying to tug Becket back out of church and finally hacking him down before the altar; the shouts of 'Strike! Strike!' and 'King's Men!' (p. 148); the archbishop's body sprawled across the floor as the monks slop blood and bits of brain into jars; the killers ransacking the dead man's possessions–books, jewellery, chalices, vest-ments, coins. Yet the shock of the killing pales before the even more shocking prep-aration of the body for burial, as the layers of fine clothes are peeled off to reveal the vermin-infested goat's hair underwear and the body sliced by whips. The gruesome asceticism that both Becket and his biographer had mostly concealed—Thomas through fine clothing, Garnier through his politically-oriented narration—becomes terribly present, reminding readers why Becket was so much more than a politician; his daily self-martyrdom was far more horrible than his quick end at the cathedral.

Though Garnier insists that he is accurate, he does not pretend to be objective. Indeed, he repeatedly interrupts his narration to rant about the issues and to scold Becket's enemies. That the archbishop's biographer should trumpet his unequivo-cal support for Becket is hardly surprising, but what is surprising is that Garnier's harangues are often at odds with the complexity of his narrative. That is, Garnier proclaims Becket's struggle to be a simple struggle between right and wrong, Church and State, even as he narrates the more complex reality of an English Church riven by clashing values and agendas. Garnier claims that, after Becket became Archbishop of Canterbury, his character 'changed in a moment' from 'bad' to 'good'; he insists that Becket 'was now utterly transformed from his previous self'; but he shows a transformation wholly in keeping with that 'previous self' (pp. 18, 16).

Garnier, indeed, portrays Becket as a complex but consistent character. As a young man, 'he applied himself constantly to honour, wisdom and goodness. He loved hounds and hawks and secular amusements; he was noble and open-handed and had a quick clear brain' (pp. 8–9). Becoming chancellor meant living and dressing lavishly and compromising his principles to please the king (p. 11). And 'perhaps', Garnier admits, 'he may have been proud and given to vanities, as far as worldly cares and in outward appearance' (p. 9). Inwardly, though, he remained deeply pious and humble. In fact, 'the more Becket climbed in the secular world, the humbler he was at heart' (p. 10): 'he kept all his inmost self for God' and was 'chaste in body and healthy in soul' (p. 9). When he did ill in the king's service, he made 'amends privately to God at night' by exhausting himself with vigils (p. 10). He continued giving generously to orphans, widows, and poor people, and was 'holy church's right hand' insofar as he was able (p. 9).

Garnier marvels that God 'should have altered a human heart so suddenly' (p. 18)—but, as he tells the story, what shifted when Becket became archbishop was not so much his heart but his public allegiance. While chancellor he had been 'entirely [Henry's], in thought and in deed' (p. 9), and as archbishop he was equally tireless in the service of what he perceived to be the best interests of the institutional Church. Opposing Henry, moreover, was fully in keeping with the private piety that Garnier shows to have persisted despite the flamboyant displays of materialism that his role as chancellor demanded (and that he may perhaps have secretly enjoyed). Though as Archbishop of Canterbury Becket adopted extreme ascetic practices—clawing, cutting, and whipping his own flesh, for example, and demanding that his confessor scourge him—this asceticism is not so much new as an intensification of the exhausting vigils and other practices he had followed privately when chancellor. As archbishop, he was as careful to conceal his asceticism as he had been as chancellor; only the confessor who beat him and the servant who washed his sweaty, vermin-infested underclothes knew his secret. To the world, he presented himself as the quintessential prelate, wearing fine clothes, eating rich foods, and sleeping beneath expensive linen sheets. Privately, he sent his sumptuous meals to the poor and subsisted on turnips, cabbage, spices, and some diluted wine; after his attendants left him for the night, he forsook his comfortable bed to pray and sleep on the bare floor.

To my knowledge, Garnier is the first medieval biographer to experiment seriously with narrative voice. He is not telling his story along with Becket's, as Adam told his story with Hugh's, or Eadmer his with Anselm's, or Jocelin his with Samson's. Indeed, he tells us little about his personal circumstances, other than that he hails from Le Pont in France and that he is itinerant ('I shall repay [Thomas's sister] by singing her praises to everyone I meet'; 'Where ever I may journey, up the world and down' he will not forget the kindness of Prior Odo and the monks of Holy Trinity Abbey (p. 165)). He presents himself not as a person but as a personality, projecting a persona reminiscent of contemporary romances. We suspect his sincerity, much as we do Béroul's in *Tristan and Isolde* or Heldris's in *The Romance of Silence*. Like these romance narrators, he comes across as something of a buffoon and seems just a bit glib. Are we really to believe that he would rather die than lie (p. 5)? The claim seems more designed to elicit eye-rolling than confidence. He complains, 'How tired I have got, putting [Becket's] sufferings into verse, but he has repaid me splendidly' (p. 164). His survivors have, in any case: for his work, Thomas's sister gave him 'a palfrey and its trappings', including the spurs. What is more, she and her nuns fed him so well that they made him 'positively fat'. 'It was a fair throw of the dice that sent me to her house', he enthuses. The only comparably flaky narrator of medieval life-writing I can think of is the John who wrote the biography of William Marshal to be discussed in Chapter Two.

Garnier's quirky narration surely has something to do with the circumstances of its delivery, which is quite different from anything we have encountered so far. He frequently addresses himself to his auditors, and while it would not be unusual for a medieval life to be read aloud in a monastery or other religious institution, he seems conscious of his work as meant not just to edify but also to entertain a diverse audience. He has read it, he claims, many times at Becket's tomb, where his listeners would presumably have included pilgrims from various walks of life, not just the career religious who were the target audience for the other biographies examined in this chapter. In composing a story to be read to a mixed audience in a public setting, the strategies of a jongleur would be handy. Vivid scenes, brisk dialogue, and plenty of gore would keep such an audience's attention. So would a blowhard narrator. I cannot help suspecting that his partisan rants express less his personal view of the controversial figure whose story he was hired to research and write than the views of his patrons, hyped just enough to prompt the more level-headed among his audience to question his sincerity, or at least his judgment, but not enough to risk offending his partisan hosts and benefactors.

'Reinventing' Autobiography

We have observed the strongly autobiographical orientation of many twelfth-century biographies. Two *bona fide* autobiographies were also composed during the first half of the twelfth century, both in France, the first such works since Augustine's *Confessions*. Guibert, Abbot of Nogent-sous-Coucy in northern France, wrote his *Monodies circa* 1115, when he was about fifty years old. The work consists of three books.[111] The first, an account of his life from his birth up to his appointment as abbot of Nogent, is the most personal, while the second is largely a history of his monastery and the third an account of an uprising that took place in 1112 in the city of Laon.[112] About fifteen years later, Peter Abelard, once the star of the Paris academic scene, now the disgraced abbot of a poor monastery in Brittany, set down the story of his life, or, as he termed it, *The Story of My Calamities*.[113] His pretext: to comfort a friend who had fallen upon hard times by convincing him that, however much he suffered, Abelard had suffered more.

Besides both being the sons of knights, and both being middle-aged abbots of small Benedictine monasteries, Abelard and Guibert shared a keen interest in psychology evinced not only in their life stories but also in their other writings.[114] Otherwise, however, they could not have been more different. Guibert had been a Benedictine for his entire adult life; his election as abbot of Nogent-sous-Coucy was a long-awaited promotion. For Abelard, a flamboyantly controversial academic forced by scandal into religious life, the abbacy of an impoverished monastery in the Breton backwater from which he had sprung was a humiliating demotion. Guibert, as Jay Rubenstein puts it, 'led a quiet and undistinguished life'; though innovative, his historical and theological writings appear to have been 'quickly forgotten', and his *Monodies* survives only in seventeenth-century transcriptions.[115] By contrast, Abelard's philosophical and theological tracts were hotly debated by his contemporaries and survived a papal decree that they be destroyed, while his

Calamities has provided grist for storytellers from Jean de Meun in the thirteenth century to modern novelists and film-makers.[116]

The autobiographies of Abelard and Guibert are as different as the men who wrote them. Guibert follows Augustine in confessing to God his spiritual peregrinations. Abelard's exposé of his calamitous celebrity life is less a confession than a brag sheet. Guibert focuses on family and monastic life, Abelard on sex and academe. Guibert recounts his subordination *to* and Abelard his subordination *of* others. Guibert meditates on his past, while Abelard analyses his. Both authors fume over the injustices done to them, but Abelard also gloats about his triumphs. Where Guibert laments his sins, Abelard acknowledges his mistakes. Abelard expresses none of Guibert's ambivalence about self and others. His conflicts are with others, not within himself.

These differences should not, however, obscure what these works have in common: a sense of alienation from most other people permeates them both, and yet both are also shaped by their authors' intense and unorthodox relationship with another individual–Abelard's with his wife and erstwhile lover Heloise, Guibert's with his unnamed mother. In their mere existence, both belie the common view that autobiography began and ended with Augustine until it re-emerged in the eighteenth century. They more than meet the minimalist definition offered by Philippe Lejeune in 1975 of a 'retrospective prose narrative written by a real person concerning his own existence, where the focus is his individual life, in particular the story of his personality'.[117] In them we see authors engaging their past in a complex process of inventing and packaging themselves. In reconstructing their past selves they provide intimate portraits of their present selves.

Guibert's Monodies

A guiding theme of Guibert's *Monodies* (*c.*1115) is the suppression of his unruly desires and the alignment of his will to the religious life he had been called to by God and family. Though his father, who had vowed his son to the Church at birth, died while Guibert was still an infant, his mother made it her mission to guide him towards his foreordained vocation, no matter that young Guibert had little inclination towards religion. She hired a private tutor who, embracing his assignment to convert a wayward boy into an ecclesiastic, transformed the dining room into a schoolroom, dressed Guibert in sombre clothes, isolated him from other boys, and forced him to study even at weekends. Guibert's resentment is palpable. He recalls sitting on the sidelines in his 'clerical attire...like some trained animal' as other boys played (p. 14). To make matters worse, his tutor, hired more for his morals than his academic qualifications, was grossly incompetent: his grammar, learned late in life, was poor, and he was 'completely ignorant of prose and verse composition' (p. 14). Nevertheless, he was determined that Guibert should master what he did not know and could not teach. Guibert rails against the injustice of his expectations and the cruelty of his floggings, declaring, 'if he actually had possessed the ability to teach what he pretended to know, I was assuredly, for a boy my age, most capable of learning what he would have taught correctly' (p. 15). His tutor's pedagogy was misguided, he complains—all work and no play dulls the mind and engenders apathy.

Yet Guibert passed up the chance to free himself from his tormentor. When his mother, discovering his arms and back blackened from a whipping, announced that she would discontinue his education, he retorted that he would rather die than quit. His mother—apparently not as indignant at the abuse as she professed—bragged of his response to his teacher, who rejoiced at Guibert's commitment. Thus, even when he took a stand, he fell in with the will of others.

Guibert asserted himself more vigorously a few years later, when he was about fourteen. His mother had resolved to adopt a quasi-religious life in a house on the property of the monastery of Saint-Germer of Fly and persuaded Guibert's tutor to enter the monastery. Feeling himself abandoned by those closest to him, Guibert repudiated everything they cherished. He mocked the religious life he had once resolved to follow and fell in with his rowdy cousins, who were training to be knights. While his mother cut her beautiful hair and donned shabby black clothing, he decked himself out in finery to cavort with his dissolute friends. While she slept poorly on straw, he slept late.

His rebellion was short-lived, though. Learning of her son's antics, Guibert's mother arranged for him to join his former tutor at the Fly monastery, where he would have few opportunities for mischief. When he wrote raunchy poetry, his tutor recalled him to propriety. His mother made him confess his carnal 'cravings and desires' and promise to reform (p. 49). 'I always obeyed her,' he recalls (p. 49). Though Guibert took monastic vows before she and his teacher felt he was ready, he was otherwise compliant. The next time he opposed his mother's will was when, in his forties, he left the monastery at Fly to become abbot of Nogent-sous-Coucy some fifty miles away. His mother was most distressed at his promotion, citing his ignorance of 'worldly affairs', especially 'business' (pp. 66-7). Though Guibert prevailed, he admits that events proved that she was right to have had misgivings.

Guibert's mother is an extraordinary character.[118] She was, to a degree, modelled on Augustine's mother Monica. Like Augustine, Guibert narrates his mother's life story within his own, emphasizing her piety and her instrumentality in guiding him towards his religious vocation. Anecdotes illustrating her impatience with gossip and her zeal for her son's religious welfare have close parallels in the *Confessions*. But where Augustine presented a mother consumed with his salvation, Guibert reveals a woman with desires and aspirations that have nothing to do with him and that were indeed at odds with his best interests. Though she worried about her son's spiritual wellbeing, she worried still more about her own: 'Her mind constantly subjected to trial all of her previous deeds: the tribunal of her reason questioned what she had done, thought, and said while she was a virgin in her early years, when she was a married woman, and now when, as a widow, she was more able to follow her inclinations' (p. 42). Guibert complains that she *knew* that pursuing her religious vocation would leave him 'an orphan' with 'no resources to fall back on' and no one to 'tend to the needs of a boy at that tender age'; she *knew* she was being 'utterly wicked and cruel' for separating herself from her child, for 'having cast off what she had once loved' (p. 41).

Guibert is not simply recording the emotions of his adolescent self. Like most autobiographers, he is grappling with the complexity of his feelings in the present. The intensity of his descriptions indicates that, years after her death, his memory of her continued to excite contradictory passions of love and resentment. Though he denounces her for abandoning him, he understands why she did so. His feelings about his teacher similarly oscillate between love and loathing. Even as he sneers at his master's cruelty and ineptitude, he acknowledges that he acts honestly and with a genuine desire for Guibert's academic success and spiritual wellbeing. He also admits to loving him like a father—and indeed, the tutor so gained his mother's trust that he *was* in effect a parent, to the point that Guibert's relationship with each of his 'parents' appears to have been complicated by their relationship with each other.[119] Though Guibert's mother and teacher had bonded over his upbringing, their relationship grew to be about them rather than just about him. When she persuaded her son's tutor to join the Fly monastery, she was thinking of his salvation—and perhaps their friendship—rather than her child's best interests. As she lay dying, the tutor, not her sons, sat weeping beside her, and when he lamented that Guibert and his brother were absent, she replied, 'I would not want either one of them, or any of my relatives, to be present at my death' (p. 96). Guibert does not record what he felt when he heard of those words, but from his presentation of their relationship, we might infer that resentment of their closeness at least partly accounts for his bitterness towards them both.

The *Monodies* registers a fascinating 'meta' contest of wills between Guibert and his mother. As she shaped (or sought to shape) his life, he shapes (or seeks to shape) her life story.[120] By divulging nothing about her place of origin or about family, he isolates her, in a literary sense, as she had literally isolated him. He says practically nothing about her other children, writing as if he were her only child. Referring to her simply as 'my mother' further reduces her to her relationship with him. At one point he even identifies her as his 'possession' (p. 95). Other family members he dismisses as 'beasts ignorant of God' (p. 8).

And yet this unnamed woman resists appropriation, emerging in Guibert's story as one who lived as she pleased, flouting the advice of blood-relatives, in-laws, friends, and clergy while customizing the institutions of family and religious life to suit herself.[121] His 'possession' paid scant attention to his wishes—abandoning him in his boyhood and later taking the veil over his strenuous objections. She may not have been able to bend him to her will in all details, but she got her way in the main, and, he admits, she was always right. She was right to put her spiritual aspirations above his needs and right to take the veil when she did. She was right in thinking that he was rushing into a monastic career, and she was right in her mis-givings about his promotion to the abbacy of Nogent (p. 101). His *Monodies* might aptly have been subtitled *Mother Knows Best*, for his life as he presents it was an extension of her will or a vindication of her judgment.

But the greatest testimony to this woman's influence is that she shaped not only his character and his actions but also the way he thought and wrote about his life. In a sense, her life edged out his. By that I mean that he divulges almost nothing about facets of his experience or stages of his career that did not involve her. Her influence permeates everything he says about himself, as he takes care to register her approval or disapproval of everything he thinks or does, from his studies to his nascent sexual urges. He reveals only enough about his troubles at Nogent to vindi-cate her judgment that he was making a mistake to assume the abbacy. By contrast, he says much about her that has nothing to do with himself. He describes her emo-tional conflicts and dilemmas; he reports incidents and conversations that occurred before he was born. Moreover, he relays an extraordinary amount of detail about her sex life, including her frustration with her husband's impotence, her distaste for marital sex, her rejection of would-be lovers, and her near-rape by a demon.[122] As Nancy Partner put it, 'he tells *her experiences* as his memories'.[123] How are we to inter-pret the fact that, when he left her to take up the Nogent abbacy, he also left the strand of his *Monodies* that dealt with his personal life, resuming it only briefly in Book Two to recount her death? Is his autobiography the story of his liberation from the influence of his overbearing parent? Or is it the story of a man who never liber-ates himself from that parent, insofar as he cannot write about his experiences with-out her? However we understand it, the first autobiography since the *Confessions* would probably not have been written were it not for the autobiographer's mother.[124]

Where Guibert does assert himself forcefully is in his appropriation of Augustine's *Confessions*. Guibert's debts are obvious: he addresses his confessions to God; he describes a 'conversion' (albeit to monasticism rather than Catholicism); he emphasizes the role his mother played in his conversion; and he narrates her life story within his own. We find in his *Monodies* Augustinian themes and even Augustinian incidents. Augustine provided the justification for the otherwise unprecedented undertaking of writing his life story by representing the understanding of oneself as a means to understand God. But Guibert shaped his model into something distinctly *un*Augustinian and thoroughly Guibertian. As we have seen, his narrative is less about sorting out his relationship with the deity than with the two human figures who loomed over his life. His mother is no Monica, just as he is no Augustine. He mastered his model as he could not master his mother, liberally adapting it to explore and meditate upon a life that is distinctly his own.

Abelard's Calamities

As the son of a knight, Abelard, like Guibert, would in the ordinary course of events himself have become a knight. But his father, like Guibert's, was responsible for redirecting his career—albeit unintentionally. A lover of letters, he provided all his sons with an education in the liberal arts, and Abelard was so taken with his studies that he resolved to become a professional academic. Though he may have rejected knighthood as a career, Abelard embraced it as a metaphor: arming himself with 'the weapons of dialectical reasoning', he 'chose the conflicts of disputes instead of the trophies of war'.[125] Where an aspiring young knight of Abelard's day might go on the tournament circuit, testing his skills in martial competitions throughout Europe, Abelard travelled from school to school engaging in disputations. The philosopher/knight ended up in Paris, academic capital of France, where he unseated William of Champeaux, 'supreme master' of dialectic, then overcame Anselm of Laon, the 'leading authority' in the field of divinity (p. 15). Professional disputes are, in his parlance, wars. He writes of 'skirmishes', and of 'setting up camp' and laying 'siege' to one of his rivals, whom he styles a 'soldier' and 'usurper' (pp. 13–15).

Such military metaphors suit Abelard's account of his rise to academic stardom, which is witty, arrogant, and nasty. He gloats about showing up senior students and established masters. How he relished humiliating his adversaries and ruining their reputations! As he pens his autobiography in middle age, he relives his victories, sneering at his feeble competition. Anselm, he jeers, 'owed his reputation more to long practice than to intelligence or memory. Anyone who knocked at his door to seek an answer to some question went away more uncertain than he came' (pp. 15–17). This is just the beginning of a tirade about an old scholar who was long dead at the time of Abelard's writing.

Abelard represents himself as a man who knew what he wanted and followed the paths he chose, beginning with his decision to be a scholar rather than a knight.

When he was ready to lose his virginity, he dispassionately selected the woman he would deflower, Heloise, the superbly educated niece of Canon Fulbert:

> In looks she did not rank least, while in the abundance of her learning she was supreme. A gift for letters is so rare in women that it added greatly to her charm and had made her very famous throughout the realm. I considered all the usual attractions for a lover and decided she was the one to bring to my bed, confident that I should have an easy success, for at the time I had youth and exceptional good looks as well as my great reputation to recommend me, and feared no rebuff from any woman.   (p. 27)

Practised at exploiting the weaknesses of others, Abelard used Fulbert's naivety, love of money, and desire to further his niece's education to persuade him to accept Abelard as a paying boarder and a tutor for Heloise. After Heloise succumbed to his charms and became pregnant, Abelard chose to marry her, making it clear to the reader—and to the furious Fulbert—that he was under no obligation to do so.

Fulbert famously took revenge by sending thugs to castrate Abelard, a calamity that cost him not only his virility but also, to an alarming degree, his agency. Wracked by humiliation, misery, and confusion, he caved in to the will of clerics urging him to take religious vows. As a monk and later an abbot, he made enemies as readily as he had as an academic, but he was less equipped to parry their thrusts. Unruly monks resisted his attempts at reform and succeeded in driving him from one post to another. His enemies conspired to have a church council declare his theological *magnum opus* heretical. Reciting the Athanasian Creed as best he could through his 'tears, choked with sobs', he flung his condemned book into the flames, reflecting that the ordeal was as terrible to him as his castration, the harm to his reputation worse than the harm to his body. In concluding the *Calamities*, he laments that he continues to suffer defamation and lives in fear of being murdered.

Unable to control the course of his life, Abelard could at least control the story he told about it. His *Calamities* is a tightly structured narration of success attained through his own merit and failure wrought through the malice of others. He deftly weaves together his amorous and academic exploits, his public and (more-or-less) private personae. Parallels are everywhere: his success in the lecture hall and comparable triumph in love; his attractiveness to pupils and to women; the end of his marriage and of his career in academe; the assault on his body and on his book.

Availing himself of hagiographical conventions, Abelard parlays his disgrace into victory by presenting himself as a latter-day saint: he and his disciples lived like the prophet Elisha and his followers (p. 89). His rivals persecuted him 'with the same cruelty as the heretics in the past did St. Athanasius' (p. 93). Jealousy caused his exile just as it did Saint Jerome's (p. 94). He cried out to God like King David (p. 95).

His relationship with Heloise once she took the veil was as chaste as Jerome's with Paula (p. 101). His disgruntled monks tried to poison him just as St. Benedict's did (p. 113).[126] His conventionality is brazenly unconventional: he is, to my knowledge, the first author to appropriate the *vita sanctorum* to promote *himself*.[127]

Through narrative, then, Abelard could impose order on experiences that might otherwise seem not just calamitous but chaotic. In narrative he could assert a degree of agency–'I *consciously* took myself from one danger to another'–even though he failed to achieve the outcomes he pursued (p. 95, my emphasis). And even as he represents himself as the victim of others' treachery, he simultaneously presents his life as an exemplum of divine justice. He was 'wholly enslaved to pride and lust', and God ordained an appropriate remedy for both: 'for lust by depriving me of those organs with which I practised it, and for pride...by the burning of the book of which I was so proud' (p. 23). He exhorts the unnamed addressee of the *Calamities* to bear his own misfortunes more cheerfully with the knowledge that, however wrongly people may behave, God ensures that everything happens in accordance with his plan. Abelard's life, thus construed, has the neatness of one of his most famous scholastic works, *Sic et Non* (*Yes and No*), designed to show unity beneath apparent contradictions, order underlying apparent chaos.

Abelard's *Calamities* are an early witness to what Paul Eakin calls 'memory's orientation to the future': 'we remodel our pasts to bring them into sync with our sense of ourselves and our lives in the present, but we also do so in view of our plans for the time to come.'[128] Scholars generally agree that Abelard's address to his friend was probably a pretext for an apology designed to rescue Abelard's reputation from ignominy and, perhaps, to prepare the way for his return to the Paris academic scene.[129] Through autobiography, Abelard could invent the self he desired to present to the world, and perhaps regain the control whose loss rendered his life calamitous. That Abelard was writing for a broad public is indicated by the fact that his *Calamities* reached the hands of Heloise, inaugurating an extraordinary exchange of letters–two by her, two by him–reflecting upon their joint misfortunes, debating the significance of those past events, and negotiating their future relationship.

Heloise and the 'Personal Letters'

In his *Calamities*, Abelard portrays Heloise as wholly his. He selected and seduced her. Even when he felt most confused and helpless about his own life, he could at least manage hers. He insisted that she become his wife when she preferred to remain his mistress. He demanded that she become a nun when she had not the least inclination towards religious life. What she wanted did not matter. And in his

telling of her story, events vindicated the choices he made for her: his former par-
amour ended up the pious and universally respected abbess of a convent, a position
that he was instrumental in securing for her. Having satisfactorily provided for her,
he ceased all contact with her.

As we might expect, the woman who emerges from Heloise's letters is rather
more complex.[130] Her initial letter to Abelard succinctly summarizes the plot of the
Calamities, while omitting herself altogether. Her only allusion to their affair is
buried in her enumeration of Abelard's many misfortunes: 'First you revealed the
persecution you suffered from your teachers, then the supreme treachery of the
mutilation of your person, and then described the abominable and violent attacks
of your fellow-students' (p. 109). Her omission is strategic: her role in Abelard's life–
past, present, and future–is precisely what she is going to contest.

We might expect Heloise to refute, or at least temper, some of the more scandalous
claims that Abelard made about her in the *Calamities*–for example, that she was
easily seduced, that she was sexually adventurous, and that she not only opposed
marrying Abelard but denounced the very institution of marriage. Her response to
Abelard instead demonstrates that, if anything, he has toned down the vigour of her
misogamy and the depth of her professed misogyny and self-loathing. She would
rather be called his concubine or whore ('concubine uel scorti') than his wife, she
declares; she would rather be his mistress than an emperor's wife (pp. 132-3). Love
is freedom and marriage a chain. The responsibility for Abelard's fall rests with her:
'What misery for me–born as I was to be the cause of such a crime! Again and
again women utterly destroy the very greatest of men!' (p. 167).

What she *does* dispute is Abelard's portrait of her as an exemplary abbess, universally admired for her 'piety and prudence', who devoted herself 'to prayer and
meditation on holy things' (pp. 101-3). To the contrary, she protests, her religious
inclinations are no greater now than they were when she took the veil, and far from
meditating on 'holy things', she fantasizes about Abelard:

The lovers' pleasures we enjoyed together were so sweet to me that they cannot displease me
and can scarcely fade from my memory. Wherever I turn they are always there before my
eyes, bringing with them awakened longings and fantasies which will not even let me sleep.
Even during the celebration of Mass, when our prayers should be purer, lewd visions of those
pleasures take such a hold on my most unhappy soul that my thoughts are on their wantonness rather than on prayer. I, who should be grieving for the sins I have committed, am sighing rather for what I have lost. The things we did and also the places and times in which we
did them are stamped on my heart, along with your image, so that I live through them all
again with you. Even in sleep I know no respite. Sometimes my thoughts are betrayed in a
movement of my body, or they break out in an unguarded word.   (p. 171)

Whereas Abelard represented his affair with Heloise as part of a past that is over and done with, for Heloise the past impinges inexorably upon the present. Her current relationship with Abelard cannot–and should not–be divorced from the fleshly union they once enjoyed.

Heloise is not trying so much to recover the past as to use it to change the present. She wants a resumption of their correspondence. To this end, she tries to provoke him into admitting that their relationship was about more than sex. She goads:

Tell me one thing, if you can. Why, since our entry into religion, which was your decision alone, have I been so neglected and forgotten by you that I have neither encouragement in conversation with you when you are here nor consolation in a letter when you are not? Tell me, I say, if you can–or I will tell you what I think and indeed what everyone suspects. It was desire, not affection, which bound you to me, the flame of lust rather than love. So, when the end came to what you desire, any show of feeling you used to make went with it. This, most dearly beloved, is not so much my opinion as everyone's, not so much a particular or private view as the common or public one....If only I could think of some pretexts which would excuse you and somehow cover up the way you hold me cheap!   (pp. 137-9)

Abelard does not take the bait. To her impassioned missive, he responds with impersonal calculation. She addressed her letter 'To her lord or rather her father, husband or rather brother; from his handmaid or rather his daughter, wife, or rather sister; to Abelard from Heloise' (p. 123). He replies 'To Heloise, his dearly beloved sister in Christ, from Abelard her brother in him' (p. 143). Deflecting Heloise's demand for his counsel and comfort, he presses for her prayers. Being Christ's bride, she needs nothing from him. He alternates between writing as if she already were and insisting that she become the devout abbess he portrayed in the *Calamities*.

Heloise has better luck with her second letter. Changing her tack, she disputes Abelard's interpretation of their lives. A capricious Lady Fortune rather than a just God decided their fate. When they made love behind her uncle's back they prospered. When they 'atoned' for their shame through an 'honourable marriage', God vented his wrath upon them (p. 165). This reinterpretation of their story draws a vigorous response from Abelard. He demands what comfort can there be in believing their fates to have been unjust (pp. 195-7). Besides, their marriage was far from honourable! When she was pregnant she donned a habit and masqueraded as a nun. Does she not remember how they made love in the corner of the refectory? Does she not recall a liaison in a spot dedicated to the Virgin Mary? When she resisted, he thrust himself upon her (p. 199). If such impieties do not deserve punishment, what does? As his rhetoric becomes more impassioned, his memories more vivid, Abelard's address becomes more intimate.

Heloise is his 'beloved' ('carissima') (pp. 198–9) and his 'inseparable companion' ('inseparabilis comes') (pp. 202–3).

If we read the personal letters as a contest of wills between two brilliant intellectuals, Heloise prevails. True, she does not make Abelard admit that their relationship had been about more than sex. His final word on the matter is this: 'My love, which brought us both to sin, should be called lust, not love. I took my fill of my wretched pleasures in you, and this was the sum total of my love' (p. 211). However, she does make Abelard revisit a past that he wished to remain past. She forces him to defend his interpretation of their lives. She complicates his view of their relationship. And she moves him to acknowledge a deeper love for her in the present—and not merely as his sister in Christ. He concludes his second letter to her by praying that God 'unite forever' in heaven those whom he has 'parted for a time on earth' (p. 217). Most critically, she has, as it turns out, successfully used the past to redirect the future. In the years that followed, Abelard wrote so copiously for Heloise and her nuns that he became 'the greatest provider of devotional literature for nuns in the twelfth century'.[131] When he died in 1142 he was buried at Heloise's convent of the Paraclete; upon her death some two decades later, her body was laid beside him.

Hildegard of Bingen's (Auto)biography

Circa 1182, Theodoric of Echternach accepted a commission to write the authorized biography of Hildegard of Bingen, the late founder and abbess of St. Rupertsberg on the Rhine. Unlike Eadmer and so many other twelfth-century biographers, Theodoric did not know his subject. Were it not for a series of misadventures, he would never have been writing her life. Yet his effort resulted in what scholars have called 'a literary watershed…without a doubt one of the outstanding *vitae* of the century', 'a hitherto unparalleled blend of first-person reminiscence with third-person representation'. [132]

Visionary, composer, and author, Hildegard was a legend in her own time.[133] Her book of visions, *Scivias* (*Know the Ways*), completed in 1151, made her a celebrity. Bishops, cardinals, abbots, abbesses, monks, nuns, and aristocrats sought her counsel. Indeed, her correspondents were a Who's Who of the twelfth century—Holy Roman Emperor Frederick Barbarossa, King Conrad III of Germany, Count Philip of Flanders, and Popes Eugenius III, Anastasius IV, and Adrian IV. In addition to her visions, she composed liturgical music and wrote on an enormous range of subjects in many different genres. Her *Ordo Virtutem* (*Play of the Virtues*) is the earliest known morality play. Her treatises covered theology, cosmology, botany, mineralogy, medicine, and human sexuality. She wrote lives of Saints Rupert and Disibod and hymns to Saint Ursula and her eleven thousand virgins. She invented an alphabet and a language. During her sixties and seventies, she undertook preaching tours, visiting monasteries along the Main, Moselle, and Rhine rivers and into Swabia.

That such a woman must have a biography was obvious to everybody, including her. Who better to write it than her scribe and close friend Volmar, who had known her most of her life and had collaborated with her on so many projects? It was to Volmar that Hildegard first confided her visions; he was her earliest advocate and an experienced biographer. To lay the groundwork, he edited her voluminous correspondence, while she prepared some notes about her life. He might have produced a personal biography in the tradition of Eadmer's *Life of Anselm*, but he died in 1173, before he could even begin writing. After his death, the project fell to Godfrey, a monk of St. Disibod, who replaced Volmar as Hildegard's assistant. But Godfrey wrote only few chapters before dying in 1176.

Guibert, a monk from the monastery of Gembloux in Brabant, took over from Godfrey. He had begun corresponding with Hildegard in 1175, and in 1177 he accepted her invitation to take up residence at St. Rupertsberg, where, in addition to conversing with Hildegard herself, he interviewed her nuns and pored over the relevant documents housed at her monastery. Shortly after her death in 1179 he began writing, but he got no further than her move to St. Rupertsberg when business recalled him to Gembloux. He never resumed the work, hence the eventual commission to Theodoric.[134]

Because Theodoric did not know Hildegard personally, he was careful to adhere closely the testimony of those who did. His life consisted of three books, the first devoted to her life, the second to her visions, and the third to her death and miracles. For the first, he drew on Godfrey's unfinished life. For the third, he quoted extensively from testimonials kept by the St. Rupertsberg nuns. In the second book, however, Hildegard speaks for herself through extended extracts from her letters, from the notes she left on her life, and from autobiographical passages in her various writings. Guibert had eschewed redundancy by omitting material 'available to be read in her books and letters', but Theodoric used that material to invent a new kind of biography.[135] Not having known Hildegard put him at a disadvantage. The commentary that cements together the autobiographical extracts, as Barbara Newman observes, 'tried to fit her life into the stereotyped pattern of female sanctity fashionable in his own age'.[136] But the cluelessness of his commentary does not diminish the power of Hildegard's story. Hildegard recounts seeing her very first vision when she was only three years old–'so great a light that my soul trembled'. She describes herself innocently prattling about her experiences until it dawns on her that nobody else sees what she does. She confides the loneliness and fears she experienced as a girl; she confesses her anxieties; and she relays her growing confidence as a *magistra* and a renowned visionary. She relates to readers her love for the young nun Richardis von Stade and her pain when her beloved friend abandons her to become abbess of a wealthy nunnery far from St. Rupertsberg. She also describes severe illnesses that recurred throughout her life, including an out-of-body experience. In addition to these incidents, Theodoric records portions of Hildegard's visions. Through her eyes, we watch a cherub pursuing spirits of the air with a fiery sword. We wander through three towers that enclose the secrets of Wisdom, traversing ramparts of precious stones and straining to see a mysterious fourth structure. We feel 'the inspiration of God…sprinkling drops of sweet rain into my soul's knowing'. (p. 179). Hildegard is omnipresent–she rejoices, complains, wonders, hurts, and gloats.

Extracts from a subject's writing had sometimes been included in lives, but never on so grand a scale; perhaps biographers generally shared Guibert's view that it was pointless to reproduce material available elsewhere. Theodoric was doing with writing what those who knew their subjects could accomplish by quoting conversations and speeches–producing at once an authentic and personal view of his subject that conveys not just her achievements and her virtues but also her personality.

* * * * *

The corpus of medieval biographies of career religious does not bespeak homogeneous exemplarity. Though the subjects of religious biography were often presented as saints, they were also presented as fellow human beings with whom readers could identify. Those readers consisted wholly or overwhelmingly of other religious, and biographers held up their subjects as guides on how to deal with the kinds of real-world challenge that religious faced: overcoming temptation and disappointment; developing intellectually and spiritually; dealing with colleagues, subordinates, sceptics, benefactors, and laypeople. The saints modelled people skills and pedagogy as well as piety. Their lives were practical as well as laudatory.

As we have seen, throughout the Middle Ages biographers writing about their acquaintances and (near) contemporaries tended to advertise their commitment to historical accuracy. During the earlier Middle Ages, however, biographers were mostly comfortable mingling the facts about their subjects that they knew from first-hand experience or that they uncovered through research with incidents lifted from Scripture or from prior saints' lives. The proportion of 'fact' and 'fiction' in early medieval lives varied: the lives of Guthlac and Cuthbert included far more miracle stories than the lives of the missionaries. It varied even within the oeuvre of a single author, as we have seen with Bede, whose miracle-laden life of Cuthbert is wholly unlike his miracle-less lives of the abbots. There were many ways to tell a 'true' story. Beginning in the eleventh century, filching miracles and other incidents became more controversial. Authors continued to borrow, but they were more self-conscious and defensive about doing so, and they risked incurring the scepticism that so infuriated Walter Daniel. But even so strident a proponent of fact-based biography as William of Malmesbury could not resist the allure of a good story with a suitable moral; after all, William reflects, just because an incident is conventional does not mean that it might not have really happened.[137]

We have looked at other broad trends in the representation of career religious. Those who called for greater objectivity on the part of biographers were also clamouring for more attention to personality and emotions. Whereas early medieval biographers showed their subjects interacting with many different people, later biographers tended to develop in particular their relationships with friends, family members, colleagues, pupils, and, not least, with the biographers themselves.

As we have seen, approaches to writing about career religious varied. Some forms are alien to our own conceptions of life-writing, such as Bede's conjoining of narrative prose with meditative verse or Byrhtferth's opaque allegories relayed in even more opaque Latin. Other medieval works anticipate fashions in life-writing that took off centuries later, such as the anonymous eleventh-century 'life and times of Bede', the proto-Boswellian memoirs of Adam or Eadmer, the autobiographies of Abelard and Guibert, or the pre-modern postmodernism of Gregory the Great's biographer, the anonymous monk of Whitby. Theodoric's hybrid life of Hildegard, though unique in its day, anticipates the Victorian practice of incorporating copious extracts from subjects' letters and diaries. From Theodoric's *Life of Hildegard*: 'As she says', 'Listen to her as she writes about it', 'It seems fitting to insert at this point some of the writings from her visions', 'this is what she says', 'she says'. From Elizabeth Gaskell's biography of Charlotte Brontë (1857): 'I shall now quote from a valuable letter', 'she writes', 'she adds', 'here follows a series of letters'.[138]

'Haloes and homely details did not go well together', Richard Altick once claimed, attempting to explain why medieval life-writings 'are neither individual nor realistic'. For Altick, medieval biography was mostly hagiography, and, he avers, 'To read very extensively in medieval saints' lives requires a special taste that few modern people have or would care to cultivate. Apart from an occasional picturesque or humanizing touch, such as an anecdote, there was no attempt to draw individualized portraits or to examine psychology.'[139] Modern biography, by contrast, offers 'an incomparably diversified gallery in which to behold the human comedy—and the human tragedy': 'Henry James gazes down a Boston vista and stammers: "Do you feel that Marlborough Street—is precisely—*passionate*?" Virginia Woolf, sick at heart, leaves her cottage and finds the death she seeks in the cold waters of a nearby stream. Wordsworth solemnly reads "The Leech Gatherer" aloud to his barber as the shears snip the poet's locks. Hart Crane, aged twenty, crouches cross-legged on the floor behind the counter of one of his father's chain of candy stores in Akron, Ohio, smoking a Cinco cigar and reading Pound's *Pavannes and Divagations*.'[140] My reply: Hugh, overweight and out of shape, rests on a makeshift seat under a pair of fir trees, mopping sweat from his brow as he entertains his companions with stories about the late archbishop.[141] Guthlac, wracked by doubts, ponders the meaning of life during yet another sleepless night. Leoba rests while her mischievous nuns read Scripture to her, occasionally misquoting it to see if she will notice. Wulfstan caresses his favourite young monks as he recalls the troublesome wet dreams of his youth. Aelred negotiates urgently with his unhappy monk, determined to keep him at Rievaulx. Willibald, touring Italy, hopes to scale a mountainside and peer into the mouth of a live volcano. Jocelin, dressed with leeches, cannot resist opining that one of his good friends would make a bad abbot. Little Guibert, clothed in black by his detested teacher, watches other children play games he is forbidden to join. Heloise and Abelard make love in the refectory of Argenteuil. Dunstan, holding vigil at the bedside of his dying friend, struggles to make sense of her mutterings.

Holy Women

The period from the late eleventh century through to the end of the Middle Ages was exceptionally rich in life-writings about Continental women—visionary nuns, urban anchoresses, beguines of the Low Countries, tertiaries of Southern Europe, and many more.[1] No such abundance of literature was written about English holy women. Though new opportunities to pursue religious vocations opened up for English women in the twelfth century, rarely were the women who pursued them written about. There were no high-profile English equivalents to holy women such as Elizabeth of Hungary, Catherine of Siena, or Bridget of Sweden, nor did English holy women have influential advocates such as James of Vitry, nor eager biographers such as Thomas of Cantimpré.[2] Rather, the overwhelming majority of late medieval English lives about holy women deal with Anglo-Saxon abbesses and legendary heroines of the early Church.

Yet, even as medieval England failed to produce a mass of literature about contemporary women comparable to that written in Italy, Germany, France, or the Low Countries during the high and late Middle Ages, it did yield lives of three extraordinary women: Eve of Wilton (d. c.1125), Christina of Markyate (d. after 1155), and Margery Kempe (d. after 1438). Each of these lives is *sui generis*. Eve of Wilton's story was told by her friend Goscelin of St. Bertin, a Flemish expatriate who brought to his project a familiarity with Continental modes of life-writing, producing a literary hybrid that is part letter, part religious rule, part (auto)biography. Goscelin's work is less a life story than the story of a friendship that, from his perspective, has gone terribly wrong, and it is coloured by his mixed feelings of love, admiration, hurt, and confusion. Christina's life was commissioned by her friend Geoffrey, Abbot of St. Alban's, but written by one who appears to have had mixed feelings about his assignment. His ambivalence made for a 'warts-and-all' portrait of a holy woman that to my knowledge was unprecedented in the lives of holy people. Lacking an enthusiastic clerical advocate who would write a proper *vita*, Margery Kempe with difficulty persuaded a priest to take down her memories. The result is a work that offers a largely unmediated glimpse into the emotional and spiritual life of a mother, wife, pilgrim, entrepreneur, and visionary.

Life-writing and Friendship: Goscelin of St. Bertin and Eve of Wilton

'To one shut in from one shut out; to one solitary from the world from one solitary in the world.' Thus begins the *Book of Encouragement* (*Liber confortatorius*, c.1080), one of the most extraordinary documents of the late eleventh century, a hybrid epistle and spiritual guide, a singular work addressed 'to a singular soul'.[3]

The 'one shut out' is the Flemish monk Goscelin, formerly of the Benedictine Abbey of St. Bertin, now residing in England. He was the most prolific and innovative of many Flemings who settled in England during the eleventh century and composed lives of Anglo-Saxon saints, their numbers making up for the dearth of native-born hagiographers at that time.[4] 'In the celebration of the English saints he was second to none since Bede', William of Malmesbury (c.1090–1143) wrote of him.[5] Goscelin and his fellow Flemings enriched Anglo-Latin hagiography with Continental methods, styles, and sensibilities: their fondness for rhymed prose, their eye for vivid, 'realistic' detail, their sense of the grotesque, and their emotionalism.[6]

The 'one shut in' is Eve, formerly a nun at the prestigious Wilton Abbey in Wiltshire and Goscelin's cherished friend, now occupying an anchorhold abutting the Church of St. Laurent in Angers, France. Goscelin had known Eve since she entered Wilton in 1065 at about the age of seven. When they met, he was a young man, perhaps in his mid-twenties, who was researching a biography of Wilton Abbey's patron saint, Edith (c.961–84), under a commission from the abbey's senior nuns.[7] Following the death in 1078 of his employer, Bishop Herman of Sherborne, Goscelin was made to understand that he was no longer welcome at Wilton for reasons he does not disclose beyond vague references to his transgressions and the envy of another (probably Bishop Herman's successor).[8] Some two years after Goscelin's departure, Eve left Wilton to become an anchoress in France. She did not consult Goscelin or even inform him of her decision; she just left. Bewildered and hurt when he learned of her departure, Goscelin resolved to pursue her in spirit since he could not do so bodily. His epistle (in four books!) would be her companion until they were reunited in the hereafter. At least, that was his plan.

Goscelin claims to be writing 'a private document' meant for Eve alone, but few documents at the time were truly private, and Goscelin expects that his will fall into the hands of others—whisperers, gossips, and cacklers (p. 99). Perhaps he expects these outsiders to be shocked by the intensity of his passion for Eve (as many of his modern readers are). Goscelin presents himself to Eve, 'soul sweetest to me', as 'your Goscelin', addressing her 'as if from a bed of pain' with the 'sighs' of 'wounded love' (pp. 101–2). He laments being 'abandoned', 'miserable', and 'inconsolable' (p. 118). This rhetoric persists throughout. Goscelin does not defend himself to his imagined maligners. 'Let him who does not love not read it', he declares as he turns his attention to Eve.

The first of the four books comprising Goscelin's 'letter' is a memoir of sorts: 'Permit me now, for mutual comfort and memory, to go over again the unbroken history of our affection and strengthen our perpetual love' (p. 102). One might expect this 'history' to take the form of a coherent, chronological narration, but what Goscelin delivers is an allusive—and, for us, *elusive*—rumination, a tissue of loosely connected memories of his beloved. He recalls Eve's kindness in giving him books and in speaking highly of his home monastery of St. Bertin. He recalls weeping as he watched her vow herself to Christ, and he remembers vivid details of the ceremony—the chants, the incense, the procession, the candles, the crowds, but above all Eve, second to last of fourteen girls, trembling and blushing with anticipation. This emotional recollection leads him to conjure up a similarly moving occasion, the dedication of a church, which he arranged for Eve to attend. The rite featured beautiful girls arrayed in bejewelled and embroidered purple garments. For Goscelin, however, their ostentatious splendour paled before the beauty of Eve in her simple black habit: 'The darts of love were fixed deeper and stuck fast; my wounded heart languished' (p. 104). Goscelin recalls their blossoming friendship—their many conversations, a dream she confided to him, the letters they exchanged, and his disappointment on the occasions when he visited and was not able to see her. He recalls how he encouraged her and kindled her passion for her heavenly bridegroom. He recalls how they comforted each other following the death of their beloved Bishop Herman and their mutual heartbreak when Goscelin was exiled from Wilton.

Any narrative that we might construct from this montage of memories will be hypothetical. The difficulty of building a coherent story is compounded by Goscelin's allusion throughout the *Book* to incidents that Eve would presumably have known but we do not. He mentions being unable speak to her on some of his visits but provides no reason (p. 104). As already mentioned, he claims, without elaborating, that envy and barbarity compelled him to leave Wilton, while also indicating that certain unspecified transgressions on his part caused their separation. He alludes to a time when she was 'wavering' (p. 173); Eve presumably would recall when or why, but we have no clue.

The gaps in Goscelin's narrative have enticed modern readers to engage in all manner of speculation about what 'really happened'.[9] Some see nothing but a deep and moving spiritual friendship, while others detect evidence of a creepy clergyman foisting his affection on a vulnerable girl. Some regard Goscelin and Eve as soul mates separated by forces beyond their control. Others have wondered whether Eve herself might have instigated the separation, perhaps alarmed at the intensity of Goscelin's passion. Some believe that Goscelin's heated language indicates sexual desire that may have scandalized those around him; others point out that intense friendships flourished at the time, both between members of the same sex and members of the opposite sex, and that missives between friends often deployed impassioned, even erotic, rhetoric. None of these hypotheses are wholly satisfactory. If Eve and Goscelin were the closest of friends, who conversed through letters when they could not do so in person, why did Eve not communicate her departure to Goscelin? Goscelin takes it for granted in his reproaches that she could have got in touch with him had she wished. If Eve and Goscelin parted on less than friendly terms, it seems unlikely that he should express such confidence that Eve's 'insatiable fervour and anxious love' for him will make his four-book 'letter' seem brief to her (p. 102). Perhaps in time the absent Goscelin simply became less important to Eve. We cannot know.

Eve, however, would. Goscelin in essence has encoded a private life story that only she can decipher. His recollections would trigger hers; the 'unbroken history' is the unwritten text engendered from the marriage of his allusions with her memories. Of course, how nearly the story Eve constructs from Goscelin's prompts resembles the story Goscelin had in mind when he wrote the *Book of Encouragement* depends on how nearly her memories of their shared experiences align with his.

In pioneering this form of unwritten 'life-writing', Goscelin drew upon the process of rumination that was routinely practised in the monasteries of his day. As Monika Otter explains, Goscelin and Eve 'were both raised in a tradition of slow, meditative, reiterative reading that aimed at committing the text to memory, savouring each word and phrase and pausing for imaginative association and emotional elaboration'.[10] Goscelin and others wrote spiritual tracts that were full of biblical allusions and metaphors that could be fully appreciated only by readers intellectually equipped to supply the missing context. Just as consuming these spiritual tracts relies on shared experiences of Scripture, consuming the 'history of our affections' relies on shared life experiences.

Though Book One is the most explicitly (auto)biographical, the subsequent three books, the heart of his 'guide', are very much tailored to the woman he thought he knew, to the life he imagines her to be living, and to the challenges he supposes her to be facing.

The situation of anchorites varied tremendously, so Goscelin could only guess at Eve's.[11] The cell, known as an anchorhold or reclusorium, that an anchorite inhabited was typically built onto a church. A window looking into the church allowed the anchorite to participate in religious services; another window, to the outside, was designed for the passage of laundry, food, drink, and other necessities; while a third window, also to the outside, permitted the anchorite to converse with visitors—friends, family, spiritual advisors, members of the faithful seeking encouragement and prayers. The cell itself might be a single room or a suite of rooms; it might have a walled garden or courtyard. There was great variety even in single-room cells, which, in England at least, we know to have been as small as 6'8" × 4'4" (2m × 1.3m) and as spacious as 29' × 24' (8.8m × 7.3m).[12] Some anchorholds housed two or more recluses, and even a servant or two; some accommodated overnight guests.

Goscelin imagines Eve inhabiting an austere eight-foot room adjoining a large church. Were he in her place, he avers, he would revel in the uninterrupted solitude that would enable him to 'escape the crowd that tears at my heart' and 'to pray, to read eagerly, to write often, to speak often' (p. 109). 'Oh, how often I sighed for a little lodging like yours', he declares. But did Eve (still) share his enthusiasm for the luxury of solitude? With the empathy of a fellow expatriate, he supposes that she might be lonely and homesick. Friends, family, places, and pastimes that she thought she would not miss would naturally grow dearer in their absence. She might find the anchoritic life wearisome once its novelty wore off. Being confined to a single room could well induce claustrophobia, and the austerity of an anchorhold would be such a change from the comforts of Wilton. In short, Eve might regret her choice and succumb to depression.

Goscelin's was the earliest of thirteen treatises for anchorites composed in medieval England.[13] Many later authors addressed their readers' perceived needs by offering them detailed instructions on how they should conduct their daily lives. Goscelin similarly exhorts Eve to be *truly* solitary, not keeping even a cat, bird, or other small pet (p. 163). He urges her to read by day, pray by night, and meditate constantly (pp. 165-9). He also offers extensive and detailed reading recommendations—Scripture, above all, but also the writings of the Church Fathers (he specifically mentions Augustine's *Confessions* and *City of God*) and lives of the saints (especially of the desert father Anthony) (pp. 162-5). In the main, however, he is less concerned with how Eve should conduct her life than with how she should think about it. If poverty frustrates her, she should imagine her wealth: she in effect inhabits her own private monastery, with her own sanctuary, oratory, refectory, dormitory, hall, bedchamber, entrance hall, pantry, and sitting room—all conveniently located in a single room (p. 161)! Goscelin, moreover, praises the solitary life in what we might think of as 'humanistic' terms, for promoting a peace of mind that has been sought by people of all faiths through the ages:

Many, such as the Brahmins and other peoples, chose such a life, not on account of the kingdom of God, about which they knew nothing, but for the sake of present peace, than which they judged nothing to be happier; using the natural benefit that the free kindness of the Creator has implanted in all they set the mind free from the lacerating cares of riches, and exercised it with the liberal arts.   (p. 156)

Like the Brahmins, Eve should luxuriate in the freedom from luxuries that 'overwhelm the mind with the burden of abundance' (p. 156).

Given that Goscelin would go on to become the most prolific biographer of his day, it is perhaps not surprising that he conveys much of his advice and consolation to Eve by telling the life stories of others, mostly men and women from the Judaeo-Christian tradition but some from the non-Christian past.[14] He sketches some lives in a few sentences, while others he relays at length. When he writes about their friendship, he tells the stories of other great friends—of the biblical David and Jonathan, of the sibling martyrs Sabinus and Sabina, of the nuns Modesta and Gertrude (pp. 118–21). When he exhorts her to courage, he tells stories of Christian martyrs, such as Perpetua (pp. 128–30) and Blandina (pp. 145–6). Goscelin declares that Eve need not be killed for her faith in order to profit from a martyr's example: 'If there are no physical struggles [in Eve's life], there are spiritual ones'; 'armies of sins' are every bit as formidable as pagan persecutors (p. 130). We can often see Goscelin tailoring the lives he tells to Eve's specific circumstances. For example, he writes of Mary of Egypt's admirable asceticism, making no allusion to her prior career as a prostitute, which is a major part of her legend (p. 158).[15] He retells as a tender love story the Church Father Ambrose's account of a Christian virgin rescued from a brothel by a young man who exchanges clothes with her: when the authorities discover the deception and condemn the youth to death, the unnamed virgin steps up to join her rescuer in martyrdom (pp. 183–5). One can see Goscelin's recurring fantasy of himself and Eve in his praise for the young martyrs: 'O in what inseparable love, in what blessed embraces they were then going to cling to one another in heaven eternally' (p. 184).

How relevant these inscribed stories are to Eve's life and/or her relationship with Goscelin we cannot determine. Most intriguing is one of the longest, which concerns an obscure anchorite, Alexander, whom Goscelin introduces as an example of 'holiness undermined by temptation, made good by falling' (pp. 190–2). Alexander had for many years lived an irreproachable life alone in a forest. Seeking to destroy him, the Devil, disguised as a monk, asked him to raise a baby girl whom he claimed was abandoned (actually the King's kidnapped daughter). When the girl matured, Alexander 'debauched her' (p. 191), and when she became pregnant, he murdered her to save his reputation. The disguised Devil, who had suggested the murder, revealed his identity and taunted Alexander with his crimes. Alexander was devastated, but God offered him an opportunity to repent by imprisoning himself in a hollow oak tree. There he remained for fifteen years until the girl's true father, the King, discovered him, realized from his story that the murdered woman was his daughter, and dug her up. The girl's body was miraculously incorrupt; moreover, she gave an unmistakable sign that she had forgiven Alexander. In the end, the King built an enormous monastery at the site and renounced his kingdom to join Alexander in religious life. Goscelin writes, 'Blessed Alexander rejoiced that, from the crime of a corrupter and murderer, he had made the fruit of a martyr, and that she would triumph in heaven for him, in the inseparable bond of love' (p. 192). The language here—Alexander's confidence in the 'inseparable bond of love' and in the girl's intervention on his behalf—echoes Goscelin's requests for Eve's prayers, his confidence in Eve's spiritual superiority to him, and his protestations of undying love (for example, pp. 108-9). I wonder whether Goscelin saw parallels between Alexander's crimes and his own unspecified transgressions, and whether he expected Eve to recognize them as well.[16] As he had written earlier concerning the martyrs, lives do not have to correspond exactly to be relevant.

Goscelin does not ask Eve to reply to his letter. Indeed, he appears to take it for granted that she will not. But he *does* expect that through his letter he will become part of her life once more. Perhaps receiving the book will prompt her to wonder how her old friend is doing: he looks the same as ever, he assures her, but he hurts more and should he live into old age she can be confident that he will be sighing still (p. 112). He asks her to imagine that they are together once again: 'accept this consolation as if I were present' (p. 102); 'look upon me sitting with you; hear me talking with you' (p. 110). He admits that, though bound to encourage her in her chosen vocation, he would most like to tear her away (p. 112)—and he imagines doing so, gently at the beginning and more forcefully at the end. At the beginning of Book One, he asks her to 'consider that I am seated with you at Wilton in the presence of our lady St. Edith' (p. 101); at the end of Book Four, he brings her back to Wilton through his vision of the hereafter, where the New Jerusalem is a transfigured Wilton of golden walls, pearly gates, a bejewelled temple, and hosts of angels and saints, singing, rejoicing, dancing, and embracing. There will be no solitude, no anchorholds. Goscelin celebrates young men and women gathered together, imagining their 'inseparable company, inestimable love, unspeakable sanctity of holy embraces and kisses' (p. 205). At this celestial Wilton, he hopes to see Eve, in her 'highest happiness, in the blessed light' (p. 207). She who is now 'far from her homeland seeking the true homeland' (p. 99) will discover that what she truly desires is the purified embodiment of what she left behind.

The *Book of Encouragement* shows how deeply Goscelin loved Eve—and how little he knew her. At the very beginning of their relationship, he appears to have misjudged her: 'You remember, soul sweetest to me, how at first I provoked your childhood, confident that I would easily correct such a pious soul' (p. 102). Even after years of close friendship, Eve remained elusive. Goscelin could not understand why she left without a word: such cruelty is at odds with her demonstrated kindness (p. 118). He could not understand why she wanted to become an anchoress, much less why she wanted to go abroad to do so (p. 112). He makes several references to her reticence: 'You, although very eloquent, used to drink in pious admonitions without speaking. Whatever I urged, I found done, not in your answers but in your acts' (p. 104). He speaks of being 'inflamed' by her 'silence' (p. 103). Little wonder, perhaps, that he should find himself 'wounded' by 'the cruelty of your silence' (p. 105).

We do not know if Goscelin's book ever reached Eve. Goscelin is our only source of information about her life in England, but we do know rather more about her life in France, thanks largely to a verse eulogy written by Hilary of Orléans following her death *circa* 1125.[17] Hilary attests that, with or without Goscelin's book to guide her, Eve remained an avid reader with a reputation for piety and asceticism. After spending about twenty years at Angers, she took up residence in a more secluded anchorhold near Vendôme, where she remained until she died. Apparently solitude was less onerous to Eve than Goscelin supposed. Yet Eve was not exactly alone at Vendôme. Her niece Ravenissa joined her there, and Eve became fast friends with another recluse, Hervé of Vendôme, a former monk. Hilary found nothing scandalous in the friendship of Eve and Hervé. Indeed, their relationship, like Eve and Goscelin's, illustrates the intense heterosocial bonds that blazed warmly and continued to burn on the Continent after the next generation's hostility towards and suspicion of friendships between women and men extinguished them in England.[18]

Goscelin's Edith: Eve Redux?

As Goscelin worked on his *Book of Encouragement*, he also returned to the life of Edith that he had been researching years ago, when he met Eve. The two works were both completed *circa* 1080 and are in many ways complementary. Like his account of his relationship with Eve, Goscelin's life of Edith is allusive, rhetorically lavish, and rich in metaphor and symbolism. Long passages of meditation and moralizing subordinate the events of Edith's life to Goscelin's interpretations of their significance. His tendency to move swiftly from the literal to the metaphorical is illustrated in his description of Edith's physical appearance:

She was of well-proportioned medium height, which she reached before she was an adult. Her holy modesty and the snow-white bird of Christ had given her those stars, her eyes— which shone from her inner radiance—the likeness of doves' eyes. Sweetness dropped down and kindness poured from her lips; honey and milk, received from the mouth of the Lord, gave their flavour. She protected the glory of her head and the rest of the harmonious work of her Creator from the Ethiopian sun...[19]

This impulse towards rhetorical embellishment and abstraction informs his work as a whole.

Goscelin interweaves prose with verse as he relays the major events of Edith's life. She was the daughter of King Edgar and his cousin Wulfthryth, who had been educated at Wilton Abbey. About two years after Edith's birth in 964, Wulfthryth returned to Wilton with her daughter in tow and took vows, shortly thereafter becoming abbess. Goscelin reports that Edith, preferring to stay at Wilton with her mother, turned down various opportunities for advancement–offers to become abbess at other religious houses and even the chance to rule England following her brother Edward's murder in 978. Edith died in 984 when she was only twenty-three years old, after overseeing the construction of a magnificent chapel dedicated to St. Denis.

When Goscelin undertook his life of Edith at the request of Wilton's senior nuns, about eighty years had elapsed since her death, and all who knew her personally were themselves deceased. However, Goscelin interviewed nuns who had heard about Edith from those who knew her well. Her 'own special places and her occupations' remained alive in the communal memory, Goscelin writes, explaining that his sources eagerly told him, 'Here she was accustomed to read, here to pray; she achieved such and such things in the Lord' (p. 24).

Those details of Edith's material life at Wilton are, however, for the most part buried within the story of her spiritual life, particularly her all-consuming desire for her heavenly bridegroom. In fact, many of the details Goscelin learned from the senior nuns appear to conflict with his portrait of Edith as the lovelorn bride of Christ, the contemplative who took little interest in worldly affairs. The nuns recalled an accomplished and urbane woman so fond of finery that Bishop Æthelwold once reproached her for wearing garments unseemly for a bride of Christ (pp. 42-3)–though they also revealed that she wore a hair shirt beneath her lavish purple habit (p. 38). Their Edith enjoyed a heated bath, kept exotic animals, and maintained diverse contacts outside the abbey, including not only clergymen and family members but also foreign diplomats and potentates (p. 39).

Modern historians have admired Goscelin because he does not invent 'facts' that would make his subjects conform more nearly to the prevailing paradigms of holiness.[20] Nor, as we see, does he appear to suppress facts that might undermine his portrait of Edith as a model contemplative–though he claims to have recorded only 'a few of the things out of the many which I have learned from the testimony of faithful people or from local books' (p. 25). Instead, he strategically contextualizes information that might undermine his ideal. After describing how powerful people valued her, he abruptly changes topic and launches into a long encomium to her devotion to the destitute (pp. 39–40). He discloses Edith's habit of wearing a hair shirt *before* relaying the bishop's rebuke, noting, 'Without doubt she made her humility more glorious by public elegance', then comparing her to the virgin martyr Cecilia, also said to have worn a hair shirt beneath her fine apparel (p. 38). Thus by the time he reports Bishop Æthelwold's criticism of Eve's 'rather ornate habit', Goscelin has already established his heroine in the minds of his readers as being all the more humble for eschewing ostentatious piety.

Goscelin similarly contextualizes Edith's menagerie, using what might be taken as evidence of an unseemly self-indulgence to illustrate her kindness towards all living creatures (p. 41). Edith, who had 'the mind of a recluse' (p. 42), visited her exotics as an escape from the demands of the world, and she cared for them with the solicitude of Saint Benedict, who was known to have provided for ravens. After praising her special rapport with animals and reminding his readers that such a rapport was common among the blessed, he reflects that she would have made an excellent martyr: 'We believe that this woman, under the persecution of Nero and Decius, would have been able to smile at the attacks of wild beasts, and to tame tigers and lions, since she knew how to quiet their fierce souls in a time of peace' (p. 42). Anybody who might criticize her for being frivolous should be ashamed: 'let him consider whether this offence might not be more holy than his virtues' (p. 42).

Stephanie Hollis has persuasively argued that Goscelin infused his Edith with the sensibility and spirituality of his own generation.[21] Goscelin wrote at a time when holy women were increasingly represented as brides of Christ. With his contemporary expatriate, Anselm of Canterbury (formerly of Bec), Goscelin and his fellow Flemish hagiographers helped bring to England the intense affective piety that would flourish during the twelfth century. Goscelin, Hollis maintains, 'ascribes to Edith the qualities of his own spiritual life which, he believed, were also shared by Eve' (p. 303). She notes that it is tempting to see in his 'depiction of Edith as a withdrawn contemplative a portrait influenced by his memory of Eve' (p. 300). Of Edith, Goscelin writes: 'clinging to [Christ] with her whole mind and struck with the holy wound of his love, from the midst of her studies she hastened towards him with her entire affection and, taking to herself the wings of a dove, she ardently desired to fly to his sanctifying embraces and to be at rest there' (p. 33). This Edith, wounded by love and rushing to embrace her beloved, embodies the ideal that

Goscelin urged upon Eve at Wilton, when he exhorted her that, 'wounded by love', she 'should desire Christ alone' (p. 103). She is the woman that Goscelin wishes Eve had become: one deeply spiritual, yet one who had not found it necessary to flee her friends and her homeland to join her heavenly spouse.

Life Friendships: Christina of Markyate

The St. Albans Psalter, produced *circa* 1125-35, is not merely a psalter—that is, one of those popular medieval prayer books that combined the biblical psalms with a liturgical calendar and sundry devotional material.[22] With 40 full-page paintings, 5 tinted drawings, and 211 decorated initials, each brilliantly designed and executed, the St. Albans Psalter is a masterpiece of English Romanesque manuscript illumination. The artists have rendered scenes from nature, from saints' legends, and from the Bible. Christ's life unfolds in vibrant colour across thirty-six pages. The guiding theme of each psalm is encapsulated in a finely wrought scene embedded within its opening initial.

Psalm 105 is an intriguing exception. Its initial 'C' depicts a veiled woman presenting a group of monks to Christ. One monk clasps the woman's shoulder as she reaches towards Christ, her fingers just touching the Saviour's. A caption positioned above the initial captures her words as she beseeches Christ: 'Save your monks.' These are presumably the Benedictines of St. Albans in Hertfordshire, where the psalter was produced, and their female intercessor is probably Christina, Prioress of the convent at Markyate, about ten miles northwest of St. Albans. The monk touching Christina might represent her close friend, Geoffrey of Gorham, who was abbot of St. Albans from 1119 to 1146.

Indeed, the St. Albans Psalter may, as the *Book of Encouragement* most certainly does, attest to the love of a religious man for a religious woman. Many scholars believe that the psalter was Geoffrey's gift to Christina.[23] The calendar indicates the consecration of her priory, along with the deaths of various friends and family members. Moreover, Geoffrey appears to have customized the psalter to suit his friend. The manuscript has a distinctly female orientation. Many of its illustrations feature women—biblical women, allegorical women, women worshipping, women facing and overcoming temptation. The feast days of numerous holy women are noted in the calendar, and the litany invokes the intercession of thirteen female saints.

Also probably included for its relevance to Christina is a verse life in French of St. Alexis, a legendary ascetic of early Christian Rome.[24] The only son of devout aristocrats who counted on him to carry on their line, Alexis consented to wed out of filial piety, but instead of making love on his wedding night, he commended his bride to Christ and fled across the sea to Mesopotamia, where he embraced anonymity and deprivation. The tinted drawing that accompanies the text shows Alexis taking leave of his grieving bride: 'Oh blessed Bride, forever bound to grief', its caption reads (p. 57).[25] Like Alexis, Christina had run away from home to avoid consummating an arranged marriage and spent years hiding from her family and spouse.

Christina's struggle to pursue a religious vocation was recounted in Latin prose by an anonymous monk of St. Albans, probably at Geoffrey's instigation.[26] Although this life lacks the conventional biographical preface indicating by whom, for whom, when, and why it was written, that the author was a monk at St. Albans is indicated by his repeated references to St. Albans as 'our monastery' (pp. 39, 79, 127).[27] Moreover, he knew Christina fairly well, for he mentions not only conversing with her but also dining with her at her priory. Among the sources he cites are her friends and family members. There can be little doubt that he is addressing Geoffrey when he writes, 'she revered you more than all the pastors under Christ' (p. 127).

If we accept that Geoffrey commissioned the life, it was begun during Christina's lifetime and probably had the twofold purpose of pleasing Christina and of creating a biography that, down the road, could be used to promote her posthumous reputation as a patron saint and protector of the abbey—the role in which the illuminated 'C' of the St. Albans Psalter projects her. The author claims Christina loved his monastery's patron, St. Alban, better than any other martyr, and he portrays her as Alban's partner, both on earth and in the hereafter: 'As our blessed patron St. Alban had her from the Lord as co-operator in building up and furthering his community on earth, so he had her afterwards as sharer of his eternal bliss in heaven' (p. 127). He emphasizes that her connection with the monastery dates back to her childhood, when she dedicated herself to Christ at 'our abbey' during a visit with her parents (p. 39). He mentions various other connections—for example, that Roger, the hermit whose abode she shared for several years, was a monk of St. Albans (p. 81). Above all, he dwells on Christina's deep and abiding friendship with Abbot Geoffrey.

Christina's biographer uses well-recognized tropes to establish her holiness. He recounts cures effected through her prayers and instances of prescience. He compares Christina, implicitly and explicitly, to saints of old, particularly the virgin martyrs and the desert fathers.[28] Yet he also departs, sometimes jarringly, both from those legendary paradigms and from the usual representation of contemporary holy people. In so doing, he portrays Christina as an imperfect woman struggling to serve God in a morally complex world. As a young adult, she exhibits a distinctive blend of naivety, cunning, obstinacy, and passion; she tries and fails to be like the saints she admires. As an older woman, secure in her vocation, she is not only pious but also manipulative, stubborn, and imperious. Instead of exalting the all-consuming love of a holy virgin for her heavenly spouse, Christina's biographer focuses on her relationships with those around her—particularly with her male friends. At a time when some male clerics were regarding friendships between religious men and women with suspicion and hostility, the *Life of Christina of Markyate* takes a hard and critical look at the feasibility and value of such relationships and delivers a resounding endorsement of them.

The *Life of Christina of Markyate* deviates in surprising ways from contemporary biographies of holy people. Following standard practice, her biographer represents her as a precociously holy child; however, her holiness springs not only from innate love of God but also from dread of the hereafter and from the influence of an elderly canon who was 'always seeking opportunities' to convince her that virginity was the route to salvation (p. 37). Christina's biographer praises her childish pieties with proto-Strachean bemusement, describing her as too young to understand 'why she should love righteousness and hate wickedness' when she takes up ascetic practices (p. 37). Having heard that 'Christ was good, beautiful, and everywhere present', she talks to him in her bed at night 'as if she were speaking to a man she could see' (p. 37). Assuming 'that if she were speaking to God, she could not be heard by man', she carries on loud nocturnal conversations until she discovers that people are making fun of her behind her back (p. 37). The biographer again plays up her naivety when he describes her near-disastrous efforts, as a young woman, to extricate herself from an unwanted marriage by imitating a fourth-century virgin martyr.[29]

Christina's naivety, though, is combined with a wiliness that rescues her time and again. When a lecherous bishop corners and propositions her, she consents to the deed, asking only to bolt the door so that nobody should catch them in the act. The bishop makes her swear 'that she would not deceive him, but that she would, as she said, bolt the door' (p. 43). Christina swears, then bolts the door *from the outside*, leaving the bishop to seethe.[30] Forced to marry by her parents, she foils their efforts to have her consummate the marriage by anticipating their tactics. When they admit her husband to her room late one night, she meets him alert, fully dressed, and prepared to talk him out of the deed. When they send prelates to extol the virtues of marriage, she is ready with counterarguments, both legal and religious. When she spots her father engaged in 'stealthy meetings' (p. 69) with the friends of a bishop sympathetic to her cause, she infers that he is bribing her ally and seeks help elsewhere. At last, she orchestrates her escape from home, forging new alliances, making bribes of her own, and disguising herself as a man.

Christina's biographer recounts experiences that are less than heroic. He describes her fear as she hides behind a tapestry while her husband ransacks the room with his friends, determined to rape her:

What, I ask you, were her feelings at the moment? How she kept trembling as they noisily sought after her. Was she not faint with fear? She saw herself already dragged out in their midst, all surrounding her, looking upon her, threatening her, given up to the sport of her destroyer. (p. 53)

He describes the ordeals she experienced while in hiding with a local hermit and forced to spend the days confined to an area so small that she could not dress warmly during the cold weather and nearly suffocated when it was hot. Fasting caused her bowels to become 'contracted and dried up', while 'her burning thirst caused little clots of blood to bubble up from her nostrils' (pp. 103, 105). Worst of all, 'she could not go until the evening to satisfy the demands of nature' (p. 105). He later shows her barely able to resist her desire for a priest who hides her in his home.[31] Christina's host begs for sex, throwing himself at her feet naked, while she struggles against her longing to accept his advances.

Even after Christina comes into her own as a holy woman, gaining fame as a healer and a visionary, her biographer deglamorizes her; he portrays her as deeply holy, but also as a bit of a crank. For example, he shows her (mis)using her visionary powers to humiliate a servant for the seemingly minor transgression of making salad with ingredients from the garden of a woman who had offended her.[32] In another unsettling episode, Christina tells her sister Matilda that she saw and heard Matilda and her husband in bed one night. The couple were at home in Huntingdon and she in her cell at Markyate, and yet 'she was able to tell each one exactly what they had said, at what time and where'; husband and wife confirmed that she spoke truly (p. 193). This intrusion into a sister's marital bedroom comes across as just a little creepy, if not downright prurient.

It is possible, likely even, that Christina's biographer was less enamoured of Christina than Geoffrey was.[33] By including a few less-than-flattering details about her, he may have been subverting a project, the idealization of Christina, with which he was not in tune. And yet it is also likely that he found much to admire in Christina and that, through humanizing detail, he was aiming for a more authentic portrait of her. His gritty descriptions of Christina's tribulations make the travails of the martyrs and desert fathers seem 'remote and "literary"'.[34] Christina inhabits a real world, where angels do not strike down would-be rapists and where saints must struggle with their bowels and bladders as well as with demons. Saints are also human beings, human beings are imperfect, and denying their imperfections may actually diminish them as saints.

In introducing his *Life of Samuel Johnson*, James Boswell, 'father' of modern biography, professed to be writing 'not his panegyrick, which must be all praise, but his Life; which, great and good as he was, must not be supposed to be entirely perfect'.[35]

In this he was following the precepts of Johnson himself, who theorized that the biographer will move readers most by reporting qualities that they can identify with—the faults and failures along with the virtues and victories.[36] Christina's biographer, I believe, understood that. To be sure, he did not discard panegyric so much as temper it with accounts of pains and pleasures that his readers might recognize as their own. He knew, perhaps, that his readers could more readily imagine being chilled, parched, constipated, tempted, and bullied than they could imagine themselves being terrorized by demons, dismembered, or boiled. He took the chance that learning of Christina's quotidian ordeals would augment rather than diminish readers' admiration for her. They might come away from *The Life of Christina of Markyate* feeling, with Johnson, that 'We are all prompted by the same motives, all deceived by the same fallacies, all animated by hope, obstructed by danger, entangled by desire, and seduced by pleasure.'[37]

The biographer's interest in character over type is evident throughout the *Life of Christina*. The men and women he describes are mostly multi-dimensional. Most are basically decent but, variously, stubborn, quick-tempered, impulsive, overly concerned with the opinions of others, or weak enough to succumb to bullying and bribes. Christina's husband Burthred is a case in point. He may be wishy-washy, but he is not a bad man. Were he left in peace, he would have been more than happy to rid himself of his unwilling spouse. Christina knows this. Before running away from home, she sends friends to him to negotiate for a formal separation. Burthred hears them out and readily agrees; he even offers to 'make provision for her' to enter a monastery 'out of my own pocket' (p. 71). Christina's parents are able 'by scolding and flattery' to harass him into changing his mind, '*but not without a great deal of trouble*' (p. 71, my emphasis); his subsequent attempts to regain his spouse are half-hearted (p. 95).

Christina's parents behave badly—very badly. Yet they, too, are not all bad. They drink too much and obsess about the opinions of others, but they also honour the saints and support religious houses. Christina's father, Autti, knows he is wronging his daughter: 'I and her mother have forced her against her will into this marriage…against her better judgment she has received this sacrament', he admits to the canons of St. Mary's (p. 59). But dreading the 'mockery and derision' of others, he nonetheless begs the canons to persuade Christina to reconcile herself to marriage. Autti and his wife have always been reluctant to abandon a course of action once chosen, her biographer explains. They fail with Christina largely because she is every bit their daughter and has inherited their stubbornness and ingenuity.

Just as Christina's biographer does not vilify her adversaries, he does not idealize her supporters. Abbot Geoffrey is a good abbot who governed his house 'with strictness and kept it flourishing in possessions', but he is also high-handed and stubborn;

Christina's biographer complains that he 'relied more on his own judgment than on that of his monks, over whose religious counsels [sic] he presided' (p. 135). Both the canon Sueno and the hermit Roger make snap judgments they later regret. Hearing of her betrothal, Sueno accuses Christina of 'feminine inconstancy' before he has even heard her side of the story (p. 55). Roger at first angrily refuses to help Christina but later regrets his hastiness, realizing that right and wrong may be contingent. Christina's supporter Alfwen is a principled pragmatist rather than an ideologue, fully able to dissemble and equivocate. When Burthred arrives at her anchorhold looking for his runaway wife, she exclaims: 'Stop, my son, stop imagining that she is here with us. It is not our custom to give shelter to wives who are running away from their husbands' (p. 95). Alfwen may not have been *accustomed* to harbouring runaway wives, but at the moment she happened to be concealing Burthred's. Christina's biographer thus shows a world in which men and women of good will equivocate, make mistakes, change their minds, and disagree about what is right and wrong, especially regarding sexual mores.

As Christina's biographer dramatizes the relationships among imperfect human beings inhabiting an imperfect world, he takes a particular interest in friendships, especially Christina's friendships with men, which are numerous and diverse. The dearest friend of her youth is Sueno, her 'only comfort' when her family turns against her: 'His friendly intimacy and sympathy had been to her such a source of strength that what she had suffered from others was accounted of little consequence' (p. 55). She could not have achieved her spiritual goals without his moral support and the material assistance of her other male friends. The recluse Eadwin helps her escape home. Roger conceals her and negotiates her formal separation from Burthred. A Cluniac monk defends her reputation when malefactors accuse her of having an affair with Abbot Geoffrey (p. 175). She remains close to her brother at St. Albans monastery. The end of the *Life* describes Christina's growing attachment to a mysterious pilgrim—handsome, courteous, modest, and abstemious—who on multiple occasions visits and delights her and her sisters with his holy conversation (pp. 183–9). The pilgrim, they later realize, can only have been an incarnation of Christ. Appearing here not as a jealous bridegroom but as one of Christina's many male friends, Jesus puts his personal stamp of approval on hetero-spiritual friendships.

Much of Christina's *Life* concerns her friendship with Abbot Geoffrey, which the author claims to have been instigated by God: 'it was through this man that God decided to provide for her needs and it was through His virgin that He decided to bring about this man's full conversion' (p. 135). Geoffrey becomes Christina's 'beloved' and 'her closest friend' (pp. 145, 149). 'With a wonderful but pure love', she cherishes him more than herself (pp. 139, 181). For his sake, she turns down offers to join prestigious monasteries in England and abroad (pp. 125, 127), and she abandons her dreams of retiring 'to some distant country where a town off the beaten track might provide a hidden refuge' (p. 147). Geoffrey's 'frequent pleadings and humble sweetness' hold her back (p. 147).

The relationship is emotionally intense and rewarding. The author writes of 'the longings, the sighs, the tears they shed as they sat and discussed heavenly matters' (p. 157). It is also materially beneficial. Geoffrey provides financial support and supervises the 'material affairs' of Christina's priory, while Christina enriches his monastery with her prayers (p. 155). Though Geoffrey, as an abbot, has more clout than a prioress, Christina has the upper hand in their relationship:

The man often visited the servant of Christ, heard her admonitions, accepted her advice, consulted her in doubts, avoided evil, bore her reproaches.…he went to the handmaid of Christ for advice as to a place of refuge and received her answer as if it were a divine oracle… If he went discomfited, he returned comforted; if weary of the vicissitudes of the world, he returned refreshed…and when he grew cold in divine love, he was glad to realize that, after speaking with her, he grew fervent.   (p. 139)

In Christina's dreams, Geoffrey is needy and vulnerable; she protects him, intercedes for him, and introduces him to her heavenly friends (pp. 157, 165). God endorses and strengthens their friendship—particularly her hold over him. In one of her visions, she sees Geoffrey, 'whom she loved above all others, encircled with her arms and held closely to her breast'. As she worries that he, being a man and therefore physically stronger than she, might escape her embrace, Jesus draws her hands together, strengthening her hold on him (p. 169). Knowing he cannot escape her vigilance, Geoffrey strives to act as Christina would wish (p. 141). Under the 'watchful care of the maiden', he becomes 'a changed man' (p. 151).

Christina's biographer does not pretend that friendship is perfect. The best of friends can also be petty, jealous, and quick to judge. Friends have misunderstandings and unrealistic expectations. They manipulate and disappoint each other. They drive each other crazy. Christina tantalizes Geoffrey with her knowledge of what he is thinking or what he is about to do. He longs to know how she does it, but she deflects his curiosity with vague replies and non sequiturs. Trying to understand her consumes him for 'whole days until evening' and causes him 'many sleepless nights' (p. 151).

Most seriously, heterospiritual relationships risk becoming sexual liaisons. Roger and Christina worry that close proximity might entice them to sin, but had they not lived together 'they would not have been stimulated by such heavenly desire, nor would they have attained such a lofty place in heaven' (p. 103). Christina very nearly sleeps with one of her protectors, but had she not taken refuge with him, she would not have escaped her persecutors. The rewards are worth the risks. Those who assume that relationships between men and women are inevitably sexual are mistaken—and often up to no good. Christina's biographer repeatedly shows people trotting out accusations of sexual misconduct to discredit those they disapprove of for whatever reason. 'Someone' tells Christina that her friend Sueno was 'still so stimulated by lust that unless he were prevented by the greater power of God he would without any shame lie with any ugly and misshapen leper' (pp. 37, 39). There is not a modicum of evidence to support this claim about a man who was introduced to us as 'advanced in age, conspicuous for his good life, and influential in his teaching' (p. 37). Christina herself becomes the target of a smear campaign:

some of them called her a dreamer, others a seducer of souls, others, more moderately, just a worldly-wise business woman; that is, what was a gift of God they attributed to earthly prudence. *Others who could think of nothing better to say spread the rumour that she was attracted to the abbot by earthly love.*   (p. 173, my emphasis)

Christina's biographer unequivocally denounces the rumourmongers:

Before they had become spiritual friends, the abbot's well-known goodness and the maiden's holy chastity had been praised in many parts of England. But when their mutual affection in Christ had inspired them to greater good, the abbot was slandered as a seducer and the maiden as a loose woman. This is not surprising, for the devil, their enemy, feared the advantage they would gain from one another and the great usefulness that would accrue through them to the Church: and so what was the cause of their extraordinary progress he wished to be considered as the cause of their falling away.   (p. 174)

Those who malign Christina are later forced to retract their calumny, her biographer shows. But suspicions and resentment probably lingered. Indeed, they may have ensured that the *Life of Christina of Markyate* ended with the premature death of Geoffrey in 1146.

Christina's life survives in a single fourteenth-century manuscript, which was badly damaged by a fire in 1731. The life, the last item in the manuscript, breaks off in mid-sentence. It is not clear how much was lost, but Rachel M. Koopmans makes a persuasive case that what remains of Christina's *vita* is very nearly all that was written and that 'love, resentment, conflicting spiritual ideals, polemics, power politics' were all 'factors in the story behind [its] missing conclusion'.[38] As we have seen, the *Life of Christina* shows that both Christina and Geoffrey were controversial figures. A contemporary letter-writer reports that in the wake of Geoffrey's death St. Albans was 'ripped apart by factionalism' caused by debate about 'the proper management of St Albans' spiritual and financial assets'.[39] It is probably no coincidence that the *Life* was discontinued—perhaps because its author shared some of his colleagues' misgivings about Christina, or because the new abbot told him to drop it, or because his work met with indifference or outright derision. No mention is made of Christina in official histories of the abbey. The monks adopted as 'co-patron' with Saint Alban not Christina but Alban's male friend and mentor, Amphibalus.

As Koopmans observes, the *Life of Christina* 'had little or no impact on its contemporaries. Abandoned in mid-composition, forgotten and unread, it was neither the basis for a medieval cult nor an influence on later readers or writers.'[40] Nevertheless, she adds, it 'provides a glimpse not only into the early career of a medieval woman but also of the complex of forces governing the production of a *Vita* in a twelfth-century religious community'. It is an important document in the history of English life-writing insofar as it attests to how it was possible to think about life.

Heterospirituality, *circa* 1200: *The Life of Saint Gilbert of Sempringham*

Eve of Wilton and Christina of Markyate lived when friendships between religious men and women thrived, despite the inevitable malicious gossip and the views of prominent churchmen such as Bernard, Abbot of Clairvaux, who declared that raising the dead would be easier than maintaining a chaste relationship with a woman (Sermon 65 on *Song of Songs*). By the end of the twelfth century, increasingly vociferous opposition had made such friendships rarer, in England at least. Indeed, influential voices within the Church had become eager to restrict all congress between the sexes.[41] The *Life of Saint Gilbert of Sempringham* illustrates the changed atmosphere that prevailed by the end of the century.[42] Though it describes events that took place in the heyday of heterospiritual relationships, the *Life* itself is the product of *fin-de-siècle* conservatism.

During the 1130s, Gilbert founded a religious order for both men and women. Gilbertine canons and nuns lived on a single 'campus', known as a 'double monastery', residing in different buildings but attending church together. Such double monasteries, which originated among the desert fathers of antiquity, had thrived in seventh-century England—Whitby, Ely, and Barking are stellar examples—and, indeed, in much of Western Europe. In 787, however, the Second Council of Nicaea condemned them and prohibited new foundations. By the Conquest, no double monasteries remained in England. Their revival was part of the burst of creativity during the first half of the twelfth century as religious visionaries such as Gilbert were figuring out ways to encourage the spiritual aspirations of women, who had fewer outlets than men to pursue religious vocations. By Gilbert's death in 1189, the Gilbertines had more female members than any other religious order in England: some 1500 of its 2200 members were women and nine of its thirteen houses were double, while only four were all-male.

Gilbert faced critics and naysayers. In 1147 he approached the Cistercians, hoping to persuade them to supervise the houses he had established so that he could become a hermit. Such a partnership seemed natural because the women were following a version of the Cistercians' rule. The Cistercians, however, demurred, not wishing to be responsible for double monasteries. Then, during the 1160s, the Gilbertines were rocked by scandal. First, there was the affair at the Yorkshire house of Watton, where one of the nuns became pregnant from a liaison with a male brother. Incensed, her spiritual sisters seized her partner in sin, forced her to slice off the offending members, and stuffed them in his mouth. Aelred of Rievaulx reported the incident with gusto in an account written *circa* 1166; for him, and doubtless for many others, the incident illustrated the insanity of allowing men and women close proximity.[43] Shortly after the Watton incident, Gilbert was forced to answer charges brought to the Pope against him by a group of disgruntled lay brothers.[44] Among other things, the brothers accused him of allowing inappropriate contact between the men and women at his institutions. Though Gilbert and his supporters insisted that rules governing the interaction between men and women were both rigorous and rigorously enforced, the Pope demanded that they become stricter still.

The *Life of Saint Gilbert* was composed *circa* 1200 as part of the case for Gilbert's canonization that his order presented to the Vatican. Amid the growing conservatism of the Church, and with memories of the scandals of the previous decades still lingering, the author anticipates and attempts to allay scepticism of or hostility towards the Gilbertine way of life. Thus he begins with an incident showcasing Gilbert's fervent virginity. When Gilbert commences his career as a priest, he lodges with a family in the village of Sempringham. One night, he dreams that he puts his hand on the breast of one of the family's beautiful daughters and cannot withdraw it. Fearing that the dream foretells an affair, he gives up his lodgings and takes up residence in the churchyard. As it turns out, his fear is unwarranted: the girl becomes one of Gilbert's first recruits to religious life, and the dream thus 'heralded not future sin but glorious merit' (p. 19). The author iterates and reiterates Gilbert's purity– 'no one has ever heard that he touched a woman, from his youth to the end of his life' (p. 15); 'he preserved unimpaired that purity of flesh which he derived from his mother's womb', rejecting as 'filth' the advancements of women (p. 59).

Having established Gilbert's credentials as a zealous virgin, his biographer documents the origins of the Gilbertines. To help seven young women who wish to commit their lives to Jesus, he arranges for their enclosure in a cell adjoining the parish church of St. Andrew. Knowing that women are easily tempted, 'he shut them away from the world's clamour and the sight of men, so that having entered the king's chamber they might be free in solitude for the embrace of the bridegroom alone' (p. 33). He arranges for female servants to pass necessities to and from the recluses via a window, but 'if humans could have lived without human things' he would have blocked all access to their sanctum. He alone is able to visit them:

There was a door, but it was never unlocked except by his command, and it was not for the women to go through but for him to go in to them when necessary. He himself was the keeper of this door and its key. For whenever he went and wherever he stayed, like an ardent and jealous lover he carried with him the key to that door as the seal of their purity.   (p. 35)

By 1139, this initial cell became the priory of St. Mary, established on land donated by Gilbert de Gant. Further donations enabled Gilbert to found more houses. Because 'women's efforts achieve little without help from men' (p. 37), Gilbert opened his order to men, first lay brothers whom he employed as servants and later canons.

Gilbert's biographer details Gilbert's care to ensure the strict segregation of the men and women in his double monasteries. The buildings housing men were 'far away from the houses of nuns' and 'had no access to them except for administering some divine sacrament when there were many witnesses present' (p. 47). When the men and women were together at church, they worshipped on opposite sides of a wall. When 'pressing reason' required a priest—even the nuns' confessor—to visit the women, he was to be chaperoned by 'several witnesses' (p. 47). In the presence of these men, the women were always to wear veils.

Gilbert's biographer, like Christina's, does not wholly idealize his subject. He admits that young Gilbert was physically unattractive, a slow learner, and lazy (p. 13). As his modern editors observe, his life is not such a 'panegyric' that it does not allow a 'concrete' image of Gilbert's personality, including his 'acute hearing', 'eloquent speech', and 'tenacious memory'.[45] But it allows little insight into Gilbert's relationship with the women he shepherded. There is no hint of give-and-take in Gilbert's dealings with his charges, no references to conversations, only to instructions and chastisements. A strict disciplinarian, Gilbert punishes a nun unwilling to confess a transgression (p. 103); he scolds nuns for not listening attentively enough to his sermon (p. 109); and, in a probable allusion to the Watton affair, he cures 'with a sharp reproof' a nun 'inflamed with an unbridled lust by the devices of the wicked Enemy' (p. 61). Whatever friendships Gilbert may have enjoyed with the nuns of his order his biographer has expunged. Underlying the narrative are the assumption that women are an unruly lot who must be kept firmly in check and a disdain for women's presumed weakness that precludes the kind of spiritual camaraderie celebrated in the *Life of Christina of Markyate*. Derogatory comments abound—for example, women's 'tender virginity is frequently and easily tempted by the serpent's cunning' (p. 33); 'simple and ignorant women…commonly promise what they do not understand and more than they can perform' (p. 35). Such comments, alongside the portrayal of Gilbert's relationship with his nuns, belie the respect for women's spirituality that the very nature of his extraordinary order bespeaks. Gilbert, after all, expected his women to follow the strict practices of the Cistercians; he promoted common practices for his canons and nuns, instructing 'that those customs observed by men but appropriate to the religious life of women and those which can be transferred from women to men should be kept by both sides' (p. 55).

Only once does the author indicate any partnership between Gilbert and a woman in his order. In a rather odd miracle story, he relates that Gilbert delays the death of Prioress Yvette 'because her life still seemed so necessary to his order'; almost immediately after his visit to her, a bowel movement releases her from the bout of constipation that has brought her to death's door (p. 101). Another episode hints at an actual friendship, but this was between Gilbert and a prioress who, the author stresses, 'belonged not to his own community but to nuns of another order' (p. 125). Following Gilbert's death, this prioress dreams she witnesses elaborate funeral preparations being made for what was surely some very great man. When she asks who is being buried, she is told that it is Gilbert. Just then, she sees Gilbert rise from the coffin and begin to sing. Of course, he is not dead, she tells her informant, for she can see for herself that he lives: 'Do you think that I do not know Master Gilbert? I know him extremely well.…my knowledge of him covers almost the whole of his life' (pp. 125–7). But this life-long female friend appears in Gilbert's biography only after his death. We learn no details of their relationship except its length.

The *Life of Saint Gilbert* evinces an obsession with virginity and a privileging of purity over humanity characteristic of its age. Pastoral literature composed for religious women in England during the thirteenth century represented men as sadists and would-be rapists, counselling women to be happy that they had escaped marriage and to protect their virtue vigilantly from sexual predators. Lives of legendary saints iterated that message.[46] On the Continent, by contrast, heterospiritual relationships continued to flourish throughout the thirteenth and fourteenth centuries, as male religious continued to encourage an extraordinarily creative female spirituality despite the inevitable naysayers. In addition to joining convents or entering anchorholds, women were leading semireligious lives as beguines or lay penitents, cohabiting with their families or with like-minded women, embracing the monastic ideals of poverty and chastity without taking formal vows.[47] In 1217, James of Vitry wondered at the 'many bands' of visionaries and ascetics doing charitable work in the diocese of Liège, keeping body and soul together by the labour of their hands.[48] James and other male admirers of such women sought to do justice to their unusual lifestyles with unusual life stories, sometimes telling their own stories along with their subjects'.[49] Thus James's life of Mary of Oignies (d. 1213) resembles 'a memoir of his relationship with her', while Peter of Dacia's 'idiosyncratic' life of Christine of Stommeln (d. 1312) reads a bit like Peter's own 'autobiography or personal memoir'.[50] Henry of Nödingen relays the experiences of Margaret Ebner (d. 1351) in fifty-six letters addressed to her—a remarkable epistolary biography. The anonymous author of the life of Angela of Foligno (d. 1309) fuses biography with mystical theology.

England, by contrast, produced no free-standing biographies of historical women during the thirteenth and fourteenth centuries, even though there is evidence that at least some equivalents of beguines and lay penitents inhabited the country.[51] John Capgrave's chronicle entry for 1337 offers this intriguing reference to a certain 'Jewet Metles', or 'Foodless Julianna':

At this time in a little town called Berwick five miles west of Walsingham there lived a woman they called 'Jewet Metles', so called because she ate no food but received the Sacrament on Sundays and lived on it all week. Priests tried to get her to take an unconsecrated host, but she knew it. She was examined by the officers of the Church and they found no fault in her faith, no sin in her behaviour.[52]

Was Jewet a laywoman? An anchoress? A nun? She comes across as more of a freak than an exemplar of piety, one who attracted sceptics rather than admirers. We know neither what she believed nor how she behaved, only that she was orthodox. The clerics who tried to trick her with unconsecrated hosts were evidently not impressed enough with her ability to detect the Real Presence to record her life.

Nor did the English visionary Julian of Norwich (d. *c*.1416) inspire a biography, unlike her Continental counterparts Catherine of Siena (d. 1380) and Bridget of Sweden (d. 1373).[53] In the initial version of her *Revelations*, Julian dropped a few hints about herself—that when she was about thirty years old a sermon on Saint Cecilia moved her to desire martyrdom, and that her prayer was answered in 1373, when she underwent a near-death experience accompanied by a series of visions. She deleted those autobiographical references in the embellished version of her visions that she produced some two decades later.[54] English women were neither written about, nor, apparently, did they feel comfortable writing about themselves. Yet the lack of enthusiastic biographers and of an environment that encouraged writing about women paradoxically enriched the very little life-writing about women that there was. As I noted earlier, the unusual frankness that characterizes the *Life of Christina of Markyate* may have stemmed from its author's mingled admiration for and disapproval of his subject, his resisting complicity in the assignment of writing about St. Albans's eccentric patroness. Three centuries later, an even more astonishing story of a native spiritual eccentric was written despite formidable obstacles: *The Book of Margery Kempe*, dictated first to a layman with dubious credentials as a scribe and then to an unwilling priest, and one of the oddest '(auto)biographies' ever written.

The Strange Case of Margery Kempe

In 1934, Colonel William Butler-Bowdon brought to the Victoria and Albert Museum an old manuscript that, as he later told a *Times* interviewer, had lain in the library of his Derbyshire manor for as long as he could remember. Hope Emily Allen, an American scholar of late medieval spirituality then researching in London, was invited to assess the colonel's document. Her reaction, scribbled on a postcard to a friend about two months into her examination runs: '[the manuscript] is too thrilling for words'.[55]

Allen had recognized the manuscript as the unabridged source of a brief devotional tract printed by Wynkyn de Worde in 1501 and labelled 'a shorte treatyse of contemplacyon taught by our lorde Ihesu cryste, or taken out of the boke of Margerie kempe of lynn';[56] Henry Pepwell reprinted the tract in 1521 as part of a devotional anthology. These printed extracts consist mostly of Christ's teachings about how to please him, prompted by the questions of a devout woman whom Pepwell assumed to be an anchoress. They give no indication of being part of a life story; one might, rather, have expected this 'boke of Margerie kempe of lynn' to be akin to the visions and meditations of Margery's contemporary Julian of Norwich.

As Allen found, the 'Margerie kempe of lynn' revealed in her complete *Book* was anything but the 'deuout ancres' Pepwell had supposed. Indeed, the *Book* fleshes her out in ways nobody could have anticipated. It relays the story of a flamboyantly singular woman—a failed entrepreneur, a wife who aspires to a born-again virginity after mothering fourteen children, a religious seeker and pilgrim who has knocked around England and ranged as far as Jerusalem on her spiritual quest, and who now, at God's command, records her experiences.

Margery's story is presented in two parts. An extended prologue introduces the first and longest part, which begins with her marriage at the age of twenty and carries the story up to *circa* 1430, when she was about sixty. It recounts her pregnancies, her business failures as miller and brewer, her mid-life religious epiphany, and her struggle to persuade her husband to forswear marital sex. It further describes her travels around England and her pilgrimages to the Holy Land, Rome, and Santiago de Compostela. Margery's eccentric brand of piety excites controversy: among other things, she weeps loudly and uncontrollably at the thought of Christ's passion, and she dons the white apparel associated with virgins. Some people—among them bishops, archbishops, and theologians—commend and encourage her devotion, while others resent her lectures on religion and her reproofs of their moral short-comings. Some even agitate to have her imprisoned and burned for heresy or sedition. In addition to these 'real world' experiences, part one of the *Book* reports Margery's many conversations with Jesus, encounters with the Virgin Mary and other saints, and visions of biblical events.

The second part of the *Book* is shorter and simpler. Begun in 1438, it is a selective continuation of Margery's life story, mostly recounting her perilous journey to escort her merchant son's widow to her home in Germany. Although visions, spiritual dalliances with Jesus, and miracles are fewer here, Margery persists in her boisterous mode of worship and alienates her fellow travellers thereby. Her return to England and a sampling of her prayers conclude this second part and the *Book*.

The discovery of the *Book of Margery Kempe* caused an even greater stir than that of the sole surviving manuscript of Malory's *Morte d'Arthur*, which was turned up in the same year in Winchester College Library.[57] Indeed, it ranks with the discovery of the *Beowulf* manuscript as one of the most important events in English literary history. Thanks to Colonel Butler-Bowdon's 1936 modernization, the *Book* immediately captured the imagination of the English-speaking public. Reviewers enthused about the remarkable life it relayed.[58] The *Times* ranked it 'among the English Classics', 'a spiritual autobiography, a travel-book, and a domestic chronicle' of a 'fearless East Anglian fifteenth-century mystic'. The *New York Times* called it the 'life tale' of a 'pioneer militant feminist and evangelist who lived 500 years ago'. Even the *Children's Newspaper* took notice, presenting Margery as 'an indomitable old tramp', the 'first known woman to write her story in English'. This warm reception reflected, in part, Butler-Bowdon's reshaping of the *Book* to align it with contemporary understandings of (auto)biography by relegating not only its concluding prayers but also thirteen chapters of 'wearisome' mystical matter to an appendix.[59]

Scholarly reception of the *Book of Margery Kempe* was less effusive. Hope Emily Allen was herself profoundly ambivalent. Though the manuscript might have been 'too thrilling for words', Margery herself was obviously a disappointment. As Allen admitted in her preface to the Early English Text Society's 1940 edition, which she prepared with Sanford Brown Meech, she at first considered the *Book of Margery Kempe* 'as merely the naïve outburst of an illiterate woman, who had persuaded two pliant men to write down her egotistical reminiscences'.[60] Upon due consideration, she allowed that Margery is 'devout, much travelled, forceful and talented', despite being 'petty, neurotic, vain, illiterate, physically and nervously over-strained'.[61] Allen trusted that her annotations to the edition would help the 'professional psychologist' make sense of Margery's 'neuroticism'.[62] For decades thereafter, the consensus among readers was that the *Book* was an invaluable mine of information about everyday life in fifteenth-century England, despite its egotistical, neurotic protagonist and lack of literary merit.[63]

The disdain that characterized the first decades of the *Book's* reception by literary scholars has yielded, since the 1980s, to more positive readings from practically every theoretical persuasion—historicist, Marxist, feminist, psychoanalytic, and queer, to name but a few.[64] As of 2017, the MLA Bibliography lists over four hundred scholarly publications on the *Book*. Editions, translations, and modernizations have appeared, and extracts are now found in the most widely-used teaching anthologies of English literature. A website developed with a National Endowment for the Humanities grant is devoted to Margery Kempe and her world.[65] The *Book* has inspired at least two novels.[66] A Kempe Society is surely forthcoming.

The *Book of Margery Kempe* endows its subject with privileges that had for centuries been associated with saints.[67] Christ promises that he will take Margery directly to himself following her death—she will never see Purgatory, much less Hell (p. 14).[68] In Heaven, she will enjoy a place of honour among the saints (pp. 16, 39). On earth, Christ appoints her an intermediary between himself and sinful humanity, authorizing her to speak in his name and telling her that 'those who worship you, they worship me; those that despise you, they despise me' (p. 18). Margery's holiness is certified with the types of plausible miracles routinely found in the lives of late holy people. For example, she discerns the secrets of others; her prayers heal the sick and obtain God's mercy for sinners; those who scorn her are punished; and she survives an accident that would have killed an ordinary person.

Yet these conventional indicators of sanctity certify a most unusual kind of saint and occur, moreover, in a life story that eschews many of the prevalent conventions for narrating the lives of holy people. Unlike the many Continental lives of holy women, which immediately name their subjects and proclaim their singularity— 'the unforgettable virgin Christina' or 'the gracious virgin Lutgard'[69]—the *Book* announces itself as a 'short' and 'comfortable' treatise wherein 'sinful wretches' may understand that the grace God 'works in any creature' by learning of 'how charitably he moved and stirred a sinful caitif unto his love' (p. 3). The prologue does not immediately specify even the gender of this 'caitif', introducing her rather as an 'Everyman' figure who had long tried, sincerely but unsuccessfully, with 'fastings with many other deeds of penance', to follow Jesus. During the course of the entire *Book*, the 'caitif' is only twice referred to by name.

As we saw in Chapter One, prologues to lives of career religious typically establish the credentials of those who wrote and/or commissioned them, but *The Book of Margery Kempe* claims no sponsor and names neither of its scribes.[70] In fact, the prologue recounts the trouble Margery had in getting anybody to record her experiences. Twenty years earlier, we are told, when she first shared her 'movings and stirrings' with respected clergymen—archbishops, bishops, and theologians—many of them urged her to have them written down, some even offering to do the job themselves (p. 4). God, however, told her to wait. Two decades later, he has charged her to 'have written her feelings and revelations and the form of her living', but she cannot find a scribe; at length, one who knows of her (probably her son) travels from Germany to assist her. When he dies, she persuades a priest to carry on his work, but he loses his nerve in the face of the 'evil' (p. 5) spoken in the community about Margery and her weeping, and he procrastinates for years before conscience moves him to fulfil his promise. Thus, in lieu of the usual endorsements by reputable clerical authors and patrons, the *Book of Margery Kempe* offers only the *remembered* endorsements that Margery claims to have obtained twenty years or more in the past; in lieu of the usual hagiographer eager to glorify his subject, we have only amateur scribes recruited to the work with great difficulty and delay.

As we have seen, lives of religious men and women typically recount events in roughly chronological order, often beginning with prenatal portents of sanctity and concluding with accounts of posthumous miracles. Christina of Markyate's biography is in this respect typical. As a girl, the holy woman (again, like Christina) usually prefers prayers to games, fasts, and hopes to consecrate her virginity to Christ. Most holy women achieve their desire to remain unwed, while those who cannot escape marriage perform their marital duties joylessly. The account of Margery's life, by contrast, begins by identifying Margery as a wife, mother, and sinner—identities that set her apart from most female holy women. We are told little of Margery's life before her marriage at the age of twenty, and that little contains no indication that she was remarkably pious—rather the opposite.[71] There is, furthermore, no indication that she had any objection to marriage; the only problem with wedding John Kempe appears to have been that marriage to this 'worshipful burgess' (p. 6) meant a step down the social ladder for the daughter of John Brunham, five times mayor of Lynn and alderman of the prestigious Trinity Guild.[72] Margery's desire for a chaste marriage appears to have arisen during her thirties. In fact, she recalls the 'great delectation' that she and John *both* took in 'using' each other's bodies: 'In her young age [she] had full many delectable thoughts, fleshly lusts, and inordinate loves for his person' (pp. 76, 132).

Repentant sinners were, of course, well represented in the ranks of the saints, and the *Book* repeatedly alludes to two of the most famous, Saints Paul and Mary Magdalene.[73]

Yet Margery's penitential experience departs fundamentally from theirs. Paul and Mary Magdalene—indeed, to the best of my knowledge, *all* of the penitents whose lives were widely known in late medieval England—pass suddenly and dramatically from sinfulness to sanctity.[74] Margery Kempe's path to holiness begins much as theirs did, with a religious epiphany. A difficult childbirth deprives her of her wits. She lashes out at her husband and friends, renounces God and the saints, and 'desire[s] all wickedness' (p. 7). This state lasts almost a year, until a vision of Jesus, 'in the likeness of a man, most seemly, most beautiful, and most amiable' (p. 8), restores her to her senses. This 'wonderful changing' (p. 3) convinces her that she is now 'bound to God and that she would be his servant' (p. 8). She goes 'obediently to her ghostly father, accusing herself of her misdeeds', and afterwards does 'great bodily penance' (p. 3). So far, her story seems to follow the usual track of the penitents; yet, unlike them, she has not arrived at holiness but only begun a journey towards it that continues for many years and never, in fact, reaches entire freedom from temptation.

The *Book of Margery Kempe* frankly recounts its protagonist's backslidings. After the period of penance immediately following her conversion, she resumes gaudy dress, unable to bear the thought that any of her neighbours should be better arrayed than she; she also tries her hand at business 'for pure covetousness and to maintain her pride', because 'all her desire was to be worshipped by the people' (pp. 8-9). Most distressingly, she cannot repress her sexual desires. Years after her conversion, she is tormented by visions of exhibitionist priests (p. 107). Though her husband's embraces repel her, she desires other men. When a certain 'man whom she loved well' propositions her for sex, she consents to the assignation, only to have him reveal that he was merely testing her (pp. 12-13).

As these examples suggest, the *Book* makes it clear that Margery is no saintly superhero. The saints' lives that she would have heard in Church cast saints as intrepid soldiers of Christ scoffing at those who seek to intimidate or harm them. The martyrs could, perhaps, afford their bravado; often their legends attest that they were extended heavenly protection from the pain that their tormentors sought to inflict, and they were always saved from threatened rape. Margery Kempe evinces no such confidence that God will intervene on her behalf. Accused of heresy in York, she tucks her hands into her sleeves so that her inquisitors will not see her tremble (p. 91). Though God may call her his 'singular lover' (p. 39) and dally in her soul, she does not expect him to save her from rape as he did Saint Cecilia and so many other virgins of old. For that, she must rely, ironically, on the earthly husband whose embraces she has spurned. Arrested in Leicester and in Beverley, she entreats her captors not to imprison her with men because 'she was a man's wife' (pp. 82-3, 98). When an angry mob in Canterbury calls for her death ('Take and burn her'), she 'stood still, trembling and quaking full sorely in her flesh, without any earthly comfort, and knew not where her husband was gone' (p. 23). Only when she cannot find her husband does she think to pray for God's help.

The *Book* presents Margery Kempe as one who knows what is expected of a saint but also knows she cannot live up to those expectations. Female saints, from the 'desert mothers' and the myriad martyrs of the early Church to the nuns, anchoresses, and beguines of her own day, were overwhelmingly virgins—yet Margery is a wife and mother of fourteen who, as we have seen, cannot fully extinguish her sexual urges.[75] Though she eventually negotiates a chaste marriage with her husband, she knows that she cannot recover her virginity, and she continually laments its loss, which she feels makes her unworthy of God's special favour. At one point, she wishes she had been killed just after her baptism, for then God would have 'had my maidenhood without end' (p. 38). Her despair moves Jesus to declare 'I love wives also' and 'I love you as well as any maiden in the world' (pp. 36-7). Spiritual chastity counts as much as physical intactness: 'forasmuch as you are a maiden in your soul…you [shall] dance in heaven with other holy maidens and virgins' (p. 39).

Similarly, Margery 'knows' that those dearest to Jesus have expressed their love through willing submission to torments. The martyrs of old were flayed, flogged, beaten, boiled, mutilated, and mangled.[76] Margery, however, cannot even imagine herself doing the same:

She imagined to herself what death she might die for Christ's sake. She thought she would have been slain for God's love, but dreaded the point of death, and therefore she imagined for herself the softest death, as she thought, for dread of her lack of endurance—that was to be bound by her head and feet to a stock and her head to be smote off with a sharp axe for God's love.   (p. 23)

Fortunately, God assures her that she need not be martyred for his sake: 'as often as you think so, you shall have the same reward in heaven as though you suffered the same death' (p. 23). In Margery's case, at least, God values 'martyrdom by slander' over martyrdom of blood.[77]

Jesus further assures Margery that she does not need to emulate the extreme asceticism found in so many of the lives of late medieval saints, especially women. Mary of Oignies (d. 1213), whose life is alluded to in the *Book of Margery Kempe*, took a knife to her own flesh.[78] Mary's contemporary, Christina 'the Astonishing' (d. 1224), whose life also circulated in England, flung herself into fiery ovens and cauldrons of boiling water, hanged herself from gallows, and submerged herself in freezing river waters; she tortured herself on the racks used to interrogate criminals and bloodied herself with thorns and brambles.[79] Bridget of Sweden (d. 1373), whom Margery seems to have viewed as something of a rival for Jesus's affection, lacerated herself with her fingernails, dripped the wax from a burning candle onto her bare skin, and wore hard knots next to her skin so that they would chafe at her continuously.[80] The *Book of Margery Kempe*, by contrast, construes self-inflicted harm as at best ineffective and at worst a sign of spiritual depravity. When Margery loses her mind and denounces God and the Virgin Mary, 'she bit her own hand so violently that it was seen all her life afterward [and] tore the skin on her body against her heart grievously with her nails' (p. 7). The acts of 'great bodily penance' that she undertakes after regaining her sanity lead to vainglory, followed by gruelling temptations, followed by despair, until Jesus calls a halt: 'You have a hair cloth upon your back. I want you to take it away, I will give you a hair cloth in your heart that shall please me much better than all the hair cloths in the world' (p. 14).

Whereas many late medieval holy women were said to be nauseated by food and to subsist on little more than the Eucharist, Margery Kempe loves to eat, and the *Book* is full of meals with friends, family, fellow travellers, and acquaintances.[81] Nor does Jesus lightly demand that she give up what she loves 'best in the world', namely 'eating of meat' (p. 14). Fasting, he avers, is an exercise for beginners (p. 65). When he does order her to forgo food, it is as a means to other, more important ends. For example, he demands that she fast so that she can more effectively bargain with her husband about taking a vow of chastity (pp. 19–20). Eating for his love is as important as fasting for his love; indeed, in order to love and serve him properly, Margery must take care of herself (pp. 118–19). 'Forget me not at your meals', Jesus says (p. 134).

As we have seen, Jesus does not want Margery to prove her devotion through suffering and deprivation, or even discomfort and inconvenience. Instead, he endorses a form of virtual holiness. *Willingness* to suffer and die is as valuable as doing so; *longing* to be a virgin is as good as being one. Likewise, contemplating the Holy Land is as spiritually efficacious as visiting it (p. 55); wishing to endow abbeys or sponsor priests is as good as laying out actual funds (pp. 148–9). God even assures her that wishing to pray is as good as praying, when she laments that the writing of her *Book* has distracted her from her devotions (p. 157).

Jesus thinks little of the prayers one learns by rote and recites by heart (p. 14). He instructs Margery to engage actively with him in 'dalliances' within her soul, where she converses with him 'as clearly as one friend should speak to another' (p. 156). Moreover, he enjoins her to participate in his life through meditation. A life of meditation, he explains, is a 'holy life' that 'pleases me more than wearing of the jacket of mail or the hair shirt or fasting on bread and water, for if you said every day a thousand Pater Nosters, you should not please me as well as you do when you are in silence and suffer me to speak in your soul' (p. 65). Good deeds she imagines while meditating are, he assures her, as valuable as if she had performed them with her 'bodily wits outwardly' (p. 148).

Margery's meditations were clearly influenced by the 'bestselling' *Meditations on the Life of Christ*, composed in the fourteenth century and available in Margery's day in an English translation by Nicholas Love. The *Meditations* provide more fully detailed accounts of Gospel events, and the author exhorts the reader to 'place yourself in the presence of whatever is related as having been said or done by the Lord Jesus, as if you were hearing it with your own ears and seeing it with your own eyes, giving it your total mental response'.[82] The author often prompts his reader not only to witness but to participate in the episodes he describes: she should hold the baby Jesus, kiss his feet, and help his mother take care of him; she should travel with the Virgin, carrying the holy infant, and accompany the holy family into Egypt: 'help carry the child, and serve in whatever way you can.'[83]

Margery Kempe does all of this and more. She engages and embellishes the templates provided in the *Meditations*, enthusiastically rescripting events narrated in the Gospels, both canonical and apocryphal.[84] Margery essentially raises the Virgin Mary: following Mary's birth, 'she busied herself to take the child to herself and keep it until it was twelve years of age with good food and drink, with fair white clothes and white kerchiefs' (p. 15). When the time comes, Margery, not Gabriel, informs Mary that she will become the mother of God. Margery, not Joseph, arranges for Mary's accommodation when the holy family travels first to Bethlehem and then into Egypt, and Margery begs food for mother and child (Joseph is presumably left to fend for himself). Margery accompanies Mary to visit her cousin Elizabeth, who declares herself as impressed with Margery's service as Mary herself is (p. 15). Margery later supports Mary through the horror of Christ's passion, practically displacing John the Evangelist (pp. 142–3).

Through meditation, Margery enters a virtual world far more satisfying than the world she inhabits bodily. She is a cherished member of a supportive community centred on the holy family. Saints, male and female, come to converse with her, and she more than holds her own among men. Paul apologizes for all the grief his disparaging pronouncements about women have caused her (p. 118), and when the Apostles tell her to cease crying at the Virgin Mary's deathbed, Margery scolds them for their insensitivity (p. 128). Unlike her husband, John, who criticizes her for wearing flamboyant clothing that antagonizes the neighbours (p. 8), Jesus orders Margery to wear the white garments of a virgin even over Margery's protests that people will ridicule her for doing so (p. 60). Wholly indifferent to malicious gossip, Jesus compares himself to the husband who truly loves his wife and makes her wear fine clothes regardless of what others might think. She even enjoys a guilt-free sex life, as Jesus commands that he must 'be homely with you and lie in your bed with you.... you may boldly, when you are in your bed, take me to you as your wedded husband' (p. 66). Like any man and wife, they can 'go to bed together without any shame or dread' (p. 155).

Margery's virtual life often intrudes into her 'bodily' life. The sight of candles on feast days or of a priest celebrating the Eucharist triggers visions that cause uncontrollable weeping. Weddings elicit meditations on Mary's marriage to Joseph or Jesus's marriage to the human soul (p. 145). An infant crying or somebody beating an animal transport her instantly and completely to the biblical world, prompting meditations on Jesus as a baby or as the suffering Saviour. When a priest tells her, 'Jesus is dead long since', she replies that, for her, 'his death is as fresh...as if he had died this same day' (p. 109).

Given these accounts of an interior life more vivid and more valued than the exterior, one cannot help but wonder whether at least some of the events that Margery seems to experience in 'bodily wits outwardly' were in fact part of her virtual life. Should we trust the account of a pilgrimage to the Holy Land that mostly records her emotional responses to famous sites, rather than their physical features? Her interrogations by clerical authorities, which are absent from scrupulously kept episcopal registers?[85] The scorn suffered from her contemporaries, or perhaps even the ostentatious religiosity that elicited such scorn? After all, the only surviving records pertaining to Margery Kempe's life document her membership, late in life, in the prestigious Trinity Guild of Lynn, somewhat undercutting her self-representation as a social pariah.[86]

The author of the *Meditations* claims that it is perfectly appropriate to embellish Jesus's life story with details, incidents, and conversations that are not attested in Scripture, so long as they are not 'contrary to faith or good morals'.[87] He urges his reader: 'Make your meditation on the Lord Jesus as if he said or did thus and so.' Could Margery have been applying the same principles when she recounted the events of her own life—as well as Christ's and the Virgin Mary's lives—to her scribes? In short, could the *Book* represent the life that Margery Kempe would have *liked* to have lived for Christ's sake—the triumphs and the slanders, the hurdles, and even the failings?

However it may have come about, the *Book of Margery Kempe* is a bold experiment in life-writing. It is radical in its rejection of the centuries-old model of sanctity as manifested through a life of celibacy and suffering. It is radical in its projection of sanctity as attainable through a life of contemplation and meditation. And it is, thus, radical in its broadening of the definition of a saint. When a man entreats Margery, 'Damsel, if ever you are a saint in heaven, pray for me', she responds, 'Sir, I hope you shall be a saint yourself and every man who shall come to heaven' (p. 96). The radical paradigm of sainthood it conveys is articulated in a radically different *form* of life-writing–a hybrid that borrows from many genres but sits uneasily in any of them.

Though the extracts printed by Wynkyn de Worde, which may have been compiled shortly after the *Book*'s completion, are usually regarded as a conservative rendering of a controversial text, I would argue that they distil its radicalism.[88] They promote the 'virtual sanctity' of desire over deeds, thus highlighting Jesus's articulation of a new form of saint's life, a life forged in the fires of the imagination. The everyday world so vividly conjured in the *Book* is reduced to fleeting allusions and to moments that trigger devotion–the sight of someone beating a child or whipping a horse, an encounter with a leper. The 'years of her youth and of her prosperity' rate barely a mention, as the extracts recount a progress that is wholly spiritual: 'the more she increased in love and in devotion, the more she increased in sorrow and contrition, in lowliness and meekness and in holy fear of Our Lord Jesus and in the knowledge of her own frailty.'[89] Yet details of Margery's imaginary life are retained: 'I would be laid naked upon a hurdle...for all men to wonder at me and cast filth and dirt on me and be drawn from town to town every day', offering a model that the reader might use in envisioning his or her own alternative life.[90]

Distilling the *Book*'s radicalism entailed taking out the details that most make the *Book* (auto)biographical in the usual sense of that term–the details, that is, mostly chosen for inclusion in modern anthologies. The medieval anthologizer, however, provided not a singular life, but a template for constructing singular lives. The *dis*embodied subject of the extracts could be *em*bodied by *anybody*– man or woman, clerical or lay, low or high born. (Though Margery is obviously female, referred to throughout as 'she' and 'daughter', nothing marks her experience as specifically feminine.) The resulting 'life' *may* have inspired a more conservative piety than Margery's–but not necessarily; the extracts also authorize pieties as eccentric as Margery's, if not more so. We cannot know, alas, how these extracts were read, but the very fact that they were made–and explicitly associated with Margery Kempe–suggests that Margery's life, performed or written, was more warmly received than the survival of her *Book* in a single manuscript might suggest.[91]

If Margery Kempe had had a clerical supporter eager to write her life, the result would probably have been far different: less idiosyncratic, more polished, more in tune with the modes of writing lives of holy people. The *Book of Margery Kempe* was blessed by being written under less than ideal circumstances. Margery had to struggle to find her scribes but she also had the freedom to determine how her memories were set down.

In the later Middle Ages, lives of contemporary English holy women were few, but they were enriched by adversity. Goscelin's portrait of Eve is the more complex for being filtered through his confusion, hurt, and resentment. Had he not been traumatized by her departure to France, he would probably never have written her story. Christina's portrait, drawn by a sceptical but usually sympathetic hand, is more vibrant than the one that would have been painted by an admirer dazzled by her holiness. And Margery, who for all we know was a holy woman in no one's eyes but her own, was free to give herself the biography that no one else would write.

3

Kings and a Marshal

Like religious figures, kings were popular subjects of medieval biography, and their lives are likewise found within histories and anthologies. Kings figure prominently in Bede's *Ecclesiastical History*, and subsequent generations of medieval authors produced histories that consisted wholly or largely of kings' biographies, from William of Malmesbury's *Deeds of the English Kings* (1125) through to the various vernacular incarnations of the sprawling English history known as the *Brut*. Lives of English kings can be found in all the major collections of saints' lives, among them the Middle English *South English Legendary*, compiled during the late thirteenth century, and the three fifteenth-century 'translations' into English of Jacobus de Voragine's thirteenth-century bestseller, *The Golden Legend*. Kings' lives constitute the bulk of the advice books known as mirrors for princes and of collections of the lives of famous men, such as John Lydgate's *Fall of Princes* (c.1439) and John Capgrave's idiosyncratic *Book of the Illustrious Henries* (1446).

This chapter focuses on lives about English kings composed by contemporaries or near-contemporaries, though I will also consider two very different anthologies of kings' lives that celebrate the deeds of rulers from the distant past. I shall begin with the earliest free-standing life of an English ruler, Asser's *Life of King Alfred the Great* (c.893), contrasting its portrait of successful kingship with the dim assessment of Edward the Confessor that emerges from the anonymous *Life of King Edward who Rests at Westminster* (1065-7), the only other free-standing life of a pre-Conquest king of England. Edward's anonymous biographer screened his criticism of the king by adopting a hagiographical form; not surprisingly, his pseudo-hagiography was reworked into a genuine saint's life when Edward was put forward as a candidate for canonization in the late 1130s. Aelred of Rievaulx's 1163 *Life of Saint Edward*, the most influential of these reworkings, illustrates the transformation of an unprepossessing ruler into a *bona fide* champion of God and England. After examining these lives of

Edward and Alfred, I shall turn to lives of the antagonists of 1066: Harold, the last
Anglo-Saxon king, and William of Normandy. William's biography, composed by his
follower William of Poitiers, presents the bellicose Conqueror as a just and prudent
prince whose greatest desire is for his subjects' wellbeing. The anonymous author of
the *Life of Harold* purports to recount Harold's life following his defeat and supposed
death at the Battle of Hastings, as reported to him by Harold's servant and close friend.
During the twelfth century there was a decline in the composition of free-standing
kings' lives and a rise in the composition of collected lives. I shall look at the two most
literary and influential of those lives, William of Malmesbury's *Deeds of the English
Kings* (1125) and Geoffrey of Monmouth's *History of the Kings of Britain* (c.1138). Many
later biographies of English kings are what I term 'regnal biographies', less concerned
with the deeds and character of the monarch than with the events of his reign, but one
of the latest surviving medieval lives of an English king, John Blacman's *Compilation of
the Meekness and Good Life of King Henry VI* (c.1480), is also the most introspective
of the English royal biographies. Blacman offers a rich portrait of a good but men-
tally unstable man who, through his manifold virtues, managed to be a disastrous
king. Blacman's rendering of an uncompromising monarch of God contrasts with
Turgot's equally introspective life of Queen Margaret of Scotland (d. 1093), who
managed to be at once worldly and saintly. I shall conclude the chapter by expanding its scope beyond monarchs to encompass William Marshal (d. 1219), Earl of
Pembroke, who served five English kings and ended his life as Regent for young
King Henry III. Marshal's life is composed in French by one who identifies himself
only as 'John'. With its idiosyncratic narrator, it ranks with Garnier's *Becket* as one of
the period's most literary lives, one that insists that biographies are no mere records
of realities but rather self-consciously constructed documents imbued with the
biases of their authors.

Asser's *Life of King Alfred*

Described by one contemporary as 'the greatest treasurer-giver of all the kings',
King Alfred of Wessex might have stepped out of the pages of *Beowulf*.[1] Alfred drove
the Vikings from his land and laid the foundation for the unification of England
under a single ruler. He was also a thoughtful man, an author, translator, and champion of education. Given the propensity of early medieval biographers to write
about teachers and scholars, it seems natural that the earliest surviving biography
of an Anglo-Saxon king should celebrate one committed to restoring in England the
tradition of learning that Bede documented in his *Ecclesiastical History*.

When Alfred became King of Wessex in 871, Vikings were on the rampage. They had slain the East Anglian king Edmund in 870 and had turned their attention to Mercia and Wessex. After many defeats and failed negotiations, Alfred routed his enemies at the Battle of Edington in 878 and took advantage of the decade of peace that ensued to build an effective defence against their inevitable return. During this time, he also set his mind to a cultural and intellectual rebuilding. In the preface to his translation of Gregory the Great's *Pastoral Care* (*c*.890), he recalls being appalled by the condition of England following his great victory of 878. Churches once filled with treasures and books had been 'ransacked and burned'.[2] Those books that survived were mostly in Latin, which few people, even clergymen, could read anymore. To remedy the situation, Alfred recruited scholars to Wessex from Mercia, Wales, and the Continent, among them the Welsh monk Asser, who was to become Alfred's biographer. Confident that literacy would lead to better government and administration, Alfred provided his household with a school. His dream was that 'all the free-born young men now in England who have the means to apply themselves to it, may be set to learning (as long as they are not useful for some other employment) until the time that they can read English writings properly'.[3] Thus laymen as well as aspiring clergymen could experience the joy that comes from studying great books. During his reign, the *Anglo-Saxon Chronicle*, the first major history written in Old English, was commenced, and Bede's *Martyrology* was translated and richly amplified. In addition to encouraging others to translate such spiritual classics as Gregory the Great's *Dialogues* and Bede's *Ecclesiastical History*, Alfred undertook translation projects himself.

How was Asser to tell the story of this hybrid monarch/warrior/scholar? Free-standing Anglo-Latin biographies had thus far dealt only with saints and professional religious. Biographies of English kings were relatively short accounts embedded within larger narratives, such as Bede's *Ecclesiastical History* or Alcuin's *Bishops, Kings, and Saints of York* (*c*.782). Asser drew upon these models, modifying each as needed, but he also had to hand something rather more relevant and 'modern': Einhard's biography of the Frankish king and emperor Charlemagne, composed most probably sometime between 829 and 836. Like Alfred, Charlemagne was at once a warrior-king and the instigator of a major educational programme.[4]

Like the biographers examined in Chapter One of this volume, Einhard emphasizes the authority of his eyewitness account: 'no one can describe these events more accurately than I, for I was present when they took place.'[5] What is more, he stresses his responsibility to Charlemagne, the patron who befriended him as a child. Uncertain that the deeds he witnessed 'will in fact ever be described by anybody else', he must ensure that Charlemagne will not 'remain unchronicled and unpraised, just as if he had never lived'.[6] Einhard's preface reads as an apology not only for the text he is presenting but also for the very endeavour of memorializing a great modern, rather than one long dead.

Einhard modelled his life of Charlemagne after one of the classics of antiquity, Suetonius's *Lives of the Caesars*, a collection of brief biographies of illustrious— and notorious—men composed around 121AD.[7] He was particularly influenced by Suetonius's treatment of Augustus, who came closest to embodying the ideal that Einhard wished to project of Charlemagne. Having no reliable information, Einhard could not describe Charlemagne's childhood in the same detail that Suetonius described that of Augustus. However, he followed Suetonius's lead in narrating Charlemagne's life not chronologically but thematically: 'his achievements at home and abroad, then his personal habits and enthusiasms, then the way in which he administered his kingdom and last of all his death'.[8] Einhard not only copied Suetonius's approach to writing the life of a public figure, but he filched details from his model with the dexterity of a hagiographer. Titbits about Charlemagne, from his habit of wearing only linen underwear to his custom of receiving followers while he bathed, come right out of the *Lives of the Caesars*.[9]

Asser, in turn, presents Alfred as something of an English Charlemagne, a courageous military leader and wise governor who prized and encouraged learning.[10] He follows Einhard's organization, too, first recounting Alfred's military achievements and then discussing his character and habits.

To tell the first part of Alfred's story, Asser adapts the genre of the annals, ongoing histories that record, year by year, momentous events such as rebellions, comets and eclipses, or the births, marriages, and deaths of kings.[11] Here Asser's immediate influence was the *Anglo-Saxon Chronicle*, which was begun during Alfred's reign, though it stretches back into the distant past with bits garnered from the Bible, from Bede's *Ecclesiastical History*, and from other sources.[12] A genre devised to relate history-in-progress might have struck Asser as appropriate for relating a life-in-progress, for Asser, unlike most earlier biographers, was treating a man who was still alive. Alfred was both his subject and his dedicatee.

Asser begins with Alfred's birth year of 849, but he apparently knew little more about Alfred's boyhood than Einhard knew about Charlemagne's, because most of the entries for the early years of Alfred's life have little to do with Alfred. Instead, Asser draws liberally from the *Anglo-Saxon Chronicle*, and much of his information concerns the doings of Alfred's future nemeses, the Vikings: for example, 'In the year of the Lord's Incarnation 855 (the seventh year of the king's life), a great Viking army stayed for the winter on the Isle of Sheppey.'[13]

After a break in 866, when Alfred turned eighteen, to describe young Alfred's character and to report a few incidents from his childhood, Asser reverts to annalistic reporting of events, focusing on the king's campaigns against the Vikings, until he arrives at the year of Alfred's marriage. He then lays aside the annalistic form for good to focus on Alfred's personality and habits. Here Asser's narration becomes distinctly hagiographical. He writes that Alfred, on his wedding day, was struck by a near-debilitating infirmity that none of his doctors could diagnose but that Asser attributes to a heavenly visitation that the king had wished upon himself. By way of background, he describes, for the first time, the king's life-long piety; though he had earlier reported that the young Alfred learned the liturgy, psalms, and many prayers, he had made clear that what Alfred had 'desired the most' was to master the liberal arts.[14] However, Asser now tells us that 'even from his childhood he was an enthusiastic visitor of holy shrines'.[15] Moreover, as a young man Alfred felt guilty because he could not subdue his sexual desires:

When in the first flowering of his youth before he had married his wife, he wished to confirm his own mind in God's commandments, and when he realized that he was unable to abstain from carnal desire, fearing that he would incur God's disfavour if he did anything contrary to His will, he very often got up secretly in the early morning at cockcrow and visited churches and relics of the saints in order to pray; he lay there prostrate a long while, turning himself totally to God, praying that Almighty God through His mercy would more staunchly strengthen his resolve in the love of His service by means of some illness.

God obliged by visiting him first with severe haemorrhoids and then, on his wedding day, with an unspecified illness that was severer still. This disease tormented him day and night until he was forty-five. Even when the symptoms abated temporarily, 'his fear and horror of that accursed pain would never desert him'. The affliction reminded him continually of the deity who alone could relieve his suffering.

Having established Alfred's piety, Asser turns to the dominant themes of the biography's second half: Alfred's intellectual pursuits and educational programmes. Asser describes in detail the school Alfred instituted for the children, including his own, living at his court, a school designed to provide the education he wished he had received growing up:

In this school books in both languages—that is to say in Latin and English—were carefully read; they also devoted themselves to writing, to such an extent that, even before they had the requisite strength for manly skills (hunting, that is, and other skills appropriate to noblemen), they were seen to be devoted and intelligent students of the liberal arts.[16]

Asser recounts Alfred's efforts to make his court a centre of culture and learning by encouraging adult education and recruiting distinguished scholars (not surprisingly, he provides a detailed account of his own recruitment). He describes Alfred's eclectic tastes in literature, which range from sacred scripture to English poetry, and the translation projects he undertakes in his free time. Alfred's love of learning and commitment to education, Asser maintains, are keys to his character.[17] This portion of Asser's *Life of Alfred* is thus very much in the tradition of biographies about career religious examined in Chapter One. Alfred may have been a warrior, a ruler, a husband, and a father, but he was also a passionate student and teacher in the tradition of Wilfrid, Boniface, and Leoba, and like them he struggled to balance intellectual cravings with secular responsibilities.

The hybrid form—part history, part annals, part sacred biography—that Asser adopted to portray a king who was himself a hybrid of warrior, ruler, and scholar does not fully succeed. The annalistic sections do not mesh smoothly with the discursive accounts of Alfred's character and achievements, and Asser must backtrack to explain the origin of Alfred's wedding-night infirmity. Despite its structural flaws, however, this first free-standing biography of an English king both memorializes and exemplifies the intellectual creativity that Alfred nurtured.

The Last Anglo-Saxon King: History and Hagiography

A wholly different approach, which breaks radically from the tradition of biographical writing examined in Chapter One, is taken in the only other pre-Conquest life of an English king, the anonymous life of Edward the Confessor. This life, entitled in its single surviving manuscript *The Life of King Edward who Rests at Westminster*, consists of two very different parts. The first, which appears to have been started about a year before Edward's death in 1066 and finished shortly thereafter, is a self-consciously literary work written in a combination of verse and rhyming prose. It begins with the Muse instructing the Poet to 'be first to sing King Edward's song'.[18] The Poet complies with a 'song' that is not only Edward's: written for the pleasure of Edward's wife, Edith, it also celebrates the deeds of her father, the powerful Earl Godwin of Wessex, and of her brothers, Tostig, Earl of Northumbria, and Harold, Earl of Wessex. Part One is, then, a 'collective life' in the tradition of Bede's *Lives of the Abbots* but organized around a person, Edith, rather than a place, Wearmouth and Jarrow.

The Poet's immediate inspiration was probably the *Encomium to Queen Emma*, composed in Latin prose *circa* 1041 in honour of Emma, Edward the Confessor's mother. The anonymous encomiast anticipates that readers will expect a narrative focused on Emma, but he protests that he can best praise the queen by also recounting the deeds of those whose lives touched hers.[19] The Poet's treatment of Edith is much like the encomiast's treatment of Emma.[20] Though she is not a major character, his affection for her is warm and unequivocal. She appears in the narrative as the ideal consort–a prudent counsellor, solicitous of her subjects, and supportive of her husband.

According to his Muse, the Poet loved Edith's kin because he loved Edith. The problem was that Edith's kin did not much love each other. Godwin had joined in league with Edward's enemies before switching sides, and Edward's marriage to Edith was meant to seal what proved an uneasy alliance. Godwin opposed the growing influence of Norman expatriates at Edward's court, and in 1051 Edward banished both Godwin and his sons Tostig and Harold. Not about to accept exile, they raised an army, returned to England the following year, and forced Edward to reinstate them. But Edith's blood kin quarrelled not only with her husband but also among themselves. In 1065, Harold took the side of Tostig's Northumbrian thanes in their dispute with his brother, and when Harold succeeded Edward as king in 1066, Tostig joined the invading Norwegian army and died at the Battle of Stamford Bridge.

Delivering a favourable portrayal of all of Edith's menfolk–Edward, Godwin, Tostig, and Harold–was a challenge that the Poet handled with great diplomacy. Though his sympathies clearly lie with Godwin and Tostig, he is careful to praise everybody and to criticize discreetly and obliquely. Part One begins not with Edward but with Godwin at the height of his power during the reign of King Cnut. The king and people alike valued Godwin for his prudent counsel, even temperament, and courage in battle. As the realm's most powerful magnate, he sagaciously discharged his duties and acted as a father to the people. After Cnut's death, he 'took the lead' in securing for Edward 'the throne that was his by right of birth' and put all his energy and his talents into the service of his new sovereign (p. 9). Conscientious, wise, and righteous, he was the victim of malicious enemies who turned the king against him by claiming that he was responsible for his brother Alfred's death (p. 20). The Poet also praises Edith's brothers in glowing terms: 'no age and no province has reared two mortals of such worth at the same time' (p. 32). Harold and Tostig were equally brave, equally handsome, and equally loyal to Edward. Of the two, Harold was more prudent, Tostig more prone to act on impulse. Harold was more even-tempered, more able to 'bear contradiction'; he was also hardier, 'well practised in endless fatigues and doing without sleep and food' (p. 31). Tostig was more righteous–he foreswore all women except for his wife, and he gave generously to religious causes.

The Poet dances around the brothers' falling out, which he recounts in the final chapter of Part One, by acknowledging minor character faults in each that led to major consequences. The Poet had observed earlier that Tostig was 'endowed with very great and prudent restraint–although occasionally he was a little over-zealous in attacking evil–and with bold and inflexible constancy of mind' (p. 32).

This over-zealousness was manifest in his treatment of his thanes, whom he 'repressed with the heavy yoke of his rule' on account of their 'misdeeds' (p. 50). They rebelled, and chaos ensued: 'all that region, which had for so long rested in the quietness of peace through the strength and justice of the famous earl, by the wickedness of a few nobles was turned upside down' (p. 51). The Poet places himself squarely on Tostig's side. His perceived 'cruelty'–that is, his willingness to mutilate or kill malefactors without regard for rank–made it possible for 'any man, even with any of his goods' to 'travel at will even alone without fear of attack' (p. 51). Yet the Poet also voices the complaints against Tostig. When King Edward took counsel with magnates from throughout his realm, 'Not a few charged that glorious earl with being too cruel; and he was accused of punishing disturbers more for desire of their property which would be confiscated than for love of justice' (p. 53). The Poet is equally circumspect in his handling of Harold. Though some lords at that same council claimed that Harold had urged the disgruntled Northumbrian thanes to rebel against his brother, the Poet expresses shock and disbelief–'Heaven forbid!' and 'I dare not and would not believe that such a prince was guilty of this detestable wickedness against his brother' (p. 53). But his surprise cannot have been wholly genuine; after reporting that Harold denied the charge under oath, he volunteers that Harold was 'rather too generous with oaths (alas!)' (p. 53).

At the beginning of Part One, Edward is idealized: 'so fair / in form', the Muse enthuses, 'so nobly fine in limb and mind'; his ascension has ushered in a 'golden age...for his English race', and he now 'blooms' with 'locks of snowy white' (p. 3). The Poet describes him directly as handsome and tall, with 'milky white hair and beard, full face and rosy cheeks, thin white hands, and long translucent fingers' (p. 12), in temperament 'pleasant but always dignified...most graciously affable to one and all' (p. 12). Edward is kind to petitioners even when he must deny their requests, appoints good judges, and replaces bad laws with good ones. But as we proceed into the narrative, a more ambivalent view emerges. Though the Poet never criticizes him directly, the king starts to look like a gullible dotard, long on good intentions but short on judgment. He errs by putting too much stock in bad counsellors, who alienate him from his father-in-law and from his wife (pp. 21, 23). By ignoring 'more useful advice', he offends 'quite a number of the nobles of his kingdom' (p. 18). In Edward's defence, the Poet explains that 'the malice of evil men had shut up the merciful ears of the king' (p. 26); however, he also intimates that the king is too detached from affairs of state, spending much of his time hunting and hawking, attending church services, and conversing with abbots and monks. That 'the most kindly King Edward passes his life in security and peace' is due in no small measure to the loyalty and vigilance of his in-laws (p. 40).

In Part Two, the Poet takes another stab at writing 'Edward's song'. He resolves first to 'briefly say something about his earlier life' (p. 60). What he says is nothing if not brief:

King Edward of happy memory was chosen by God before the day of his birth, and conse-quently was consecrated to the kingdom less by men than, as we have said before, by heaven. He preserved with holy chastity the dignity of his consecration, and lived his whole life dedicated to God in true innocence.

From there he moves directly to accounts of the numerous miracles that indicate God's approval of Edward's life. He anticipates that his portrait of Edward as a pious old man will please Edith, who often spoke of Edward as a father and of herself as his child (p. 60).

Though early medieval biographers, as seen in Chapter One, often used miracles to illustrate their subjects' character, the Poet says little of the sentiments that motivate Edward's miracles or the qualities they demonstrate. Instead, he focuses on sometimes banal and sometimes grisly minutiae. For example, he details how Edward rid a young woman of a pox by treating her with water he had bathed in: after moistening the infected area, he applied pressure until 'worms together with pus and blood came out of various holes'; ignoring the stench, 'the good king kneaded with his holy hand and drew out the pus' (p. 62). The Poet moves from the miracle stories to a conclusion in which the dying Edward prophesies that God will visit His anger upon England following his death.

In 1161, just over one hundred years after Edward's death, he was canonized by Pope Alexander III. Numerous hagiographies celebrated his sanctity, and it would be easy—and wrong—to view *The Life of King Edward who Rests at Westminster* as the first of them. As the *Life*'s editor and translator put it, Part One 'cannot be regarded as in any way a saint's life', while Part Two is at most 'a rudimentary and perhaps slightly hesitant saint's life' (pp. xx–xxi). The Poet, a savvy observer of the eleventh-century political scene, is shrewd, cynical, and cognizant of what was 'advanta-geous…in the theatre of the world' (p. 32). Edward's holiness is not so much his theme as it is his stratagem to escape writing a conventional biography of the king. In Part One, he redefines his task from writing 'Edward's song' to writing the song of Edward and his in-laws. Unable to praise Edward's governance, he praises his piety; Edward is otherworldly rather than incompetent, innocent rather than unjust. When, at the beginning of Part Two, the Muse (perhaps representing Edith) asks again for 'Edward's song', he supplies Edward's miracles.

It is hardly surprising that the promoters of Edward's cult produced drastically revised lives, and their revisions demonstrate the difference between the Poet's political biography and royal hagiography, a major genre of medieval biography. Osbert of Clare composed the first life of *Saint* Edward in 1138, as part of the initial (failed) campaign for Edward's canonization. In 1163, to honour the newly minted saint, Aelred of Rievaulx elaborated Osbert's work into the biography that soon became the authoritative source of all subsequent medieval lives of Edward.[21] Aelred's is *bona fide* hagiography: it begins with Edward's holy childhood, follows him through a life filled with signs of God's favour in the form of cures and prophecies, and ends with post-mortem miracles. Adhering to hagiographical convention, Aelred associates Edward with established saints such as King Oswald and biblical patriarchs such as Moses.

Whereas the Poet associates Edward's piety with his old age, Aelred claims that Edward enjoyed praying, attending church, and conversing with monks even as a child, and most crucially that he longed to commit his virginity to God. True, the Poet had praised Edward's chastity, but chastity was not virginity; one could be chaste by merely confining one's desires to one's spouse, and indeed, though Edward had no children, the Poet does not suggest that he was childless by choice. Aelred, however, transforms the Poet's blandly chaste Edward into a fervent virgin. Urged by his lords to marry after his ascension to the throne, Edward

was struck with fear that by the heats of passion the treasure he kept in an earthen vessel might be lost. But what to do? If he refused stubbornly, he was afraid that the secret of his pious resolve might be betrayed: if he agreed to their pressure, he dreaded the shipwreck of his chastity.[22]

Seeing no recourse, he trusts God and agrees to wed.

Many of the pieties that Aelred praises are not prudent in a king. Edward's celibacy is the prime example. Edward is also generous to a fault. Aelred describes him watching a serving boy raid the money chest that his chamberlain has left unattended and intervening only to warn the boy of the chamberlain's imminent return.

Some royal hagiographers do not care whether their subject is a good king so long as he is a good saint, but Aelred is not one of them. Though his Edward is innocent, naive even, he is not ineffectual.[23] Aelred omits the controversies, so prominent in the Poet's narrative, that show Edward as an indifferent governor of questionable judgment: he says nothing of Edward's failed attempt to help Tostig regain Northumbria, nor of his estrangement from his wife. The king's imprudent generosity has no adverse consequences, if for no other reason than that his conscientious chamberlain does not make a habit of leaving the royal coffers open. As for Edward's virginity, that is part of God's plan and so beyond criticism: the Bishop of Glastonbury informs Edward of a vision in which he has seen St. Peter anoint Edward king while urging him to remain a virgin, and God duly provides him with a wife who readily assents to a celibate union. Edward's innocence is not the liability it was in the anonymous life because God—not the Godwin clan—is continually watching out for his interests. Thus as the Danish king is readying his fleet to attack England, he trips, falls overboard, and drowns; correctly seeing in this event a sign of God's favour towards Edward, 'not only the Danes but other nations as well sent ambassadors and gifts to sue with him for peace' (p. 39).

God also protects Edward from treachery at home, which in Aelred's account takes the form of the iniquitous Earl Godwin and his spawn. Edward's canonization took place under Norman rule, and the Norman promoters of his cult, Aelred among them, were naturally unsympathetic to Earl Godwin and his sons. From their perspective, Godwin's son Harold was a usurper who reneged on his promise to support William of Normandy as Edward's heir. Nor did they approve of Godwin's attempts to undermine the influence of Edward's Norman counsellors. Aelred duly represents Godwin as 'traitor to both king and kingdom', a perpetrator of 'abominable crimes' including the murder of Edward's brother Alfred (p. 74). A skilled liar, he thinks to bind Edward to him through marriage, little suspecting that God has from childhood instilled in Edith a desire for virginity (p. 35). Through 'deceit, falsehood and deviousness', Godwin alienates Edward's true friends, i.e. his Norman supporters, intending thereby to force Edward to rely wholly on his judgment. Edward plays along, confident that God will deal with Godwin. And at last the deity does strike with 'vengeful anger': at a feast, Godwin calls on God to witness that he was not responsible for Alfred's death and forthwith chokes to death on a morsel of bread (pp. 74–5). Tostig and Harold are no better than their father. Both are schemers; Harold is a bully and an oath-breaker (pp. 72, 89).

Though Aelred praises Edith effusively, likening her to a rose among thorns, she is a far cry from the Poet's wise counsellor. As a girl, she led a sheltered life, reading and embroidering, uncontaminated by any interaction with the opposite sex. As queen, she delights in her husband's chaste embraces. Aelred lovingly depicts the alternative form of marriage that she and Edward enjoy, teasing readers with what I think is an unprecedented peek into the marital bedroom:

She was a wife in heart, but not in flesh: he a husband in name, not in deed. Their conjugal affection remained, without their conjugal rights, and their affectionate embraces did not rupture her chaste virginity. He loved, but was not weakened; she was beloved but, untouched, and like a second Abishag, warmed the king with her love but did not dissipate him with her lust; she bowed to his will, but did not arouse his desires.   (p. 36)

Aelred leaves his readers to imagine how this all transpired, but the feelings he imputes to Edith are certainly not those of a daughter for her father. Aelred's Edith plays no role in Edward's life beyond that of his beloved virginal bedfellow. He does not even describe her abetting his good works.

The Life of King Edward who Rests at Westminster and Aelred's *Life of Saint Edward the King* thus represent differing approaches to the writing of kings' lives, each of which flourished in post-Conquest England: what I will call a 'secular' tradition whose principal concern is the king as a ruler and a hagiographical tradition whose principal concern is the king as a saint. That said, the demarcation between these two approaches is not always sharp; writers concerned principally with history and politics often ascribe to their protagonists an extraordinary piety, as we have already seen both in Asser's life of Alfred and in the anonymous *Life of King Edward who Rests at Westminster*.

The Norman Conquest: Winners and Losers

William of Normandy: A Peaceable Conqueror

William of Poitiers, one of the Conqueror's chaplains, drew upon personal experience to produce a text that, in the words of its modern editor, has 'more in common with the reminiscences of a Victorian statesman than with the monastic chronicles of his own day'.[24] Composed between 1071 and 1078, *The Deeds of William* survives in only one damaged manuscript, missing both its beginning and its end. It consists of two books, the first covering William's career as duke of Normandy and the second his reign as king of England.

Like so many medieval biographers, William of Poitiers touts the veracity of his account, contrasting biographers' duty to the truth with poets' licence 'to amplify their knowledge in any way they liked by roaming through the fields of fiction' (p. 29). Unlike those roaming poets, he avers, he will not take 'a single step beyond the bounds of truth'–though in fact he embellishes his account liberally and omits incidents that present William as anything but a merciful and judicious prince.[25] 'Truth' is as much a convention in the biography of royals as it is in the biography of religious.

William of Poitiers, who had trained as a knight and seen combat prior to entering the Church, was fully at home writing about William of Normandy as a military leader and strategist. The Conqueror emerges from his account like the hero of some *chanson de geste*. A brave and skilled warrior and a charismatic leader, he inspires his followers with his own valour, thinking little of personal safety. The author, like the biographers of holy men and women, compares the duke to heroes of old–though his heroes are, of course, warrior kings such as Caesar or Xerxes rather than hermits or martyrs (p. 111). Moreover, he borrows from the classics to reinforce the parallels, just as hagiographers borrowed from Scripture. For example, he lifts from the Roman historian Sallust the gist of the rousing speech that he claims William gave before the Battle of Hastings.

Yet, even as he celebrates the Conqueror's military victories, William of Poitiers is careful to depict him as the champion of peace. The protagonist of the *Deeds* goes to war only in just causes and only when he has exhausted all alternatives. His invasion freed England from the tyranny of Harold, but it should never have been necessary (p. 173). William of Normandy, his biographer avers, had always dealt fairly with Harold and had even proposed to settle the succession by single combat in order to avoid loss of life on both sides: 'For this brave and good man preferred to renounce something that was just and agreeable rather than cause the death of many men, being confident that Harold's head would fall since his courage was less and his cause unjust' (p. 123). He is even loath to shed the blood of criminals: 'He preferred to punish with exile, imprisonment, or some other penalty which did not cost life, those whom other princes, in accordance with custom or established law, put to the sword' (p. 39).

Despite its title, *The Deeds of William* is at least as interested in William's character as it is in his deeds. The author paints a complex portrait of strategic affability: 'there was in him something that won the love of his household, his neighbours, and those far away. He, for his part, strove to the utmost of his ability to be an honour and support for his friends, and *he took care also that his friends should owe him as much as possible*' (p. 17, my emphasis). Readers are made privy to the Conqueror's thoughts, motives, and even spiritual meditations. Acknowledging that many of William's English subjects enthusiastically—and understandably—supported Harold against an invading foreigner, the author insists that, if only they had known what William was like, their hostility would have dissipated.

Of all the lives of English kings, the *Deeds of William* most fully models the ideal praised in 'mirrors for princes'. Though known as a warrior, the Conqueror employs force only for the common good; he considers the welfare of *all* constituencies, including clergy, townspeople, soldiers, and lords; he cares deeply about the powerless and destitute; he deals fairly with adversaries and honourably with hostages; and his appointments to public office are credits to his prudence and character judgment.

Though focused on the secular sphere, William of Poitiers also effuses about the Conqueror's piety. Even in his youth, William 'took part devoutly in religious services' (p. 81). As an adult, he 'venerated the Eucharist', lent 'an eager ear to readings from Holy Writ' (p. 81), brought up his children as devout Christians, and, in his role as a prince, served God by championing just causes, 'suppressing sedition, rapine, and brigandage' (p. 81), and safeguarding the wealth of God's Church while astutely advising its ministers. A moral man, he honours his wife—'he had learnt that marriage vows were holy and respected their sanctity' (p. 149)—and he prohibits prostitution and drunkenness among those who serve him (p. 159).

Harold: The Untold Story

Harold Godwinson's story was also told, though over a century after his defeat at Hastings.[26] As we might expect, his is the most idiosyncratic life of an English king, for it says practically nothing about his reign. Not that there was much to say; crowned on 6 January 1066, the day after the death of Edward the Confessor, he ruled England for less than a year before his death on 14 October.

The anonymous *Life of King Harold Godwinson* begins with a story about Harold's father that has all the earmarks of romance. The Danish king Cnut, having usurped the English throne, sees the young Godwin as a threat and schemes to destroy him. He dispatches Godwin to Denmark with sealed letters that order the recipients to slay the bearer. Suspecting foul play, Godwin opens the letters and confirms his suspicions; he then replaces them with forgeries ordering that the bearer be given Cnut's sister in marriage. This deceit is justifiable, the author states, because Godwin commits it to save his life. Moreover, Cnut himself benefits from it, for he gains in Godwin a loyal soldier and prudent counsellor. With this anecdote, then, Harold's biographer establishes that deceit *can* be justifiable, even laudable. Much of the ensuing narrative deals with laudable deceits practised by Harold following his defeat at the Battle of Hastings.

Of course, everybody 'knows' that Harold died at Hastings; the most famous account of the battle, preserved in the Bayeux Tapestry (1070s), shows him falling, pierced by a Norman arrow, and today's visitors to Battle Abbey in Sussex can view the very spot where he supposedly fell. Few doubted the reports of Harold's demise during the late eleventh century, either. Yet Harold's biographer claims that Harold's wife Edith, sent to retrieve his body from the battlefield, mistook another's hacked, bloodied, and decomposing corpse for her husband's.[27] In fact, he explains, the king, though gravely wounded, was spirited away and restored to health by an Arab woman skilled in surgery (p. 13). After failing to raise support for his cause abroad, Harold set his sights on the Kingdom of Heaven. He spent years as a pilgrim, 'his soul like a bride seeking her bridegroom' (p. 18), before returning to Britain in his old age incognito, settling first not far from Hastings before moving to Wales. To those who inquired whether he was present at the great battle, he replied, 'I was certainly there' (p. 32). If pressed by somebody who suspected he actually *was* Harold, he added, 'there was nobody dearer to Harold than myself.' He did not lie, his biographer points out—he merely failed to tell the whole truth.

Harold's biographer is as evasive as his subject. His digressive narrative privileges issues over incident. He surveys the debate over whether Harold was justified in reneging on his vow to support William of Normandy's claim to the English throne. He addresses at length the question of how Harold could have been defeated if he were truly the 'lawful king', 'rightfully and lawfully crowned' (p. 3). He energetically defends the legitimacy of his biography, identifies his sources, documents the evidence that Harold survived Hastings, and explains how his survival could have been so thoroughly concealed. He offers apologies and excuses for his 'excessive' digressions (p. 13) and promises to get back on track. Yet he leaves enormous gaps in his account of Harold's deeds.

A case in point is his coverage of the many years Harold spent as a pilgrim. He first mentions Harold's peregrinations as he is establishing the credibility of his principal source, a hermit by the name of Sæbeorht who served Harold for many years. Following Harold's death, Sæbeorht resolved to follow his late master's example by going on pilgrimage:

He eventually left England, intending to approach the Lord's Cross in the place where that cross was fashioned and to adore the place where his feet rested. And hoping, as Harold had done, to moisten with his tears the resting-places of other holy men, to listen to strange languages which he did not understand, and joyfully to endure no small tribulation for Christ's sake, he entered a foreign land. Eventually, after many wanderings which there is not space her [sic] to mention, he fulfilled his vow and returned to his native land as Harold had done.   (p. 11)

Note that the author does not say that Sæbeorht visited the Holy Land—only that he *intended* to do so—and one must infer that he wished to travel to the Holy Land because Harold did. The author specifies neither the graves Sæbeorht visited, nor the foreign languages he heard, nor the foreign land he entered.

We might expect that the author would be more explicit about Harold's journeys within the body of his biography, but he is not. Following his failed attempts to rally support among the Saxons and Danes, Harold has a complete change of heart, accompanied by a radical change of appearance:

The hand which was accustomed to bear weapons he supports with a spear cut down to form a staff. Instead of a shield, a pilgrim's wallet hangs from his neck. His head, which he was accustomed to equip with a helmet and adorn with a crown, is shaded with a cowl. In place of boots and greaves, his feet and legs are either completely bare or wrapped in thin leggings. For the rest, let me be brief. The whole armour, the entire adornment of this mighty and powerful man is either left off altogether, or else worn for the humiliation of the penitent. The coat of mail is not thrown off from his shoulders, arms, loins and sides; but it is brought even closer to the body; for the underclothes being taken off and cast aside, the roughness of the metal comes next to the bare flesh. Thus when asleep he did not lie supported by a bed but enclosed in a breast-plate.   (pp. 15-16)

After reflecting at length on the significance of Harold's changed appearance and marvelling at his asceticism, the author turns to Harold's travels—but without specifying where he actually goes: 'this man then departed to a remote country to visit the holy places in order that he might reverence the relics of the saints on their own home ground and in their own shrines' (p. 17). At this point, the author flashes back to a pilgrimage to Rome that Harold had undertaken before he became king. Of his post-Hastings travels, he writes:

I will…follow, as we began to do, our new pilgrim with Christ for a guide. And if we are not able to accompany him to every place and on every single day as he traverses so many provinces of Christendom and spends his time so profitably, or if we do not know and cannot recount every single thing he did or endured on his lengthy pilgrimage, let us at least go and meet him as he returns to us with all speed, accompanying him while still far from our shores.   (p. 18)

That the author cannot report 'every single thing he did' goes without saying, but why he does not report *anything* Harold did 'as he journeys through many places' 'while still far from our shores' is a mystery. These repeated instances of 'un-narration' suggest a deliberate strategy. The dearth of detail about Harold's deeds contrasts with the abundance of detail about his dress—his pilgrim's garb, for example, and the 'hair shirt' he makes from his chain mail. The author also twice describes the veil that Harold wore in front of his face so that those he encountered would not recognize his scarred visage (pp. 29, 31).

   The Life of King Harold Godwinson, then, has the earmarks of a biography without actually being one. Indeed, the author appears to be using the telling of Harold's life as a generic veil of sorts for his real agenda, which was to promote some very specific claims about his subject: that he had been the legitimate king of England, that God favoured him even though he allowed William to conquer England, that he survived Hastings, that he led a saintly life, and that his intercession can now aid sinners on earth (p. 37).

Bio-History

The first half of the twelfth century witnessed a flowering of biographically-oriented histories in the tradition of Bede's *Ecclesiastical History*.[28] Historians of the period saw themselves both as reviving a genre that had languished after Bede's death and as continuing the story that Bede had begun. Bede's twelfth-century followers were 'specialists', mostly focusing on the lives of kings. Through this focus, historians 'created a biographical thread which held history together, and thereby provided the social and political continuity which enabled the present to engage directly with and make sense of the past', as Chris Given-Wilson has put it.[29] Four major king-centred histories were composed during the 1120s and 1130s: William of Malmesbury's *Gesta Regum Anglorum* (*Deeds of the English Kings*), Henry of Huntingdon's *Historia Anglorum* (*History of the English People*), John of Worcester's *Chronicon* (*Chronicle*), and Geoffrey of Monmouth's *Historia Regum Britanniae* (*History of the Kings of Britain*). William, Henry, and John recast much of Bede's history and continued it into their own time. Geoffrey of Monmouth, by contrast, wrote a prequel to the *Ecclesiastical History*, beginning with Brutus, the legendary survivor of the fall of Troy and founder of Britain, and concluding with Cadwallader, the last Briton king; in the process, he introduced into mainstream history the story of King Arthur. All four works were widely circulated and helped ensure that the writing of history for centuries to come would centre on the lives of exceptional men.

Here I will focus on the two most influential and 'literary' of England's twelfth-century's bio-historians: William of Malmesbury and Geoffrey of Monmouth. These contemporaries took wholly different approaches. Along with Henry of Huntingdon and John of Worcester, William appears to have belonged to a coterie of monastic historians committed to the writing of sober, factual history. As William's modern editor Edmund King puts it, William's may be

the first generation of which we may speak of the existence of a historical profession within England, a group of scholars in regular contact, collecting material, distributing drafts of their writings to one another for comment, confident both of their methodology and of the market for their work.[30]

Geoffrey was an outlier. Indeed, Valerie Flint has proposed that Geoffrey was parodying the values and methodologies of monastic historians such as William.[31] He claims as his source for the *History of the Kings of Britain* an ancient book that was almost certainly spurious.[32] As Derek Pearsall notes, his 'inventions are dressed up as perfectly sober matter-of-fact history'.[33] His contemporaries disagreed hotly on his reliability, and he has remained a controversial figure up to our own times.

In his *Deeds of the English Kings*, William covers the pre-Conquest period by looking in turn at the rulers of each of England's four major kingdoms, Kent, Wessex, Northumbria, and Mercia. His lives range from brief notices to elaborate cradle-to-grave narratives. Some recount major life events, while others focus on character and habits.[34] Some are simple paeans to great men, but most offer nuanced views of their subjects that consider changes in their circumstances and personalities. William Rufus changed for the worse over time yet maintained 'real greatness of spirit' (p. 565).[35] Edward the Confessor, 'handicapped by illness and burdened by old age', became almost 'an object of contempt' (p. 467). As Björn Weiler observes, 'good kings could turn into bad ones' and sinners could atone for their transgressions in a work that everywhere evinces a 'subtle understanding of human nature'.[36]

William is as interested in personal habits as in deeds and politics. His tone is often gossipy, with comments on his subjects' health, appearance, and relationships, and he has an eye for the quirky and offbeat.[37] From him we learn that William Rufus stammers and Henry I snores (pp. 567, 747). Henry I is muscular, William Rufus paunchy, and William the Conqueror (in his later years) corpulent (p. 747). William's lives are full of action and vividly rendered scenes. A splendid example is his rendering of the White Ship Disaster that killed Henry I's son William in November 1120—the tragic outcome of monumental stupidity. The seventeen-year-old prince and his high-spirited friends, all revved up on booze, were speeding through the waters off Barfleur in the dead of night on a spanking-new ship driven by drunken oarsmen:

The ship sped swifter than a feathered arrow, and skimming the sea's curling top, she struck, through the carelessness of her besotted crew, a rock projecting from the surface not far from the shore. Hapless souls, they jump to their feet and in a babel of shouting unship iron-shod poles for a long struggle to push their vessel off the rock....Already some were being washed overboard, and others drowned by the water that came in through the cracks.   (p. 761)

A boat was dispatched towards the shore with young William aboard, but hearing the cries of his half-sister, the prince ordered it back to the scene of the wreck, hoping to rescue her. Mobbed by the desperate, his little boat sank. One man lived to tell the story.

William frequently uses anecdote to illustrate character. A case in point is his illustration of the prodigality of clueless William Rufus. A lavish spender with no sense of what goods and services ought to cost, he was constantly being cheated by those around him. He prided himself on sparing no expense on his wardrobe:

One morning when he was putting on some new shoes, he asked his valet what they had cost. 'Three shillings', the man replied, at which the king flew into a rage. 'You son of a bitch!' he cried; 'since when has a king worn such trumpery shoes? Go and get me some that cost a mark of silver.' The servant went off and returned with a much cheaper pair, pretending they had been bought at the price specified. 'Why,' said the king, 'these are a good fit for the royal majesty.'   (p. 557)

Thenceforth, the servant bought the king's clothes at bargain rates, claimed to have paid a princely sum, and pocketed the difference.

Though William criticizes digression in other biographers, he is himself easily distracted from the main thread of his narration. He interpolates genealogies, descriptions of faraway places, and even hair-raising stories of ghostly visitations and demonic possession (p. 571). He opines about politics, history, and culture, waxing eloquent about the differences between the Normans and the Anglo-Saxons. He expatiates on the difference between liberality and prodigality (pp. 556–7).

William's digressions often take the form of miniature life stories, which can be as complex and nuanced as his longer biographies. Consider his treatment of Matilda, Henry I's consort, whose life he embeds within that of her husband (p. 757). Matilda encouraged William to write his *Deeds of the English Kings*, though she died before he finished the project. In letters accompanying the completed manuscript, William enthuses unequivocally about her love of 'good literature' and her promotion of 'those who were devoted to it' (p. 5), citing her premature death as her only flaw. We might thus expect his embedded life to be a simple paean to a great woman, and that is how it starts out. The first part reads almost as hagiography: Matilda grew up in a convent and rejected multiple offers of marriage before accepting Henry I; she apparently had little interest in sex, and after she bore the obligatory two children she was 'satisfied' when the king was 'busy elsewhere'; she was a holy woman who wore a hair-shirt beneath her royal garments and engaged in various acts of asceticism and piety. But midway through, William's tone changes, at first subtly, as he notes that Matilda's pleasure in hearing divine service led her to esteem 'clerks with sweet voices' more than was 'wholly wise' (pp. 756–9). Her reputation for generosity attracted hordes of 'scholars who had a name for singing or for turning verses' whom she 'kept dangling with promises that were sometimes honoured, and sometimes—indeed, more often—empty'. At this point, William's tone becomes outright censorious, as he confirms reports that Matilda succumbed to 'the vice of prodigality': '[she] laid all kinds of claim against her tenantry, used them despitefully and took their livelihood, winning the name of a generous giver but ignoring the wrongs of her own people.' Although William immediately blames her failings on her 'cunning' servants, this excuse, coming *after* such harsh criticism, smacks of insincerity; could he really believe it could undo the damage done by his censure? Or was William's belated exculpation part of a strategy to present his deceased patroness as a holy but gullible—and rather vain—woman? We might well wonder whether William himself was one of the scholars Matilda kept dangling with empty promises.

Though William says little of the period that predated Bede's *Ecclesiastical History*, he acknowledges that the distant past and its heroes deserve commemoration.

He singles out King Arthur, particularly, who has been 'the hero of many wild tales among the Britons even in our own day, but assuredly deserves to be the subject of reliable history rather than of false and dreaming fable' (p. 27). His fellow historian, Henry of Huntington, echoes these sentiments. Explaining why he chose to begin his *History of the English People* with Julius Caesar and 'omitted the flourishing kingdoms that existed from Brutus down to the time of Caesar', he writes, 'although I searched again and again, I was unable to find any report in those times, either oral or written.'[38] Only after he had completed his *History* did he discover 'a written account of those very matters': Geoffrey of Monmouth's *History of the Kings of Britain.*

Surviving in over two hundred manuscripts, not counting extracts and translations, Geoffrey of Monmouth's *History of the Kings of Britain* (1136) was the most widely disseminated and influential of the post-Conquest medieval British histories.[39] Geoffrey claimed knowledge of the past that eluded other historians thanks to 'a certain very ancient book in the British language' given to him for translation by his antiquarian friend Walter, Archdeacon of Oxford, which 'narrated in the most refined style an orderly and unbroken relation of the acts of all the kings, from Brutus the first king of the Britons to Cadwallader the son of Cadwallo'.[40] That book, most modern historians agree, was Geoffrey's invention, a literary device to secure authority for his fabrication of the Britons' past.[41]

Geoffrey's 'translation' includes characters who are well known to us today, some drawn from Welsh legend, others invented.[42] There we can read about Coel ('Old King Cole'), though it would be hard to recognize the nursery rhyme's 'merry old soul' with his pipe and his fiddlers three in Geoffrey's erstwhile duke of Colchester who slew King Asclepiodotus and seized his kingdom. Geoffrey appears to have originated the story of Leir (Lear), best known to us from Shakespeare. As in Shakespeare, Leir foolishly divides his kingdom between his two eldest daughters, who profess to love him more than life itself, while disinheriting his youngest, the wise Cordelia, who claims to love him just as much as a daughter ought. In Shakespeare's tragedy, of course, all the principals die in the battle to recover Leir's rights. In Geoffrey's telling, however, Cordelia and her husband restore Leir to the throne. He rules three years, and Cordelia rules peacefully for fifteen years following his death. Her nephews, however, 'outraged that Britain was now subject to a woman', oust her from power. Devastated by the loss of her realm, she commits suicide in prison.

In the tradition of Bede, Geoffrey tailors the life stories he narrates to the overarching agenda of his *History*. Like Bede, he is concerned with the decline of the Britons as a people, but instead of following Bede in attributing that decline to religious failures (particularly the Britons' failure to preach to the Anglo-Saxons), he attributes it to the seemingly endemic internal dissent and treachery that ruined even the greatest kings and left their people open to conquest. That Geoffrey should have been preoccupied with the dangers of strife, particularly within families, is no wonder. He was composing his *History* during the late 1130s, on the eve of the civil war that commenced in 1139 between Matilda, the daughter and designated heir of Henry I, and her cousin Stephen, who seized the throne following Henry's death in 1135.

The appearance of numerous powerful and politically savvy women bespeaks Geoffrey's sympathy for Matilda, though his political allegiance may have oscillated.[43] I have already mentioned Cordelia, who governed peacefully for fifteen years following her father's death. Her overthrow by nephews who claimed that women ought not to be allowed to rule rehearses the dispute between Stephen and Matilda. It is hard not to see Matilda also in Geoffrey's portrait of King Coel's beautiful and learned daughter Helen: 'Her father had no other heir to whom he could pass the throne of the kingdom; he had therefore taken great care to instruct her in the ruling of the realm so that she could run things more easily after his death' (p. 102). Though Henry I's designation of his daughter as his heir may have been unprecedented in the history chronicled by Bede and his successors, Geoffrey shows that it was not uncommon among the early Britons. His other female governors include Queen Gwendolen, who rose up against the husband who repudiated her and ruled for fifteen years following his death in battle, and Queen Marcia, 'learned in all the arts', 'mighty in counsel and wisdom', and author of the code known as the Marcian Law (p. 79).

Geoffrey's abhorrence for familial friction shapes the lives he narrates. For example, his life of King Leir focuses on the king's wrong-headed distribution of his realm among his daughters and has less to say about Cordelia's peaceful fifteen-year reign than about her overthrow by her jealous nephews. Geoffrey's most detailed and famous life story—that of King Arthur—demonstrates both the glory the Britons were capable of and the tragedy wrought by familial disloyalty.

Geoffrey by no means invented Arthur.[44] The *History of the Britons* (*Historia Brittonum*) and *Welsh Annals* (*Annales Cambriae*) of the ninth and tenth centuries celebrate him as a great warrior who defeated the Saxons at the Battle of Badon (late 490s or early 500s), although earlier historians who covered that battle, including Bede, do not mention him. Arthur, his queen, and several of his followers are alluded to in the cryptic Welsh Triads, which date from the early twelfth century but may have taken shape centuries earlier, and in Welsh romances such as *Culhwch and Olwen*, which probably originated before the eleventh century.[45] Welsh hagiography of the late eleventh and twelfth centuries often cast Arthur as the 'bad boy king', lusty, greedy, and headstrong, chastened by the puissant saint for such transgressions as attempting to steal his tunic, appropriating his portable altar for a dinner table, or slaying one of his kinsmen.[46]

Geoffrey was the first to endow this misty figure of Welsh chronicle and legend with a comprehensive and coherent biography, beginning with his conception and concluding with his apparent death following the Battle of Camlann.[47] Through detailed descriptions of Arthur's deeds, Geoffrey elucidates the character that made him Britain's most successful king: his generosity to his followers, his acuity as a military strategist, his prowess in battle, his ability to inspire others with his stirring rhetoric, his willingness to listen to advice, and his ability to manipulate his advisors into recommending the course of action upon which he had already settled. Geoffrey shows him scrupulously filling administrative offices and dispensing gifts. As a judge, Arthur is stern but fair, ruthless in punishing treason but compassionate enough to be 'moved to tears', as well as to mercy, by genuine remorse (p. 169). He respects worthy opponents and honours those on both sides who die in battle (p. 196). A friend to the Church, he founds religious houses and rebuilds churches that have been destroyed in war (p. 170).

Geoffrey, however, does not wholly idealize the king. Arthur maintains the loyalty of his followers by dispensing wealth, and when wealth runs out, he attacks the Saxons 'so that he could distribute their riches among his men'. Geoffrey adds, almost as an afterthought, 'Justice spurred him on as well, since by right of inheritance he ought to have had control over the entire island' (p. 163). Arthur's priorities—gaining wealth first, pursuing justice second—indicate that the great king was more an imperialist than an idealist. Geoffrey's Arthur, indeed, is a predator who smells fear and preys on the vulnerable:

The fame of Arthur's generosity and prowess…spread to the furthest ends of the earth, and great fear beset the kings across the sea that Arthur would invade them and seize the lands under their rule. Spurred on by these concerns, they refortified their cities and towers and built castles in strategic locations so that, in the event that Arthur attacked them, they would have a safe refuge. *When Arthur learned of these things, he rejoiced at being universally feared, and he desired to submit all Europe to his rule.* (p. 171, my emphasis)

Geoffrey intimates that Arthur's fall might be due at least in part to overreaching. When the Romans demand tribute from Britain, Arthur goes to war against them, protesting, 'Nothing that is acquired by force or violence can be justly possessed by anyone' (p. 178). Given his raid on the Saxons, not to mention his invasions of Scandinavia, Ireland, and Gaul, one might detect a whiff of hypocrisy here. Should readers have missed the irony, Geoffrey has one of Arthur's vassals iterate the point: 'whoever attempts to take from another that which is not his shall lose what he seeks to take' (p. 179). That is, of course, exactly what happens to Arthur. Spoiling for a fight, he and his troops attack the Romans, ousting them from their holdings on the Continent. Arthur is about to lead his army into Rome itself when he learns that his regent and nephew, Mordred, has usurped his throne and wife. He returns forthwith to England for his fateful encounter with the traitor. Was Arthur's fall caused wholly by the treason of his nephew, or might his own greed have played a role? Geoffrey's celebration of an expansionist king conveys a discreet caution to ambitious princes.

Though Geoffrey focuses on Arthur's numerous military campaigns, offensive and defensive, not everything about Arthur's story is martial. Between accounts of military engagements, Geoffrey describes the development of Arthur's court into a cultural centre, setting trends in fashion and entertainment. Yet Arthur himself seems curiously detached from civilizing pursuits. His court is full of ardent lovers 'inspired' by the 'madding flames of love' (p. 176), but he shows no interest in the opposite sex. Geoffrey says nothing of Arthur's feelings for the Roman beauty, Guinevere, whom he weds (p. 170). In fact, Geoffrey reveals little of Arthur's opinions about anything. It is perhaps emblematic of Geoffrey's exclusive concern with Arthur's public persona that he describes his armour in intricate detail but says practically nothing about the king's character or physical appearance (pp. 166-7). For all the detail Geoffrey provides about Arthur's achievements, Arthur the man remains an enigma.[48]

Although the *History of the Kings of Britain* represents Arthur, like all of its subjects, as a historical figure, it does hint at Arthur's fictionality through his modernity. Geoffrey's representation of Arthur, more so than any other of his other kings, is flamboyantly anachronistic. The Arthurian court, with its knights competing in tournaments and languishing for *amour*, is a twelfth-century court. Arthur's Britain is an idealized version of Geoffrey's Britain, which 'surpassed all other kingdoms in its courtliness, in the extravagance of its fineries, and in the polished manners of its citizens. Every individual knight of fame and virtue in the kingdom bore a livery and arms of a unique colour' (p. 176). In fact, Geoffrey's is the earliest description of the tournament as a spectator sport whose players were identified by their armorial bearings.[49]

Despite this egregious anachronism, Geoffrey's representation of King Arthur was widely accepted as factual, as was the rest of his *History*.[50] Henry of Huntingdon incorporated 'facts' he learned from Geoffrey into a revised version of his own history, and Geoffrey's *History* soon was translated into English and French, the vernaculars of England: the Norman historian Wace produced a version in French verse, the *Roman de Brut*, in 1155, which was in turn translated into English verse by Layamon *circa* 1200.[51] Both Wace and Layamon adapted their Latin source liberally, adding episodes and tweaking incidents and characters. They differ from each other–and from Geoffrey–in their renderings of Arthur, but both offer more insight into Arthur's character. Geoffrey's *History* and its early verse translations were also adapted into French and English prose, and these vernacular *Bruts* continued Geoffrey's story of Britain into the fifteenth century.

Geoffrey's 'biography' of Arthur also inspired a rich tradition of fiction, though much of it marginalized Arthur to focus on his knights and on the tournaments, love, and magic that were incidental in Geoffrey. That tradition included chivalric romances recounting discrete adventures undertaken by Arthur's knights, such as *Sir Gawain and the Green Knight*, as well as more expansive lives, such as *The Rise of Gawain, Nephew of Arthur*.[52] At the end of the medieval period, Thomas Malory's massive life–or, literally, 'death'–of Arthur, the *Morte d'Arthur*, offered a sprawling epic of the Arthurian world that incorporated elements of both the romance and the chronicle traditions. As Caxton's preface to his 1485 edition of the *Morte* attests, fifteenth-century readers were divided over the issue of Arthur's historicity: 'diverse people hold the opinion that there was no such Arthur and that all the books about him are just feigned and fables.'[53] Caxton himself refutes these naysayers, putting forth various arguments for Arthur's existence and concluding, 'no one can reasonably deny that there was a king of this land named Arthur.' Whether a historical figure underlies the Arthur of popular culture continues to be debated today, though few would deny that the Arthur known in popular culture was brought to life largely by the brilliance of Geoffrey of Monmouth, one of the great practitioners of bio-fiction.

Regnal Biography

In addition to producing royal biographies as free-standing lives and as components of histories, medieval authors composed another type of king's story that was less concerned with the deeds and character of a particular ruler than with events that took place during his reign.[54] These works usually begin not with the king's birth but with his accession, and when they do cover earlier events, it is generally to provide background for the political issues that defined the king's reign rather than personal background for the king. Thus in these 'regnal biographies' the king is less the subject than a convenient device for bracketing a certain period in history, much as legal and official documents, as well as chronicles, marked time in regnal years that commenced with the monarch's accession. *The Deeds of Stephen* (1148–55), then, is not so much about Stephen as about the civil war that engulfed England while he and his cousin Matilda fought to succeed Henry I. *The Deeds of*

Henry the Fifth (1416–17), likewise, is less Henry's story than an account of his war in France. Regnal biographers offer little insight into the thoughts and motives of their purported subjects. For example, Henry V's biographer can only speculate about what the king might have been thinking as he processed in his regalia at the celebration in London of one of his victories: 'from his quiet demeanour, gentle pace, and sober progress, *it might have been gathered* that the king, silently pondering the matter in his heart, was rendering thanks and glory to God alone, not to man.'[55] But like most regnal biographers, he rarely even hazards such guesses about the king's state of mind. It may be that regnal biographers say so little about their subjects' thoughts or backgrounds because successful kingship requires setting the individual aside to become a new man, as Shakespeare's Hal does at the end of *Henry IV, Part 2*. In this view, it matters little what a king thinks so long as he acts properly. Thus the problem with Edward II, as his biographer so clearly demonstrates, is that he puts personal desires and interests above his responsibilities as king; the barons who oppose him are represented as acting not in Edward's interests but rather in the interests of the crown he wears.[56]

Despite their different emphases, regnal biographers have much in common with king-centred biographers. Both broadly agree on the qualities of a good king: he is wise and discerning, understands how to temper justice with mercy, and always puts the welfare of the realm over self-interest. Kings whose reigns are marked by war are nonetheless celebrated as champions of peace. Stephen desires peace but is forced to defend his throne against the warmongering Matilda; Henry V 'sought not war but peace' and does all he can to minimize loss of life in his righteous war with France.[57] The good king is devout and expresses his piety by safeguarding the material interests of the Church and respecting its ministers; his devotion does not interfere with his secular responsibilities but rather makes him a better, more vigilant steward of his kingdom. Though regnal biographers may divulge little about their subjects' thoughts, they are as eager as other royal biographers to voice their own opinions about the events they relate, the people they describe, and, more broadly, the spirit of the age.

Blacman's Henry VI: The Private Life of a King

One of the last medieval English kings' biographies, John Blacman's *Compilation of the Meekness and Good Life of King Henry VI*, differs substantially in form and content from its predecessors. Blacman, a priest and later a Carthusian monk, was one of Henry's spiritual advisors.[58] With some of the king's closest confidants among his friends and patrons, Blacman could draw on a wealth of eyewitness testimony in composing his biography of one of the least successful kings in English history.

Henry VI became king of England in 1422 at only nine months of age, and two months later he became king of France as well. Despite the treaty promising him the latter throne, his claim to France was resisted, and his reign was marked by significant defeats there, as well as by turmoil in England. In 1453, he succumbed to the first of several bouts of madness, and his cousin Richard, Duke of York, was made regent. Henry recovered in 1454, but Richard sought to retain the reins of government, and the 'Wars of the Roses' began. When Richard was killed in 1460, his son Edward took up the fight, defeated Henry's supporters decisively in 1461, and was crowned Edward IV. By allying with disaffected adherents of Edward, Henry's wife and son managed to restore Henry to the throne in 1470, but Edward regained power only six months later. Henry's son was killed in battle in May 1471, and later that month Henry himself died under mysterious circumstances in the Tower.

The chaos that marked Henry's reign would have lent itself to a regnal biography after the fashion of the *Deeds of Stephen*. Blacman might have delved into the roots of the dynastic dispute, reported battles, and chronicled the changing fortunes of the houses of York and Lancaster. Instead, he produced the most intimate free-standing biography yet written of an English king.[59]

In his prologue, Blacman announces that he will pass over some of the traditional material of biography—'of his most noble descent, how he was begotten according to the flesh of the highest blood and the ancient royal stock of England, and how in the two lands of England and France he was crowned the rightful heir of each realm' (p. 25)—on the grounds that these matters are well known.[60] He also passes over the political events that shape most royal biographies. He says nothing of Henry's rule, nor does he recount 'that most unhappy fortune which befell him against all expectation in after-times' (p. 25). He refers to major events of Henry's reign obliquely and only insofar as they illustrate Henry's character. For example, he mentions that Henry married and had a son in the process of describing Henry's chastity: Henry eschewed sex until marriage; he restrained himself physically within marriage, as evinced by the fact that the couple had only one son; and he never indulged in extra-marital affairs, even though his wife was absent often, and sometimes for long periods (p. 29). In lieu of major events, Blacman recounts characteristic incidents—for example, Henry's anger that a Christmas entertainment included scantily clad women and his embarrassment at seeing naked men bathing at Bath (pp. 29-30). He also recounts habits. Henry 'would keep careful watch through hidden windows of his chamber' (p. 30) to make sure that no women sneak in and corrupt his servants. He safeguarded the chastity of his stepbrothers Jasper and Edmund, along with all other dependents, so that they did not fall into the 'untamed practices of youth' (p. 30). He berated those who swore (p. 38).

The virtues Blacman highlights add up to an 'ideal' most unlike the ideal of kingship that underlies royal biographies, an ideal that persists regardless of whether the biographer praises or censures his subject and of whether his chief concern is the monarch himself or his reign. It is not that the virtues Blacman praises are not *part* of the princely ideal. The topics of his chapters–piety, chastity, generosity, humility, pity, patience–were praised in all of the royal biographies discussed above. But Blacman does not, as other royal biographers routinely do, expatiate on the public benefits of such private virtues. Moreover, he omits altogether the public virtues that royal biographers and theorists of kingship praise in a monarch, such as prudence, dignity, and restraint. Blacman says virtually nothing about Henry's ability to govern well, either through his wise policies and appointments or through his judicious use of force. He says nothing of Henry's concern for the welfare of his subjects. The best he has to say of Henry in his capacity as ruler is that 'he was both upright and just, always keeping to the straight line of justice in his acts. Upon none would he *wittingly* inflict any injustice' (p. 26, my emphasis). Blacman gives no specific examples of Henry's justice, though he copiously illustrates such virtues as patience, piety, and chastity. Instead, his phrasing raises the spectre of enough unwittingly inflicted injustices to be worth exculpatory remark. It is hard to imagine how Henry found time to govern, for Blacman describes him as 'continually occupied either in prayer or the reading of the scriptures or of chronicles' (p. 27). Though Blacman claims that he treated 'the business of the realm with his council as need might require', he immediately adds that the king resented being distracted by business from his perusal of religious books, and he attests that he himself witnessed the king's impatience with those who disturbed his study (p. 38).

Biographers of pious kings from Asser to the anonymous author of the *Deeds of Henry V* extolled an ability to balance piety with public obligations. Even those who wrote about bishops and other professional religious took pains to show that their subjects made concessions to worldly values and expectations, throwing banquets for their visitors even when fasting, or nursing a glass of wine so as not to draw attention to their abstinence. Henry refused to act–or even to dress–the part of king. He 'always wore round-toed shoes and boots like a farmer's' and 'a long gown with a rolled hood like a townsman' (p. 36). He would have nothing to do with hunts, banquets, or other aristocratic pastimes (p. 40). His actions–for example, refusing a substantial gift meant to 'relieve the burdens and necessities of the realm' (p. 32)–demonstrate his indifference to the state of his land. Not surprisingly, he bore his eventual loss of both England and France with equanimity (p. 33).

Like *The Life of King Edward who Rests at Westminster*, the *Compilation* was written about a king who became a candidate for canonization, but *before* that campaign was launched; in 1480, when Blacman was writing, Henry's nemesis Edward IV still reigned. Even by then, however, an informal cult had begun forming around Henry; pilgrims were visiting his grave, and miracles were attributed to his intercession. Blacman may have been encouraging this nascent cult.[61] Yet his account is far from simple hagiography. As Roger Lovatt has argued, Blacman 'gave an almost comprehensive picture of the king's defects as a ruler', but he 'chose to interpret such public inadequacy as private rectitude'.[62] In essence, Blacman used the king's private virtues in much the same way that the Poet used miracles—as a way of skirting around the problems with Henry's rule, while at the same time drawing attention to them by their glaring omission. His portrait of Henry VI, 'far from being one of bland sanctity, is both precise and pregnant with meaning'.[63]

Blacman's life of Henry contrasts strikingly with another life of a holy royal that focuses on character and habits rather than life events, the life of Margaret of Scotland (c.1046-93), wife of Malcolm III.[64] Margaret's daughter Matilda, consort of Henry I of England, commissioned her mother's life from Turgot of Durham, who had been her mother's confessor and close friend. Knowing she was dying, Margaret confided to Turgot her 'conscience' and recounted her life 'in sequence'.[65] Turgot's purpose, then, and his position *vis à vis* his subject, were not unlike Blacman's.

As Turgot presents her, Queen Margaret had much in common with Henry VI: she chastised wrongdoers and imposed a strict morality on those in her charge; she fasted, prayed, and engaged in various acts of charity. She was at least as eager as Henry to converse with priests and other religious men and to spend her time studying and meditating on Scripture and other holy books. And yet, she differed radically from Henry in her ability to reconcile her spirituality with her pubic obligations. Turgot recalls:

What I used to admire greatly in her was that, *amid the tumult of cases and the multiple cares of the realm*, she attended to her holy reading with wonderful eagerness, about which she would confer with the most learned men, often about delicate questions.[66]

He enthuses as much about her public as about her personal pieties, pointing to the material as well as spiritual benefits she accrues for her people:

All things proper were done by the rule of the prudent queen; by her counsel the laws of the realm were dispensed, and by her work the divine religion was bolstered and the people rejoiced in the prosperity of their affairs.[67]

When she felt that something needed doing, she summoned a council, with the king present, 'prepared to say and do' 'whatever she ordered'.[68] Among the ways she promoted her people's wellbeing was by encouraging trade—indeed, *luxury* trade:

> She had provided that merchants from diverse regions coming by land and by sea brought with them many and precious types of things for sale, and varieties which were unknown up until then. Among these things the local people bought were robes with diverse colours and a variety of clothing and ornaments, and as the king instructed and the queen urged, they paraded around in such diverse styles of clothing that they were believed to have been renewed in a certain way by such beauty.[69]

Though she encouraged her husband to pray, keep vigils, and weep over his sins, she also nurtured his public dignity: she made sure that his servants were both well trained and clothed in brightly coloured uniforms, that their palace was opulently furnished, and that their table glittered with silver and gold vessels. Turgot explains that she did this not because 'she was delighted by worldly honour or pride' but because 'she was mindful to fulfil what royal dignity required of her'.[70] As she walked in the splendour befitting a queen, she remembered that 'under those gems and gold' she was 'nothing but dust and ashes'.[71] Unlike Margaret, Henry did not distinguish between what he wore and what he was—if he disdained the world he had to dress accordingly.

Modern readers often consider lives of kings, like lives of saints, much of a muchness. That judgment is not wholly without basis. Almost all of the kings' lives examined here reflect a common ideal of kingship, so much so that royal biographers might be said to be guided by their sense of a universal *life of the kings* analogous to the *life of the saints* that Gregory of Tours posited. Kings' lives, like saints' lives, could be highly formulaic. And yet, as I hope this sampling has also established, there was variety within this biographical genre. That variety is evident in the kinds of kings commemorated, in the approaches used to tell (or, as in the case of Henry VI and Harold, strategically *not* to tell) their stories, and in the motivations that underlay the tellings. Kings were commemorated as saints, conquerors, scholars, and losers. Their biographers might be royal apologists or political dissidents, who might be attempting to kindle admiration or trouble, to provide models or anti-models for behaviour.

William Marshal, Advisor to Kings

I turn now from kings to a man called by his latest biographer 'the power behind five English thrones', William Marshal (*c*.1127–1219), the ambitious younger son of a minor lord who rose to become the advisor to Henry II, his three sons, and his grandson.[72] That he should gain and retain the confidence of these Angevin kings was no small achievement, for they were frequently at odds with each other.[73] Among his many accomplishments, Marshal helped broker the truce between King John and his barons that resulted in the Magna Carta in 1215. Following John's death in 1216, he repelled an invasion of England by Prince Louis of France, thus securing the throne for the young King Henry III. Though seventy years old, Marshal rode into battle with the courage that had carried him to fame in his youth.

Shortly after Marshal's death, his eldest son, also William, enlisted a professional writer by the name of John to record his father's life story.[74] The result was a narrative poem in French of some twenty thousand lines, completed around 1226, that is the earliest surviving life of a layperson who was neither a saint nor a member of the royal family in any European vernacular. John claims to have consulted both written and oral sources, among the latter John of Earley, Marshal's oldest and dearest friend, whom John claims as his chief informant. Some of the events John the poet claims to have witnessed himself. Having no precedents to work from, he adapted conventions of the popular genres of his day—chivalric romance, *chanson de geste*, dynastic history, and hagiography—producing a distinctive form of life-writing.

As in some chivalric romances, John's *History of William Marshal* begins not with William but with his father, John, who supported Henry I's daughter and designated heir Matilda in her struggle against Stephen of Blois.[75] Though loyal to Matilda (at least after he switched to her side from Stephen's), the elder Marshal was wholly unscrupulous with his family: he abandoned his first wife when a better match presented itself, and he abandoned his son William, held hostage by Stephen, to a near-certain death, figuring that 'he still had / the anvils and hammers / to produce even finer [sons]' (ll. 513-5).

John Marshal's cavalier perfidy sets in relief his son's integrity: William emerges from the narrative as a courageous soldier, a charismatic leader, a crafty military strategist, and a skilled diplomat. His honour is unimpeachable, his loyalty to family, to friends, and to princes unwavering. When, as an old man, his friends urge him to consider his health and decline the guardianship of King John's beleaguered son Henry, he replies:

> If all the world deserted the young boy,
> Except me, do you know what I would do?
> I would carry him on my shoulders
> And walk with him thus, with his legs astride,
> I would be with him and never let him down,
> From island to island, from land to land,
> Even if I had to look for my daily bread.

> (ll. 15,690-6)

Though inclined to mercy, he can be ruthless when the occasion demands. A hard-ened soldier, he can be 'saddened and troubled' by the sight of a wailing woman retrieving belongings from her burning home (ll. 8757–8). The only flaws John admits in this exemplar of chivalry are an indifference to his own safety, a willing-ness to trust rulers unworthy of his loyalty, and an occasional failure to heed sound advice. These 'flaws', of course, only highlight his virtues of courage, loyalty, and resolve. The risks he takes always pay off in the end.

Surrounding Marshal are a cast of sharply drawn characters, among them his prudent wife Isabel, his outspoken but loyal friend John of Earley, and his many pol-itical allies and adversaries, including shrewd Eleanor of Aquitaine and wily Prince Louis of France. The kings Marshal serves, though only supporting actors in the drama of Marshal's life, display more personality than we generally find in regnal biographies. The profligate 'Young King', the crusading Richard the Lionheart, and the capricious John come to life not only as monarchs but also as men.

Among the most carefully crafted scenes of the *History* are those dealing with Marshal's death, which John rates 'the best amongst 'his' many fine and splendid adventures' (ll. 18,899–900). John charts Marshal's deterioration over the last few weeks of his life: his loss of appetite and bodily functions, his bouts of delirium, his claims to be visited by winged figures in white that nobody else can see. John describes his end-of-life pieties and his final acts: settling who should succeed him as young King Henry III's guardian, providing for his children, and determining charitable bequests. John of Earley inquires how William wishes to dispose of his eighty-plus fur-trimmed cloaks. The proceeds from the garments could deliver Marshal from his sins, a priest suggests, to William's disgust. The Church expects too much from knights, he complains. Whatever sins he may have committed as a man of arms, he cannot undo; he can only present himself to God as a penitent. The coats, he says, should be distributed among his men. When all is settled, Marshal bids farewell to friends and children and kisses his wife for the last time.

John's writing is vigorous, full of dialogue, action, and vivid description. Readers listen in on the deliberation of great lords and watch as sailors, rich in plundered booty, squabble over whose clothes are finer—one boasting that his cloak is made entirely of squirrel fur, another countering that his is all ermine, sewn with gold threads (ll. 17,541–68). John prompts his readers to experience warfare by conjuring up the sights and sounds of combat:

> Had you been there, you would have seen great blows dealt,
> Heard helmets clanging and resounding,
> Seen lances fly in splinters in the air,
> Saddles vacated by riders, knights taken prisoner.

> You would have heard, from place to place,
> Great blows delivered by swords and maces
> On helmets and on arms,
> [And seen] knives and daggers drawn
> For the purpose of stabbing horses;
> Their protective covering was not worth a fig…
>
> (ll. 16,883–92)

Through his eyes we witness the slaughter of livestock, the burning of homes, the injury of civilians, and the ubiquitous frenzy and fear. Though John draws on romance conventions, he glamorizes neither the battlefield nor the tournament arena. Arresting similes abound: mercenaries parade their prisoners about 'like greyhounds on leashes' (l. 11,273); a hypocrite's face is yellower 'than a kite's claw' (l. 11,445); in his maiden battle, William 'smote and hammered / like a blacksmith on iron' (ll. 1102–3); in a tourney, he 'struck and hammered / like a woodcutter on oak trees' (l. 2858–9).

John divulges nothing about his own material situation beyond his allusion to being a professional writer.[76] He provides no surname, no place of origin; he identifies no family members and names no friends. He gives no indication of how or when he knew Marshal. Yet he is omnipresent as a narrative voice, and that voice radiates personality. He passes judgment on the various characters, praising the prowess of this knight, the integrity of that one, the skills of another. He denounces those who schemed against Marshal (ll. 5366–71) and gloatingly anticipates Marshal's triumph over his enemies (ll. 5669–92). He opines about politics, human nature, and the spirit of the age ('in those days the world was not / so proud as nowadays', ll. 763–4). He moralizes about envy (ll. 5109–26) and cupidity (ll. 8071–82), and he laments the vicissitudes of Fortune and the hazards of war (ll. 9113–37, 15,839–48). Death, he says, is proud, ravenous, indifferent to rank, while God is 'wise and courtly' (ll. 15,013–22, 1363–4). Bearing arms, he lectures his presumably clueless readers, is not like wielding a sieve, winnow, axe, or mallet; furthermore, not all knights are chivalrous (ll. 16,845–68). Proverbs pepper the *History*–'a man coveting all loses all' (l. 4274); 'the pocket always smells of herrings / and a good cup smells of good wine' (ll. 14,706–7); 'The saying goes that a man who bandages his finger / when it is whole will find it again when he chooses to take the bandage off' (ll. 13,277–8). And John is not above indulging in an off-colour pun–a papal legate is in such a hurry to leave the presence of an angry King Richard that he would not return to retrieve his cross ('sa croiz') lest he lose his testicles ('les croiz') (ll. 11,625–6). John never allows readers to forget that he is *constructing* Marshal's story.[77] References to himself are everywhere–'as I have told you', 'I can tell you', 'I know that full well', 'I shall undertake to prove to you', and so forth. As John becomes more engrossed in his storytelling, his I-can-tell-you's escalate—'I can vouch for the fact that' (l. 16,643), 'I can tell you for a fact that' (l. 16,655), 'I can tell you' (l. 16,666), 'I can tell you' (l. 16,672), 'I can assure you' (l. 16,673)—to indicate his mounting excitement. He constantly anticipates objections and argues with his imagined critics. He explains (often at length) what he cannot, will not, or must not tell. He justifies (again, often at length) what he includes, what he omits, and the order in which he narrates his facts. 'What a most forgetful man I am!' (l. 2151), he exclaims when he realizes a gap in his story. 'I do not dare give my opinion on the matter,' he protests at another point. He alludes to his written sources repeatedly (ll. 4539, 16,466, 16,784), points to places where those sources disagree, and bemoans the impossibility of following them all (ll. 16,401–12).

His scruples often seem more narratorial tics than sincere caution. Though he passes over Marshal's two-year pilgrimage to Palestine on the grounds that he was not present and has no sources, he also says that people still talk of Marshal's exploits there, so presumably his ignorance is willing, if not feigned, and merely a handy excuse for passing over a period about which he chooses not to write (ll. 7276–88).

Elsewhere, John claims that he cannot report a meeting between kings because 'the kings and those others present / did not invite me to take part in their deliberations' (ll. 7377–80). Yet he *does* report words exchanged at other meetings that he would neither have attended nor known about—the conversations among Marshal's enemies, for example, as they conspire against him. Sometimes, he be labours the obvious:

> Of all the tournaments fought;
> It would be very difficult to know about them all,
> For almost every fortnight
> Tournaments were held from place to place;
> That is why I think nobody could know about them all.
>
> (ll. 4971–5)

Sometimes he explains at length that he will not elaborate for fear of wearying his readers—imagining, it would seem, readers more interested in the mechanics of storytelling than in the story itself. Though, as we saw in Chapter One, Garnier employed an intrusive narrator in his life of Thomas Becket, he confined his comments to the content of his story. John's extended meanderings on the craft of narration are, to my knowledge, unprecedented in medieval biography, though they have precedents in contemporary romance.[78]

Having no literary models to constrain him and nobody to please but the family of the deceased gave John tremendous freedom. His ebullient narration suggests that he relished that liberty, enjoyed the challenge of writing the first life of a non-royal, non-holy layman, and expected his efforts to be warmly received. There is no evidence that *The History of William Marshal* circulated beyond his patrons, certainly no evidence that it influenced other life-writers. The text survives only in a mid-thirteenth-century manuscript, perhaps 'the author's original and unrevised draft', that 'lay untouched and unnoticed' in a private collection until the nineteenth century, when it emerged to capture the imagination of modern audiences yearning to know what the 'age of chivalry' was 'really like'.[79] The five biographies and quartet of historical novels that it has inspired since its first edition appeared in the late 1890s testify to its enduring fascination.[80]

Authors and Poets

Early Literary Biography

Bede died just before Ascension Day in 735 of an illness that came on around Easter.
One of his students, Cuthbert of Jarrow, recounted his last days in a letter to a
colleague at another monastery.[1] Cuthbert presents Bede as a holy monk, a dedicated
teacher, and, above all, an author labouring to complete work in progress. A sense
of urgency drives the narration as Cuthbert describes Bede racing against time to
finish two writing projects: his translations into English of the Gospel of John and of
a selection from Isidore of Seville's *On the Wonders of Nature*. For the sake of his
students, he feels that he cannot leave his work undone. On Bede's last day, after a
morning of frenetic dictation, his young disciple Wilberht points out that a chapter
remains unwritten and doubts that Bede is up to finishing it. Bede replies, 'Take
your pen and mend it, and then write fast.'[2] That evening Wilberht says, 'There is
still one sentence, dear master, that we have not written down.'[3] Bede relays the
sentence, then echoes Jesus's dying words: 'It is finished' (John 19: 30). He expires
moments later. The 'it' that was finished was thus at once the book and the life of
early England's most illustrious author, whose staggering corpus includes scriptural
commentaries, linguistic treatises, hymns, epigrams, poetry, a history, a martyrology,
and several biographies.[4]

Cuthbert's letter has some of the characteristics of literary biography: Cuthbert
presents Bede specifically as an author rather than as a great man who happens to
write; he discusses Bede's work-in-progress and his literary tastes; and he explains
what motivated Bede to write. Yet it relays nothing about Bede's life before his
illness; it is thus really more a 'literary death' than a 'literary life'.

Cuthbert promised in his letter to write 'a fuller account' of Bede that might have
been England's first free-standing literary life, but as far as we know he never did.[5]
Indeed, literary lives were rare in the Middle Ages. To be sure, many subjects of
the free-standing medieval biographies examined in Chapter One were prolific

authors, among them Gregory the Great, Anselm of Canterbury, and Aelred of Rievaulx. However, with the exception of the anonymous author of the eleventh-century life of Bede discussed in Chapter One, their biographers portrayed them mainly as great men of God and only incidentally as authors.

We find a few early prototypes for literary biography embedded in histories. Bede, for example, provides the earliest life of an Old English poet: Caedmon, a seventh-century monk at Whitby Abbey renowned for his ability to turn any passage of Scripture into moving poetry.[6] Though he writes briefly, Bede covers the topics that we expect to find in literary biography today: the subject's background and character; how he came to write; and what he wrote about and why. Until he was an old man, Bede tells us, Caedmon knew nothing of poetry, and this ignorance put him at a disadvantage at banquets, where a harp was often passed from guest to guest so that each might entertain the company with a song. Whenever Caedmon saw the harp coming near, he would sneak away in shame. One night, though, he dreamed that a man stood next to him, calling him by name and enjoining him to sing. Because his heavenly visitor would not take no for an answer, Caedmon complied. To his astonishment, he produced a beautiful original song about Creation. When he awoke, he remembered that song and found that he could easily compose others. Bede goes on to report the many spiritual topics Caedmon wrote about, and he includes a Latin translation of lines from the poem Caedmon 'dreamed'. Bede concludes by describing Caedmon's death. This earliest surviving life of an Old English poet also preserves the earliest surviving poem in English; although Bede rendered Caedmon's poem in Latin, a number of manuscripts of his *History*, including the very early 'St. Petersburg Bede' (*c*.746), relay it in Old English.

Bede's life of Caedmon, enshrined as it is in literary anthologies, is perhaps the best-known example of a medieval 'literary life'; however, Bede and his fellow historians usually treated Latin authors. Bede's chapter on Aldhelm, Abbot of Malmesbury and Bishop of Sherborne, recounts how Aldhelm came to write his first book, a treatise on the observance of Easter; he describes Aldhelm's *On Virginity*, coining the term *opus geminatum*, or *twinned work*, to convey its conjunction of prose and verse; he praises the many other books that showcase Aldhelm's 'wide learning', 'polished style', and broad familiarity with 'biblical and general literature'.[7] His retrospective on the life of Pope Gregory the Great is largely a discussion of Gregory's commentaries, homilies, epistles, and other writings that includes both detailed summaries of some of these works and the kind of personal detail that later readers would expect of literary biographies: 'The extent of [Gregory's] writings is all the more amazing when one considers that throughout his youth, to quote his own words, he was often in agony from gastric pain, perpetually worn out by internal exhaustion and frequently troubled by a slow but chronic fever' (p. 97).

Bede's twelfth-century admirer, William of Malmesbury, shared his interest in authorship. In his *Deeds of the English Bishops* (c.1125), William elaborated Bede's life of Aldhelm into a more detailed portrait of the bishop as a poet and author. Not only does William summarize Aldhelm's writings, from his treatises on Easter and on virginity to his essays on metre and scansion, but he also mixes literary criticism and life-writing by analysing Aldhelm's style and various formal innovations and by quoting copiously from his writings. Though Aldhelm was best known as a Latinist, William points out that he was also a reader and creator of poetry in his mother tongue: 'no one has ever in any age rivalled him in the ability to write poetry in English, to compose songs and to recite or sing them as occasion demanded.' To illustrate, he tells us that, to seduce the frivolous laity loath to linger for spiritual instruction after Mass, Aldhelm sang English ditties and gradually smuggled bits of Scripture into them, thus cultivating in his flock an appreciation for 'sound sentiments'.[8]

William's chief interest is in fellow historians and biographers. Not surprisingly, he writes at length about Bede, whose scholarship he much admires and strives to emulate.[9] Adopting the 'life-and-times' approach taken by the anonymous author of Bede's first life, William writes about the Northumbrian Church and about people Bede would have known; he also quotes at length from Cuthbert's letter. As we would expect of a literary biography, he discusses Bede's subject matter and style, along with his posthumous reputation and legacy. Symeon of Durham inscribes a similar life of Bede within his *Tract on the Origins and Progress of this Church of Durham*.[10]

We learn little from medieval historians about secular authors, especially those who wrote in the vernacular—unless, as in Aldhelm's case, their 'ditties' were written to achieve higher ends. William does embed the life story of William IX of Aquitaine (1071–1126), Count of Poitou, whose repertoire includes some of medieval Occitan's raunchiest poetry, and the deeds he relates are consistent with the count's randy poetic persona, but William mentions his compositions only in passing.[11]

The literary interests of the fifteenth-century historian John Capgrave were more eclectic. In his Middle English *Abbreviation of Chronicles* (c.1462), he treats not only patristic and biblical authors but also classical Greek and Roman poets, philosophers, and playwrights. Indeed, he mentions so many writers that his *Chronicles* might be considered an early attempt at literary history. Yet his sketches of authors are far less detailed than Bede's and William of Malmesbury's; most indicate only when, where, and what an author wrote. Occasionally, as with Terence, he quotes from an author's work, or he might provide a titbit or two about the author's circumstances, as he does with Plautus, who 'despite his eloquence was compelled by poverty to live with a baker and grind his corn at a hand-mill, and when he had leisure he would write very insightful tales' ('tales of ful grete sentens').[12]

In his *Book of the Illustrious Henries* (*c.*1446), Capgrave writes at greater length about Latin authors Henry of Ghent and Henry of Urimaria.[13] He admits that he knows almost nothing about Henry of Ghent beyond Henry's writings, but he fleshes out his chapter with an impassioned celebration of authorship. We know about illustrious persons of the past, he reminds us, only because authors wrote about them. As for those authors, their writings are their biographies, the most perfect tribute to their accomplishments, and one that ensures that they will live long after they have died.

Capgrave knew much more about Augustine of Hippo, putative founder of Capgrave's order and the subject of one of his free-standing biographies. From among the many different approaches he might have taken to Augustine's life, he chose to emphasize authorship. Combining a celebration of Augustine's scholarly achievements with summaries of his books, Capgrave's life of Augustine is, as I have written elsewhere, 'at once a biography of the saint and an annotated bibliography of his writings'.[14]

A very few lives of secular authors, mostly from ancient Greece and Rome, are found in late medieval anthologies from the Continent and in their Middle English adaptations. Boccaccio and Christine de Pizan treat several female authors in their respective anthologies, *Famous Women* (1374) and the *Book of the City of Ladies* (1405). Both combine biographical information (albeit invented or inferred from their subjects' writings) with discussions of content, style, and contribution to literature. Praise of the women's accomplishments and analysis of their methods of composition figure more prominently than narrative. This focus is consonant, as I shall discuss in Chapter Five, with the polemical orientation of the collections: both Boccaccio and Christine were chiefly interested in justifying their subjects' claim to fame and, in Christine's case, supporting the proposition that women are capable of producing poetry as finely wrought as men's.

Troubadour *Vidas* and *Razos*

The earliest surviving lives of medieval secular authors from anywhere in Western Europe date from the middle of the thirteenth century. They concern the troubadours, those itinerant balladeers of Southern France who praised, or lamented, love and its complications. Some hundred lives, or *vidas*, of individual troubadours survive.[15] Composed in Provençal during the thirteenth and fourteenth centuries, but referring to subjects who lived decades to centuries prior, they are, like so many saints' lives, more what we would consider biographical fiction than biography.

The *vidas* range from terse notices to complex narratives of their subjects' lives, loves, careers, and deaths. In tone, they are as varied as the songs themselves, ranging from romantic to sarcastic. Many have a tabloid quality, retailing salacious titbits about noblemen (and occasionally women); gamblers who took up songwriting to support their habit; knights who became troubadours because they could not afford knighthood; monks turned lovers, lovers turned monks. Some are stories of war, others of jealousy, prostitution, suicide, and domestic violence. Anticipating our modern literary biographies, the *vidas* often indulge in proto-criticism: this poet wrote 'good melodies but poor words'; that one 'sang badly, and invented poetry badly, and played the fiddle badly, and spoke still more badly, but he wrote words and melodies very well'.[16] Some troubadours were rated good storytellers, others good versifiers, others good linguists, while some were good for nothing: 'His songs had no great value, nor did he.'[17]

The *vidas* often purported to explain a troubadour's lyrics by reference to the poet's life. For example, Jaufre Rudel, who wrote songs pining for a distant lady, is the subject of a romantic *vida* recounting his infatuation with the Countess of Tripoli, his foolhardy voyage to see her, and his happy death in her arms. Though some biographical details in the *vidas* have been corroborated, in most cases these lives do not reveal the author behind the work so much as they extrapolate a suitable author *from* the troubadour's lyrics.[18] Nonetheless, their underlying assumption that an author's life can illuminate his or her work is remarkable in a time when most imaginative writing was still anonymous.

A related biographical form, the *razo*, purports to explain what the troubadour had in mind when composing a specific song.[19] These stories were probably used to spice up live performances, much as musicians and poets today often introduce songs and readings with personal anecdotes. However, scholars believe that most of the *razos* that have come down to us originated not with the composers themselves but with later performers or admirers who, like the writers of *vidas*, freely inferred life events from the poet's songs. *Razos* often offer a cheeky take on the songs they 'explain'. For example, the *razo* associated with Bernart de Ventadorn's famous song of a lark beating its wings joyfully against a sunray informs us that the song is 'really' about a lady nicknamed 'Lark' opening her cloak for her lover, 'Ray', as they tumble into bed.[20]

Uc de Saint-Circ, himself a troubadour, wrote, revised, or edited many of the surviving *razos* around the middle of the thirteenth century. He further composed a *vida* of Bernart de Ventadorn, and he may have composed his own *vida*,[21] which would then be the earliest 'autobiography' of a secular poet and biographer. According to this *vida*, Uc was the wayward son of a minor nobleman. Sent to Montpellier to study for the Church, he frittered away his time learning songs and instead became a minstrel. Though his pretty verses could fool the ladies, he was never truly great because he never truly loved, and after he married, he stopped writing songs altogether.

The earliest *vidas* and *razos* occur in anthologies of troubadour songs, known as *chansonniers*, with each *vida* introducing a selection of the poet's work and the *razos* introducing individual songs.[22] In *chansonniers* of the fourteenth century, however, we find *vidas* dissociated from the troubadours' songs and assembled into sections of their own. This segregation suggests, Elizabeth Poe argues, 'a growing appreciation of the intrinsic literary worth of the biographies'.[23]

The taste for writing and reading literary biography, however, never really blossomed. The practice of writing lives of poets or other authors of imaginative literature certainly did not spread to England, though literary tributes abound for the 'triumvirate' of later Middle English literature, Geoffrey Chaucer, John Gower, and John Lydgate. These tributes evince a broad familiarity with the authors' works and an appreciation for their style, but little interest in them as people.[24] More concerned with incident are the headnotes that the scribe and editor John Shirley wrote for his anthologies of the writings of Chaucer, Lydgate, and other Middle English authors.[25] These headnotes are somewhat akin to the troubadour *razos*, explaining when, where, why, and for whom particular works were composed. Unlike the fanciful *razos*, though, they generally seem informed by Shirley's first- or second-hand knowledge of the circumstances he describes. Though hardly life stories, they do suggest that Shirley, at least, felt that the works he collected would be better appreciated with an understanding of the lived experience that produced them, even if that experience was partly invented or obtained through gossip, innuendo, or rumour.[26] The logical next step—a cohesive biography of a Middle English author—was not taken until 1598, when Thomas Speght introduced his collected works of Chaucer with a chapter reconstructing 'the Life of our learned English poet' from available 'chronicles and records'.[27]

Historian Autobiographers

Medieval writers in Latin or the vernacular were more likely to write about themselves than to write at any length about their fellow authors. Bede concludes his *Ecclesiastical History* (731) with an autobiographical epilogue that supplies a few personal details: he was born on the property of the double monastery of Wearmouth and Jarrow in Northumbria; his family entrusted his care to the monastery's founder and abbot, Benedict Biscop, when he was seven years old; at nineteen he became a deacon and at thirty a priest; and he spent his entire life at

Wearmouth and Jarrow, reading, writing, teaching, and worshipping. Bede says little of what he felt beyond noting that 'it has always been my delight to learn or to teach or to write.'[28] He devotes the bulk of the epilogue to listing his many works, sometimes summarizing their contents and sometimes explaining what he was trying to accomplish in a particular piece. His epilogue is thus both the earliest English literary autobiography and a prototypical bio-bibliography.

Perhaps inspired by Bede, Orderic Vitalis concludes his own *Ecclesiastical History* (1141) with a similar autobiographical epilogue.[29] He includes the kinds of personal details that Bede disclosed: when and where he was born, who taught him, when he became an oblate, and so forth. He also follows Bede's manner of indicating his age at different life events–started school at five, sent abroad at ten, became an oblate at eleven, ordained subdeacon at sixteen, became a priest at thirty-three, now sixty-seven. But though he says much about himself as a monk, he says nothing about himself the author. Given that his *Ecclesiastical History* was his corpus, he could not have included a bibliography, but there are other ways to write about oneself as an author than to list works, as William of Malmesbury demonstrates.

William was indeed the only one of Bede's admirers to write extensively about himself as an author. His story, woven into the body of his *Deeds of the English Kings* (1125), has little to do with deeds and dates and everything to do with his intellectual development, as this sample drawn from the beginning of Book Two indicates:

It is many years since I formed the habit of reading, thanks to my parents' encouragement and my own bent for study. It has been a source of pleasure to me ever since I was a boy, and its charm grew as I grew. Indeed I had been brought up by my father to regard it as damaging to my soul and my good repute if I turned my attention in any other direction.[30]

William ruminates on the different branches of knowledge he studied–logic, medicine, ethics, and history. History he cherished more than all the other disciplines because it 'adds flavour to moral instruction by imparting a pleasurable knowledge of past events, spurring the reader by the accumulation of examples to follow the good and shun the bad'. He skips from the memories of his childhood and youth to some unspecified time in adulthood when he used his own money to accumulate a 'library of foreign historians'. His voracious reading of foreign histories led him to wonder about his own land's past and kindled in him the urge to research and write. As he begins Book Four, he returns to his own life, admitting that he had intended to end his account without treating the events of his own day until the urging of his friends and the boredom of being retired changed his mind: 'my old love of study plucked me by the ear and laid its hand on my shoulder, for I was incapable of doing nothing, and knew not how to devote myself to those business cares which are so unworthy of a man of letters [*homine litterato*].'[31]

William's account of his life seems rather more 'modern' than Bede's and Orderic's. Where they mostly impart facts, William interprets his experience. We understand why he became a historian and why he is writing the kind of history he is writing. From his narration, we can understand the love of learning evinced everywhere in his *History*—in his inscribed lives of authors, in his artfully crafted characters and scenes, in his numerous allusions to and echoes of literary classics, and in his weaving of paeans, lampoons, and even doggerel into his narration. William's literary orientation is by no means inevitable in a history of kings of England, and he often has to digress to tell readers about a favourite poet or historian. This meandering history is exactly the kind of work that the *homo litteratus* who looks out at us from William's self-portrait would write. William conveys through his autobiographical interludes a distinct sense of self and a conviction that his upbringing and past experience led him to develop as he did.

Francesco Petrarch and Christine de Pizan

For much of the Middle Ages, vernacular authors had little to say about themselves. The only thing we know about the author of the Old English *Fates of the Apostles*, *Elene*, and *Juliana* is the acrostic C-Y-N-E-W-U-L-F woven into the closing verses of each, but by the standards of his time, Cynewulf was forthcoming: his fellow poets did not even name themselves. Anonymity remained common throughout the medieval period. We know nothing of the authors of some of the best-loved works of the Middle Ages, from *Beowulf* to *Sir Gawain and the Green Knight*.

The most fully developed literary autobiographies were Continental. Francesco Petrarch (1304–74) was the first—and to my knowledge the only—medieval author to undertake anything resembling a free-standing autobiography.[32] Writing at the end of a distinguished career as a scholar, poet, and essayist, he *expected* future generations to wonder about him, and he began a Latin epistle 'To Posterity' to satisfy their curiosity.[33] In his brief and incomplete epistle, he relates the major events of his life in chronological order, beginning with his birth in Arezzo at dawn on Monday 20 July 1304, and abruptly ending with the death of a patron, Jacopo II da Carrara (Giacomo the Younger), lord of Padua, in 1350. He documents his movements precisely—a year at Arezzo, six at Ancisa, four at Montpellier studying law, and so forth. Throughout, he emphasizes those experiences most relevant to his *literary* identity, including the accolades his writings garnered and the patrons who abetted his career. He reminisces about the places most (and least) congenial to his creative spirit. He fondly recalls his time in the Sorgue River valley, about fifteen miles from Avignon, where 'almost every bit of writing which I have put forth was either accomplished or begun, or at least conceived'.[34] Even as he professes a seemly modesty, he trumpets his fame: 'The greatest kings of this age have loved and courted me. They may know why; I certainly do not'; 'my style, as many claimed, was clear and forceful; but to me it seemed weak and obscure.'[35]

After Petrarch's death, a longer, messier—and more intriguing—account of the poet's experiences came to light, an autobiographical dialogue that he called *The Secret*, written when he was about forty years old.[36] By then he had established his reputation as a poet; indeed, two years earlier, he had been crowned Poet Laureate of Rome, the first to hold that title since antiquity. He was working on *Africa*, an epic poem in Latin about the Second Punic War, as well as on a collection of biographies of famous Romans in Latin prose. Though his employment in the Church precluded marriage, he had fathered two children, and he was nursing an unrequited passion for Laura, a married woman who had haunted his imagination since he first saw her more than fifteen years earlier in the Church of Saint Claire of Avignon. Petrarch had been memorializing his unconsummated love in the poems that he would assemble into his collection *Il Canzoniere* (*The Songbook*), completed shortly before his death.

Petrarch modelled *The Secret* on one of the most influential works of late antiquity, Boethius's *Consolation of Philosophy* (c.524).[37] Boethius, an author of theological and philosophical tracts and formerly a high-ranking official at the court of Theodoric the Great, wrote the *Consolation of Philosophy* as he was awaiting execution for treason. It begins when the imprisoned Boethius, bemoaning his misfortune, is startled to see standing beside him a resplendent woman who turns out to be none other than Lady Philosophy. Boethius complains to her that he has been disgraced and ruined for nothing more than being a zealous and honourable public official. Philosophy, through a kind of Socratic dialogue, brings him around to the view that the things he laments losing—fame, friends, wealth, power—were never worth having in the first place. They are ephemera bestowed by Lady Fortune, who metes out rewards and punishments without regard to merit: as Lady Fortune spins her enormous wheel with all of humanity ranged along its rim, those on top fall, while those below rise. Through Lady Philosophy's help in cultivating an indifference to Fortune's gifts, Boethius acquires wisdom and peace.

As this summary indicates, the *Consolation of Philosophy* is autobiographical, but Boethius speaks only in general terms about his background, private life, and career except to detail the circumstances leading to his political ruin; the *Consolation* attempts to understand life in broad terms. Petrarch's *Secret* likewise is less concerned with biographical particulars than with the meaning of life generally.

Petrarch's interlocutor is not Lady Philosophy but rather Augustine of Hippo, one of Petrarch's favourite authors, a man who shared his love of classical literature and who knew what it was to struggle with untoward passions. Who better to guide and goad the melancholy poet along the path to self-understanding? Augustine had in his *Confessions* described his 'inner self' as 'a house divided against itself'.[38] How fitting, then, that Petrarch should convey his own inner conflicts by imagining a debate between 'Augustinus' and 'Franciscus'.

Petrarch claims that *The Secret*, as its name suggests, was meant to be for himself alone. Addressing himself to his book, as medieval authors often did, he declares, 'flee from public places [and] stay with me...for you are my secret.'[39] The work is full of unelaborated references to events in Petrarch's life and conveys little sense of place or time. He recalls forsaking his happy life in the country to return to the city, but he indicates neither the location of his country retreat nor the city to which he returned (pp. 79-80). Writing as if in private dialogue with one who knows him intimately allows Petrarch to omit information he would be expected to supply were he addressing posterity. When he laments that in a single day Fortune 'dashed me to pieces along with my hopes, my resources, my family, my home' (p. 97), Augustinus, as if not wishing to further upset him, changes the subject, leaving the reader in the dark as to the nature of the calamity. It is likewise when Augustinus alludes in passing to 'long journeys through which you came to the threshold not only of imprisonment but also of death' (p. 118). Franciscus would of course know what he is referring to, but we do not.

Easier to comprehend are the intellectual issues Petrarch raises. Franciscus complains that reading no longer comforts him, and Augustinus responds by suggesting strategies that will enable books to improve his life, or at least his outlook on life. References to the classics—Seneca, Cicero, Terence, Virgil, Ovid, Juvenal, and the ancient tragedies—abound as the literati discuss the ethics of reading and consider such matters as whether a work can mean something other than what its author intended (p. 100). Augustinus quotes from Petrarch's writings as well as from his own oeuvre. When Franciscus mentions how hard he has found it to govern his passions, Augustinus responds that he knows exactly what he means, alluding to a moment in Book Eight, Chapter Seven, of the *Confessions* when he entreated God to make him chaste—but not yet (p. 88).

The Secret reads in part like a medieval version of 'talk therapy', with Augustinus leading a more-or-less docile Franciscus to a greater understanding of himself and his current malaise and prompting him to re-evaluate his priorities and redirect his energies. But at many points, this therapeutic dialogue erupts into a spirited clash of wills. When Augustinus criticizes Franciscus for being greedy, Franciscus replies that he is merely being prudent by pursuing enough wealth to support himself in his old age (pp. 77, 80). When Franciscus accuses Augustinus of picking fights,

Augustinus retorts that his attitudes make him want to vomit (p. 110). The two men vigorously debate Franciscus's love for Laura, which Augustinus decries as a distraction and Franciscus defends as his inspiration.

Time management is another major bone of contention. Augustinus insists that Franciscus, at his stage of life, should be thinking more of death than of the pursuit of glory. The common division of time into units (minutes, hours, days, years) and of life into ages (child, youth, middle age, and old age) only perpetuates the illusion that we have longer than we do, Augustinus warns; how, he demands, would Franciscus spend his time if he knew he had just a year to live? When Franciscus replies that he would take care to occupy himself only with serious pursuits, Augustinus wonders why he is not doing that now, when for all he knows, he has not a year, or even a day, left (p. 139). He goes on to berate Franciscus for wasting his time on *Africa*. Authors aplenty have covered the subject; he ought to be working on projects that enhance his understanding rather than his celebrity. Though the Franciscus of *The Secret* protests vigorously, the historical Petrarch followed Augustinus's advice: he never finished *Africa*, and his later literary production took a religious and moralistic turn.

Some sixty years after Petrarch wrote his *Secret*, Christine de Pizan, an Italian expatriate living in France, whose father was a humanist in the tradition of Petrarch, appropriated Boethius once more.[40] Like Petrarch, Christine was a prolific and celebrated author, indeed the first medieval woman to earn a living from writing.[41] Her oeuvre spans a wide range of genres, including political theory, allegory, dream vision, conduct literature, history, lyric poetry, feminist polemic, and life-writing, and her life-writings were themselves abundant and diverse. At the end of 1403, Philip the Bold, Duke of Burgundy, commissioned her to write the life of King Charles V of France, a project she completed in 1405. That same year, she published her *City of Ladies*, a dream vision in which, with the help of the Ladies Reason, Rectitude, and Justice, she constructs an allegorical city from the life stories of virtuous women past and present. In 1405–6 she also produced an extended account of her own life as the third and final book of another allegorical work, the *Vision*.[42]

Wandering through a magnificent palace dedicated to learning, the Christine of the *Vision* happens upon a resplendent lady, who identifies herself as the very Lady Philosophy whose consolation had delivered her 'dearly beloved son Boethius' from despair (p. 91). Hoping for a similar deliverance, Christine recites the story of her life. Like Boethius, she claims to be the victim of the cruel and capricious Lady Fortune, but unlike Boethius (or Petrarch), she provides a detailed chronological account of her life, from her childhood to the present.

Christine begins, conventionally enough, by reminiscing about her fortunate youth. She was born to noble and virtuous parents in Venice. Obviously proud of her intellectual lineage, she notes that her maternal grandfather was a scholar and that her father, Thomas, was so distinguished a physician and astrologer that the kings of France and Hungary vied to entice him into their service. Thomas chose the king of France, and Christine recalls being presented to Charles V at the Louvre in December, her mother, sisters, and herself decked out in their 'richly ornamented Lombard clothing and headdresses' (p. 92). Her father prospered under King Charles, and when she was only fifteen, knights, gentlemen, and wealthy scholars were already seeking her hand in marriage. Valuing character over money, Thomas wed his daughter to a well-born young scholar, Étienne du Castel, 'whose virtues surpassed his wealth' (p. 93). Étienne rewarded Thomas's confidence by working hard and thriving in his position as notary at court.

At the height of Christine's happiness, though, Fortune struck, depriving her during the 1380s of the three most important men in her life. King Charles's unexpected death in 1380 cost her father, now elderly and infirm, his pension, forcing him to make do on a straitened income until his own death in 1387. Two years later, Fortune snatched away Christine's husband Étienne, just as he was 'on the point of rising to a high rank' (p. 95). Years of misery ensued. Ignorant of Étienne's finances, she was exploited by unscrupulous men and impoverished by fourteen years of litigation over his estate. She recounts her frustration with hours wasted in law courts and antechambers to gain nothing but 'ambiguous replies and false hopes'. She describes suffering through tedious speeches and misogynist jokes that she pretended not to understand. She recalls skimping on underclothes to afford costly outer garments, preferring to shiver than to be shunned for looking poor, until she at last hit on the idea of writing laments and courtly lyrics and succeeded in attracting patrons intrigued by the novelty of a female poet.

As much as Christine rails against Fortune, though, her *narration* makes clear that *human* idealism, optimism, and lack of planning were largely to blame for her unhappiness. Consider the passage in which she explains that, although her father made good money, his expenditure chronically exceeded his means:

Despite the fact that as is customary with philosophers, there was no saving of my father's money and possessions–which (may he rest in peace) I do not hold to be a laudable custom of husbands who must manage the care of their household, which may be impoverished after them by their prodigality–yet despite the liberality of his habits, the good king's provision would not let his favourite's household lack for any necessity.   (p. 93)[43]

The tangled and indirect language– 'there was no saving of my father's money' rather than 'my father did not save money', 'which I do not hold to be a laudable custom' rather than 'which I deplore'–hints at Christine's discomfort in criticizing her own father. She further softens her criticism by subsuming her father into the broader category of 'philosophers' who naturally lack personal prudence and by structurally subordinating her criticism within a sentence whose main clause praises King Charles's generosity. She again touches on human agency, and again with restraint, in adding that the family's loss of income resulted not merely from the misfortune of Charles's 'untimely death' but from 'the failure of the good king's memory' that kept him from making good on his promise to settle additional lands and benefits upon Thomas and his heirs (p. 94).

Étienne, too, played a role in her tribulations, and Christine criticizes her beloved husband with the same delicacy she used to speak of her father's and the king's faults. She begins by lamenting the misfortune that kept her from being present at Étienne's death and thus from being apprised of 'the condition of his finances', yet she later indicates that husbands (and by implication Étienne) should 'declare all their business affairs to their wives' as a matter of course in order to avoid 'misfortune' later on (p. 96).

Interwoven with Christine's tale of personal ill fortune is the story of her rising good fortune as an author—a turn in her life that proceeded directly from her misfortunes. In her misery, Christine resumes the long-abandoned pleasure of study. She returns to the literature she once loved, and she writes poems to assuage her grief at the loss of her husband and also to vent her frustrations at the indifference of others to her plight. Exhorted by Nature to 'forge pleasant things', she brings forth books as she once brought forth children—fifteen 'principal volumes' between 1399 and 1405, she boasts, along with many individual poems, 'which all together are contained in around seventy large quires' (p. 105). She begins presenting her works to princes and nobles, who discuss them among themselves and circulate them among friends and acquaintances abroad. Soon, Christine acquires an international reputation. Though she modestly attributes the success of her writings to the novelty of having been composed by a woman, the respect she commands is evinced in prestigious commissions she receives, such as the authorized biography of Charles V.

Lady Philosophy voices the subtext of Christine's complaint. Asked for her opinion, she replies that Christine whines like a 'spoiled child' (p. 112). Lady Fortune has blessed, not cursed, Christine. Her children are beautiful, and though her wise father may have left her poor in goods, he left her rich in wisdom. As for her mother, Christine is lucky still to *have* a mother whose comfort and consolation have conferred inestimable benefits. 'Why do you ungratefully complain of the blessings you have received?' she demands (p. 110). What is more, Lady Philosophy (rather cruelly) reminds her, the loss of her husband provided the leisure to write that brought her personal gratification as well as fame:

By your own words, there is no doubt that if your husband had survived until the present, you would have spent less time on your studies; for the household chores would not have allowed it, this benefit of scholarship…Then you should not consider yourself wretched when you have among other blessings one of the worldly things that it most delights and pleases you to have, namely, the sweet taste of knowledge.   (p. 116)

Christine is hardly the first—we need only think of the virgin martyrs—and would scarcely be the last to find freedom from the traditional role of wife and mother essential to personal fulfilment; but her Philosophy here verges on a Panglossianism that the Philosophy of Boethius could scarcely approve.[44] Far from being a Boethian indictment of the gifts of Fortune and a call for transcendence, Christine's *Vision* is a call to pragmatic *action*—to spend wisely, to save, to care for one's dependents, to plan for misfortune, and, above all, to apply one's talents to transforming one's circumstances. Christine's Lady Philosophy eventually gets around to elaborating the lesson of the *Consolation of Philosophy*, namely that Fortune cannot harm those who do not desire what she offers (pp. 122–32). But by this point Christine has thoroughly supplanted the Boethian view that humans can only prevail against Fortune by cultivating indifference to her gifts with a call to make the most of those gifts.

Though we might adduce from the *Vision* a straightforward moral, we cannot adduce from it a straightforward self. We obviously cannot equate the Christine who discusses her life with Lady Philosophy with the Christine who created both 'herself' and her interlocutor. Petrarch generated the same ambiguity when he chose to have Franciscus discuss his values and priorities with Augustinus. And in that, of course, he followed Boethius. All three authors have to some degree fictionalized themselves; all three have used dialogue to register inner turmoil. The self-portrait constructed by the author of such a dialogue reveals *a* self, part of a more complex identity that includes the interlocutor. But the three writers' uses of dialogue vary. Lady Philosophy talks Boethius around to her view of life's meaning, one wholly at odds with the view he claimed to hold at the beginning of the *Consolation*. Christine, like Boethius, ultimately capitulates to Lady Philosophy, thanking her for setting her straight, but as we have seen, Lady Philosophy only articulates a view of life that was implicit in Christine's biographical narration. Lady Philosophy spurs Christine's self-examination and airs views that Christine could not bring herself to say directly—for example, that she might be better off, or at least happier, as a widow. And though the historical Petrarch takes Augustinus's advice, within the world of the *Secret* Franciscus and Augustinus part ways agreeing to disagree, thereby vesting the dialogue with the indeterminacy characteristic of the late medieval debate poetry that was designed to air different sides of issues without necessarily privileging one.[45]

Autobiographical Impulses in Middle English Texts

No Middle English author—not even John Lydgate, who enjoyed a prestige in his day that was comparable to Petrarch's—told his own life story with the detail and thoroughness of Petrarch or Christine de Pizan. Yet fourteenth- and (especially) fifteenth-century English authors were eager to write about themselves. They did so discreetly, obliquely, often playfully and always in the process of writing about other matters.

Middle English authors were most likely to write about themselves in prologues, epilogues, or in autobiographical interludes, and most of their self-references are fleeting.[46] In his *Morte d'Arthur* (1469-70), Thomas Malory tantalizingly identifies himself as 'a knight prisoner' but says nothing further about himself or about the circumstances of his incarceration. A few are more forthcoming. The author of a finely crafted verse life of Saint Christine reveals in an epilogue that his name is William Paris and that he is the squire of Sir Thomas Beauchamp, Earl of Warwick. Paris boasts that he was the only one of Beauchamp's followers to remain true when, in 1397, the earl was imprisoned for treason on the Isle of Man.[47] There, when he was not attending to his lord's needs, Paris passed the time writing 'Christine'. Before relating her *Vision*, Julian of Norwich describes the events that immediately preceded it.[48] Hearing the story of Saint Cecilia in church one day made her desire to suffer as the early virgin martyr had. Her desire was granted when she became deathly ill at the age of thirty and a half. She recalls receiving the last rites during three days of delirium; she remembers the parson, accompanied by a child, holding a cross up so that her final vision would be of her saviour. She then relays the visions she experienced before regaining her senses.

John Capgrave, Osbern Bokenham, John Lydgate, and William Caxton are among many fifteenth-century authors who wrote prefaces or epilogues divulging who persuaded them to undertake a particular writing project and why. In this, they were doing what Anglo-Latin biographers and historians had been doing since the eighth century and what Anglo-French biographers had been doing since the twelfth. These earlier prefaces could be simple—the author wrote at the command of such-and-such a bishop, abbot, or community—or rather more ornate. French prologues and epilogues often tease readers with bits of stories. In one of the more colourful epilogues in Anglo-French, Garnier of Pont-Sainte-Maxence recalls his patrons plying him with good food and fine gifts: a palfrey and its trappings, clothes, and much more.[49] Yet French authors, such as William Marshal's John (see Chapter Three), generally come across more as disembodied personalities than as social persons.

One of the most elaborate accounts in Latin of an author and his patron was given by William of Malmesbury in a letter written to accompany his *Deeds of the English Kings*. William claims to have written at the instigation of Henry I's late consort Matilda, an intellectual 'devoted...to literary studies'.[50] He recalls the genesis of his *opus magnum* from a discussion he had with the queen about Saint Aldhelm (*c*.640-709). Being related to the saint, the queen was curious about his genealogy, and upon learning that he was related to the West Saxon kings, she asked William to write a 'short essay' about his family history. With perhaps feigned modesty, she declared herself 'unworthy to receive the tribute of a volume...on the history of the English kings'. In any case, she evidently reconsidered her unworthiness, for when William presented her with the brief sketch she had requested, she charmed him into embellishing it into a 'full history of her predecessors'. William's letter goes well beyond the usual fact of the commission to convey a sense of his patron's personality and of their rapport.

In the fifteenth century, Osbern Bokenham, an Augustinian friar from Suffolk and fifteenth-century England's most prolific writer of saints' legends, took an approach comparable to William's in the prologue to his *Life of Mary Magdalene*. Going further even than William, Bokenham located his conversation with his patron within a scene so vibrant and intense that it is practically cinematic, one that imparts not just the gist of conversation but conversation itself. On Twelfth Night, 1445, the friar is attending a party at the castle of Isabel Bourchier, Countess of Eu. Merriment fills the hall as guests revel, decked out in their finest apparel, blue, white, green; the room glistens like a field in May. As Bokenham watches Isabel's four sons disporting themselves on the dance floor, his hostess stops by and asks him about the lives of female saints she hears he has been writing. After rattling off the names of seven women whose stories he has told, he mentions his work-in-progress, a life of Elizabeth of Hungary for the most excellent Elizabeth Vere, Countess of Oxford. Perhaps feeling a bit competitive, Isabel interjects a request for the life of her own favourite saint, Mary Magdalene. Bokenham hums and haws—he is an ignorant old man with little experience as a poet, he protests (insincerely, we must suspect, given the list of verse saints' lives he has just rehearsed!). At last, however, he acquiesces—on the condition that the countess should not expect him to take up the project until he has returned from his upcoming pilgrimage to the shrine of St. James in Santiago de Compostela.

Bokenham was one of late medieval England's most colourful 'prologuers'. Autobiographical passages such as the one I have just described permeate his oeuvre, offering priceless insight into the experiences of a fifteenth-century poet and friar who enjoyed an active social life and worked on literary projects for his

friends and acquaintances between trips abroad.[51] Bokenham mentions travels in
Wales, Spain, and Italy. Halfway through his *Life of Saint Margaret*, he pauses to
complain of his blotting pen and to bemoan the infirmities of old age: tremors, dull
wits, and failing eyesight (he would be blind without his spectacles, he declares).
His *Margaret* is especially rich in anecdote. He relates that he obtained some of his
material during a stay at Montefiascone, some fifty miles outside Rome, where 'they
entertain weary pilgrims with Tribian wine instead of Muscatel'.[52] Severe flooding
waylaid him at Montefiascone, but the delay gave him the chance to write up some
information about the saint that he had discovered by chatting with the locals and
perusing books housed at her nearby shrine. Elsewhere in *Margaret* he confesses
that he would have been in serious trouble on a recent trip to Venice had he not
taken the precaution of paying homage to a relic of the saint's foot before he left
England. The foot, he recalls, still had flesh on its bones—through the 'bright, pure
crystal' of the reliquary, one could see everything 'except the great toe and the heel,
which are in a nunnery called Reading' (p. 5).

One of *Margaret*'s greatest charms is the easy-going camaraderie it reveals between
Bokenham and his friend and fellow friar Thomas Burgh, who requested the life. As
we have seen, Bokenham reveals much about himself in *Margaret*—that he is an
Augustinian friar, that he has visited Rome and Venice, that he appreciates good wine,
that he wears glasses, and that he is no longer young. But he will not divulge his name,
claiming to fear ridicule. He exhorts Burgh not to share the work with anybody, but
should he do so, to 'say you believe it was sent from Ageland [Lincolnshire] from a
friend of yours who sells horses at fairs and who dwells near the castle of Bolingbroke
in a town called Borgh where you first took the name of Thomas' (p. 6). Burgh is to say
that he obtained the *Life of Saint Margaret* from a horse trader? We can imagine the poet
and his friend chuckling over some private joke whose meaning is forever lost to us.
Burgh, by the way, did not lay much weight on Bokenham's injunction to secrecy. In
1447, four years after Bokenham wrote *Margaret* for him, he commissioned as a gift to
a 'convent of nuns' a volume containing the lives of Margaret and other female saints,
'translated into English by a doctor of divinity named Osbern Bokenham, Austin friar
of the convent of Stoke Clare' (p. 195).

The stories Bokenham tells about the genesis of his lives of Margaret and Mary
Magdalene are entertaining and hefty, unfolding in hundreds of lines. For modern
scholars, they have proved more interesting than the texts they introduce precisely
because of the insight they provide into Bokenham's life and social network.
However, they were still what we might call 'functional' prologues. Their value was
tied to the text they introduced—perhaps even to a particular iteration of that text.
Would anybody besides the text's dedicatee appreciate the story of its genesis?
Bokenham apparently thought not, because he removed his prologues to 'Mary

Magdalene', to 'Margaret', and to his other lives of female saints when he included them in an anthology of saints' legends that he was preparing for a broader audience.[53] Stripped of their prologues, 'Margaret' and 'Mary Magdalene' read like most other anthologized saints' lives. But where the lives could survive perfectly well without their prologues, the prologues without the stories they were designed to introduce would be like sentences that ended mid-word, jokes without a punch line, or riddles without answers. Their 'plot' could only be completed by the story they promised.

'Master Chaucer' and the Anti-autobiographical Prologue

Bokenham's colourful autobiographical prologues may have been inspired by the man he extolled as the rhetorician par excellence, one of medieval England's cagiest and *least* forthcoming authors: Geoffrey Chaucer (c.1343–1400).[54] Thanks to copious surviving public records, we know more about Chaucer than about almost any other medieval author.[55] We know that he was born around 1343 to the wealthy wine merchant John Chaucer and his wife Agnes; that in 1357 he was in the service of Elizabeth de Burgh, Countess of Ulster, and that his wardrobe that year included a pair of red and black hose and a short jacket. We know that he took part in Edward III's unsuccessful invasion of France in 1359 and that he was briefly a prisoner of war. We know that in 1366 he married Philippa de Roet, whose sister Katherine Swynford would become the mistress and later the wife of John of Gaunt, King Richard II's uncle and the most powerful man in the realm. Extant records document Chaucer's various activities from the 1370s until his death in 1400, including his participation in diplomatic missions to France and Italy, his twelve-year tenure as a customs controller at the port of London, and his service as Justice of the Peace and Member of Parliament for Kent. We know that Chaucer had at least two sons. And we know that in 1380, one Cecily Chaumpaigne released him of 'all kinds of actions' pertaining to her 'rape' (*raptus*) (though what this 'release' means remains the subject of heated debate among Chaucerians).[56]

Yet medieval England's best-documented poet was also intensely private. Unlike his contemporary, John Gower, he directly divulges none of his views on current political, social, or religious issues.[57] Allusions to topical events are few, fleeting, and oblique. Chaucer says nothing of his experiences of parliament or the civil service, though a mention in the *House of Fame* of going home after making his 'reckonings' is a possible reference to his job at the customs house. He alludes to friends in some of his poems and claims to have written his *Treatise on the Astrolabe* at the request of his ten-year-old son Lewis, but he says nothing of his wife or other children—much less of Cecily Chaumpaigne.

Nonetheless, Chaucer injects himself—or at least a version of himself—into all of his fiction, particularly through 'autobiographical' prologues. In the *House of Fame* and the *Book of the Duchess* he purports to recount dreams; in the *Canterbury Tales* he claims to tell of the people he met and the stories he heard while on a pilgrimage. His prologues are intricately rendered. In his *Legend of Good Women*, for example, Chaucer claims to have dreamed that he was meandering in a field one beautiful day in May when he encountered the God of Love and his consort, Alceste. The God of Love berated Chaucer for writing stories that reflect poorly upon women, angrily dismissing the poet's protestations of innocence. At last, Alceste intervened, proposing that Chaucer atone for his sins against womankind by writing a book extolling constant women who were betrayed by men. The *Legend*, he tells us, is that book.

Though the Chaucer we meet in the *Canterbury Tales*, the *Legend of Good Women*, and other writings has characteristics of the historical Chaucer—he reads widely and eclectically, has a day job that involves 'reckoning', is the author of *Troilus and Criseyde*, etc—Chaucer the character cannot be equated with Chaucer the author.[58] Chaucer the dreamer does not understand his dreams. Chaucer the pilgrim misjudges his companions, misinterprets their stories, and contributes an egregiously awful romance to their storytelling contest.[59] This quasi-fictive Chaucer interacts with fictional characters but does not meet actual people, at least not directly. Scholars identify the grieving Black Knight about whom Chaucer claims, in the *Book of the Duchess*, to have dreamed with the recently bereaved John of Gaunt, but nobody believes that the conversation he 'dreamed' is one he held with the actual duke.[60] Only in the *Treatise on the Astrolabe* does he give a plausible (in both senses) account of his 'real' life leading him to write a work: that his son Lewis importuned him to write it. But as John Reidy cautions in his introduction to the *Treatise*, Chaucer may simply have been 'wishing his own enthusiasms onto his children'.[61]

Chaucer, I think, would have had no trouble comprehending and endorsing the view that all writing is to some degree autobiographical. In his *Canterbury Tales* he shows that the stories people tell are all, in one way or another, about themselves. People fictionalize their experiences and their fantasies. They narrate out of spite, or in retaliation for some perceived insult, or to impress others. Sometimes they tell the kind of story they think their listeners expect from them; sometimes they tell the kind of story they think their listeners expect a person of their status or profession to tell. Chaucer is also well aware of the dangers of revealing too much. Tellers who talk about themselves get in trouble, as the Pardoner does when he first boasts that he is a fraud and then tries to defraud his fellow pilgrims. Garrulous authors risk revealing that they are not quite what they claim they are—or even, perhaps, what they *think* they are: though the Wife of Bath declares unequivocally that what

women want most is mastery over their men, in the course of her rambling prologue she lets slip that the husband she loved best was the one who beat her up and
sweet-talked her into giving him her wealth.[62] Chaucer has created such a complex
portrait of a proto-feminist who fancies bad boys (the hero of her tale is a rapist) that
readers might forget to wonder why *Chaucer* would tell such a tale and attribute it
to a woman like the Wife of Bath.[63]

Chaucer complicates self-disclosures by never speaking directly of his professional and private lives and by constructing his persona from easily recognizable
literary tropes.[64] Aware that people reveal themselves by the fiction they tell, he
conceals himself by presenting his writings as the self-revelations of *others*, whether
those others are the pilgrim narrators of the *Canterbury Tales* or the dreamer who
both can and cannot be identified with himself. It is not that Chaucer's first-
person references can *never* be associated with the 'historical author'; it is just
that it is often not obvious when they should be. This ambiguity has generated a
considerable body of criticism.[65] For example, does the 'Retraction' that concludes the *Canterbury Tales*, in which Chaucer boasts of his moral, philosophical,
and religious writings and repudiates his romances, dream visions, and other
secular work, express Chaucer's sincere valuation of his oeuvre or the assessment
of his clueless persona?[66] Chaucer's 'autobiographical' prologues and interludes
are, in that sense, *anti*-autobiographical.

Chaucer had many admirers. Some, such as John Metham, imitated him by
prefacing their works with vivid and fanciful accounts of how those works came to
be written.[67] Others, like Bokenham, described with Chaucer's eye for detail real
places and reported with Chaucer's vivacity conversations with real people.
Chaucer may also have supplied the inspiration for one of his most vocal admirers
to experiment with ways of making 'autobiographical' prologues less functional and
more integral to the stories they introduced. That admirer was Thomas Hoccleve
(c.1367-1426), a clerk of the Privy Seal who loudly advertised his discipleship of the
late great master.[68] Hoccleve may have been struck by how thoroughly Chaucer
integrated discussions of himself into the fictions he introduced. Whereas
Bokenham's 'Mary Magdalene' and 'Margaret' could—and did—stand alone perfectly well without their prologues, Chaucer's *Book of the Duchess* or *Legend of Good
Women* could not: the narratives were too securely embedded in their frame, too
reliant on their narrator's predicament. Thomas Hoccleve strove for a similar
integration. He adapted Chaucer's self-deprecatory persona as well as his means of
insinuating that persona into his works, but he departed from Chaucer by investing
his inscribed 'self' with the kinds of personal and professional detail that Chaucer
scrupulously eschewed.[69]

Hoccleve's Runaway Prologues

Hoccleve's *Male Regle* (1405–6) is an odd generic hybrid with strong autobiograph-ical content.[70] Hoccleve introduces himself as one whose profligacy has cost him health and wealth. He rues the sins of youth and fills his memoir with particular-izing details that vivify his experience as a low-level royal bureaucrat.[71] We see him playing truant from his job at the Privy Seal after overindulging in the taverns of Westminster; we see him flattered into over-tipping tavern cooks and Thames boatmen who call him 'Sir' or 'Master'; we glimpse the girls whom he plies with sweet wine and wafers for...kisses, not sex, he piously insists.

Given its penitential themes, the *Male Regle* 'ought' to conclude with stern warnings against excess, but it does not.[72] Though Hoccleve vows to abandon his vices, poor health and poverty in fact leave him no choice. He enviously notes that most of his Privy Seal colleagues continue in great shape despite following the same riotous lifestyle—a circumstance that he petulantly (and irrationally) attributes to skill in pleasing great lords rather than to resilient livers. He then abruptly shifts from a penitential to a practical gear. Addressing the treasurer, Lord Furnival, he requests the ten pounds in salary that he is owed and that, he avers, will cure his problems and his health. Hoccleve's exemplum on the dangers of indulgence, but-tressed by his 'confession' of his own youthful follies, turns out to be an extended prologue to a begging poem!

Chronically strapped for cash, Hoccleve also wrote several more conventional begging 'ballades' during the early 1400s.[73] They generally consisted of three or four eight-line stanzas succinctly requesting reimbursement. One entreats the 'wise and prudent' Lord Chancellor to expedite the payment of money owed to Hoccleve, while another prays that the Lord of the Exchequer make the Privy Seal clerks' Christmas merry by paying their salaries.[74] Yet another informs the king that, absent intervention, Hoccleve and his fellow clerks will be 'trotting off' to a debtors' prison;[75] one addressed to a town clerk of London complains that Hoccleve is sleepless with worry about bills he cannot pay and fears that jail is in his future.[76] Begging poems thus naturally have autobiographical components insofar as they describe the circumstances they hope that cash will remedy. In the *Male Regle*, Hoccleve simply elaborates the autobiographical detail into about four hundred lines, obscuring the poem's real object. The reader thus experiences the 'gotcha' of a practical joke when Hoccleve shifts his pleas from God to Lord Furnival, morphing from a penitent to a petitioner who hints that he would be happy to resume his profligate lifestyle if only his means allowed.

Hoccleve's first major work, the *Regiment of Princes* (1411–12), also begins with a 'runaway prologue' that turns into a begging ballade before in turn becoming the introduction to a mirror for princes, a genre of didactic literature popular in his day.[77] The Prologue to the *Regiment* is 2016 lines—more than a third of the work's total of 5463 lines. Much of it purports to recount a conversation between Hoccleve and an unnamed old man whom he encountered while walking in a field early one morning following a restless night. Hoccleve first tries to ignore the old man but cannot. His unwanted companion speculates about his state of mind, regales him with unsolicited advice, and opines about everything from fashion to politics. His persistence pays off: Hoccleve finds himself divulging his own political and religious views as well as details about his finances, marriage, and job, not to mention the sources of his current distress. He confesses that King Henry IV bestowed upon him a generous annuity, but that he is having trouble collecting it. More than two decades of working at the Office of the Privy Seal have taken their toll on his health—his back aches from the hours spent hunched over his desk, his eyesight has deteriorated from the strain of reading, and he suffers from stomach pains that he attributes to the stress of his employment. Soon he will no longer be able to work, but once he retires, collecting his annuity will be even trickier. Poverty and loneliness will haunt his old age.

The old man's first advice is that Hoccleve accept his fate, but Hoccleve's offer of half the profit if he can suggest a more lucrative alternative produces a plan. Having learned that Hoccleve considers himself a disciple of the late great Chaucer, the old man proposes a literary solution: Hoccleve should join his appeal to Prince Henry for help securing his annuity with a work that would please his lordship—perhaps a treatise on the qualities befitting a good ruler. Hoccleve concurs, and after inquiring where to find the old man again (presumably to deliver his share of the proceeds), he goes home to commence the *Regiment*.

In both the *Male Regle* and the *Regiment* Hoccleve prefaced works that could have stood alone—in the *Male Regle* a begging poem and in the *Regiment* a mirror for princes—with long and anecdotal stories about himself, much as Bokenham prefaced his 'Margaret' and 'Mary Magdalene'. But unlike Bokenham's prologues, Hoccleve's prologues could *also* stand alone. Had he concluded his *Male Regle* at line 408, Hoccleve would have had a moral poem bewailing the consequences of misspent youth. Likewise, the *Regiment*'s lively Dialogue, an ingenious blend of memoir and social satire, reads like a permutation of the popular genre of literary debate, in which disputants address such issues as labour, justice, love, and marriage without necessarily arriving at any conclusions.[78] Fewer than 150 of the Dialogue's 2016 lines directly pertain to the *Regiment*, although it does anticipate key themes, including justice, self-control, and social order.[79]

Hoccleve experimented still more radically with prologues and dialogues some fifteen years later in his *Series* (1419-21), an anthology of sorts consisting of two moralized stories and a prose treatise on dying that are preceded by Hoccleve's complaint about his current circumstances and bound together by his Dialogue with an unnamed friend. Where Hoccleve had, in the Dialogue preceding the *Regiment*, inveighed against the poor working conditions of the Privy Seal–boredom, physically taxing labour, the bullying of the great lords' flunkeys–in the *Series* he dramatizes through dialogue the challenges facing an author.

The *Series* begins with Hoccleve lamenting the loneliness that has followed what appears to have been a nervous breakdown five years earlier. His friends no longer want anything to do with him; when he sees them at Westminster Hall or around London, they avert their gaze and pretend not to have noticed him. Those few who do ask how he is doing do not listen to his answer. He hears talk behind his back, remarking on his strange gesticulations and wild looks and predicting a relapse. Thus, despite looking normal enough to himself in the mirror, he dreads going out in public. At last, however, he talks himself into thanking God for his recovery, setting aside his depression, and getting on with life.

At this point, an unnamed Friend comes calling. Hoccleve shows his Friend the Complaint he has just written (i.e. the first 413 lines of the *Series*), and the Friend is aghast to learn that Hoccleve plans to publish it. In a rambling dialogue reminiscent of Hoccleve's conversation with the Old Man, the Friend and Hoccleve discuss matters personal and public, from Hoccleve's illness to the recently outlawed practice of 'coin clipping', or shaving bits of metal from currency. But they mostly talk about what Hoccleve should, or should not, write.[80] Hoccleve wants to translate a treatise on dying–he is getting on in years and ought to be thinking of the end–but his Friend persuades him to write the story of a good woman on the grounds that he has offended women mightily with one of his previous works. When Hoccleve completes the assignment, the Friend insists that he add a moral that transforms the story of a good woman into an allegory about Christ and the soul. Having appeased his Friend, Hoccleve translates the treatise on dying, but scarcely has he laid down his pen when his Friend turns up again, this time insisting that he translate the story of a deceitful woman and pooh-poohing Hoccleve's objection that he has just insisted on the importance of flattering women. The *Series* thus ends up a mishmash of what Hoccleve purportedly wanted to write (the Complaint and treatise on dying) and what his Friend pushed him to write (the stories about women and their moralizations).

The richness of Hoccleve's eclectic collection has been abundantly recognized in the decades since Derek Pearsall dismissed it as 'an attempt to make a longish poem out of nothing'.[81] Readers today are more prone to concur with David Watt's judgment of it as 'a sophisticated compilation of texts linked by its narrator's account of making the book that preserves them'.[82] Interpretations of the poem's autobiographical orientation have been provocative and varied. Christina von Nolcken has read it as the work of a fifty-something poet in ill health who is preparing himself emotionally and spiritually for his impending death.[83] John Burrow has interpreted it as Hoccleve's attempt to rehabilitate himself after an embarrassing mental breakdown.[84] Others have viewed the *Series* as the work of an author *still* in the throes of mental illness. For Matthew Goldie, 'Hoccleve attempts to authorize a stable self but instead writes a fragmented and incoherent identity, one characterized by illness instead of integrity.'[85] Similarly, Marion Turner sees in the *Series* Hoccleve's attempt to understand his breakdown; his Friend's doubts about his recovery express his own fear that he is 'still tainted' by mental illness: 'his self remains fractured and incomprehensible to anyone *including* himself.'[86] Other critics see Hoccleve less in conflict with himself than with his unruly readers. For Sebastian Langdell, Hoccleve strikes back at a censorious public, embodied in the person of the Friend, which demands of authors a narrow morality and prejudges works it has not read.[87]

For most interpreters, Hoccleve's end was not the treatise and stories per se but rather the series of beginnings, the preambles to its various components. Within the *Series*, the constituent poems come across, as D. C. Greetham put it, like 'digressions in the portrayal of the poet's psyche'.[88] Hoccleve's chief interest is his struggle to come to terms with his personal demons, with his mortality, with the expectations of friends and colleagues, and with his readership, real and imagined. The inscribed texts give him the opportunity to tell that story, *his* story.

Not everybody cared about that story. Though Hoccleve tried to make his life story integral to the *Series*, five anthologizers freely extracted the treatise on dying and the inscribed stories from their autobiographical frame; six manuscripts preserve the complete work.[89] Reception of Hoccleve's *Male Regle* was even more tepid.[90] The only person (besides Hoccleve) to have copied the poem made radical cuts, 'depersonalizing' it and transforming it from a mischievous begging poem into 'a resolutely moral piece on the necessity of moderation in youth and the necessity of accepting good counsel'.[91] The *Regiment* was another story. Surviving in forty-three manuscripts, it was something of a bestseller (only four other Middle English texts survive in more copies: the *Prick of Conscience*, Chaucer's *Canterbury Tales*, Gower's *Confessio Amantis*, and Langland's *Piers Plowman*).[92] Its success was surely in no small measure due to the general popularity of mirrors for princes, but that does not explain why the overwhelming number of manuscripts preserve the dialogue along with the mirror. Perhaps, as M. C. Seymour suggests, the 'interesting autobiographical dialogue' was actually part of its appeal.[93] Perhaps there was, after all, an audience for literary lives, well told and properly packaged.

Autobiographical Hybrids and Interpolations

The Testaments of Thomas Usk and John Lydgate

Like Hoccleve, Thomas Usk and John Lydgate indulged their autobiographical impulses within literary works that defy categorization. Though Lydgate's and Usk's generic hybrids both present themselves as 'testaments', they exemplify different approaches to narrating lives. In *The Testament of Love* (1385-6), Usk confesses his political missteps in the course of a Boethian dialogue; in *The Testament* (1449), Lydgate confesses his moral failings in the course of a religious meditation. Usk hopes for an improvement in his worldly circumstances; Lydgate hopes for Christ's mercy as he contemplates the hereafter. Usk turns to Lady Love and Lydgate to Jesus Christ. Both authors invoke the last will and testament, perhaps the most widely practised form of life-writing in their day.[94] But whereas wills resonate with the material life of the testator—friends, family, valued institutions and charities, specific items to be bequeathed—both Lydgate and Usk pointedly subordinate the particular to allegory and conventions in ways that conceal even as they reveal.

In 1385, Usk was in an unenviable predicament, caught in the crossfire between John Northampton, mayor of London from 1381 to 1383, and his rival Nicholas Brembre.[95] Northampton had in 1383 enlisted Usk as lobbyist and propagandist in a campaign to keep Brembre from becoming mayor even though Brembre had won the election. When Brembre prevailed, both Northampton and Usk ended up in prison. Usk secured his freedom by testifying against Northampton, but this treachery to an erstwhile employer was hardly apt to win him the trust of the ascendant faction.[96] To recuperate his good name and convince members of the Brembre party to take him into their service, he took a singular measure: he wrote a philosophical dialogue, *The Testament of Love*.

Usk obviously modelled his work on Boethius's *Consolation of Philosophy*.[97] The *Testament* begins with the imprisoned author lamenting his misfortunes. He fears that his wrongful incarceration has discredited him in the eyes of the one he loves more than anything, his Margaret, or pearl.[98] As he despairs, he is surprised by the appearance of the beautiful Lady Love. Usk and Love discourse on many topics, philosophical and amatory, and at one point Usk recounts the circumstances that led to his disgrace—a thinly disguised allegory of his dealings with Northampton. Without naming anybody, he speaks of bad governors, mighty senators, conspiracies, and accusations. As Paul Strohm points out, Usk is after remediation rather than consolation, and Lady Love, herself a 'factionalist', helps him shore up his damaged credibility by providing a receptive audience for his apology and by agreeing that he did what seemed reasonable under the circumstances.[99] His unjust punishment, she opines, should not degrade him in the eyes of his beloved—for which read in the eyes of potential benefactors.

Although we do not know whether the *Testament* helped Usk ingratiate himself to Nicholas Brembre's royalist faction, we do know that in October of 1387, the year he completed the work, he was appointed under-sheriff of Middlesex. But this success was short-lived, and so was Usk. By the end of the year, the tide had turned against Usk's new allies, and his former friends were not inclined to have mercy on the man who had betrayed them. On 4 March 1388, Usk, convicted of treason, was drawn and hanged, then cut down while still alive and beheaded—or, more accurately, bludgeoned to death (witnesses said that it took more than thirty strokes to decapitate him).[100]

As my summary of it suggests, Usk's *Testament of Love* so wraps events in allegory that anybody not acquainted with his career would find the 'plot' difficult to follow. R. Allen Shoaf, one of its modern editors, characterized it as 'incoherent', noting that the actions it relates are 'frustratingly unclear', especially 'those surrounding Usk's arrest and imprisonment'.[101] So oblique, indeed, was it that William Thynne, who first printed *The Testament* in 1530, attributed it to Chaucer, and for the next three-hundred years, readers assumed that its autobiographical elements referred to some obscure episode in Chaucer's past.[102]

Interpretive challenges of a different sort confront readers of *The Testament*, composed in 1449 by John Lydgate, a man who could not have had less in common with the unhappy Usk. Lydgate was England's Petrarch, 'a proto-professional poet who for all practical purposes was an acting laureate'.[103] Though a Benedictine monk, he was a savvy propagandist and diplomat and a celebrated poet whose patrons included kings, nobles, and wealthy merchants.[104] A jack-of-all-genres, he produced a vast oeuvre that includes epics of ancient Greece and Thebes, saints' lives, religious meditations, allegories, satires, love poetry, dream visions, debates, lyrics, occasional poems, and propaganda. He composed *The Testament*, his most autobiographical work, shortly before his death.

Whereas Usk confines the account of his misfortunes to two chapters of his *Testament* (Book One, Chapters 6-7), Lydgate tells his story in fits and starts, with deferrals and frustrations everywhere. Following a two-hundred-line meditation on the name of Jesus, we encounter Lydgate as an old man plagued by stiff joints and cloudy eyesight who is contemplating his mortality, lamenting the wasted time that is forever lost to him, and intending to make Jesus the 'chief surveyor / of my last will and testament' (ll. 211–12).[105] As he begins his 'last testament' (l. 239), an allegorical lady, 'Remembrance of Misspent Time', approaches, accompanied by her sister, 'Thoughts of Old Excesses' (ll. 269–73). But any expectations we form of a Boethian dialogue are soon dashed. Lydgate's melancholy visitors offer no comfort; rather, they silently present Lydgate with a 'bill' enumerating his past follies. Instead of revealing the bill's contents, as we might expect him to do, the poet begins musing on the joys of springtime. Over a hundred lines later, he declares himself ready to confess the transgressions of his youth, but he defers his confession for more than 150 further lines as he prays for Jesus's mercy; it is not until line 609 that he divulges any specifics about his past.

Those specifics are the stereotypical follies of youth.[106] The young Lydgate was rambunctious and self-indulgent, moody, hot-tempered, and lazy. He stayed up late and rose late, sloughed off his studies, preferred playing cherrystones to going to Mass, favoured stealing grapes from another man's vineyard over attending Matins. Hating correction, he blamed others for his misdeeds and made excuses for his failings. What led a boy so ill disposed to piety or study to become a Benedictine? Parental pressure? Persuasion? Was he convinced, perhaps, that monasticism guaranteed a life of indulgence? Lydgate does not say. One wonders, indeed, whether he was as naughty and frivolous as he claims to have been. Yet he insists that he continued his dissolute lifestyle within the walls of Bury St. Edmunds. Ignoring the lessons and exhortations of his teachers, he became a hypocrite in a black habit who preferred parties to contemplation, good wine to pious literature (ll. 726-32). Frivolous stories and malicious gossip were favourite pastimes (ll. 721-22).

As Ruth Nisse has observed, 'the Testament, as autobiography, is more notable for what it leaves out than for what it includes'.[107] Lydgate does not recount his career as a Benedictine, much less his remarkable *extra*-monastic career as poet laureate, propagandist for the Lancastrian kings, and diplomat. Eschewing the particular, he conveys the *essence* of a life—which may or may not have actually been his—and explores the relationship between youth and old age, between experience and memory. Memory is present from the very first lines of the poem, which read, 'Oh how wholesome and glad is the memory / Of Jesus Christ' (ll. 1-2), and it binds together the disparate segments of *The Testament*: Lydgate's memory of Jesus, Lydgate's memory of his youth, and Jesus's memory of his passion. Like the workings of memory, Lydgate's journey through his past is circuitous, his progress hindered by an inability, or unwillingness, to disengage from the present. His past profligacy, real or imagined, enhances the portrait of his present self as a pious and penitent Benedictine, a representation that everywhere overlies the memories of an impious youth.

Lydgate's narration of his youth gives way, in the final 143 lines of *The Testament*, to a narration of Christ's passion. This narration is rooted in Lydgate's memory of an image on a cloister wall of the crucified Christ with gaping wounds, which bore an inscription exhorting him to look ('vide'): 'Behold my meekness, oh child, and forsake your pride' (ll. 745-6). As a young monk, Lydgate did not understand (ll. 747–8), but the recollection prompts him to take up his pen and write verses in Christ's voice that explain the image and its inscription. Christ recalls the events of his passion in eighteen stanzas replete with the specificity of character and incident that Lydgate suppressed when recounting his own life. Like Hoccleve's *Regiment* or Bokenham's saints' lives, this narration could stand alone as a separate poem;[108] one might even read the first 754 lines of *The Testament* as a Hocclevian 'runaway prologue' to the 143-line passion poem that concludes it.

Like Hoccleve's *Series*, Lydgate's *Testament* is a carefully constructed work that gives the impression of disorderliness. Julia Boffey notes its alternation between devotional and autobiographical sections, underlined by a corresponding formal alternation between different stanza types.[109] As with the *Series*, its structural complexity mirrors the poet's complex self-presentation. The *Testament* can be read as Lydgate's repudiation of his career as a court poet and propagandist.[110] It can be read as an act of self-abnegation, with Lydgate substituting literary tropes for personal experience, and ultimately Christ's life and voice for his own.[111] Yet the *Testament* can also be read as Lydgate celebrating his diverse career as court poet and Benedictine in a poem that expresses a suitable piety while combining the forms and tropes of both his secular and his religious oeuvre in a literary tour de force.[112] We would do well to consider that Lydgate created the deity who speaks at the end of the *Testament* just as Christine and Boethius created Lady Philosophy and Petrarch created Augustinus. It is thus not clear whether Christ's life absorbs Lydgate's, or whether Lydgate claims the ultimate authority by ventriloquizing the Saviour.

Lydgate's *Testament* was well received by his contemporaries.[113] Six manuscripts preserve the work intact, while six more include extracts or condensations. Although some redactors of the *Testament*, like those of the *Series*, liberated the devotional portions from their autobiographical frame, others underscored the autobiography by omitting some or all of the purely devotional sections. Julia Boffey points out that the *Testament*, in its abridged or unabridged form, occurs in several anthologies of Lydgate's writings whose editors appear to 'highlight its status as an autobiographical document'.[114] Like the compilers of the troubadour songbooks who included the *vidas* and *razos* along with the poetry, these Middle English editors appear to have judged that knowing about an author's life enhances the pleasure of reading his or her work.

Towards 'Literary (Auto)Biography'

In his 1965 history of literary biography, Richard D. Altick proposed that there were no literary biographies before the eighteenth century because earlier periods lacked a sense of the 'man of letters as a distinct type of social being'.[115] 'Man of letters' is an imprecise term, which Altick does not define. Yet under any reasonable definition, men (and women) of letters clearly inhabited the Middle Ages and were recognized as such. William of Malmesbury identified himself as '*homo litteratus*'. If there were no 'sense' of a person of letters, Petrarch would not have been crowned poet laureate, and Christine de Pizan would not have been inundated with commissions. The many who expressed their appreciation of Chaucer, Gower, and Lydgate understood these 'masters' as men of letters. Hoccleve actively sought to join their ranks by linking his name with Chaucer's and publishing his collected works.[116] What truly distinguishes the Middle Ages from later periods is that nobody appears to have thought authors appropriate subjects for extended, free-standing biographies and autobiographies. There were no conventions for writing lives of authors, as there were for writing lives of prelates, potentates, and saints; there was no 'life of the authors'. Those who tentatively told their own stories or those of their fellow poets and historians were on their own.

Given the lack of precedent and the long tradition of authorial anonymity, it makes sense that these early experiments in literary biography should almost always be part of something else, some work whose legitimacy would be generally accepted—a history or a saint's life, a dream vision, an allegory about politics or love, a moral or penitential tract. Thus situated, lives of poets and authors, from Caedmon to Lydgate, could blend, chameleon-like, into their literary, historical, moral, or philosophical backdrops. Even less surprising is that authors should so often write about themselves in the course of describing interactions with their patrons, who could reasonably be counted on to enjoy being a part of the work they had commissioned.

As we have seen, several of the pioneers of literary autobiography chose the dialogue form. It was a natural vehicle. Through dialogue, they associated their work with the esteemed *Consolation of Philosophy*, even when they presented as their interlocutor a supercilious Friend or a nagging Old Man; they created the polite fiction that they were being pressed to speak by eager listeners rather than presuming to impose their personal anecdotes on readers; they granted themselves licence to explore their experience from diverse perspectives and voice opinions that they might not wish to express directly. They could express anxieties, dilemmas, and fears; they could promote themselves and legitimate their endeavours.

5

Polemical Anthologies

One of the earliest forms of biography in the West, and one of the most enduring, was the biographical collection. We have already encountered variants of this form in the histories constituted from lives: monks such as Bede chronicled their institutions by recounting the lives of their abbots, while William of Malmesbury and many other historians relayed British history as a procession of sovereigns. The practice of writing history through biography extended back into antiquity, as Suetonius's *Lives of the Caesars* demonstrates, and survived long after the Middle Ages, as reflected in Carlyle's (in)famous dictum 'The history of the world is but the biography of great men.' Lives were also used to vivify places: John Capgrave's *Solace of Pilgrims* (1451) describes the churches and monuments of Rome through the stories of the people associated with them. Many such collections develop, through a succession of examples, unstated arguments. As I noted in Chapter Three, Geoffrey of Monmouth repeatedly emphasized the dangers of intrafamilial dissent as he told the lives of British kings. Similarly, in his *Deeds of the English Kings*, William of Malmesbury repeatedly praised sovereigns' learning, or deplored the lack thereof, to make the case that erudition makes for good governance.

Defining Sainthood

Anthologies of saints' lives, the most common type of biographical collection in the Middle Ages, are also implicitly polemical. The creators of those collections promoted particular views of sainthood by their choice of which lives to include, by how they adapted their sources, and by how they presented the saints whose lives they largely invented. Some hagiographers emphasized their subjects' prayerfulness and spirituality, others their struggles against pagan persecutors or worldly vanities, others their emotions and dilemmas, others their passive endurance of afflictions, others their teachings, still others their performance of miracles. Through the celebration of similar virtues and behaviours in saints ranging from fictional virgin martyrs to historical popes, the producers of these collections were in fact arguing their view of what it means to be holy.

Such arguments can be discerned even in collections of very brief lives. Consider the martyrologies produced in pre-Conquest England. Meant to remind worshippers of the date on which each saint should be commemorated, martyrologies were originally mere lists of saints' names beside the dates of their feasts. When Bede introduced the genre to Britain in the eighth century, he added a modicum of information about each saint, thus inventing what is known as the 'historical martyrology'.[1] Bede says little about the saints' personalities, virtues, backgrounds, or careers, though he sometimes praises their studiousness; instead, his focus is on their deaths, so much so that his stories might better be called 'death-writing' than 'life-writing'. Rarely does he even indicate the circumstances that induced persecution before conjuring the spectre of the saint bludgeoned, blinded, racked, maimed, mutilated, nailed, boiled, or burned. The cumulative impression left by his portrayals is that what is most commendable—or at least most remarkable or relevant—about a saint is passive submission to violence: 'after the very many torments of prison, of various lashings, of red-hot plates, [Lawrence] at last completed his martyrdom by being roasted on an iron griddle' (August 10). Even the relatively few lives of confessors that Bede includes in his *Martyrology* have more to do with death than with life: 'Paul the first hermit…remained alone in the wilderness from his sixteenth year until his one hundred and thirteenth: Anthony saw his soul carried by angels to heaven among a chorus of apostles and prophets' (January 10). When an anonymous ninth-century author 'translated' Bede's Latin martyrology into Old English, he added many lives, confessors as well as martyrs, and emphasized what they did over what they endured, elaborating Bede's deaths into lives.[2] From him, we obtain the details Bede withheld—for example, how Paul lived during his ninety-seven years as a hermit, or what Alban did to bring about his execution. In this *Old English Martyrology*, holiness consists at least as much in deeds as in suffering, as suggested through stories of saints who refuse unwanted marriages, defy tyrants, travel, proselytize, and perform acts of charity and asceticism. Virginity, an attribute Bede mentions only in passing, is here so frequently praised and so central to the plots that it becomes a crowning virtue of female saints.[3]

Later, more expansive legendaries similarly express their own preoccupations. In his *Lives of the Saints* (992–1002), Ælfric, Abbot of Eynsham, pays far more attention to the saints' character and qualities than does the *South English Legendary*, the most widely circulated collection of lives in post-Conquest England.[4] For example, Ælfric's Sebastian is educated, passionate, prudent, truthful, judicious, righteous, reliable, a good intercessor, trusty counsellor, and 'in all his ways honourable'.[5] By contrast, the *South English Legendary* calls Sebastian 'a very honourable man' but does not elaborate.[6] Where Ælfric praises saints as scholars and preachers, the *South English Legendary* celebrates miracle workers and strident crusaders against evil, whether that evil comes in the form of pagan persecutors or worldly temptation.[7] Ælfric's saints are admirable *and* imitable; the *South English Legendary*'s martyrs, at least, are only admirable. Much like the *South English Legendary*, the 'bestselling' Latin collection of the late thirteenth century, Jacobus de Voragine's *Golden Legend*, also stressed miracles, holding the saints up as heroes whose perfection is unattainable by the rank-and-file faithful.[8]

Some legendaries, including the *South English Legendary* and Jacobus's *Golden Legend*, were very long-lived.[9] As they were copied and/or translated, these classics were frequently updated to reflect the tastes of their adapters and publics. Thus during the fifteenth century, when less strident and more exemplary saints became fashionable, some lives were rewritten and others added.[10] When he wrote his Middle English *Golden Legend* in the 1450s, Osbern Bokenham included many lives that developed the saints' emotions and explored their ethical quandaries:[11] his Audrey must decide whether to abandon her dream of entering a convent in deference to her beloved parents, who want her to marry; his Barbara ponders whether her conscience will allow her to pretend to honour idols in order to please her father; his Winifred wonders whether it would be sinful to lie to a would-be rapist to preserve her virginity. In his 1483 *Golden Legend*, William Caxton balanced Jacobus's martyr-heavy compendium by adding the stories of dozens of confessors who embody values prized by his London clientele, such as charity, discipline, compassion, studiousness, patience, humility, and social responsibility. Seventy of the 250 lives in Caxton's *Golden Legend* were not in Jacobus's, and many of those that were have been radically changed.[12]

When we further scrutinize the recurring themes in hagiographical collections, we find their producers taking positions on a host of religious and social issues. What exactly does it mean to be a saint? Does sanctity make one immune to temptation? How important is virginity? Does holiness require Christians to renounce worldly responsibilities along with frivolous pleasures? Is compromise acceptable? To what extent, if any, do men and women embody different ideals of holiness? What about laypeople and religious? Should ordinary people try to imitate the saints or confine themselves to admiration and veneration? Legendaries, then, are more polemics than the repositories of 'facts' about the saints they claim to be.

While the authors of legendaries make their arguments implicitly, authors of other kinds of biographical collections were overtly polemical. My focus in the rest of this chapter is the treatment in such polemical anthologies of two popular topics: the nature of women and the depredations of fortune. The collections I shall be discussing generally relay the lives of characters from Greek and Roman legend or from a remote and shadowy historical past. Like the authors of legendaries, whose subjects also hail mostly from a murky past, authors of these collections took a fair amount of licence with the stories they inherited. Just as, say, Saint Margaret could be a strident virago in one legendary and a paragon of decorous femininity in another, Medea could be a traitor and murderess here and a paragon of loyalty there. Though the creators of these polemical collections openly subordinate the lives they tell to larger moral agendas, they also sometimes subvert those agendas, either by telling 'inappropriate' stories or by supplying interpretations at odds with the stories they have told. In some cases, the subversion is egregious and obviously intentional, but in other cases it is unclear whether the writers are mischievously undercutting pious sentiments that they never subscribed to in the first place or whether they are wrestling with truly mixed feelings about their subjects and with unacknowledged competing impulses and agendas.

On the Nature of Women

In the prologue to her eponymous *Tale*, the Wife of Bath, one of Chaucer's most flamboyant Canterbury pilgrims, recalls how her husband Janekyn used to infuriate her by reading aloud from his 'book of wicked wives', an anthology of 'legends and lives' of women who had mistreated their husbands in myriad ways—killing them, cheating on them, haranguing them, tempting them into sin, betraying them to their enemies. Janekyn's book may sound fanciful, but it belongs to a tradition of catalogues rehearsing the deeds of women that reaches back into antiquity.[13] While some offered examples of virtuous conduct for women to admire and emulate, others were concerned with arguing that women's conduct stemmed from their inherent nature, which in most cases was held to be vicious.[14] Misogynist anthologies were often specifically *misogamous*, discouraging men from marriage on the grounds that women throughout history have made their husbands' lives miserable.[15] Jerome's influential *Against Jovinian* (*c.*393) argues both sides, cataloguing examples of vicious wives to discourage men from marriage and examples of virtuous maidens to encourage women to remain celibate. Women's detractors and defenders both made their case by overwhelming readers with examples.

Many classical and medieval polemicists recited only one or two illustrative deeds from their exemplars' lives. The earliest medieval author to use full lives to explore the nature of women was Giovanni Boccaccio, best known today for his framed fiction, *The Decameron* (1349-51).[16] Boccaccio composed his *Famous*

Women (*c*.1361) late in life, when he gave himself over to writing encyclopedic tomes in Latin. Inspired by Petrarch's *Lives of Famous Men* (begun in 1337), *Famous Women* comprises 106 chapters, each recounting the life of a different woman. Boccaccio drew most of the lives from Greek and Roman history and mythology, a handful from the Old Testament and from medieval European history; his sources, stated or unstated, include the Bible, Jerome, Livy, Ovid, Suetonius, and Virgil. Although his subjects are varied—wives, sovereigns, artists, and sibyls—the lives generally follow a common template: Boccaccio begins by summarizing the subject's claim to fame and identifying her progenitors, where known. He then recounts her principal accomplishments and concludes with some sort of moral.

As he dedicates the *Famous Women* to Andrea Acciaiuoli, Countess of Altavilla, Boccaccio asserts that he aims both to delight his reader with instances of feminine virtue and to furnish her with examples to either emulate or shun. By applying the lessons gleaned from the examples of non-Christian women, she will surpass even the best of them and thus please her Maker. Boccaccio is careful to distinguish between fame and virtue, emphasizing that his topic is 'famous' women, 'whatever might be the cause of their renown' (p. 203). As to women's nature, he states, 'almost all are endowed by nature with soft, frail bodies and sluggish minds'; only a few exceptions (among whom he naturally numbers his dedicatee) are able to 'take on a manly spirit' by showing 'remarkable intelligence and bravery'. Through the lives of individual women he illustrates what he defines as specifically feminine faults, including 'fickleness', 'temerity', 'cunning', 'wantonness', 'lasciviousness', 'stinginess', and 'avarice'.[17] 'The female', he declares, 'is a very suspicious creature, either because of the weakness of her sex or because she does not have a good opinion of herself' (p. 313). Marked by 'excessive softness, flattery, petulance, and tears', women are 'accustomed to faint on their husbands' bosom at the slightest noise of a mouse' (pp. 409, 411). Women have no aptitude for arts such as painting, which require 'great intellectual concentration' (p. 251). Men 'have greater aptitude for everything' (p. 329).

Boccaccio uses the lives even of praiseworthy women as occasions for castigating women generally. Argia was 'generous beyond the nature of women' (p. 114).[18] Sempronia distinguished herself as a poet by writing with 'discernment'—'not the way women usually do' (p. 177). Boccaccio claims to focus on women of the past because exemplary women are rare in his own time. Contemporary women, he laments, are 'constantly excusing their weaknesses' and indulge their 'itching lust' like prostitutes, while girls are 'giddy' and of 'loose morals' (pp. 403, 449).

To be sure, Boccaccio perceives as naturally feminine not only certain vices but also certain virtues—decency, modesty, honour, and shame—and these he occasionally commends, but for the most part, he lauds women who are able to overcome their female nature. He decries those who engage in 'womanly occupations' such as spinning and weaving, which he equates with 'idleness' (p. 275), and praises women who pursue the arts of warfare, government, and painting, thereby offering an alternative ideal of femininity.[19] In fact, he proposes Camilla, who 'disdain[ed] all womanly work' and died in battle, as a model of 'proper demeanour' for girls of his own day (p. 157). However, his repeated assertion that women generally are unable to carry out 'masculine' occupations undermines that alternative paradigm and reaffirms gender difference.

Boccaccio's attempt to impose a value-charged binary between male and female, however, is strained.[20] He undercuts the biological difference between the sexes that supposedly accounts for gender difference when he calls brave women 'tried and true men' and weak men 'women' (p. 129), or when he points out that practical experience can change natural dispositions, making women 'more manly in arms than those born male who have been changed into women–or helmeted hares–by idleness and love of pleasure' (p. 131). Sometimes Boccaccio complicates his distinction between good and bad qualities, as when Penelope uses her 'feminine cunning' to ward off the men who wish to take Odysseus's place in her bed. By the end of *Famous Women*, readers have encountered a more confused but also richer view of women's abilities and of gender difference than Boccaccio had allowed for in his introduction. One wonders whether he might not have meant to entertain the women among his readers with his incompetence as a maligner of their sex.[21]

The many readers of Boccaccio's *Famous Women* included Geoffrey Chaucer, who based his own *Legend of Good Women* (1385-7), the earliest collection of lives of women written in English, on it.[22] Chaucer presents his work as a defence of women, but, as with so many disquisitions on women, including Boccaccio's, this claim of intent is of dubious sincerity.[23] Chaucer purports to undertake his *Legend of Good Women* at the instigation of the God of Love and his consort Alceste as a penance for writing *Troilus and Criseyde* and other stories that reflect poorly on women. The *Legend*, Love insists, should celebrate constant women who were betrayed by men, beginning with Cleopatra. Chaucer complies, and his tale of Cleopatra is followed by the stories of Thisbe, Dido, Hypsipyle, Medea, Lucretia, Ariadne, Philomela, Phyllis, and Hypermnestra. Borrowing terms from Christian hagiography, he introduces each of his lives as a 'legenda' and designates six of his heroines 'martiris', or martyrs (Cleopatra, Thisbe, Dido, Hypsipyle, Medea, Lucretia).[24] We do not know whether his offering satisfied the god and/or Alceste, because Chaucer never completed the collection, which breaks off mid-sentence near the end of his story of Hypermnestra: 'This tale is told to this end–.'

Chaucerians have vigorously debated what 'end' the anthology as a whole is 'told to'.[25] Many have pointed out that the *Legend of Good Women* hardly passes muster as a pro-female anthology. To begin with, Chaucer's wronged women include two of the ancient world's most notorious villainesses, Medea and Cleopatra, whom other writers routinely cited as examples of female iniquity.[26] Chaucer's readers would surely have balked at pitying Medea, who slew her own children (a detail Chaucer omits) because their father misbehaved, or Cleopatra, whom Boccaccio, following tradition, denounces as 'malicious', 'avaricious', and 'insatiable' for her 'greed, cruelty, and lust' (pp. 363, 361, 365). Some Chaucerians have found Chaucer's praise for innocent women wronged by men either wearisome or excessive, with woman after woman homogenized into victimhood. A related hypothesis is that Chaucer abandoned the project out of boredom. For many, *The Legend of Good Women* is less a tribute to women's constancy than to a wily author's ability to subvert the demands of the meddlesome and overbearing 'patron' who misread his *Troilus and Criseyde* and assigned such a ridiculous 'penance'.[27]

Yet, as we have seen, actual medieval legendaries homogenize saints in much the same manner, extolling the same virtues in a bishop as in a virgin martyr, and some critics have accordingly argued that Chaucer's treatment of women would not have been read by his medieval readers as sarcasm, and should not be read by us as evidence that his project bored him.[28] Indeed, views of Medea and Cleopatra were not universally negative, and Chaucer might have been tapping into those alternative traditions to produce revisionary rather than ironic stories.[29] Even if he was subverting the God of Love's assignment, he might have been doing so to a feminist end.[30] Given Chaucer's caginess and propensity for 'game', I find myself inclined to Catherine Sanok's proposition: that Chaucer's objective was to craft a 'legendary' whose bias, whether pro- or anti-women, is indeterminable.[31]

Men wrote most medieval collections of women's lives. The first known female to contribute to the genre was Christine de Pizan, whose *Book of the City of Ladies* (1405) is a direct response to the authors of the kind of misogynist anthologies that infuriated the Wife of Bath.[32] Christine recounts how one day as she is contentedly reading in her study she happens upon a most disturbing volume—a book by one Mathéolus that rehearsed the iniquities of womankind. Mathéolus's book per se does not bother her ('it was of no authority' and 'had a bad name anyway and was intended as a satire'), but it does cause her to wonder why so many men—philosophers, poets, scholars, and orators too numerous to name—agree that 'the behaviour of women is inclined to and full of every vice' (pp. 3–4).[33] Though her own experience convinces her that they are wrong, she cannot help wondering how so many distinguished men could be mistaken. Thus beset by doubts about herself and her sex, she has a vision of three crowned women. Identifying themselves as Lady Reason, Lady Rectitude, and Lady Justice, they scold her for believing the testimony of books even though it contradicts the evidence of her own experience. Under their tutelage,

Christine constructs an impregnable 'City of Ladies', built from the stories of the myriad good women of the past and the present.

The Book of the City of Ladies is divided into three parts, each associated with a different allegorical lady. In the first book, Lady Reason helps Christine erect the wall and the enclosure for the city, which she does by recounting the lives of women who distinguished themselves in the public sphere as sovereigns, generals, and judges. In the second, Rectitude helps Christine construct the buildings within the walls—the houses, palaces, streets, squares, and public buildings—from the stories of devoted wives, mothers, and daughters. Finally, Lady Justice provides roofs and towers of the finest gold, crafted from the lives of the saints. In each book, Christine and her interlocutors discuss the lives, and the ladies insist that the virtues manifested in the illustrious heroines of the past continue to be manifested in women today. The lives Christine relates thus illustrate the potential for greatness and virtuous behaviour that *all* women *naturally* have. Through these examples, Christine also attacks double standards, antifeminist stereotypes, and defamatory beliefs (for example, that women really want to be raped).

Boccaccio's *Famous Women* was Christine's principal source for stories of women from antiquity.[34] In her adaptations, Christine praises many of the same qualities as Boccaccio does, among them leadership, courage, intellect, creativity, responsibility, chastity, and loyalty; however, she also reshapes and often drastically revises, using Boccaccio's own material to refute his larger claims about women.[35] Where he calls his famous women exceptions, she calls them normative. She systematically attacks negative stereotypes that Boccaccio rehearsed in *Famous Women*—for example, that women are 'naturally' lascivious, greedy, vain, fearful, frivolous, and frail. In Christine's world, misbehaving women are acting 'contrary to the natural disposition of women' (p. 33). Christine's criticism of Boccaccio is sly and surreptitious. She professes nothing but admiration and enthusiasm for her predecessor, whose 'credibility is well-known and evident' (p. 78), even as she quotes him out of context to support claims he would not endorse. Whereas Boccaccio repeatedly belittles 'feminine' occupations, such as spinning, weaving, or sewing, Lady Reason takes to task those who sneer at sewing, 'an occupation necessary for divine service and for the benefit of every reasonable creature' and one that should redound to women's 'great credit, honour, and praise' (p. 30).

Yet Christine is not immune to the prejudices she decries, as we see when she discusses her own life. She recalls bitterly (or rather, Lady Rectitude reminds her) that her father encouraged her education, while her mother exhorted her to occupy herself 'with spinning and silly girlishness, *following the common custom of women*' (pp. 154–5, my emphasis). Thanks to her mother's 'feminine opinion', Christine was not 'more involved in the sciences', though her mother could not altogether extinguish her 'natural inclination' (pp. 154-5). Though Christine criticizes her mother for pressing her into 'feminine' pursuits, she, too, endorses gender-specific pursuits. Asked why women are not lawyers and judges, Lady Reason argues that it would be inappropriate for them to practise those professions as long as competent men are on hand, for God has 'ordained man and woman to serve Him in different offices': to men he has given 'strong and hardy bodies for coming and going as well as for speaking boldly' (p. 31). Public roles that Boccaccio claimed most women *cannot* fulfil, Christine avers they *should not* fulfil—even as she provides myriad lives to demonstrate that women have a 'natural sense for politics and government' and that 'a woman with a mind is fit for all tasks' (p. 32). Christine's view of gender roles is, upon examination, as muddled as Boccaccio's. Needless to say, her endorsement of divinely ordained gender roles does not sit well with some modern feminists, who have sharply questioned whether she deserves her reputation as a proto-feminist.[36]

To complicate matters further, Christine includes, alongside undisputed exemplars of female virtue, some of the most infamous 'wicked wives' of the past. Among them is Socrates' wife, Xanthippe, made notorious by Jerome for dumping a chamber pot upon her husband's head.[37] As Christine de Pizan retells the tale, Xanthippe's 'great learning and goodness' prompted her to marry 'the greatest philosopher', despite his advanced age and bookishness (pp. 130-1). Though he cares more for his research than 'obtaining soft and new things for his wife', the 'valiant lady' delights in his learning, virtue, and constancy. Upon learning that he is to be executed, she rushes to his side, snatches the cup of poison he is about to drink, and dashes it to the floor. Thus, in Christine's hands, shrewishness in Jerome's telling becomes righteous indignation, and derision admiration; the urine Xanthippe dumped over Socrates' head becomes the poison she spilled in a vain effort to save his life. Christine concludes, 'the grief in the heart of the woman who loved him did not abate for the rest of her life' (p. 131).

Christine offers an equally radical revision of Medea, though in this case she, like Chaucer, suppresses rather than changes elements of the story she inherited. Medea, indeed, appears twice in the *City of Ladies*. In Book One, she is a paragon of learning whose knowledge enables Jason to win the Golden Fleece. In Book Two, her only fault is her 'too great and too constant love' for Jason (pp. 189-90). Christine emphasizes that Medea does not rashly throw in her lot with a Greek adventurer (as Boccaccio implies) but rather calculates that Jason's fame, lineage, and good looks would make him a good husband. After Jason betrays her for another woman, 'Medea, who would rather have destroyed herself than do anything of this kind to him, turned despondent, nor did her heart ever again feel goodness or joy'. Christine does not contradict the traditional story; after all, Medea presumably did *not* 'feel goodness or joy' when she murdered her two children. Christine advocates for other maligned women, too: Circe changes Odysseus's men into swine because she mistook them for enemies; Semiramis sleeps with her son because there was no taboo against incest, and she reasonably judges that she cannot find a worthier consort than her own flesh and blood.

Christine de Pizan's *City of Ladies* has been contrasted with Chaucer's *Legend of Good Women* for its 'consistently serious defence of women'.[38] Yet I detect some playfulness in Christine's treatment of infamously bad women, and I suspect that she expects readers who know the usual story of Xanthippe to enjoy the transgressive mind that would think of transforming urine into poison and her husband's tormentor into his advocate.[39] Such playfulness, however, does not negate the overall seriousness of her project. Her far-reaching encyclopedia of women's lives anticipates the revisionary history and revisionist biography that occupied pioneering feminists of the twentieth century who sought to bring to light women's manifold contributions to history and to rehabilitate the reputations of women defamed by 'accusations and slanders' (p. 185). The *City of Ladies* puts me in mind of Judy Chicago's *The Dinner Party*. Unveiled in 1979 and now housed at the Brooklyn Museum, *The Dinner Party* features elaborate place settings for thirty-nine legendary and historical women, with the names of 660 more women inscribed on the floor. Chicago called Christine de Pizan's *City of Ladies* a 'precursor to *The Dinner Party*', and some of her heroines, like Christine's, would surely raise eyebrows.[40] In the brief lives written about each woman, Chicago, like Christine, often omits well-known parts of traditional stories. Her life of Dido, for example, says nothing of Aeneas, and she says nothing about Semiramis's love life. Acts traditionally characterized as iniquities—Clytemnestra's killing of Agamemnon, for example—are presented as righteous. No doubt anticipating critics, Chicago emphasized that her 'narrative' is 'woven from fact and fancy'; 'It does not attempt to be a precise or objective history but, rather, an imagined chronicle based upon historical fact.'[41] 'Even if the history symbolized by *The Dinner Party* is found to suffer from inaccuracies of fact or detail,' she iterates, 'its greater importance rests in its reminder that women have a rich heritage.' Had Christine de Pizan defended her principles of selection and her storytelling, she might have done so in similar terms. She knew, Chaucer knew, Boccaccio knew, and their audiences knew that much of what is 'known' about denizens of the distant past is invention. What has been invented can be reinvented. Being faithful to one's sources is not necessarily the same thing as being faithful to history. And she is just as authorized as her sources to appropriate a story to the needs of the present, whether for inspiration or for entertainment.

Another proto-feminist remaking of Boccaccio's *Famous Women* consists of an adaptation of twenty-one of his 106 lives into Middle English verse *circa* 1440.[42] The anonymous poet's strategies are much like Christine's. The achievements Boccaccio attributes to 'some women', mostly women in the distant past, the anonymous translator attributes to women generally, who 'have been—*and are*' as good as men 'or better' in their intelligence and abilities (ll. 9-11, my emphasis). The Middle English writer mostly removes Boccaccio's deprecations of women, and where he retains them he distances himself from them by attributing them specifically to his source.[43] Gone are Boccaccio's references to 'feminine' weaknesses of cunning, greed, lust, and such; it is likewise as regards characterizations of women's virtues and abilities as 'masculine'. Where Boccaccio usually regarded cunning as negative, the Middle English translator praises women for using their wits to benefit others (l. 486). Indeed, he imputes cunning in the negative sense to *men* rather than women, as when Cyrus overcomes his enemies through 'wily deceit' ('wily trayne' l. 1592). Most of the women chosen for inclusion are admirable, and wrongdoers are shown to have transgressed for a good cause. Instead of using the misfortunes and misdeeds of his heroines to excoriate feminine frailty, the anonymous translator uses them as occasions to impress upon his female readers the importance of the judgment and good sense that, his exhortations imply, they are fully capable of exercising (ll. 1093-9, 1380-6).

The translator's revisionist impulse is evident from the first of his lives, that of Eve. Boccaccio expresses nothing but contempt for the beauty who threw away Paradise and led her gullible husband into sin so that she might achieve greater glory. The Middle English author, by contrast, presents a sympathetic Eve walking hand-in-hand with her husband in Paradise. Instead of condemning her foolishness, the translator laments the fate that befell her when she ate the forbidden fruit—'Alas, alas the hour! / Your great joy is turned to sorrow'—in an impassioned address to Eve herself (ll. 298-9). The Fall unfolds as a *human* tragedy that smote two basically decent people. Eve was enticed to sin not because she hungered for glory but because the devil promised her 'knowledge', which she considered 'a noble thing', 'better than all worldly riches' (ll. 295-6). Continuing on with the story of Semiramis, the writer recounts the Assyrian queen's wise and just rule and her magnanimity. Gone are Boccaccio's disparaging references to her 'feminine cunning' and 'womanly deceit' (l. 19); gone too is his long account of her sexual history, particularly the incest that, for Boccaccio, tainted all the good she had ever done. Indeed, in the Middle English version, her example demonstrates that women should not be dismissed, for they may equal or even exceed men in their wit, prudence, and leadership ability. Likewise, the Middle English author expresses none of Boccaccio's ambivalence about Ceres's 'ingenuity', but rather praises the 'compassion' that moved her to apply her 'wits and mind' to help humanity (ll. 568-74). He customizes Boccaccio's life of Venus, the purported institutor of brothels, 'which the English call stews' (l. 806), and launches into a discussion, wholly his own, about whether brothels might be useful in that the patrons might indulge in 'more uncleanness' and 'more sin' elsewhere (ll. 810, 816).

The poet concludes by declaring that he will not translate the rest of Boccaccio's narratives until he has circulated the stories he has written so far and received feedback. If his work is received favourably, he will translate the rest. If not, continuing the project will get him 'more labour than thanks' (l. 1792). Only a single manuscript of the partial translation has come down to us, and whether he discontinued the project or whether all copies of the finished product were lost we cannot know. In any case, this lone surviving manuscript stands in stark contrast with the over one hundred surviving copies of Boccaccio's *Famous Women*, the twelve copies of Chaucer's *Legend of Good Women*, and the twenty-five copies of Christine de Pizan's *City of Ladies*.

Of Princes and Fortune

At about the same time that he was writing his *Famous Women*, Boccaccio was working on another trend-setting anthology of life stories, *Of the Falls of Illustrious Men*, completed *circa* 1360. *Falls* consists of fifty-six mini-biographies of famous people who fell from the pinnacle of worldly prosperity. Boccaccio's expressed purpose was to convince present-day princes never to take their good fortune for granted. Contemplating the misfortunes of others should spur them on to behave prudently; though fortune is, by nature, transient, one can at least lead one's life with integrity.[44] Aware that a succession of narratives with the same prosperity-followed-by-ruin plot might weary his readers, Boccaccio intersperses his life stories with edifying interludes. In some he moralizes, praising virtues and denouncing such ruinous vices as pride, deceit, selfishness, credulity, and gluttony. He offers tips for prolonging prosperity: rule as a father rather than a tyrant, do not give in to lust or greed, avoid bad women, and so forth; he discourses on patriotism, poverty, and rhetoric; and he engages in a 'discussion' with Fortune.

Boccaccio presents his *Falls* as a vision of sorts. Once he has determined to write about those who have fallen, he finds himself beset by the shades of the unfortunates themselves, clamouring for his attention. Adam and Eve materialize first, demanding 'the right to stand at the beginning of your work' (p. 3). Elsewhere, he is accosted by hordes of the weeping dead—far too many to address. For the most part, Boccaccio shows little sympathy for their plight, instead wondering at the stupidity that ruined men and women who had everything. Though he maintains at various points that fall is inevitable—'whoever rose up, had *always* fallen' (p. 88, my emphasis)—he also asserts the capacity of humans to determine their own fortunes, declaring that 'each person decides where he can achieve his own happiness as he wishes' (p. 104). Though he claims 'where virtue is, Fortune has no power' (p. 125), he also laments the many times omnipotent Fortune crushed those who loved virtue and elevated those who cared only for vice (p. 226). Boccaccio's ambivalence towards his stated moral—that Fortune ultimately ruins those she favours—is shared by most of his imitators.

Boccaccio narrates most of his life stories in the third person, but a few of his subjects speak for themselves. One is the Frankish queen Brunhilda, whose story Boccaccio at first declines to tell on the grounds that he has heard nothing about her. Impatiently, the queen replies that she will enlighten him. But she is a woman, Boccaccio protests; how can he believe anything she says? She promises to tell him the truth, if she deems it 'appropriate', and he counters that he will record her tale if she speaks 'only the truth' (pp. 220-1). As Brunhilda proceeds, Boccaccio repeatedly interrupts, revealing that he has heard more about her than he initially admitted. 'I heard you were married to Chilperic or Childepert', he claims when she speaks of her husband Sigebert. He goes on to contradict her account of her deeds and motivations; he challenges her claim that Clothar fathered her son; he further supplies 'facts' that she supposedly omitted (p. 224). Brunhilda recoils at his audacity. 'A little while ago', she exclaims, 'this man did not know my name, and now suddenly he is a judge of my nature'; how dares a man who lived centuries later presume to know 'better what took place than I who was there!' (p. 222). 'I know whereof I speak', he asserts, citing the testimony of 'many others', none of whom he names (p. 224).

In his meta-biography of Brunhilda, Boccaccio exposes both the prejudice of the biographer and the self-interest of his subject. Brunhilda has every reason for wanting a sympathetic biography, and frankly admits that she may lie. Boccaccio champions 'truth', but how can one trust an author who at first claims to know nothing about the Frankish queen and then claims to know all about her? How can we assume that his unnamed sources trump her confession—especially when his judgments about Brunhilda are coloured by his openly expressed opinion that women are by nature duplicitous and prone to evil (pp. 220, 223)? Though Boccaccio has the final word, his argument with Brunhilda invites readers to question the reliability of everything he has written. How fitting, though, that an author who has subverted his book's original 'thesis' should end up impugning his own credibility. Here, as in his *Famous Women*, Boccaccio suggests that he is less interested in making an argument about Fortune than in demonstrating the uses and abuses of lives as polemical tools.

Boccaccio's *Of the Falls of Illustrious Men* inspired numerous translations and adaptations.[45] In England, Chaucer appropriated several of his mini-biographies for the Monk's contribution to the *Canterbury Tales*. Following Boccaccio, the Monk recites a series of stories of those who fell from prosperity to ruin thanks to Fortune's caprice. Through his accumulated 'old and true examples' he promises to demonstrate that 'when Fortune desires to flee / No man may stay her course' (ll. 3186-8).[46] Some of Fortune's victims did nothing to earn their fate: for example, Ugolino of Pisa was imprisoned on false charges, and his three young sons perished along with him. Yet the overwhelming majority of the Monk's stories indicate that individuals make their own fortunes. Lucifer fell 'on account of his sin' (l. 2202), Adam 'for misconduct' (l. 3202). Nebuchadnezzar offended God, and his son Belshazzar failed to learn from his father's example. Nero was cruel, Antiochus proud, and Alexander overreaching. Samson might never have fallen had he shown better sense, the Monk intimates, as he admonishes men to beware of revealing secrets to their wives (ll. 3281-2). The Monk never gets to finish his tale: 'No more of this!' exclaims the Knight, who finds the recitation too depressing and would prefer to hear of unfortunates who prospered and *remained* prosperous. Irritated and bored, Harry Bailly, the self-appointed supervisor of the storytelling, concurs. It does no good to talk without an audience, he chides (ll. 3991-2).

Though the *Monk's Tale*, like the *Legend of Good Women*, has been read as a collection of egregiously bad stories, Chaucer actually offers a well-wrought version of the biographical collection in miniature with his sequence of seventeen verse stories, ranging in length from a single eight-line stanza to sixteen such stanzas.[47] He captures the diversity of medieval micro-lives, which range from birth-to-death accounts to narratives focused on an incident or period of a life. His mixture of lives of ancients and moderns reproduces the variety of subjects commonly found in collections. Most critically, he illustrates the difficulty of arguing that people are the victims of Fortune, showing, as Emily Jensen puts it, that 'life...cannot be reduced to a single principle' even if *readers* are driven by a 'need to abstract generalized meaning from particulars'.[48]

We know that some medieval readers, at least, found much to admire in the *Monk's Tale*, which was excerpted twice from the *Canterbury Tales*.[49] In both instances, it appears in manuscripts that also include John Lydgate's *Fall of Princes*–another work in the tradition of Boccaccio's *Falls*. Whereas Chaucer produced a miniature *Falls*, Lydgate embroidered Boccaccio's work into a poem of over thirty-six thousand lines, 'perhaps the longest poem in the English language'.[50] In that work, Lydgate warmly praised the Monk's 'old and new stories' for showing 'how princes were overthrown for their trespasses' (ll. 349, 3422-7).[51] As David Wallace has suggested, Lydgate may have seen himself in 'Chaucer's portrait of a travelling monk who is keen to English Italian-derived *de casibus*'.[52]

Lydgate undertook the *Fall of Princes* at the request of Humphrey, Duke of Gloucester. Duke Humphrey asked for a translation of Boccaccio's *Falls* because he wanted a work that would demonstrate the vicissitudes of Fortune (1.432–4). Freely adapting Laurent de Premierfait's 1407 French translation of Boccaccio's *Falls*, Lydgate describes Boccaccio's encounters with the unhappy victims of Fortune, embellishing and interpreting their stories, adding material of his own, and at times contesting Boccaccio's judgments about the lives he related. As Maura Nolan writes, 'Lydgate has ambitions that exceed the mandate he receives from Humphrey…he is burdened by an awareness of the impossibility of reducing all history to a single moral.'[53] Following Boccaccio and the Monk, he bewails Fortune's variance, but, like them, he mostly shows princes making their own fortunes through their choices.[54] They prosper by practising prudence, patience, justice, and humility. When they become arrogant, cruel, or deceitful, they fall. To reinforce that message, Lydgate supplies moralizing envoys to the lives he recounts.

Lydgate may have had the criticisms of the Monk's fellow pilgrims in mind when he worried at the beginning of Book Two that readers might find so many stories of fallen princes hard to take. As if answering the objections of the Knight and Harry Bailly, he points out that reading about the falls of princes can benefit everybody, great and small, by teaching them how to avoid the same miserable outcomes. Fortune, Lydgate declares, does not ruin people; misconduct does. The inexorable Wheel of Fortune is a myth perpetrated by people wishing to absolve themselves of responsibility for their lives.

Lydgate's is the most complex rendering of Boccaccio. As he describes and editorializes about Boccaccio's encounters with the fallen, he becomes as much a presence in his *Fall of Princes* as Boccaccio had been in his *Falls*. Lydgate's negotiations involve not only his source but also his patron.[55] At the beginning of Book Two, just after Lydgate has defended his project and begun writing the life of Saul, Duke Humphrey intervenes. Like Chaucer's Knight, he has had enough sad stories of fallen princes—even though he had expressly demanded such tales. Lydgate should explain how princes can *avoid* falling, he suggests, apparently having failed to notice that Lydgate has been doing that all along! Nor, evidently, has he heeded Lydgate's impassioned apology for his project, which proclaims Fortune a myth. Lydgate promises compliance but in fact continues on his course, finishing the story of Saul and following it with the lives of still more fallen princes. The book concludes with the assurance that Duke Humphrey will prosper if he follows the path of virtue, 'despite Fortune's mutability' (l. 3548). The *Fall of Princes* thus resembles Hoccleve's *Series* and Chaucer's *Legend of Good Women*: each is an anthology of stories that tells the story of its own making; each is quasi-autobiographical; each describes the author's encounters with an overbearing, capricious, and clueless patron; and each is the outcome of a contest of wills between the author and his patron. What distinguishes Lydgate's *Fall of Princes* from the others is that Lydgate's patron is a named historical figure, and a prince at that. How appropriate it is that the voice of a living prince should resound through Lydgate's gallery of portraits. Humphrey's interventions at various points in the *Fall* are sketches of a prince, studies for some future portrait whose final form may hinge on how well the Duke absorbs the lessons of the work he has commissioned and whose message he has dictated.

Collections of lives demonstrate the malleability of life stories more powerfully than any other biographical genre. Lives are the building blocks—literally, in the *City of Ladies*—for polemics and for moral lessons. In some collections, diverse lives iterate and reiterate the author's message, burying readers under a mass of evidence. It does not matter whether the stories are historically accurate: lives serve the living.

The creators of polemical collections are ostensibly the most reductive practitioners of life-writing, or at least they are the most unapologetic and transparent about their intention of reducing lives to morals. Yet among their ranks we find some of the slipperiest life writers. They court criticism by claiming to fit life stories into particular patterns while intentionally choosing (or creating) stories that do not fit that pattern. Through their misadventures and blunders, they suggest that, while one may reduce life stories to a formula, one cannot thereby reduce life. Neither Fortune nor free will can wholly explain why people succeed or fail; women are neither inherently good nor bad. Authors and their publics already know this. The pleasure of arguing for platitudes may reside not in succeeding but in being foiled, over and over, thereby affirming and reaffirming the irreducible richness of human experience.

6

Fictional Lives

Throughout this survey, we have seen that, as much as medieval writers valued the biographical form, and as much as they at least claimed to value historical accuracy, many were by our standards surprisingly cavalier about intermingling fact with legend and with inventing not only incident and character but also documentation and witnesses. In some histories, in anthologies of saints' lives, and in the polemical anthologies discussed in Chapter Five, mostly factual biographies of historical figures freely mix with lives that are little more than myth accreted around a name from the distant past (Arthur, Semiramis) if not indeed invented from whole cloth (Medea, Katherine of Alexandria). Most of the lives examined in Chapter Five were those of legendary figures, stripped down to fit an anthology's larger theme. In this chapter I shall look at works that take the opposite approach to telling legendary lives, embellishing them into elaborate biographical fictions that give close attention to characterization as well as to history, politics, and culture. The authors of these works had a keen sense of the complexity of human experience, and they were experimenting with ways of capturing that experience through life narrative.

This chapter samples a handful of what I consider the most remarkable English life-fictions of the Middle Ages. The first is *Beowulf*. That classic of Old English literature has been appreciated as a genre-bending narrative, part epic, part elegy, part horror, part fantasy, part allegory.[1] I propose that it is also a stunning instance of avant-garde life-writing, in which the poet conveys in fragments a cradle-to-grave story of its eponymous hero. The task of piecing together Beowulf's life from the bits of information relayed out of chronological order is complicated because Beowulf is a singularly unreliable narrator of his own past. Through him, the poet reflects on how and why people tell their stories and on how and why they misremember—or misrepresent—their pasts. For my second example, I return to Geoffrey of Monmouth. Though best known for his *History of the Kings of Britain* discussed in Chapter Three, which furnished King Arthur's biography (itself a splendid example of biographical fiction), Geoffrey also wrote a free-standing *Life of Merlin* in Latin hexameters that is a study in mental illness unmatched elsewhere in medieval literature. For my final example, I shall consider two fifteenth-century saints' lives about unsuccessful sovereigns: Lydgate's *Lives of Saints Edmund and Fremund* and Capgrave's *Life of Saint Katherine*. These lives were part of a broader trend in late medieval hagiography, which, anticipating the biographical fictions of later centuries, invested legendary figures with detailed back stories and complex personalities, using a density of historical reference to create the illusion of scrupulously researched biography. Lydgate and Capgrave not only flesh out the characters and contexts of their protagonists; by drawing attention to those protagonists' weaknesses and failures, they problematize what has long been accepted as the *sine qua non* of hagiography: exemplarity.

Beowulf: Writing Life in Old English Poetry

Beowulf survives in a single manuscript, an anthology of imaginative and religious works that dates from about 1000.[2] When this codex was first catalogued for the British Library in 1705, bibliographer Humfrey Wanley described the story we now call *Beowulf* as that of Beowulf the Dane who fought with Swedes.[3] Like so many medieval works, the story had no title in the manuscript, and Wanley had to deduce what it was about from a cursory reading. He was, of course, mistaken: *Beowulf* begins by describing the exploits of Danish kings in olden days, and Wanley mistook the poet's allusion to a Danish prince 'Beowulf' (l. 4) as referring to the Geatish (i.e. southern Swedish) monster-slayer whose adventures comprise most of the work.

The first sixty lines of *Beowulf* read like a combination of chronicle and advice book for princes. The poet begins with the glorious deeds of the warrior king Scyld Scefing, who struck terror into the hearts of his enemies and made tributaries of peoples far and wide before dying of old age. 'That was a good king' (l. 11), he declares.[4] He extols Scyld's son as an example of how a wise prince lays the foundation for future success: 'a young man ought by his good deeds, by giving splendid gifts while still in his father's house, to make sure that later in life beloved companions will stand by him, that people will serve him when war comes' (ll. 20–4). Scyld's grandson, 'fierce in battle', upheld the glory of his forbears (ll. 57–8). Sixty lines into the narrative, the poet zeroes in on Scyld's great-grandson Hrothgar, who follows his predecessors' formula for success, triumphing in battle and liberally rewarding his followers. Though the poet had declared, perhaps a little too glibly, that 'through deeds that bring praise, a man shall prosper in every country' (ll. 24–5), Hrothgar's praiseworthy deeds bring not only wealth but also a man-eating monster, Grendel, who drives him from his magnificent mead-hall. After sixty years of successful government, he endures a decade of terror before Beowulf, the Geatish warrior, arrives on line 194 to deliver the Danes from Grendel. When Beowulf accomplishes his mission and returns to Geatland, the poet follows him home and carries on his story. It is thus less accurate to say that the poem *is* about Beowulf than that it *becomes* about Beowulf.

Even when we disregard *Beowulf*'s first 193 lines and examine only the part that deals with Beowulf, it reads less like a life story than an adventure story of a hero's encounter with three monsters. And yet *Beowulf* is about so much more than its linear plot. The narrative digresses constantly, veering 'off track' with stories within stories, flashbacks, flash-forwards, and ruminations.[5] At the many feasts, scops or professional storytellers recount the story of Creation, the friendship of Sigemund and Fitela, Sigemund's dragon-slaying, and the tragic story of Hildeburh, who lost her husband, brother, and son in the strife between the Danes and the Frisians. The poet relays, often at length, past and future treacheries, battles, and feuds. Little wonder that the earliest literary critics considered it a mishmash that might be important to historians, linguists, and folklorists but was hardly great art—nothing at all like the *Iliad*, *Aeneid*, or *Nibelungenlied*.[6] When J. R. R. Tolkien rescued it from scholarly disdain in a famous 1936 lecture, he declared, '*Beowulf* is not an "epic"....if we must have a term, we should choose rather "elegy".'[7] The poem, he argued, is not so much about a hero battling monsters as it is about *life*—and in particular about the two pivotal points in a man's life, youth and old age. To those who declared its structure 'curiously weak', he replied that it is 'curiously strong': through numerous digressions and allusions, the poet sets his hero in an 'antiquity with a greater and yet darker antiquity behind'.[8] Writing more recently, Michael Lapidge similarly characterized *Beowulf* as a reflection 'on human activity and conduct, on the transience of human life'.[9]

Bits and pieces of Beowulf's life are mapped, mostly out of chronological order, onto the chronological account of his three encounters with monsters. From these bits, we can piece together a remarkably detailed life of Beowulf—the most detailed life story found anywhere in Old English poetry.[10] Extracting Beowulf's life from *Beowulf* is somewhat like solving a riddle, requiring the same attention to detail and nuance and the same processes of deduction and inference. The challenge is compounded by the poet's allusion to the same events at different points in the narrative, supplying new details in each rendering. For example, the battle against the Frisians that claimed the life of his friend and uncle Hygelac is told thrice.[11] The first mention occurs as the poet describes a splendid necklace given Beowulf at the feast celebrating his killing of Grendel (ll. 1192–1211). In a stunning move, he flashes forward to what became of the necklace: Hygelac wore it when he 'sought trouble' by attacking the Frisians, and it was taken from his corpse by battlefield plunderers (ll. 1199–1211). How did Hygelac come to wear the necklace that Wealhtheow gave Beowulf? The poet relates, some thousand lines later, that Beowulf 'gave [Hygelac's wife] Hygd the neck-ring, the wonderfully wrought treasure, that Wealhtheow had given him' (ll. 2168–70). We are left to infer that Hygd in turn gave the necklace to her husband. The poet returns to Hygelac's death before narrating Beowulf's encounter with the dragon by declaring that Beowulf had in the past taken great risks, as evinced by his heroics at the battle that claimed Hygelac's life (ll. 2349–63). In this second telling, Beowulf recalls one episode of that battle, his slaying of the Frisian champion Daeghrefn (ll. 2496–504). Following Beowulf's death, a messenger offers still another perspective on Hygelac's last battle in the course of relaying the history of the enmity between the Geats and their neighbours, the Franks and the Frisians. In keeping with the non-linearity of the poem as a whole, he relays this history in reverse chronological order (ll. 2896–3023).

The poet uses Beowulf's fights with monsters to anchor not only Beowulf's life but also an era.[12] Beowulf's story touches, directly or indirectly, upon historical feuds, wars, and failed truces among Frisians, Franks, Danes, Scylfings, Heatho-Bards, Geats, and others. The poet also reaches back into the legendary Germanic past peopled by Sigemund and Fitela, Hama and the Brosings. From a narrative perspective, *Beowulf* complements histories such as Bede's: where Bede constructs history from discrete lives, the *Beowulf*-poet constructs a discrete life from the moments of history that impinged upon it. Underlying both the *Ecclesiastical History* and *Beowulf* is the sense that writing history and writing lives are closely connected processes.

John Leyerle has famously described the structure of *Beowulf* as 'a poetic analogue of the interlace designs common in Anglo-Saxon art of the seventh and eighth centuries'.[13] In stone and metalwork of the period, and on the ornate carpet pages of manuscripts such as the *Lindisfarne Gospels*, interwoven lines bend, curve, and twist, disappearing and reappearing to form complex patterns. The poet's meandering narration is more than a matter of aesthetics. It evinces the view that lives and the events that constitute them are only comprehensible piecemeal and in relation to other events and other lives, past, present, and future. Present deeds are informed by past actions, or at least from *memories* of past actions. A linear narrative cannot adequately convey the sense of a present shaped by the past and haunted by the future.

There is something we might call proto-Modernist not only in the poet's narration of Beowulf's life but in Beowulf's narration of his own past. The long passage in which Beowulf recollects his life anticipates the stream-of-consciousness narration that we associate with the novels of James Joyce and Virginia Woolf. The old king, sensing that his life is about to end, says to those around him, 'In youth I lived through many battle-storms, times of war. I remember all that' (ll. 2421-2). But instead of describing the battles, Beowulf recalls being taken from his father at age seven to be fostered by King Hrethel (ll. 2423-9). He mulls over the tragedy of his foster-brother Haethcyn's accidental slaying of his brother Herebeald. The memory of Hrethel's grief makes him think about the plight of a man whose son has been executed; like Hrethel, he cannot avenge his boy's death (ll. 2430-66). He imagines the hypothetical father's grief:

Always with every morning he is reminded of his son's journey elsewhere. He cares not to wait for another heir in his hall, when the first through death's force has come to the end of his deeds. Sorrowful he sees in his son's dwelling the empty wine-hall, the windy rest-ing place without joy—the riders sleep, the warriors in the grave. There is no sound of the harp, no joy in the dwelling, as there was of old. Then he goes to his couch, sings a song of sorrow, one alone for one gone. To him all too wide has seemed the land and the dwelling.

(ll. 2450-62)

Such grief killed Hrethel, he reflects, before his mind turns to Haethcyn's death in battle and Hygelac's vengeance (ll. 2467-85). Only then does he recall those 'battle-storms' he faced in his youth, particularly his fight against the Frisian champion Daeghrefn (ll. 2484-504). Why he singles out that engagement is not clear. The pas-sage as a whole is a tissue of free association that powerfully conveys the meandering 'dark thoughts' of an anxious old man who knows that he will soon die.

The poet is acutely aware that people are not accurate tellers of their own stories, as he demonstrates abundantly with Beowulf. There are, throughout the poem, discrepancies between what the narrator (whose reliability we are given no reason to suspect) relates about Beowulf and what Beowulf relates about himself. Of Beowulf's youth, the narrator says, 'He had long been despised...nor would the lord of the Weather-Geats do him much gift-honour on the mead-bench' (ll. 2183-6). But before facing the dragon, Beowulf recalls to his Geatish followers only Hrethel's kindly treatment: 'King Hrethel had me and kept me, gave me treasure and feast, mindful of kinship. During his life I was no more hated by him as a man in his castle than any of his own sons' (ll. 2430-4). The narrator tells us that the Danish venture was Beowulf's initiative (ll. 194-204), but Beowulf tells the Danish king Hrothgar that 'the best wise earls' of his people urged him to help Hrothgar (ll. 415-24). The narrator reports a singularly unheroic struggle between Beowulf and Grendel's mother, wherein the 'mighty mere-woman' yanks Beowulf to the ground, sits on him, and almost polishes him off with her knife (1541-8).[14] Beowulf elides Grendel's mother altogether when he recounts the fight to Hrothgar; he instead speaks vaguely of 'the war under water' and his triumph over the 'house-guardians' (ll. 1651–66). Most significantly, Beowulf's account to Hygelac and Hygd of his journey differs substantially from the narrator's. The narrator shows him charged with spying by Hrothgar's guard, insulted by Hrothgar's thane Unferth, and (ever so tactfully) threatened by Hrothgar's wife, Wealhtheow, who fears he might have designs on the Danish throne. Beowulf discloses none of this to Hygelac. Instead, he reports receiving an effusive welcome: Hrothgar 'at once…gave me a seat with his own sons. The company was in joy: I have not seen in the time of my life under heaven's arch more mead-mirth of hall-sitters' (ll. 2010–16). He describes the feasting, harp-playing, singing, storytelling, and revelry that followed his victories. As he shows off the splendid gifts he received, he praises Hrothgar's 'good customs' and Wealhtheow's hospitality.

Beowulf's accounts of his own doings reveal a complex personality. Certainly, the warm welcome he describes to Hygelac and Hygd is more flattering than the mixed reception that he actually received among the Danes. And the story he tells Hrothgar of his encounter with Grendel's mother is patently self-serving, though eminently understandable: what self-respecting warrior would wish to admit that a woman–even a monster woman–nearly slew him? These 'adjustments' to the 'truth' lead us to wonder about other stories he tells about himself that the narrator does not confirm. When he boasts, on arriving in Denmark, of having slain a family of five giants and sundry water monsters (ll. 419–22), might that involve a certain padding of his curriculum vitae? Are we to believe his explanation when he is belittled for losing a swimming match, that while the winner swam unimpeded towards the finish line, Beowulf was pulled underwater by a 'fierce cruel attacker' and beset by 'loathsome assailants' (ll. 548–61), in the end slaying no fewer than nine sea-monsters before reaching the safety of shore?

Yet self-aggrandizement is not all that Beowulf is after. He passes up the chance to boast of his heroics by saying that his encounter with Grendel is a tale 'too long to tell' (l. 2093), and he frankly admits to his friend that a swamp-woman nearly bested him in a fight. Repeatedly, he demonstrates sensitivity, tact, and a willingness to defuse rather than exacerbate tension. Telling Hrothgar that the Geatish lords have urged him to help with Grendel makes him seem an emissary of goodwill rather than an opportunist out to use the Danes' misery to enhance his fame. He assuages concerns that he might have designs on the Danish throne by indicating that he took Hrothgar's reference to him as his 'son' to mean only that Hrothgar would look after Beowulf's followers should he die. When lent an heirloom sword for his fight against Grendel's mother, the sword proves worthless, but when Beowulf returns it, he nonetheless thanks the man who lent it and tells him it was 'a good war-friend, strong in battle', leading the narrator to remark, 'he was a thoughtful man' (ll. 1810–12).

As Beowulf departs for Geatland, he assures Hrothgar of Hygelac's support should he need it, but we later find that Hygelac had *discouraged* Beowulf from taking on Grendel, advising him to let the Danes take care of their own troubles (ll. 1994-8); could Beowulf really have believed that Hygelac would be eager to help Hrothgar with men and spears? Upon returning home, Beowulf conceals information that might tempt his impulsive uncle to attack the vulnerable Danes while emphasizing their generosity and the honours they showed him, details that would favourably dispose his lord towards them. One bit of his account is pure invention–that Hrothgar implored Beowulf, *by Hygelac's life*, to pursue Grendel's mother (ll. 2131-2). In short, Beowulf is not merely a warrior, he is a diplomat and a peace-weaver.[15]

Beowulf presents two contrasting ideals of heroism and kingship by beginning with one king's life story and ending with another's. The life of Scyld Scefing unfolds in about fifty lines, Beowulf's in about two thousand. The modes of narration are not altogether different; the poet interpolates bits about Scyld's childhood into the otherwise chronological account of his adulthood, anticipating in a small way his tangled narration of Beowulf's story. But otherwise Scyld's life story is compact and tidy. It celebrates an uncomplicated warrior ethos: conquer, reward, and thrive. It has a moral: 'Through deeds that bring praise, a man shall prosper in every country' (ll. 24-5). It even has parallelism: the Danes found Scyld as a baby adrift in a treasure-laden ship, and when he dies, they return him to the sea in a ship laden with equally magnificent treasure.

Beowulf's story is so much messier. The poet portrays him as a decent man, considerate of others, diplomatic, restrained, and unwilling to seek trouble, a wise king who looks out for his people and distributes gifts generously. He dies fulfilling his roles as 'shielder of warriors' and 'ring-giver'. Yet only one man stands by him when he faces the dragon. And Beowulf is by no means perfect. His companion Wiglaf, his only supporter in his battle with the dragon, laments his overconfidence; and Beowulf's only legacies are a treasure that his people will bury with him and a reputation that will not save them from their enemies.

What lessons are we to draw from his life? The primary one, I think, is that, despite the poet's earlier platitudes, giving treasure does *not* guarantee loyalty and that praiseworthy deeds do *not* ensure success. Kings and heroes, however courageous their deeds and extraordinary their achievements, are, upon inspection, flawed and mortal. Beowulf embodies a more humane model of kingship and heroism than Scyld, one more compatible with a pacifist Christianity. The final lines of the poem show us that war is not glorious when viewed from the perspective of those whose mead-benches are taken, complementing the proof through Beowulf's example that heroism need not be predicated on slaughter and conquest. And yet the poet does not suggest that having a Beowulf will fix the world's problems because people, on balance, are greedy and prone to violence—a 'reality' kept constantly before us by the stories of feuding, treachery, fratricide, and war that form the backdrop of Beowulf's story. Many of *Beowulf*'s original readers would probably have inferred from it the message that another Old English elegy, the *Wanderer*, makes explicit in its concluding lines: 'It will be well for him who seeks mercy, / consolation from the Father in heaven, where for us all security stands' (ll. 114-15). This same message is iterated and reiterated in the Anglo-Saxon poems of saints that portray their heroes as warriors who triumph through suffering and martyrdom.

Geoffrey of Monmouth's Merlin and the Life of the Mind

We have already met Geoffrey of Monmouth as the author of the *History of the Kings of Britain* (1138), discussed in Chapter Three as an example of the biohistorical approach to writing kings' lives. Geoffrey's *History* was written in the manner of contemporary histories and greatly influenced later historians of England, but (as already remarked in Chapter Three) much of its content was invented.[16] I therefore might equally have discussed this 'essentially literary' work in this chapter as an illustration of biohistorical fiction.[17] Instead, I shall examine another of Geoffrey's historical inventions, just as audacious as the *History of the Kings of Britain* though not nearly as well known, his verse *Life of Merlin* (1150), which one modern historian has called 'a strange and horrifying fairy-story'.[18] In contrast to the *History*, the *Life of Merlin* does not mimic a single well-established genre; rather, it appropriates the conventions of various literary forms, from romance to prophecy, to create a unique life story.[19]

In the *History*, Merlin figured as an advisor to kings—first to Vortigern and later to the brothers Ambrosius and Uther Pendragon. The supposed offspring of an incubus and a human woman, he could foresee the future, and Geoffrey included a long sequence of his prophecies. He later described how Merlin arranged the transport from Ireland to Salisbury Plain of the massive rocks that would come to be known as Stonehenge, and how he devised a means for Uther to bed Duke Gorlois's closely guarded wife, Igerna, and so to beget the future King Arthur.

The *Life of Merlin* begins long after the events recounted in the *History*. Merlin, still a renowned prophet, is now also a king in south Wales. In the opening scene, he becomes so distraught at seeing beloved warriors slain in battle that he loses his mind and flees human society for the wilderness. There he remains, despite the best efforts of his wife, Gwendolena, his sister, Ganieda, and her husband, King Rhydderch of Cumbria, to bring him to his senses. Only after drinking from a certain spring does he become whole again. Considering himself now too old to resume the reins of government, he retires to the forest to devote himself to God by pursuing a quasi-monastic way of life in the company of his now widowed sister and two friends. Facets of Merlin's story prior to his breakdown—his youthful affair with a vindictive woman, his passion for Gwendolena, his pleasure in hunting, his kindness and generosity to his companions—are revealed fleetingly through reminiscences. In that respect, Geoffrey's approach to writing a life is somewhat like the *Beowulf*-poet's.

By devoting most of his narrative to the period when Merlin was 'outside' himself, having lost 'the peace that is natural to the human mind' (p. 268), Geoffrey provides a compelling early exploration of mental illness.[20] What strikes me as most interesting is that Merlin's madness is not manifest in incoherent raving, hallucinations, or random behaviour; rather, Geoffrey constructs Merlin's malady as a set of symptoms that we might today see as signs of major depression. To me this suggests that Geoffrey was not drawing solely on imagination or literary convention but also on observation or experience. Merlin sobs uncontrollably. Music soothes him, but only temporarily. He barely tolerates his anxious family members and loathes everybody else. He loses his appetite, becomes listless, and spurns help. His moments of lucidity are rare, his mood swings extreme. For example, he tells his wife, reasonably, that she should remarry, but learning that she has taken his advice distresses him. All alone under the stars, the unhappy prophet seethes about a 'love…now divided':

Gwendolena, perhaps, has abandoned me because I have been away, and she now cleaves to another man and finds joy in a new husband's embraces. Thus am I defeated and another man occupies her. My legal rights have been snatched from me while I have tarried here, for a slothful lover is often supplanted by one who is not slothful and who is near at hand. But I am not jealous. Let her marry now while the omens are favourable, and let her take on a new husband with my permission.   (p. 252)

Merlin's thoughts in this passage are as divided as the love he laments. His talk of defeat and abandonment bespeak the jealousy he denies. Indeed, though resignation prevails in this late-night monologue, rage ultimately carries the day. Appearing at Gwendolena's castle the next morning to congratulate her with gifts, he ends up killing her bridegroom.

The Merlin of Geoffrey's *History* is obviously the same legendary character as the Merlin of his *Life*. There is a clear disjunction, however, between the two works' representations of him. Only once in *Merlin* does Geoffrey allude to Merlin's role in events he had described in the *History*: after delivering a series of prophecies, Merlin says, 'All these things have I already sung to Vortigern in explicating for him the riddle of the two warring dragons when we sat together by the sides of the drained pool' (p. 258). Later, however, when Merlin gives an extended summary of the reigns of British kings, he says nothing of his involvement with Vortigern. In that same historical summary, Merlin likewise refers to Arthur's conception–Uther 'sired a child' (pp. 266-7)–without mentioning that he arranged the tryst that led to the child's conception. When Merlin's friend Taliesin speaks of demons who may 'have intercourse with women and impregnate them' (p. 260), neither he nor Geoffrey makes any allusion to Merlin's own supposed paternity.

At least as interesting are the psychological dissonances and resonances between Geoffrey's two accounts of Merlin. In the *History*, Merlin is omniscient but also compassionate. His foreknowledge of suffering causes him to weep (p. 131). Moreover, he uses his knowledge to help others–even those, such as King Vortigern, whom he has every reason to dislike–advising them on how they might gain fortune or avoid misfortune (p. 143). Sympathy prompts him to help Uther obtain the woman he desires: 'he perceived the torment that the king suffered for his great love of that woman' (p. 158). A sombre figure who never laughs, he refuses to use his knowledge of the future for 'amusement or vanity', declaring that 'hidden matters must not be revealed unless the greatest need demands it' (p. 150).

The pre-madness Merlin we meet briefly at the beginning of Geoffrey's *Life* is also a serious and compassionate man. Indeed, as I mentioned, it is compassion that drives him to insanity. But when Merlin loses his mind, he also loses his capacity for empathy. Uncontrollable tears at the suffering of others give way to malicious laughter at their misfortunes. He repeatedly reveals 'hidden things' for 'amusement or vanity'. With such unsolicited revelations, he stirs up mischief between his happily married sister and her husband. Just to entertain and impress those around him, he foretells how others will die. The sight of a poor man begging sends him cackling–the beggar has no idea that he is sitting atop a hoard of buried treasure, and Merlin is not about to enlighten him. Yet once cured of his madness, he regains the compassion that had been his defining trait. Demonstrating that 'the feelings that had for so long been dormant within him returned' (p. 268), Merlin's first act as a healed man is to rescue a madman from jeering bystanders and lead him to the curative spring waters.

Geoffrey's *Life of Merlin* is remarkable not only in terms of its content but also in terms of its form. Though labelling itself a *vita*, it lacks the conventional brackets of birth and death. Moreover, the narrative about Merlin is repeatedly interrupted by long digressions, including prophecies made by Merlin and others as well as disquisitions on natural phenomena, animals, and history. Within this jumble Geoffrey retells his most famous life story, that of Arthur, much as he had done in the *History*. Formally and thematically, that embedded life story is everything Merlin's framing life story is not: in neat chronological order, Geoffrey recounts the life of an illustrious public figure, a man whose career was spent leading the kinds of battles that drove King Merlin mad.

Yet in one respect, the accounts of the two kings' lives are similar: both narratives end by recounting not their subjects' deaths but their retirements from kingship into a natural world. After the Battle of Camlann, Arthur's friends deliver him into the expert hands of the healer Morgan, who governs the Eden-like Isle of Apples and assures them of his probable recovery. Like Merlin, Arthur *could* reclaim his kingship, but, like Merlin, he will not. Though death dominates much of the *Life of Merlin*, causing Merlin's madness and his sister's retreat from the world, Geoffrey ultimately affirms life: he leaves Merlin, peaceful and content, in the forest, just as he leaves Arthur recovering at the Isle of Apples.[21] The two very different narrations about completely different kinds of king converge.

Geoffrey's two wholly different kinds of lives—one traditional in its genre if not its content, the other experimental—reveal his dexterity as a biographer. His life of Arthur as told within his *History of the Kings of Britain* and retold within his life of Merlin is orderly, chronological, and more concerned with events than emotions. His life of Merlin, by contrast, is an unruly account of actions propelled by mental imbalance. His life of Arthur recounts the making of a king, while his life of Merlin recounts a king's unmaking. The *Life of Merlin* might indeed be termed an 'un-life', taking as its subject a man who has lost not only the trappings of his rank but even his humanity. Defying chronology with a life story relayed through memory and allusion, a story interrupted frequently by digressions about history, prophecy, the natural world, and even other lives, the *Life of Merlin* offers a pre-modern glimpse of postmodernity. It is perhaps not surprising that Geoffrey's more conventional *History* survives in hundreds of manuscripts, his idiosyncratic *Life of Merlin* in just one complete version and a handful of extracts.

Hagiographical Fictions

It is fitting to conclude by considering the genre that is so often equated with medieval life-writing. That much hagiography is fiction is well known, but the widespread view is that its fictive elements reflect not authorial creativity so much as the rote filling in of gaps according to formulas, producing a mass of encomia unreliable as history and dull as literature. Yet many daring experiments in life-writing can be found within the enormous corpus of hagiography. Hagiography's legendary saints include both figures invented from scratch as well as figures who survive in the historical record only as names in early martyrologies (lists of martyrs), as inscriptions on ancient monuments, or as persons mentioned briefly in annals or histories.[22]

The lives supplied for them make up the bulk of the stories comprising such popular collections as the *South English Legendary* and the *Golden Legend*, and numerous longer, free-standing lives of legendary saints were also written. Though many of these constructed lives are formulaic, others reveal astonishing originality.

In England, long lives of legendary saints, enriched by historical detail and characterization, were written in Latin throughout the Middle Ages, in French during the twelfth and thirteenth centuries, and in English during the fifteenth. These intricate narratives have much in common with the biographies of historical men and women examined in the first four chapters of this volume. Their protagonists are often multi-dimensional; they inhabit a complex moral universe; they worry about pleasing their families and dependents as well as God; they make mistakes; they mature. The thirteenth-century hagiographer Guillaume de Berneville, as Delbert Russell has observed, traced the '*evolving spirituality*' of the hermit Giles to demonstrate that 'the quest for a spiritual life must also include engagement with the lay world, rather than a flight from it'.[23] Matthew Paris (d. 1259), best known as a chronicler but also a prolific author of French-language hagiography, embroidered the story of Britain's proto-martyr Alban into a 1846-line life that focuses on Alban's conversion from a sceptical Roman official into a champion of Christianity and that describes his close friendship with Amphibalus, the priest who converted him.[24] Another of Paris's achievements was an elaborate fictional biography of Edward the Confessor.[25] One would not recognize the Poet's incompetent or Aelred's naïf in Paris's courteous and wise Edward, judiciously governing England with God's aid; in Paris's hands, Edward is an exemplar not just of holiness but also of righteous rule.

During the first decades of the fifteenth century, Middle English hagiographers began writing similarly elaborate lives. John Lydgate helped make this approach fashionable with his two five-book epics, *The Lives of Saints Edmund and Fremund* (1436) and *The Life of Saints Alban and Amphibalus* (1439).[26] During the 1440s and 1450s, Osbern Bokenham composed numerous saints' lives that emphasize emotional conflicts and ethical dilemmas. Similarly detailed and introspective saints' lives continued to be written into the early modern period, as Alexander Barclay's *Life of Saint George* (1515) and Henry Bradshaw's *Life of Saint Werburga* (1521) attest.

The narrative range and moral complexity of Lydgate's *Lives of Saints Edmund and Fremund* was unmatched in any previous Middle English saint's life. St. Edmund, the patron of Lydgate's abbey of Bury St. Edmunds, was a shadowy figure from the Anglo-Saxon past; the only near-contemporary reference to him is an entry in the Anglo-Saxon Chronicle that King Edmund of East Anglia died fighting the Danes in the year 870. Later hagiographers transformed Edmund into a martyr-king who chose to die rather than to give up his religion.[27] None, however, were much inclined to say much about his accomplishments as a king. The sparsest account, which circulated in the *South English Legendary*, reports that 'holy king' Edmund was captured by 'hateful' Danish princes while walking alone outside the gates of his city.[28] Christ-like, he submitted to being bound, beaten, and shot full of arrows. The entire story unfolds in a mere hundred lines of verse.

Lydgate, by contrast, develops a politically charged narrative in 3500 lines.[29] His Edmund, the son of an illustrious warrior king, assumes the reins of government while still a youth. Although deeply religious, he is also astute, just, amiable, and skilled at arms; in short, he embodies all the qualities that mirrors for princes urge sovereigns to cultivate. Lydgate describes him attending to the business of his realm, presenting him implicitly as a suitable role model for young King Henry VI, to whom he dedicated the life.[30] But Lydgate does not fully idealize Edmund; rather, he uses Edmund's death as a caution against letting piety overwhelm judgment. When the Danes invade his country, Edmund at first acts as a good monarch should: he raises an army and slaughters Danes with a most unsaintly ferocity. But the sight of the battlefield strewn with the bodies of heathens who have lost all chance of salvation fazes him: 'God's law forbids the shedding of blood', he declares.[31] Thus, when the Danes regroup for an offensive, Edmund declines to resist. He instead surrenders himself to the Danish princes, who kill him for refusing to renounce Christianity.

Lydgate is conventional enough while praising Edmund's courage and faith, but he conjoins his account of Edmund to a lengthy second life–that of Fremund–that functions as a sequel, chronicling the consequences of Edmund's martyrdom.[32] With Edmund no longer around to protect his land, the Danes attack with even greater savagery, robbing, raping, killing, burning churches. Edmund may be enjoying heavenly bliss, but his erstwhile subjects are enduring hell on earth. In desperation, old King Offa of Mercia sends messengers to implore his only son Fremund–who had renounced his heritage to become a hermit–to marshal an army against the Danes. Though Fremund at first demurs, God sends an angel to affirm in no uncertain terms that he must fight the miscreants. Battle is joined, and miraculous intervention enables Fremund's band of twenty-four to slaughter an army of forty thousand. This happy result (from the Mercian, if not Danish, point of view) casts Edmund's pacifism in a new light: was it piety or mere squeamish-ness that led him to give up the fight? Even the late Edmund seems to reconsider: in the first of many post-mortem miracles that Lydgate relates, the ghost of Edmund, fully armed, spears King Svein of Denmark in his bed for presuming to attack East Anglia in 1013.

Lydgate's many admirers included John Capgrave, an Augustinian friar from King's Lynn in Norfolk who was also a prolific author.[33] Capgrave's 1445 *Life of Saint Katherine of Alexandria* extends Lydgate's experimentation, presenting a saint whose holiness is even more fraught, and who is even more an anti-model of sovereignty.[34]

Katherine of Alexandria was one of late medieval Europe's most beloved saints.[35] Though she was said to have been martyred in Alexandria during the fourth century, the earliest mention of her dates from the seventh century, and the earliest surviving account of her passion was composed during the tenth century. According to the most widely circulated and influential version of her legend, the so-called 'Vulgate passion', Katherine, the learned only child of the late King Costus of Alexandria, confronts the Emperor Maxentius when, on a visit to Alexandria, he orders a lavish celebration honouring the pagan gods. Astonished by her learning and loveliness, the emperor summons the fifty greatest scholars of his realm to refute her errors in a public debate. Much to everybody's surprise, Katherine converts the philosophers; what is more, she goes on to convert the emperor's wife and his best friend. When the frustrated emperor resorts to physical persuasion, she survives unscathed his attempt to mutilate her with enormous spiked wheels. Following her martyrdom by decapitation, angels bear her body to Mount Sinai, where miracles continue to be performed at her tomb.

Katherine's unusual representation as both a king's daughter and a scholar may underlie her extraordinary popularity during the Middle Ages. The authors of saints' lives may have identified with her bookishness, while her royalty may have given her a celebrity status that appealed broadly to men and women, religious and lay. To augment her appeal, her adversary was no less than the emperor himself. Whatever the reasons, representations of Katherine are distinguished by both their abundance and their variety. From the thirteenth century onwards, authors and artists embellished her legend with accounts of her conversion to Christianity and her mystical marriage to Christ. In art, Katherine appears in a wide range of roles: from a pious lay reader to a preacher and theologian, from the victim of horrific atrocities to a sword-wielding virago, from a sovereign to a bride of Christ.[36] Katherine's popularity extended well beyond the Middle Ages. John Foxe, stalwart debunker of fraudulent Catholic legends, was so adamant that Saint Katherine existed that he included her in his *Acts and Monuments*, despite his insistence that all the elements of her legend are lies.[37] Her legend's modern reincarnations include a 1997 novel and a 2014 movie.[38]

Comprising over eight thousand lines of verse divided into five books, Capgrave's *Life of Saint Katherine* is, to my knowledge, not only the most extensive rendering of Katherine's life but the most elaborate medieval rendering of any saint's life.[39] Capgrave situates Katherine's life in a lavish, if unreliable, history of Egypt and Syria. He describes the major cities of her realm, Amaleck in Cyprus and Alexandria in Egypt, supplying information about their histories, topographies, and demographics, their political and economic importance, and their customs and government. He describes the conquests and kingship of Katherine's father, King Costus, and he later recounts at length the imperial politics that led to Maxentius's expulsion from Rome, his rise to power in the East, and his eventual confrontation with Katherine in Alexandria. Looking beyond Katherine's death, he reports Maxentius's ignominious defeat at the hands of the Roman Emperor Constantine. But history and politics are by no means Capgrave's only interests. He relays the minutiae of Katherine's world, from the manner of raising a royal baby to the customs surrounding the burial of a king to the provisioning of a city for a coronation. He describes the purview and challenges of each of the disciplines comprising the liberal-arts curriculum. His characters expatiate on and debate theology along with such issues of social and political theory as proper methods of government and appropriate gender roles. At the centre of this richly detailed tapestry of history and culture, of course, is the saint herself. Though Capgrave relies on a plot of Katherine's life that had by his time already been embellished considerably to include such episodes as her mystical marriage to Christ, he develops her character with unprecedented nuance.[40]

Capgrave praises Katherine's virtues, but he also exposes her vulnerabilities. One of his innovations is to show how Katherine's upbringing shapes her character as an adult. King Costus, thrilled that his wife had conceived and borne a child despite her advanced age, stops at nothing to give his daughter the best of everything, including a superb liberal-arts education. Unwilling to distract her from the scholarly pursuits she adores, the king leaves her alone with her teachers. Thus isolated from the world, she grows into a brilliant but wayward recluse who spends her days happily studying in the palace her father designed just for her. Having been groomed neither for marriage nor for government, she wishes nothing to do with either. When, upon her father's death, her subjects and mother urge her to marry so that her husband can govern the country while she ensures the succession by bearing children, Katherine balks. Capgrave deftly describes the turmoil his heroine experiences, knowing that her petitioners' requests are reasonable and yet determined to resist. Thanks to her superb rhetorical training, Katherine outmanoeuvres her pragmatic advisors in a lengthy debate about whether women are fit to be rulers and whether her status as a queen obliges her to marry. Nevertheless, her insistence on remaining single has disastrous consequences for her realm: Maxentius's arrival in Alexandria, the reinstatement of paganism as the state religion, and her own deposition and execution. Katherine's behaviour, like the pacifist Edmund's, may be laudable in a martyr, but it is lamentable in a ruler.

Capgrave's *Life* is not just about Saint Katherine and her world; it is also about the very mechanics of putting together a biography.[41] As if expecting that readers might question the authenticity of his text, so unlike the accounts of Katherine's life and passion that they would have encountered elsewhere, Capgrave claims to be translating the long-lost eyewitness account composed by Katherine's convert Athanasius. In his prologue, he explains that he obtained Athanasius's account from a now-deceased English priest, who had made writing Katherine's life his own life's work. The priest, as Capgrave represents him, approached his project much as a modern biographer might–he spent years researching Katherine's life, learning her native tongue, and travelling to her native land to discover more about her background. At last, guided by a revelation, he unearthed a codex containing a Latin translation of Athanasius's life of Katherine. The translation had been undertaken by another of Katherine's devotees, a knight named Arrek, who, like the English priest, had spent years researching Katherine's life before discovering Athanasius's account. According to Capgrave, the unnamed English priest died before he could finish translating Arrek's Latin translation into English; moreover, what he had translated was barely intelligible thanks to his obscure dialect. Capgrave's task, then, was to translate the priest's obscure language into proper English and to supply the missing ending.

As he proceeds with the narrative proper, Capgrave continues to assure readers of the reliability of his account. Adopting a persona that he uses nowhere else in his oeuvre, that of a fussy editor, he interrupts Katherine's story to tell of the sources he has consulted, the points on which they disagree, and how he has resolved discrepancies. He notes which eyewitnesses supplied which bits of information. He quotes from characters' letters. He concludes by telling readers that he will not relay certain miracles that purportedly occurred at Katherine's tomb for fear of 'poisoning' everything he has written by including material for which he has no 'authority' (ll. 1960–79).

Capgrave thus validates his *Life of Saint Katherine* with every authorizing device in a medieval biographer's repertoire, claiming that it is the product of scrupulous research, eyewitness testimony, credible written sources, conservative editing, and careful fact-checking. The problem is that he deploys these authorizing strategies in ways that do not add up, are redundant, or undermine each other. Though it was common for medieval biographers to establish the reliability of their source(s), I can think of no other instance of a medieval biographer tracing the history not only of his source, but also of his source's source, and of his source's source's source. Capgrave's Prologue reads less like a sober scholarly introduction than a romance of scholars-errant questing for a marvellous treasure. Their scrupulous research is rendered superfluous: Arrek and the English priest ultimately translate a life written by the saint's disciple, a text miraculously revealed to them as God's reward for their years of scholarly effort. At times, Capgrave contradicts himself. For example, he begins his story of Katherine's conversion in Book Three by reminding readers who might 'doubt whether this account is true' that it derives from a long-lost source (ll. 22–3); a dozen lines later, though, we find him reconstructing her conversion from sundry 'old books' (l. 43). With his characteristic obsession with detail, he notes that the hermit who escorted Katherine to Heaven for her mystical marriage was either not present for or unable to see many of the proceedings; however, he later declares the hermit the sole source for what transpired: 'for how else would it come to our ears? How would we have learned about it?' (ll. 1147–8). How indeed? Capgrave seems to be daring readers to question his account, importing the literary playfulness that Chaucer loved into the serious business of writing a saint's life.[42]

What Capgrave was doing had precedents, as we have seen in previous chapters. Authors since the earliest life of Cuthbert had advanced spurious truth claims. We have encountered obtrusive narrators in Garnier's *Life of Thomas Becket* and John's *History of William Marshal*. Geoffrey of Monmouth claimed a rare source for his *History of the Kings of Britain*, using the '*topos* of translation' to 'hide a fiction'.[43] But no other biographer that I know of subverted his own truth-claims as egregiously as Capgrave. And Capgrave does nothing similar in his more sober and conventional biographies of Norbert, Gilbert, and Augustine. In *Katherine*, Capgrave is consciously and unabashedly elaborating the legend he inherited into a compelling biographical fiction, whose invention, he trusts, will not vitiate its merit and relevance to his readers.

Notes

Introduction

1. Donald Stauffer, *English Biography Before 1700* (Cambridge, MA: Harvard University Press, 1930), p. 3.
2. Margaretta Jolly, 'Biography and Autobiography', in *Oxford Bibliographies: British and Irish Literature* (http://www.oxfordbibliographies.com). Last modified 20 September 2012.
3. *Teaching Life Writing Texts*, ed. Miriam Fuchs and Craig Howes (New York: The Modern Language Association of America, 2008), pp. 34-6. Kempe's name is misspelled ('Marjorie') in the Index (p. 395).
4. Clarissa Atkinson, *Mystic and Pilgrim: The Book and the World of Margery Kempe* (Ithaca, NY: Cornell University Press, 1983), p. 23.
5. Hermione Lee, *Biography: A Very Short Introduction* (Oxford: Oxford University Press, 2009), p. 18.
6. The following surveys indicate other medieval forms of life-writing: Julia Boffey, 'Middle English Lives', in *The Cambridge History of Medieval English Literature*, ed. David Wallace (Cambridge, UK: Cambridge University Press, 1999), pp. 610-34; and Kathleen M. Ashley, 'Accounts of Lives', in *A Companion to Medieval English Literature and Culture, c. 1350-c. 1500*, ed. Peter Brown (Malden, MA: Blackwell, 2007), pp. 437-53.
7. For a good introduction to this genre and its many forms, see Thomas J. Heffernan, *Sacred Biography: Saints and Their Biographers in the Middle Ages* (New York: Oxford University Press, 1988) and Thomas J. Head, 'Hagiography', *The ORB: On-line Reference Book for Medieval Studies* (http://the-orb.arlima.net/encyclop/religion/hagiography/hagindex.html). *Medieval Hagiography: An Anthology*, ed. Thomas Head (New York: Garland, 2000) includes translations of many classics of the genre.
8. *Acts of the Christian Martyrs*, ed. and trans. Herbert Muserillo (Oxford: Clarendon, 1972), pp. 7 and 13.
9. Gregory of Tours, *Life of the Fathers*, trans. Edward James (Liverpool: Liverpool University Press, 1986). The sense of such a *vita sanctorum* continued to govern the composition of Reformation hagiography, as Foxe's *Acts and Monuments* attests. See Alice Dailey, *The English Martyr: From Reformation to Revolution* (Notre Dame, IN: University of Notre Dame Press, 2012).
10. For a translation, see Head, *Medieval Hagiography*, pp. 1-30.
11. Translations of these lives, along with other important *vitae* from late Antiquity, can be found in *Early Christian Biographies*, ed. Roy J. Deferrari (Washington, DC: Catholic University of America Press, 1952).
12. The classic study of hagiographic invention is Hippolyte Delehaye, *Legends of the Saints*, trans. Donald Attwater (New York: Fordham University Press, 1962).
13. For the virgin martyrs, see my *Virgin Martyrs: Legends of Sainthood in Late Medieval England* (Ithaca, NY: Cornell University Press, 1997).

Chapter 1

1. Willibald, 'The Life of Saint Boniface', trans. C. H. Talbot, in *Soldiers of Christ: Saints and Saints' Lives from Late Antiquity and the Early Middle Ages*, ed. Thomas F. X. Noble and Thomas Head (University Park, PA: Pennsylvania State University Press, 1995), pp. 109-10.
2. In his *The Lives of Thomas Becket* (Manchester: Manchester University Press, 2001), Michael Staunton dates and describes each of these lives (pp. 6-11) and provides extracts from them; see quote at p. 6. He notes that one of Becket's early apologists—Alan of Tewkesbury—explicitly presents his account as an explanation, or *explicatio*, of the archbishop's sanctity.
3. For a comprehensive account of this process, and the kinds of biographies it generated, see André Vauchez, *Sainthood in the Later Middle Ages*, trans. Jean Birrell (Cambridge, UK: Cambridge University Press, 1997).
4. Elisabeth van Houts, 'The Flemish Contribution to Biographical Writing in England in the Eleventh Century', in *Writing Medieval Biography: Essays in Honour of Frank Barlow*, ed. David Bates, Julia Crick, and Sarah Hamilton (Woodbridge, Suffolk: Boydell, 2006), pp. 111-27.
5. Richard of Ely claims to base his life of the eleventh-century outlaw Hereward on an account written in English by Hereward's former chaplain, Leofric; William of Malmesbury claims to have translated an Old English life of Bishop Wulfstan of Worcester composed by the bishop's pupil Coleman. Both of the Latin 'translations' of these Old English sources may be found in *Three Lives of the Last Englishmen*, trans. Michael Swanton (New York: Garland, 1984).
6. Jocelyn Wogan-Browne discusses these and other lives of professional religious in her *Saints' Lives and Women's Literary Culture, 1150-1300: Virginity and its Authorizations* (Oxford: Oxford University Press, 2001).
7. For an introduction to and a catalogue of these free-standing *vitae*, see E. Gordon Whatley *et multi*, 'Acta Sanctorum', in *Sources of Anglo-Saxon Literary Culture, Volume 1: Abbo of Fleury, Abbo of Saint-Germain-des-Prés, and Acta Sanctorum*, ed. Frederick M. Biggs, Thomas Hill, Paul E. Szarmach, and E. Gordon Whatley (Kalamazoo, MI: Medieval Institute Publications, 2001), pp. 22-486. See also Michael Lapidge, 'The Saintly Life in Anglo-Saxon England', in *The Cambridge Companion to Old English Literature*, ed. Malcolm Godden and Michael Lapidge (Cambridge, UK: Cambridge University Press, 1991), pp. 251-72.
8. Colgrave, *Two Lives of Saint Cuthbert: A Life by an Anonymous Monk of Lindisfarne and Bede's Prose Life* (Cambridge, UK: Cambridge University Press, 1940), p. 63.
9. Colgrave, *Two Lives of Saint Cuthbert*, p. 143.
10. Colgrave, *Two Lives of Saint Cuthbert*, p. 145.
11. Felix, *Felix's Life of Saint Guthlac*, ed. Bertram Colgrave (Cambridge, UK: Cambridge University Press, 1956), p. 65; and *The Anglo-Saxon Missionaries in Germany, Being the Lives of SS. Willibrord, Boniface, Leoba and Lebuin together with the Hodoepericon of St. Willibald and a selection from the correspondence of St. Boniface*, ed. and trans. C. H. Talbot (London and New York: Sheed and Ward, 1954), p. 27.
12. Talbot, *Anglo-Saxon Missionaries in Germany*, p. 153.
13. Talbot, *Anglo-Saxon Missionaries in Germany*, p. 205.
14. Talbot, *Anglo-Saxon Missionaries in Germany*, p. 206.
15. Talbot, *Anglo-Saxon Missionaries in Germany*, p. 206.

16. Colgrave, *Two Lives of Saint Cuthbert*, pp. 63, 65.

17. Byrhtferth of Ramsey, *The Lives of St Oswald and St Ecgwine*, ed. and trans. Michael Lapidge (Oxford: Clarendon Press, 2009), p. 209.

18. The context of Cuthbert's promotion as a premier saint of England is explored in *St Cuthbert: His Cult and His Community to AD 1200*, ed. Gerald Bonner, David Rollason, and Clare Stancliffe (Woodbridge, Suffolk: Boydell, 1989).

19. On the significance of the four-book life, see Walter Berschin, '*Opus deliberatum ac perfectum*: Why Did the Venerable Bede Write a Second Prose Life of St Cuthbert?' in *St Cuthbert: His Cult and His Community*, p. 98.

20. Colgrave, *Two Lives of Saint Cuthbert*, p. 111.

21. Colgrave, *Two Lives of Saint Cuthbert*, p. 331. Colgrave indicates the borrowings in his apparatus.

22. Colgrave, *Two Lives of Saint Cuthbert*, pp. 74-7.

23. Colgrave, *Two Lives of Saint Cuthbert*, pp. 69, 71.

24. Colgrave, *Two Lives of Saint Cuthbert*, p. 73.

25. Felix, *Life of Saint Guthlac*, p. 81.

26. Felix, *Life of Saint Guthlac*, p. 81.

27. Felix, *Life of Saint Guthlac*, pp. 81, 83.

28. Felix, *Life of Saint Guthlac*, p. 97. Felix's description of a saint wracked by self-doubt may have been inspired by the *Life of Saint Anthony*–Athanasius reports Anthony's warning that the devil attempts to instil despair in the hearts of ascetics and attests that Anthony himself is troubled by various temptations; however, he provides no description of the nature of Anthony's troubles. See Chapter Five of the *Life of Saint Anthony*. Anthony has this to say about despair: 'they [the devils] may say that asceticism is useless…to make men disgusted with the solitary life on the grounds that it is burdensome and very grievous', *Early Christian Biographies*, ed. Roy J. Deferrari (Washington, DC: The Catholic University Press of America, 1952), p. 159. Note that Guthlac, mostly haunted by the memory of past sins, experiences despair differently.

29. *The Earliest Life of Gregory the Great*, ed. Bertram Colgrave (1968; reprint, Cambridge, UK: Cambridge University Press, 1985), p. 77.

30. Colgrave, *The Earliest Life of Gregory the Great*, p. 85.

31. Colgrave, *The Earliest Life of Gregory the Great*, pp. 131, 133.

32. For anthologies of these lives, see Noble and Head, *Soldiers of Christ* and Talbot, *Anglo-Saxon Missionaries in Germany*.

33. Noble and Head, *Soldiers of Christ*, p. 201.

34. Talbot, *Anglo-Saxon Missionaries in Germany*, p. 36.

35. For an edition and facing translation of this *vita*, see Stephen of Ripon, *The Life of Bishop Wilfrid by Eddius Stephanus*, ed. Bertram Colgrave (1927; reprint, Cambridge, UK: Cambridge University Press, 1985).

36. Talbot, *Anglo-Saxon Missionaries in Germany*, p. 154.

37. Michael Lapidge, *Anglo-Latin Literature, 600–899* (London: Hambledon Press, 1996), p. 12.

38. Talbot, *Anglo-Saxon Missionaries in Germany*, pp. 158, 172.

39. Bede, *Ecclesiastical History of the English People*, ed. Bertram Colgrave and R. A. B. Mynors (Oxford: Clarendon Press, 1969), p. 3.

40. The lives extracted from the *Ecclesiastical History* include lives of Alban, Oswald, Aidan, Fursa, Etheldryd, Cuthbert, and Aldhelm. The most frequently extracted of them all is Bede's autobiographical postscript. See M. L. W. Laistner, *A Hand-List of Bede Manuscripts* (Ithaca, NY: Cornell University Press, 1943), pp. 103–11.

41. See Bede's *Lives of the Abbots of Wearmouth and Jarrow*, in *The Age of Bede*, trans. D. H. Farmer (1965; reprint, New York: Penguin, 1983), pp. 185–208.

42. Bede, *Lives of the Abbots*, p. 186.

43. This digression is of special interest to students of English literature because it is the subject of the 'Battle of Maldon', the only surviving heroic poem composed in Old English besides *Beowulf.*

44. Byrhtferth, *The Lives of St Oswald and St Ecgwine*, p. lxxiii.

45. For an overview of this genre, which had its roots in Classical Latin literature, see Bill Friesen, 'The *Opus Geminatum* and Anglo-Saxon Literature', *Neophilologus* 95 (2011): 123–44. See also Lapidge, 'The Saintly Life', pp. 258–9. Other Anglo-Saxon practitioners of this genre include Alcuin, who wrote prose and metrical lives of Willibrord, and, in the later tenth century, Frithegod of Canterbury, who rewrote Stephen's *Life of Wilfrid* in both prose and verse.

46. Friesen, 'The *Opus Geminatum*', p. 140.

47. For a detailed analysis of Byrhtferth's Latin style, see Lapidge's Introduction to *Lives of St Oswald and St Ecgwine*, pp. xliv–lxi.

48. Byrhtferth, *Lives of St Oswald and St Ecgwine*, p. 59.

49. Talbot, *Anglo-Saxon Missionaries in Germany*, p. 215.

50. Talbot, *Anglo-Saxon Missionaries in Germany*, p. 223.

51. Talbot, *Anglo-Saxon Missionaries in Germany*, p. 32.

52. Talbot, *Anglo-Saxon Missionaries in Germany*, p. 176.

53. Wulfstan of Winchester, *The Life of St Æthelwold*, ed. and trans. Michael Lapidge and Michael Winterbottom (Oxford: Clarendon Press, 1991), pp. 47, 49.

54. Walter Daniel, *The Life of Ailred of Rievaulx*, trans. Maurice Powicke (Oxford: Clarendon Press, 1950), pp. 4, 62. This volume includes editions with facing-page translations both of Daniel's *Life* and of his response to Maurice.

55. Daniel, *Life of Ailred*, p. 66.

56. Daniel, *Life of Ailred*, p. 76.

57. Daniel, *Life of Ailred*, p. 77.

58. For a thoroughgoing study of Aelred's life and writings, see Aelred Squire, *Aelred of Rievaulx: A Study* (Kalamazoo, MI: Cistercian, 1981).

59. Thomas Head, *Hagiography and the Cult of the Saints: The Diocese of Orléans, 800–1200* (Cambridge, UK: Cambridge University Press, 2005), p. 95.

60. Eadmer, *The Life of St Anselm, Archbishop of Canterbury*, ed. and trans. R. W. Southern (Oxford: Clarendon Press, 1962), p. 149.

61. Catherine Keene, *Saint Margaret, Queen of the Scots: A Life in Perspective* (New York: Palgrave Macmillan, 2013), pp. 108–9.

62. Adam of Eynsham, *The Life of St Hugh of Lincoln*, ed. Decima L. Douie and Hugh Farmer O.S.B., 2 vols (London: Thomas Nelson and Sons, 1961, 1962), Vol. 2: pp. 229–30.

63. Adam of Eynsham, *Life of St Hugh*, Vol. 2: p. 230.

64. Adam of Eynsham, *Life of St Hugh*, Vol. 2: p. 230.

65. Adam of Eynsham, *Life of St Hugh*, Vol. 2: p. 200.

66. Antonia Gransden discusses and contextualizes the related commitment of William and his contemporaries to realistic descriptions of persons, places, and objects in 'Realistic Observation in Twelfth-Century England', *Speculum* 47 (1972): 29-51.

67. William of Malmesbury, *Saints' Lives*, ed. and trans. M. Winterbottom and R. M. Thomson (Oxford: Clarendon Press, 2002), p. 169.

68. William of Malmesbury, *Gesta Pontificum Anglorum: The History of the English Bishops*, ed. and trans. M. Winterbottom (Oxford: Clarendon Press, 2007), p. 499.

69. William of Malmesbury, *Saints' Lives*, p. 169.

70. Hugh of Fleury expresses a similar view on the importance of carefully researching the lives of early saints in his *Life of Saint Sacerdos*. See Thomas Head's discussion in *Hagiography and the Cult of the Saints*, pp. 91-5.

71. William of Malmesbury, *Gesta Pontificum Anglorum*, pp. 503-5.

72. R. W. Southern, *Saint Anselm: A Portrait in a Landscape* (Cambridge, UK: Cambridge University Press, 1990), p. 424.

73. Adam of Eynsham, *Life of St Hugh*, Vol. 2: p. 225.

74. 'The Life of the Venerable Beda by an Unknown Author of Great Antiquity', in *The Historical Works of the Venerable Bede*, trans. Joseph Stevenson (London, 1853), pp. xxxix-xlviii.

75. Antonia Gransden, 'Bede's Reputation as an Historian in Medieval England', *Journal of Ecclesiastical History* 32 (1981): 425. On Bede's reputation as a saint, see also Richard W. Pfaff, 'Bede among the Fathers? The Evidence from Liturgical Commemoration', *Studia Patristica* 28 (1993): 225-9.

76. Adam of Eynsham, *Life of St Hugh*, Vol. 1: p. 23.

77. Adam of Eynsham, *Life of St Hugh*, Vol. 1: p. 29.

78. Adam of Eynsham, *Life of St Hugh*, Vol. 1: p. 26.

79. Adam of Eynsham, *Life of St Hugh*, Vol. 1: p. 3.

80. Adam of Eynsham, *Life of St Hugh*, Vol. 1: p. 28.

81. Adam of Eynsham, *Life of St Hugh*, Vol. 2: p. 271.

82. On the introspectiveness of twelfth-century biographies, see also Ineke van 't Spijker, 'Saints and Despair: Twelfth-Century Hagiography as "Intimate Biography"', in *The Invention of Holiness*, ed. Anneke B. Mulder-Bakker (London: Routledge, 2002), pp. 185-205.

83. William of Malmesbury, *Saints' Lives*, pp. 119, 21.

84. Eadmer, *Life of St. Anselm*, pp. 50-4.

85. Adam of Eynsham, *Life of St Hugh*, Vol. 1: p. 6.

86. Matthew Paris, *Life of St Edmund*, trans. C. H. Lawrence (Stroud, Gloucestershire: Sutton Publishing, 1997).

87. Aelred of Rievaulx, *Spiritual Friendship*, ed. Marsha L. Dutton, trans. Lawrence C. Braceland (Collegeville, MN: Cistercian, 2010). Aelred's treatise takes the form of a conversation, with Daniel as one of the interlocutors. On the period's interest in friendship, see also Southern, *Saint Anselm*, p. 65. Brian Patrick McGuire discusses the decline of monastic friendship after the twelfth century and its effect on monastic biographies in 'The Collapse of a Monastic Friendship: The Case of Jocelin and Samson of Bury', *Journal of Medieval History* 4 (1978): 369-97.

88. Daniel, *Life of Ailred*, p. 24.

89. Daniel, *Life of Ailred*, p. 31.

90. Daniel, *Life of Ailred*, p. 36.

91. For more on this phenomenon, see Jay Rubenstein, 'Biography and Autobiography in the Middle Ages', in *Writing Medieval History*, ed. Nancy Partner (London: Hodder Arnold, 2005), pp. 22–41.

92. Adam of Eynsham, *Life of St Hugh*, Vol. 1: p. 43.

93. Adam of Eynsham, *Life of St Hugh*, Vol. 1: p. xiv.

94. Eadmer, *Life of St Anselm*, p. 150.

95. As mentioned in Note 5 to this chapter, Coleman's life survives in a translation by William of Malmesbury. See William of Malmesbury, *Saints' Lives*, p. 95.

96. Rubenstein, 'Biography and Autobiography in the Middle Ages', p. 27.

97. Jocelin of Brakelond, *Chronicle of the Abbey of Bury St Edmunds*, trans. Diana Greenway and Jane Sayers (Oxford: Oxford University Press, 1989), p. 3.

98. Greenway and Sayers call Jocelin 'almost a diarist and in part a biographer' (p. x). In Brian Patrick McGuire's estimation, Jocelin renders Samson 'in a detail hardly ever seen for any other medieval figure' in 'some of the best biographical passages in medieval Latin prose' ('Collapse', pp. 378, 388). Historians generally share McGuire's admiration of Jocelin as Samson's biographer. Antonia Gransden, for example, praises his 'lifelike' portrait in *A History of Bury St Edmunds, 1182-1256: Samson of Tottington to Edmund of Walpole* (Woodbridge, Suffolk: Boydell and Brewer, 2007), p. 2. Daniel Gerrard cautions that the vivacity and the apparent artlessness of Jocelin's narration have led–or more properly misled–scholars into accepting his interpretation of Samson at face value in 'Jocelin of Brakelond and the Power of Abbot Samson', *Journal of Medieval History* 40 (2014): 1-23.

99. McGuire, 'Collapse', p. 396.

100. It was a common practice at monastic houses to periodically apply leeches to draw blood, a practice thought to contribute to the monks' health.

101. Jocelin, *Chronicle*, p. 15.

102. Jocelin, *Chronicle*, p. 39.

103. Jocelin, *Chronicle*, p. 33.

104. Jocelin, *Chronicle*, pp. 32, 38-9.

105. Gerrard, 'Power', p. 23.

106. That manuscript, London, British Library Harley MS 1005, dates from the second half of the thirteenth century. Portions of Jocelin's *Chronicle* survive in three other manuscripts.

107. Jocelin, *Chronicle*, pp. 121-2. Jocelin is quoting from Ovid's *Art of Love*, Book One, line 444.

108. On this point, see Gerrard ('Power'), who trusts Jocelin's account of Samson's deeds far more than his interpretation of Samson's personality.

109. McGuire, 'Collapse', pp. 388-92.

110. Garnier of Pont-Sainte-Maxence, *Garnier's Becket*, trans. Janet Shirley (London: Phillimore, 1975), p. 5.

111. The complete title is *De vita sua sive monodiarum suarum libri tres*, or *On his life, or his monodies, in three books*. For quotations and page references, I am using the translation by Joseph McAlhany and Jay Rubenstein: Guibert of Nogent, *Monodies and On the Relics of Saints* (New York: Penguin, 2011).

112. For a provocative discussion of the outward turn Guibert takes in the *Monodies* and its relationship to his personal confession, see Heather Blurton, 'Guibert of Nogent and the Subject of History', *Exemplaria* 15 (2003): 111–31.

113. For the definitive biography of Abelard, see M. T. Clanchy, *Abelard: A Medieval Life* (Oxford: Blackwell, 1997).

114. Jay Rubenstein explores in depth Guibert's understanding of psychology and compares his autobiography with Abelard's in his *Guibert of Nogent: Portrait of a Medieval Mind* (New York: Routledge, 2002).

115. See Guibert, *Monodies*, p. vii.

116. Among their appearances in modern films, Abelard and Heloise were the stars in *Stealing Heaven* (1988, directed by Clive Donner) and puppets in *Being John Malkovich* (1999, directed by Spike Jonze).

117. Philippe Lejeune, *On Autobiography*, trans. Paul John Eakin and Katherine Leary (Minneapolis, MN: University of Minnesota Press, 1989), p. 4.

118. On her life and spirituality, see Anneke B. Mulder-Bakker, *Lives of the Anchoresses: The Rise of the Urban Recluse in Medieval Europe*, trans. Myra Heerspink Scholz (Philadelphia, PA: University of Pennsylvania Press, 2005), pp. 24–50; and Nancy Partner, 'The Family Romance of Guibert of Nogent: His Story/Her Story', in *Medieval Mothering*, ed. Bonnie Wheeler and John Carmi Parsons (New York: Garland, 1996), pp. 357–77.

119. On this point, see also Mulder-Bakker, *Lives of the Anchoresses*, p. 26.

120. On Guibert's proprietary representation of his mother, see Partner, 'Family Romance'. Partner's compelling reading of Guibert and his mother has much shaped my thinking about their relationship. Partner notes that her death liberated him to take 'full possession of her' by 'writing her life into his' (pp. 360, 369).

121. For a more elaborate discussion of this point, see Partner, 'Family Romance', pp. 370–6.

122. On Guibert's fixation with his mother's sex life, see especially John F. Benton, 'The Personality of Guibert of Nogent', *Psychoanalytic Review* 57 (1970): 568–70.

123. Partner, 'Family Romance', p. 361.

124. Georg Misch discussed Guibert's *Memoirs* as the first medieval autobiography in his 1959 *Geschichte der Autobiographie* (Leipzig: G. B. Teubner, 1959), pp. 108–62. To my knowledge, his judgment has not been challenged. For a restatement of Guibert's importance in the history of medieval autobiography, see Rubenstein, *Guibert de Nogent* and 'Biography and Autobiography'.

125. For all quotes and parenthetical references, I am using *The Letter Collection of Peter Abelard and Heloise*, ed. David Luscombe, trans. Betty Radice (Oxford: Clarendon Press, 2013). Abelard was perhaps inspired by hagiographies, like that of Martin of Tours, wherein literal soldiers of the emperor become metaphorical soldiers of Christ; as we shall see, hagiographical tropes explicitly shape Abelard's account of his monastic career.

126. In a letter to Heloise, he continues this hagiographical self-presentation, requesting that, should his enemies succeed in killing him, she and her nuns might follow in the footsteps of the biblical women who tended Christ's body after the Crucifixion (p. 155).

127. Yet it is fully in character. In a letter written *circa* 1118, that is, about the time Abelard entered religious life, Fulk of Deuil accused Abelard of considering himself better than the saints. See Clanchy, *Abelard*, p. 327.

128. Paul John Eakin, *How Our Lives Become Stories: Making Selves* (Ithaca, NY: Cornell University Press, 1999), pp. 214, 26.

129. Mary M. McLaughlin, 'Abelard as Autobiographer: The Motives and Meaning of His "Story of Calamities"', *Speculum* 42 (1967): 463-88. Tracts disguised as letters of advice written to friends were common at the time; a famous example is Andreas Capellanus's *Art of Courtly Love*.

130. Important studies of Heloise's life and letters include Barbara Newman, 'Authority, Authenticity, and the Repression of Heloise', in *From Virile Woman to Woman Christ* (Philadelphia, PA: University of Pennsylvania Press, 1995), 46-75; and the essays in the collection edited by Bonnie Wheeler, *Listening to Heloise: The Voice of a Twelfth-Century Woman* (New York: St. Martin's Press, 2000).

131. Clanchy, *Abelard*, p. 153. On the evolution of their relationship, see also Linda Georgianna, '"In Any Corner of Heaven": Heloise's Critique of Monastic Life', in Wheeler, *Listening to Heloise*, pp. 187-216.

132. I am quoting, respectively, from Anna Silvas, 'Introduction' to *Jutta and Hildegard: The Biographical Sources*, ed. and trans. Silvas (Turnhout, Belgium: Brepols, 1998), p. xxii, and Barbara Newman, 'Three-Part Invention: The *Vita S. Hildegardis* and Mystical Hagiography', in *Hildegard of Bingen: The Context of her Thought and Art*, ed. Charles Burnett and Peter Dronke (London: Warburg Institute, 1998), p. 189.

133. For a thorough introduction to Hildegard's life, times, writings, art, and music, see the essays in *Voice of the Living Light: Hildegard of Bingen and Her World*, ed. Barbara Newman (Berkeley, CA: University of California Press, 1998).

134. For a fascinating discussion of the vexed relationship between Hildegard and Guibert, see John W. Coakley, *Women, Men and Spiritual Power: Female Saints and Their Male Collaborators* (New York: Columbia University Press, 2006), pp. 44-67. Coakley proposes that Guibert may have become disenchanted with Hildegard when she rebuffed his attempts to construe himself as her collaborator. For a translation of Guibert's *vita*, see Sivlas, *Jutta and Hildegard*, pp. 89-111.

135. Sivlas, *Jutta and Hildegard*, p. 115.

136. Barbara Newman, 'Sibyl of the Rhine: Hildegard's Life and Times', in *Voice of the Living Light*, pp. 1-29; quote at p. 4.

137. William is explaining his inclusion of what he expects readers to consider a dubious posthumous miracle story concerning Wulfstan's rescue of imperilled mariners (*Saints' Lives*, p. 101).

138. On nineteenth-century biography and the 'zeal for documents' that prevailed since Boswell, see A. O. J. Cockshut, *Truth to Life: The Art of Biography in the Nineteenth Century* (London: Collins, 1974), quote at p. 17.

139. Richard Altick, *Lives and Letters: A History of Literary Biography in England and America* (New York: Knopf, 1965), p. 7.

140. Altick, *Lives and Letters*, p. x.

141. Adam of Eynsham, *Life of St Hugh*, Vol. 1: p. 39.

Chapter 2

1. *Medieval Holy Women in the Christian Tradition, c.1100-c.1500*, ed. Alastair Minnis and Rosalynn Voaden (Turnhout, Belgium: Brepols, 2010); Anneke B. Mulder-Bakker, *Lives of*

the Anchoresses: The Rise of the Urban Recluse in Medieval Europe, trans. Myra Heerspink Scholz (Philadelphia, PA: University of Pennsylvania Press, 2005); *New Trends in Feminine Spirituality: The Holy Women of Liège and Their Impact*, ed. Juliette Dor, Lesley Johnson, and Jocelyn Wogan-Browne (Turnhout, Belgium: Brepols, 1999); Gertrud Jaron Lewis, *By Women, for Women, about Women: The Sister-Books of Fourteenth-Century Germany* (Toronto: Pontifical Institute of Mediaeval Studies, 1996); and Caroline Walker Bynum, *Holy Feast and Holy Fast: The Religious Significance of Food to Medieval Women* (Berkeley, CA: University of California Press, 1987).

2. John W. Coakley, *Women, Men and Spiritual Power: Female Saints and Their Male Collaborators* (New York: Columbia University Press, 2006).

3. For all quotations and references, I am using the translation of the *Liber confortatorius* by Michael Wright and Kathleen Loncar in *Writing the Wilton Women: Goscelin's Legend of Edith and Liber confortatorius*, ed. Stephanie Hollis (Turnhout, Belgium: Brepols, 2004), pp. 97–212. *Writing the Wilton Women* includes valuable contextualizing essays and analyses of Goscelin's *Book of Encouragement* and *Life of Edith*.

4. Elisabeth Van Houts, 'The Flemish Contribution to Biographical Writing in England in the Eleventh Century', in *Writing Medieval Biography: Essays in Honour of Frank Barlow*, ed. David Bates, Julia Crick, and Sarah Hamilton (Woodbridge, Suffolk: Boydell Press, 2006), pp. 111–27. Van Houts also discusses the popularity of English and Celtic saints in Flanders during the early to mid-eleventh century (pp. 118–19), which was evinced both in the acquisition of their relics and in the writing of their lives. Other Flemish hagiographers of Anglo-Saxon saints included Drogo of Saint-Winnocksbergen and Folcard of Saint-Bertin.

5. William of Malmesbury, *Gesta Regum Anglorum: The History of the English Kings*, ed. and trans. R. A. B. Mynors, completed by R. M. Thomson and M. Winterbottom, 2 vols (Oxford: Clarendon Press, 1998), Vol. 1: p. 593.

6. Van Houts discusses these features of Flemish hagiography in 'The Flemish Contribution', see especially pp. 119–22.

7. Stephanie Hollis, 'Goscelin's Writings and the Wilton Women', in Hollis, *Writing the Wilton Women*, pp. 217–44.

8. Goscelin writes of 'these torments of separation, which were owing to my crimes' (p. 101); shortly thereafter, he writes, 'with the rise of a king who did not know Joseph, by serpent envy and a stepfather's barbarity, your devoted one was compelled to wander a long way away' (p. 104).

9. Rebecca Hayward surveys scholarly interpretations of Goscelin's and Eve's relationship in 'Spiritual Friendship and Gender Difference in the *Liber confortatorius*', in Hollis, *Writing the Wilton Women*, pp. 341–53.

10. Monica Otter, introduction to her translation, *The Book of Encouragement and Consolation [Liber Confortatorius]: The Letter of Goscelin to the Recluse Eva* (Woodbridge, Suffolk: Boydell and Brewer, 2004), p. 11. The classic study of this culture of rumination is Jean Leclerq, *The Love of Learning and the Desire for God: A Study of Monastic Culture*, trans. Catharine Misrahi (New York: Fordham University Press, 1961).

11. Ann K. Warren, *Anchorites and Their Patrons in Medieval England* (Berkeley, CA: University of California Press, 1985), pp. 29–41.

12. Warren, *Anchorites and Their Patrons*, p. 32.

13. For a listing of these guides, their authors, and their dates, see Warren, *Anchorites and Their Patrons*, pp. 294-8.

14. For a survey of Goscelin's career, see Frank Barlow's 'Goscelin of St Bertin', Appendix C of his *The Life of King Edward who Rests at Westminster* (London: Thomas Nelson and Sons, 1962), pp. 91-111. On Flemish hagiographers' particular sensitivity to women, 'lay and ecclesiastical, alive and dead', see Van Houts, 'The Flemish Contribution' (quote on p. 112). For a facing-page edition/translation of Goscelin's lives of female saints, see *The Hagiography of the Female Saints of Ely*, ed. Rosalind C. Love (Oxford: Clarendon Press, 2004).

15. On this point, see Rebecca Hayward and Stephanie Hollis, 'The Female Reader in the *Liber confortatorius*', in Hollis, *Writing the Wilton Women*, p. 396.

16. Rebecca Hayward and Stephanie Hollis also wonder whether this embedded life might be 'the narrative reflex of a guilty conscience' in 'The Female Reader in the *Liber confortatorius*', p. 397.

17. For a discussion of this eulogy, see Hollis, 'Goscelin's Writings and the Wilton Women', pp. 229-30.

18. On this shift in attitudes, see Sharon K. Elkins, *Holy Women of Twelfth-Century England* (Chapel Hill, NC: University of North Carolina Press, 1988).

19. For all quotations and references, I am using the translation by Michael Wright and Kathleen Loncar in Hollis, *Writing the Wilton Women*, pp. 21-67.

20. On this point, see Barbara Yorke, '"Carriers of the Truth": Writing the Biographies of Anglo-Saxon Female Saints', in Bates, Crick, and Hamilton, *Writing Medieval Biography*, pp. 49-60. Yorke notes that in his life of Edith, Goscelin 'often seems to be battling against the tenor of his source material in order to present Edith as a model of humility and correct monastic behaviour' (p. 56). Susan J. Ridyard describes Goscelin's intimate familiarity with Wilton and assesses the reliability of his life of Edith in her *The Royal Saints of Anglo-Saxon England: A Study of West Saxon and East Anglian Cults* (Cambridge, UK: Cambridge University Press, 1988).

21. Stephanie Hollis, 'Edith as Contemplative and Bride of Christ', in Hollis, *Writing the Wilton Women*, pp. 281-306.

22. For a facsimile, transcription, translation, and study of the St. Albans Psalter, see the website developed at University of Aberdeen, *The St Albans Psalter*, http://www.abdn.ac.uk/stalbanspsalter/english/index.shtml. See also *The St Albans Psalter: A Book for Christina of Markyate*, ed. Jane Geddes (London: British Library, 2005); and Kristine Haney, *The St. Albans Psalter: An Anglo-Norman Song of Faith* (New York: Peter Lang, 2002).

23. For arguments associating the psalter with Christina and Geoffrey, see Jane Geddes, 'The St Albans Psalter: The Abbot and the Anchoress' in *Christina of Markyate: A Twelfth-Century Holy Woman*, ed. Samuel Fanous and Henrietta Leyser (London: Routledge, 2005), pp. 197-216; and Morgan Powell, 'Making the Psalter of Christina of Markyate (The St. Albans Psalter)', *Viator* 36 (2005): 293-336. For challenges to the long-standing view linking the psalter with Christina, see Haney, *The St. Albans Psalter* and Donald Matthew, 'The Incongruities of the St Albans Psalter', *Journal of Medieval History* 34 (2008): 396-416. These studies also treat the debate over whether the psalter was

originally designed for Christina, or whether a pre-existing psalter was adapted for her use.

24. Tony Hunt, 'The *Life* of St Alexis, 475-1125', in Fanous and Leyser, *Christina of Markyate*, pp. 217-28. For a translation of the life, see 'Life of St. Alexis', trans. Nancy Vine Durling, in *Medieval Hagiography: An Anthology*, ed. Thomas Head (New York: Garland Publishing, 2000), pp. 316-40.

25. See p. 57 in 'Transcription and Translation', *The St Albans Psalter*, http://www.abdn.ac.uk/stalbanspsalter/english/index.shtml.

26. For an introduction to all facets of Christina's life and biography, see the essays in Fanous and Leyser, *Christina of Markyate*.

27. For all quotations and citations, I am using *The Life of Christina of Markyate: A Twelfth Century Recluse*, ed. and trans. C. H. Talbot (Oxford: Clarendon Press, 1959).

28. On the influence of these two genres of hagiography on the *Life*, see Samuel Fanous, 'Christina of Markyate and the Double Crown', in Fanous and Leyser, *Christina of Markyate*, pp. 53-78.

29. See my discussion of this scene in *Virgin Martyrs: Legends of Sainthood in Late Medieval England* (Ithaca, NY: Cornell University Press, 1997), pp. 19-21.

30. For more on Christina's persecutor, see R. I. Moore, 'Ranulf Flambard and Christina of Markyate', in Fanous and Leyser, *Christina of Markyate*, pp. 138-59.

31. See Kathryn Kelsey Staples and Ruth Mazo Karras, 'Christina's Tempting: Sexual Desire and Women's Sanctity', in Fanous and Leyser, *Christina of Markyate*, pp. 184-96.

32. For a fascinating discussion of this episode, and of the biographer's critical take on Christina, see Rachel Koopmans, 'Dining at Markyate with Lady Christina', in Fanous and Leyser, *Christina of Markyate*, pp. 143-59.

33. See Koopmans, 'Dining at Markyate' and 'The Conclusion of Christina of Markyate's *Vita*', *Journal of Ecclesiastical History* 51 (2000): 663-98.

34. Winstead, *Virgin Martyrs*, p. 20.

35. James Boswell, *The Life of Samuel Johnson*, ed. David Womersley (New York: Penguin, 2008), p. 21.

36. 'Biography', *The Rambler* 60, in *Samuel Johnson: The Major Works*, ed. Donald Greene (Oxford: Oxford University Press, 2009), pp. 204-7.

37. Johnson, 'Biography'.

38. Koopmans, 'Conclusion', p. 666.

39. Koopmans, 'Conclusion', pp. 692-3.

40. Koopmans, 'Conclusion', p. 698.

41. For more on this development, see Elkins, *Holy Women of Twelfth-Century England*.

42. For an edition with facing-page translation, see *The Book of St Gilbert*, ed. Raymonde Foreville and Gillian Keir (Oxford: Clarendon Press, 1987). I am using this edition for all citations. The Introduction provides a detailed survey of Gilbert and his order to which the following discussion is indebted. See also Brian Golding, *Gilbert of Sempringham and the Gilbertine Order, c. 1130-c. 1300* (Oxford: Clarendon Press, 1995).

43. See Giles Constable, 'Aelred of Rievaulx and the Nun of Watton: An Episode in the Early History of the Gilbertine Order', in *Medieval Women*, ed. Derek Baker (Oxford: Blackwell, 1981), pp. 205-26.

44. Documents pertaining to this incident are edited and translated in Foreville and Keir, *Book of St Gilbert*, pp. 134–67.

45. Foreville and Keir, *Book of St Gilbert*, p. lxxviii.

46. Winstead, *Virgin Martyrs*, pp. 40–57.

47. Studies of this phenomenon include Mulder-Bakker, *Lives of the Anchoresses* and Dor, Johnson, and Wogan-Browne, *New Trends in Feminine Spirituality*. Fortunately, many of these lives are now translated as part of the 'Medieval Women: Texts and Contexts' series published by Brepols. On heterospiritual friendships from *circa* 1170-1240, see also Brian Patrick McGuire, *Friendship & Community: The Monastic Experience, 350–1250* (Kalamazoo, MI: Cistercian Publications, 1988), pp. 388–98.

48. James reports his observations in the Prologue to his *Life of Mary d'Oignies*. See James Vitry, 'The Life of Mary of Oignies by James of Vitry', trans. Margot H. King, in *Mary of Oignies: Mother of Salvation*, ed. Anneke B. Mulder-Bakker (Turnhout, Belgium: Brepols, 2006), pp. 39–50.

49. Coakley, *Women, Men and Spiritual Power*.

50. Coakley, *Women, Men and Spiritual Power*, pp. 71, 97.

51. Norman P. Tanner, *The Church in Late Medieval Norwich, 1370-1532* (Toronto: Pontifical Institute of Medieval Studies, 1984). Brenda Bolton compares insular and Continental women's religious life and considers reasons for the differences in 'Thirteenth-Century Religious Women: Further Reflections on the Low Countries "Special Case"', in Dor, Johnson, and Wogan-Browne, *New Trends in Feminine Spirituality: The Holy Women of Liège and their Impact*, pp. 129–57. See also Anne Clark Bartlett, 'Holy Women in the British Isles: A Survey', in Minnis and Voaden, *Medieval Holy Women in the Christian Tradition c.1100–c.1500*, pp. 165–93.

52. John Capgrave, *Abbreuiacion of Chronicles*, ed. Peter J. Lucas, Early English Text Society OS 285 (Oxford: Oxford University Press, 1983), p. 159.

53. For an introduction to Julian and her context, see Nicholas Watson, 'Julian of Norwich' in *Medieval Women's Writing*, ed. Carolyn Dinshaw and David Wallace (Cambridge, UK: Cambridge University Press, 2003), pp. 210–21.

54. On reading Julian of Norwich's visions autobiographically, see Christopher Abbott, *Julian of Norwich: Autobiography and Theology* (Woodbridge, Suffolk: D. S. Brewer, 1999).

55. Marea Mitchell, *The Book of Margery Kempe: Scholarship, Community, and Criticism* (New York: Peter Lang, 2005), p. 16. John C. Hirsh provides a detailed account of the discovery of the manuscript, its reception, and the events leading to the publication of the first scholarly edition in 1940 in his *Hope Emily Allen: Medieval Scholarship and Feminism* (Norman, OK: Pilgrim Books, 1988). For a reflection on Hope Allen's complex relationship with Margery Kempe, see Carolyn Dinshaw, *How Soon is Now? Medieval Texts, Amateur Readers, and the Queerness of Time* (Durham, NC: Duke University Press, 2012), pp. 105–27.

56. The extracts comprise Appendix 2 (pp. 353–7) of Margery Kempe, *The Book of Margery Kempe*, edited by Sanford Brown Meech with a prefatory note by Hope Emily Allen and Notes and Appendices by Sanford Brown Meech and Hope Emily Allen. Early English Text Society OS 212 (Oxford: Oxford University Press, 1940). Studies of the extracts include Sue Ellen Holbrook, 'Margery Kempe and Wynkyn de Worde', in *The Medieval Mystical Tradition in*

England: Exeter Symposium IV, ed. Marion Glasscoe (Cambridge, UK: D. S. Brewer, 1987), pp. 27–46, and Allyson Foster, 'A *Shorte Treatyse of Contemplacyon: The Book of Margery Kempe* in its Early Print Contexts', in *A Companion to The Book of Margery Kempe*, ed. John H. Arnold and Katherine J. Lewis (Cambridge, UK: D. S. Brewer, 2004), pp. 95–112.

57. For a comparison of these two literary events, see Mitchell, *The Book of Margery Kempe*, pp. 55–60.

58. Mitchell, *The Book of Margery Kempe*, pp. 57–9, from which are drawn the headlines that follow.

59. William Butler-Bowdon, *The Book of Margery Kempe* (London: Jonathan Cape, 1936), p. 16. Butler-Bowdon makes his text more accessible, too, by providing chapter titles. The American edition, published in 1944 by the Devin-Adair Company, sets 'chapters entirely devoted to mystical matters…in a smaller type to keep them distinct from the narrative text' rather than putting them in an appendix. The impulse to excise features of the *Book of Margery Kempe* that might alienate modern readers and to render the *Book* a more recognizable autobiography has persisted. Two 'translations' have changed the *Book's* third-person narration to first-person: *The Autobiography of the Madwoman of God: The Book of Margery Kempe*, trans. Tony D. Triggs (Tunbridge Wells, Kent: Burns & Oates, 1995) and *The Book of Margery Kempe*, trans. John Skinner (New York: Doubleday, 1998). Justifying this radical departure from the original, Triggs writes that he made a 'confident choice in favour of allowing Margery to speak for herself throughout; we hear her account in the first person, just as her scribes must have heard it themselves' (p. 12). Skinner silently changes all the third-person references to first-person.

60. See the 'Prefatory Note' to Kempe, *The Book of Margery Kempe*, ed. Meech, p. lvii.

61. 'Prefatory Note', p. lxiv.

62. 'Prefatory Note', p. lxv.

63. For succinct surveys of Kempe scholarship, see Mitchell, *The Book of Margery Kempe*, pp. 73–93, and Barry Windeatt, 'Introduction: Reading and Re-reading *The Book of Margery Kempe*', in Arnold and Lewis, *A Companion to The Book of Margery Kempe*, pp. 1–16.

64. Arnold and Lewis, *A Companion to The Book of Margery Kempe* provides a good sample of approaches, with special attention to the work of historians.

65. Sarah Stanbury and Virginia Raguin, *Mapping Margery Kempe: A Guide to Late Medieval Material and Spritual Life* (http://college.holycross.edu/projects/kempe/).

66. Robert Glück, *Margery Kempe* (New York: High Risk Books/Serpent's Tail, 1994) and Mark Schroeder, *The Book of Margery Kempe* (Amazon Digital Services, 2012).

67. For a useful overview of the *Book of Margery Kempe's* hagiographical qualities, see Katherine J. Lewis, 'Margery Kempe and Saint Making in Later Medieval England', in Arnold and Lewis, *A Companion to the Book of Margery Kempe*, pp. 195–215.

68. For quotations and references, I am using Margery Kempe, *The Book of Margery Kempe*, ed. and trans. Lynn Staley (New York and London: W. W. Norton, 2001).

69. Thomas of Cantimpré, *The Collected Saints' Lives*, ed. Barbara Newman, trans. Barbara Newman and Margot H. King (Turnhout, Belgium: Brepols, 2008), pp. 123, 215. For examples of other lives of late medieval saints translated into modern English,

see *Living Saints of the Thirteenth Century*, ed. Anneke B. Mulder-Bakker (Turnhout, Belgium: Brepols, 2011). For an edition of three lives of late medieval holy women that were translated into Middle English, see *Three Women of Liège*, ed. Jennifer N. Brown (Turnhout, Belgium: Brepols, 2008).

70. On the close relationship between medieval women and their confessors and biographers, see Coakley, *Women, Men and Spiritual Power*. Sebastian Sobecki reviews scholarship about the identity of the scribes and presents documentary evidence supporting the hypotheses that the first scribe is Margery's son John and that the second scribe is Robert Spryngolde in '"The wryting of this tretys": Margery Kempe's Son and the Authorship of Her Book', *Studies in the Age of Chaucer* 37 (2015): 257-83. See also the provocative 'dialogue' on the making of the book and its status as autobiography: Nicholas Watson's 'The Making of *The Book of Margery Kempe*' and Felicity Riddy's 'Text and Self in *The Book of Margery Kempe*' and 'Afterwords', in *Voices in Dialogue: Reading Women in the Middle Ages*, ed. Linda Olson and Kathryn Kerby-Fulton (Notre Dame, IN: University of Notre Dame Press, 2005), pp. 395-434, 435-53, 454-7 respectively.

71. Margery's summary of her childhood suggests that she was anything but a child prodigy of holiness: 'how unkind she had been against our Lord Jesus Christ, how proud and vain she had been in her bearing, how obstinate against the laws of God, and how envious against her fellow Christians' (pp. 29-30).

72. On the importance of this step down to Margery's self-conception, see Nancy Partner, 'Reading the Book of Margery Kempe', *Exemplaria* 3 (1991): 29-66.

73. On the importance of the Apostle Paul and Mary Magdalene as models for Margery Kempe, see Sarah Salih, 'Staging Conversion: The Digby Saint Plays and *The Book of Margery Kempe*', in *Gender and Holiness: Men, Women and Saints in Late Medieval Europe*, ed. Samantha J. E. Riches and Sarah Salih (London: Routledge, 2002), pp. 121-34.

74. Augustine of Hippo famously recounts his prolonged conversion process in his *Confessions*, but that process was radically abbreviated in the versions of his life that were most readily available in late medieval England. See, for example, the account in Jacobus de Voragine's 'bestselling' hagiographical collection, *The Golden Legend*, trans. William Granger Ryan, 2 vols. (Princeton, NJ: Princeton University Press, 1993), Vol. 2: pp. 116-25.

75. On the importance of virginity in medieval saints' lives, see Winstead, *Virgin Martyrs*; Jocelyn Wogan-Browne, *Saints' Lives and Women's Literary Culture: Virginity and its Authorizations* (Oxford: Oxford University Press, 2001); and Sarah Salih, *Versions of Virginity in Late Medieval England* (Woodbridge, Suffolk: D. S. Brewer, 2001).

76. On the popularity in Margery's England of saints who died violently, see Lewis, 'Margery Kempe and Saint Making', pp. 206-7.

77. Gail McMurray Gibson, *The Theater of Devotion: East Anglian Society and Drama in the Late Middle Ages* (Chicago: University of Chicago Press, 1989), p. 47.

78. Mary's life, indeed, was translated into Middle English. See Brown, *Three Women of Liège*, pp. 85-190 (for instances of self-mutilation, see Book One, Chapter 7 and Book Two, Chapter 7).

79. For the Middle English translation of Christina's life, see Brown, *Three Women of Liège*, pp. 51-84 (the account of her self-inflicted torments can be found in chapters 6-14).

80. For a Middle English life of Bridget, see Bridget of Sweden, *Liber Celestis*, ed. Roger Ellis, Early English Text Society OS, 291 (Oxford: Oxford University Press, 1987), pp. 1–5. Bridget's feats of asceticism are described on p. 1.

81. On the importance of fasting for medieval holy women, see especially Bynum, *Holy Feast and Holy Fast* and Rudolph M. Bell, *Holy Anorexia* (Chicago: University of Chicago Press, 1985). Gail Gibson notes Margery's competitiveness with Bridget in *Theater of Devotion*, p. 47.

82. John of Caulibus, *Meditations on the Life of Christ*, trans. Francis X. Taney, Anne Miller, and C. Mary Stallings-Taney (Asheville, NC: Pegasus Press, 2000), p. 4.

83. John of Caulibus, *Meditations*, pp. 28, 40, 45.

84. See Gail Gibson's discussion of this refashioning in *The Theater of Devotion*, pp. 47–65.

85. Lynn Staley discusses the absence of such corroborating documentation in *Margery Kempe's Dissenting Fictions* (University Park, PA: Pennsylvania State University Press, 1994), pp. 173–4.

86. The relevant entries in the Account Roll of Trinity Guild are given in Appendix III of the Early English Text Society's *Book of Margery Kempe*, ed. Meech, pp. 358–9.

87. John of Caulibus, *Meditations*, p. 4.

88. The extracts are printed as Appendix II, 'Printed Extracts from *The Book of Margery Kempe*', of Kempe, *The Book of Margery Kempe*, ed. Meech, pp. 353–7; the translations are my own. See the studies of Holbrook and Foster (cited in Note 56 of this chapter). For me, an indication that the redactor did not intend a conservative rewriting of the *Book* is the preservation of Jesus's elevation of his 'daughter' above the clergy, a pronouncement that concludes the text. When Margery remonstrates that 'you should show these graces to religious men and to priests', Jesus replies, 'No, no daughter, for I love best what they love not, and that is shames, reproves, scorns, and despites of the people, and therefore they shall not have this grace, daughter, for he who dreads the shames of this world may not perfectly love God' ('Printed Extracts', p. 357).

89. 'Printed Extracts', p. 357.

90. 'Printed Extracts', p. 356.

91. On this point, see also Foster, 'A Shorte Treatyse of Contemplacyon', p. 112.

Chapter 3

1. Alfred was described thus by his friend Wulfsige, Bishop of Sherborne, in the verse preface to Bishop Werferth of Worcester's translation of the *Dialogues* of Gregory the Great. Wulfsige also refers to Alfred by the Old English kenning 'ring-giver'. Wulfsige's preface is given in *Alfred the Great: Asser's Life of King Alfred and Other Contemporary Sources*, ed. and trans. Simon Keynes and Michael Lapidge (New York: Penguin, 1983), pp. 187–8. For an introduction to Alfred and his contributions, political and cultural, see Richard Abels, *Alfred the Great: War, Kingship and Culture in Anglo-Saxon England* (London and New York: Longman, 1998). See also the essays comprising *Alfred the Great: Papers from the Eleventh-Centenary Conferences*, ed. Timothy Reuter (Aldershot, UK, and Burlington, VT: Ashgate, 2003).

2. Keynes and Lapidge, *Alfred the Great*, p. 125.

3. Keynes and Lapidge, *Alfred the Great*, p. 126.

4. For an overview of Charlemagne's rule, see Roger Collins, *Charlemagne* (Toronto: University of Toronto Press, 1998).

5. Einhard and Notker the Stammerer, *Two Lives of Charlemagne*, trans. Lewis Thorpe (New York: Penguin, 1969), preface, pp. 51–2.

6. Thorpe, *Two Lives*, pp. 51–2.

7. On Einhard's use of Suetonius, see Matthew Innes, 'The Classical Tradition in the Carolingian Renaissance: Ninth-Century Encounters with Suetonius', *International Journal of the Classical Tradition* 3 (1997): 265–82. For a discussion of the influence of Suetonius on Charlemagne as well as on his biographer, see E. K. Rand, 'On the History of the *De vita Caesarum* of Suetonius in the Early Middle Ages', *Harvard Studies in Classical Philology* 37 (1926): 1–48.

8. Thorpe, *Two Lives*, p. 59.

9. Janet L. Nelson discusses Einhard's specific borrowings from Suetonius in 'Did Charlemagne have a Private Life?' in *Writing Medieval Biography: Essays in Honour of Frank Barlow*, ed. David Bates, Julia Crick, and Sarah Hamilton (Woodbridge, Suffolk: Boydell Press, 2006), pp. 15–28.

10. For quotations and citations, I am using the translation of Keynes and Lapidge in *Alfred the Great*. Keynes and Lapidge discuss the meagre information that survives on Asser's life in their introduction (pp. 48–58), where they also consider and refute the claim that Asser was not in fact the life's author.

11. See Sarah Foot, 'Finding the Meaning in Form: Narrative in Annals and Chronicles', in *Writing Medieval History*, ed. Nancy Partner (London: Hodder Education, 2005), pp. 88–108; Antonia Gransden, *Historical Writing in England, c. 550–c. 1307* (Ithaca, NY: Cornell University Press, 1974).

12. Michael Swanton, trans. *The Anglo-Saxon Chronicle* (New York: Routledge, 1998).

13. Keynes and Lapidge, *Alfred the Great*, p. 67.

14. Keynes and Lapidge, *Alfred the Great*, p. 75.

15. For this episode (and all quotes), see Keynes and Lapidge, *Alfred the Great*, pp. 89–90.

16. On Alfred's court school and the intellectual pursuits of his children, see Keynes and Lapidge, *Alfred the Great*, pp. 90–1.

17. Keynes and Lapidge, *Alfred the Great*, p. 110.

18. *The Life of King Edward the Confessor who Rests at Westminster*, ed. and trans. Frank Barlow (London: Thomas Nelson and Sons, 1962), p. 3. Subsequent page references will be given in the body of the text.

19. *Encomium Emmae Reginae*, ed. Alistair Campbell (London: Royal Historical Society, 1949). See the author's 'argument', pp. 6–9, which concludes that the discerning reader will understand that 'the course of this book is devoted entirely to the praise of Queen Emma' (p. 9).

20. For more on the representation of Emma and Edith, see Pauline Stafford, 'The Portrayal of Royal Women in England, Mid-Tenth to Mid-Twelfth Centuries', in *Medieval Queenship*, ed. John Carmi Parsons (New York: St. Martin's Press, 1993), pp. 143–67.

21. On Aelred's reworking of the previous lives of Edward, see Katherine TePas Yohe, 'Aelred's Recrafting of the Life of Edward the Confessor', *Cistercian Studies Quarterly* 38 (2003): 177–189.

22. Aelred of Rievaulx, *Life of St. Edward the Confessor*, trans. Jerome Bertram (Southampton, UK: Saint Austin Press, 1990), p. 34. Subsequent page references will be given in the body of the text.

23. John P. Bequette, 'Aelred of Rievaulx's *Life of Saint Edward, King and Confessor*: A Saintly King and the Salvation of the English People', *Cistercian Studies Quarterly* 43 (2008): 17-40.

24. William of Poitiers, *The Gesta Guillelmi of William of Poitiers*, ed. and trans. R. H. C. Davis and Marjorie Chibnall (Oxford: Clarendon Press, 1998), pp. xix-xx. Subsequent page references will be given in the body of the text.

25. On the selectivity of William of Poitiers's account, see David Bates, 'The Conqueror's Earliest Historians and the Writing of his Biography', in Bates, Crick, and Hamilton, *Writing Medieval Biography*, pp. 129-41. Bates hypothesizes that William did not complete his biography because he found it impossible to reconcile the Conqueror's deeds with his ideal of a just prince. See also Emily Albu, *The Normans and their Histories: Propaganda, Myth and Subversion* (Woodbridge, Suffolk: Boydell Press, 2001), pp. 82-8.

26. For discussions of Harold's kingship, and of the *Vita Haroldi*, see the essays in *King Harold II and the Bayeux Tapestry*, ed. Gale R. Owen-Crocker (Woodbridge, Suffolk: Boydell & Brewer, 2005). See especially Stephen Matthews, 'The Content and Construction of the *Vita Haroldi*', who reads the life as secular hagiography (pp. 65-73).

27. 'The Life of King Harold Godwinson', in *Three Lives of the Last Englishmen*, trans. Michael Swanton (New York: Garland, 1984), p. 34. Subsequent page references will be given in the body of the text.

28. Nicholas Vincent has proposed that twelfth-century chroniclers were following Bede when they chose to write of the Plantagenet kings as a collective entity, rather than to compose biographies of individual kings and queens in 'The Strange Case of the Missing Biographies: The Lives of the Plantagenet Kings of England, 1154-1272', in Bates, Crick, and Hamilton, *Writing Medieval Biography*, p. 246.

29. Chris Given-Wilson, *Chronicles: The Writing of History in Medieval England* (London: Hambledon, 2004), p. 157.

30. From King's introduction to William of Malmesbury, *Historia Novella: The Contemporary History*, ed. Edmund King and trans. K. R. Potter (Oxford: Clarendon Press, 1998), p. xxiv. Martin Brett describes the workings of that network of scholars in 'John of Worcester and his Contemporaries', in *The Writing of History in the Middle Ages: Essays Presented to Richard William Southern*, ed. R. H. C. Davis and J. M. Wallace-Hadrill (Oxford: Clarendon Press, 1981), pp. 101-26.

31. Valerie I. J. Flint, 'The *Historia Regum Britanniae* of Geoffrey of Monmouth: Parody and Its Purpose. A Suggestion', *Speculum* 54 (1979): 447-68.

32. R. W. Leckie, Jr, *The Passage of Dominion: Geoffrey of Monmouth and the Periodization of Insular History in the Twelfth Century* (Toronto: University of Toronto Press, 1981); Nancy F. Partner, *Serious Entertainments: The Writing of History in Twelfth-Century England* (Chicago: University of Chicago Press, 1977), pp. 63-8; and Robert W. Hanning, *The Vision of History in Britain from Gildas to Geoffrey of Monmouth* (New York: Columbia University Press, 1966), pp. 121-72.

33. Derek Pearsall, *Arthurian Romance: A Short Introduction* (Oxford: Blackwell, 2003).

34. On William's methods as a historian and on the influence of biography on his approach to writing history, see Gransden, *Historical Writing in England, c. 550–c. 1307*, pp. 166–85.

35. For all quotations and references, I am using William of Malmesbury, *Gesta Regum Anglorum: The History of the English Kings*, ed. and trans. R. A. B. Mynors, completed by R. M. Thomson and M. Winterbottom, 2 vols (Oxford: Clarendon Press, 1998), Vol. 1.

36. Björn Weiler, 'William of Malmesbury on Kingship', *History* 90 (2005): 3–22. For close readings of William's complex portraits, see also Kirsten A. Fenton, *Gender, Nation and Conquest in the Works of William of Malmesbury* (Woodbridge, Suffolk: Boydell and Brewer, 2008).

37. Antonia Gransden discusses the penchant of William and his fellow historians for realistic detail in 'Realistic Observation in Twelfth-Century England', *Speculum* 47 (1972): 29–51.

38. 'The Letter to Warin the Breton', in Henry of Huntingdon, *Historia Anglorum: The History of the English People*, ed. and trans. Diana Greenway (Oxford: Oxford University Press, 1996), p. 559.

39. For an overview of Geoffrey's work, see Michael J. Curley, *Geoffrey of Monmouth* (New York: Twayne, 1994). For studies of Geoffrey's place in medieval British historiography, see Laura Keeler, *Geoffrey of Monmouth and the Late Latin Chroniclers, 1300–1500* (Berkeley, CA: University of California Press, 1946) and the studies of Hanning and Leckie cited in Note 32 of this chapter.

40. For all quotations and line references, I am using Geoffrey of Monmouth, *The History of the Kings of Britain*, ed. and trans. Michael A. Faletra (Plymouth, UK: Broadview Press, 2008), p. 41.

41. In his Introduction to *The History of the Kings of Britain* (pp. 8–36), Faletra provides a good overview of controversies surrounding Geoffrey's writings, including a review of the opinions on his spurious source.

42. Helen Cooper considers some of Geoffrey's contributions in her *The English Romance in Time: Transforming Motifs from Geoffrey of Monmouth to the Death of Shakespeare* (Oxford: Oxford University Press, 2004).

43. Fiona Tolhurst reads Geoffrey's representation of women as 'a response to the political career of Empress Matilda' in *Geoffrey of Monmouth and the Feminist Origin of the Arthurian Legend* (New York: Palgrave, 2012), p. 7, but also as evidence of his 'personal interest' in strong female characters (p. 113).

44. For a succinct overview of Arthurian materials that predate Geoffrey, see Ronald Hutton, 'The Early Arthur: History and Myth', in *The Cambridge Companion to the Arthurian Legend*, ed. Elizabeth Archibald and Ad Putter (Cambridge, UK: Cambridge University Press, 2009), pp. 21–35. For essays exploring facets of Geoffrey of Monmouth's place in the Arthurian tradition, see *The Arthur of Medieval Latin Literature: The Development and Dissemination of the Arthurian Legend in Medieval Latin*, ed. Siân Echard (Cardiff: University of Wales Press, 2011).

45. For an overview of the Celtic materials, see Ceridwen Lloyd-Morgan, 'The Celtic Tradition', in *The Arthur of the English: The Arthurian Legend in Medieval English Life and Literature*, ed. W. R. J. Barron (Cardiff: University of Wales Press, 2001), pp. 1–9.

46. These episodes occur, respectively, in the lives of Padarn, Carannog, and Gildas. For more on Arthur in Welsh saints' lives, see Andrew Breeze, 'Arthur in Early Saints' Lives', in Echard, *The Arthur of Medieval Latin Literature*, pp. 23–44; Jeff Rider, 'Arthur and the

Saints', in *King Arthur through the Ages*, ed. Valerie M. Lagorio and Mildred Leake Day (New York: Garland, 1990); and Siân Echard, *Arthurian Narrative and the Latin Tradition* (Cambridge, UK: Cambridge University Press, 1998), pp. 198-200.

47. Geoffrey is cagey about Arthur's fate—implying at once that he was healed and that he died: 'He was carried away to be healed of his wounds on the isle of Avalon....May his soul rest in peace' (p. 199).

48. Geoffrey's silence about Arthur's private life is not just 'his style' of representing kings. He provides intimate details about many of his other rulers, including Arthur's father, Uther.

49. Richard Barber and Juliet Barker, *Tournaments* (Woodbridge, Suffolk: Boydell Press, 1989), pp. 17-18.

50. On this point, see Laurie A. Finke and Martin Shichtman, *King Arthur and the Myth of History* (Gainesville, FL: University Press of Florida, 2004), pp. 38-46.

51. See Wace and Layamon, *Arthurian Chronicles*, trans. Eugene Mason (Toronto: University of Toronto Press, 1996).

52. For translations of these and other Arthurian romances, see *The Romance of Arthur*, ed. Norris J. Lacy and James J. Wilhelm, 3rd ed. (New York: Routledge, 2013). For a succinct overview of the tradition of Arthurian romance and its relation to Geoffrey, see Pearsall, *Arthurian Romance*.

53. For Caxton's prologue, see Thomas Malory, *Le Morte Darthur*, ed. Stephen H. A. Shepherd (New York: Norton, 2004), pp. 814-19.

54. For more on these lives and chronicles of reigns, see Gransden, *Historical Writing in England, c. 550-c. 1307* and *Historical Writing in England, c. 1307 to the Early Sixteenth Century* (Ithaca, NY: Cornell University Press, 1982).

55. *Gesta Henrici Quinti: The Deeds of Henry the Fifth*, ed. and trans. Frank Taylor and John S. Roskell (Oxford: Clarendon Press, 1975), p. 113 (my emphasis).

56. *Vita Edwardi Secundi: The Life of Edward the Second*, ed. and trans. Wendy R. Childs (Oxford: Clarendon Press, 2005), p. 103.

57. *Gesta Henrici Quinti*, pp. 35, 67.

58. For more information about Blacman, his relationship with Henry VI and members of his circle, and the dating of his *Compilation*, see Rogert Lovatt's essays, 'John Blacman: Biographer of Henry VI', in Davis and Wallace-Hadrill, *The Writing of History in the Middle Ages*, pp. 415-44, and 'A Collector of Apocryphal Anecdotes: John Blacman Revisited', in *Property and Politics: Essays in Later Medieval English History*, ed. Tony Pollard (New York: St. Martin's Press, 1984), pp. 172-97.

59. Blacman may have been inspired in his approach by John Capgrave's brief biography of Henry in his 1446 *Book of the Illustrious Henries*. In striking contrast to his biographies of other monarchs, Capgrave's entry on Henry has little to say about the events of his reign. See my *John Capgrave's Fifteenth Century* (Philadelphia, PA: University of Pennsylvania Press, 2007), pp. 157-61.

60. For all quotations and page references, I am using M. R. James's edition and translation, *Henry the Sixth* (Cambridge, UK: Cambridge University Press, 1919).

61. Lovatt, 'John Blacman', p. 417.

62. Lovatt, 'John Blacman', p. 435.

63. Lovatt, 'John Blacman', p. 438.

64. See Catherine Keene, *Saint Margaret, Queen of the Scots: A Life in Perspective* (New York: Palgrave Macmillan, 2013). Keene translates Turgot's life of Margaret in Appendix A (pp. 135-221). Chapter 7 (pp. 81-93) analyses Turgot's work.

65. Keene, *Saint Margaret*, p. 211.

66. Keene, *Saint Margaret*, p. 183 (my emphasis).

67. Keene, *Saint Margaret*, p. 178.

68. Keene, *Saint Margaret*, p. 189.

69. Keene, *Saint Margaret*, p. 185.

70. Keene, *Saint Margaret*, p. 186.

71. Keene, *Saint Margaret*, p. 186.

72. Thomas Asbridge, *The Greatest Knight: The Remarkable Life of William Marshal, the Power Behind Five English Thrones* (New York: Ecco, 2014). For earlier biographies, see David Crouch, *William Marshal: Knighthood, War and Chivalry, 1147-1219* (London: Longman, 2002); Georges Duby, *William Marshal: The Flower of Chivalry*, trans. Richard Howard (New York: Pantheon, 1986); Jesse R. Raven, *William the Marshal: The Last Great Feudal Baron* (London: P. Owen, 1962); Sidney Painter, *William Marshal: Knight-errant, Baron, and Regent of England* (Baltimore, MD: Johns Hopkins University Press, 1933); Thomas L. Jarman, *William Marshal: First Earl of Pembroke and Regent of England* (Oxford: Blackwell, 1930). Marshal's life has also inspired a tetralogy of novels by Elizabeth Chadwick; see Note 80 of this chapter.

73. On the period and its conflicts, see Robert Bartlett, *England under the Norman and Angevin Kings, 1075-1225* (Oxford: Oxford University Press, 2000).

74. In lines 19,195-6, the author identifies himself as 'John' and in line 11,101 claims to be a professional writer. For all references and quotations, I am using *The History of William Marshal*, ed. A. J. Holden, trans. S. Gregory, Anglo-Norman Text Society, Occasional Publications Series 4-6 (London: Anglo-Norman Text Society, 2002, 2004, 2006).

75. Examples of such romances include *Cligès* by Chrétien de Troyes and *Parzival* by Wolfram von Eschenbach.

76. David Crouch discusses what can be deduced about him in 'Writing a Biography in the Thirteenth Century: The Construction and Composition of the "History of William Marshal"', in Bates, Crick, and Hamilton, *Writing Medieval Biography*, pp. 221-35.

77. Compare his obtrusiveness with Chandos Herald's relative reticence in his *Life of the Black Prince*, composed between 1376 and 1387. *The Life and Campaigns of the Black Prince*, ed. and trans. Richard Barber (Woodbridge, Suffolk: Boydell Press, 1979), pp. 84-139.

78. John bears a particular resemblance to the garrulous 'Master Heldris' who narrates the roughly contemporary *Romance of Silence*.

79. Crouch, *William Marshal*, pp. 2-3.

80. That first edition was published by Paul Meyer, who discovered the manuscript at a Sotheby's sale room in 1861. See *L'Histoire de Guillaume le Maréchal, comte de Striguil et de Pembroke*, ed. Paul Meyer, 3 vols. (Paris: Librairie Renouard, H. Laurens, successeur, 1891-1901). For the story of the work's discovery, see Crouch, *William Marshal*, p. 3. See the biographies cited in Note 72 of this chapter by Asbridge, Crouch, Duby, Raven, Painter, and Jarman; the William Marshal quartet was written by Elizabeth Chadwick: *A Place Beyond Courage* (London: Sphere, 2007), *The Greatest Knight* (New York: Time Warner, 2005), *The Scarlet Lion* (Boston, MA: Little, Brown & Co., 2006), and *To Defy a King* (London: Sphere, 2010).

Chapter 4

1. Cuthbert of Jarrow, 'Letter on the Death of Bede', in Bede, *Ecclesiastical History of the English People*, ed. Bertram Colgrave and R. A. B. Mynors (Oxford: Clarendon Press, 1969), pp. 579-87.

2. Cuthbert, 'Letter', p. 585.

3. Cuthbert, 'Letter', p. 585.

4. For a guide to Bede's life and oeuvre, see George Hardin Brown, *A Companion to Bede* (Woodbridge, Suffolk: Boydell Press, 2009). On Bede's reputation, see Antonia Gransden, 'Bede's Reputation as an Historian in Medieval England', *Journal of Ecclesiastical History* 32 (1981): 397-425; Joyce Hill, 'Carolingian Perspectives on the Authority of Bede', in *Innovation and Tradition in the Writings of the Venerable Bede*, ed. Scott DeGregorio (Morgantown, WV: West Virginia University Press, 2006), pp. 227-49; and Malcolm B. Parkes, 'The Scriptorium of Wearmouth-Jarrow', in *Scribes, Scripts, and Readers: Studies in the Communication, Presentation, and Dissemination of Medieval Texts* (London: Hambledon, 1991).

5. Cuthbert, 'Letter', p. 587.

6. Bede, *Ecclesiastical History*, Book 4, Chapter 24.

7. Bede, *Ecclesiastical History*, p. 304.

8. William of Malmesbury, *Gesta Regum Anglorum: The History of the English Kings*, ed. and trans. R. A. B. Mynors, completed by R. M. Thomson and M. Winterbottom, 2 vols (Oxford: Clarendon Press, 1998), Vol. 1: p. 507.

9. William of Malmesbury, *Gesta Regum Anglorum*, Book 1, Chapters 54-62.

10. Symeon of Durham, *Libellus de Exordio atque procursu istius, hoc est Dunhelmensis ecclesie: Tract on the Origins and Progress of this the Church of Durham*, ed. and trans. David Rollason (Oxford: Clarendon Press, 2000), pp. 65-77.

11. William of Malmesbury, *Gesta Regum Anglorum*, Book 5, Chapter 439. For more on William IX, known as the first troubadour, and his poetry, see *The Poetry of William VII, Count of Poitiers, IX Duke of Aquitaine*, ed. and trans. Gerald A. Bond (New York: Garland, 1982).

12. John Capgrave, *Abbreuiacion of Chronicles*, ed. Peter J. Lucas, Early English Text Society OS 285 (Oxford: Oxford University Press, 1983), p. 44 (my translation).

13. John Capgrave, *Book of the Illustrious Henries*, trans. Francis Charles Hingeston (London: Longman, 1858).

14. I discuss Capgrave's representation of Augustine as scholar and author with reference to other treatments of the Church Father in *John Capgrave's Fifteenth Century* (Philadelphia, PA: University of Pennsylvania Press, 2007), pp. 22-31 (quote at p. 31).

15. For an introduction to this fascinating genre, see Elizabeth W. Poe, 'The *Vidas* and *Razos*', in *A Handbook of the Troubadours*, ed. F. R. P. Akehurst and Judith M. Davis (Berkeley, CA: University of California Press, 1995), pp. 185-97. For translations into modern English, see *The Vidas of the Troubadours*, trans. Margarita Egan (New York: Garland, 1984).

16. Egan, *Vidas of the Troubadours*, pp. 61 (Jaufre Rudel) and 31 (Elias Cairel).

17. Egan, *Vidas of the Troubadours*, p. 81 (Peire de Valeira).

18. Paul Zumthor discusses the authors' interpretation of the conventional 'I' of lyric poetry as an autobiographical 'I' in 'Autobiography in the Middle Ages?' *Genre* 6 (1973): 29-48.

19. For translations of troubadour lyrics with their *razos* and *vidas*, see *Proensa: An Anthology of Troubadour Poetry*, ed. George Economou, trans. Paul Blackburn (Berkeley, CA: University of California Press, 1978).

20. Poe, 'The *Vidas* and *Razos*', pp. 190–1.

21. Egan, *Vidas of the Troubadours*, pp. 109–11. Uc's *vida* of Bernart de Ventadorn is one of only two signed *vidas*; the other is the *vida* of Peire Cardenal by Miquel de la Tor.

22. For these conjoinings, see Economou, *Proensa*.

23. Poe, 'The *Vidas* and *Razos*', p. 188.

24. For example, Osbern Bokenham praises the rhetorical skill of John Lydgate, 'who is still alive unless he died recently'. See Osbern Bokenham, *A Legend of Holy Women*, trans. Sheila Delany (Notre Dame, IN: University of Notre Dame Press, 1992), p. 10 (lines 416–18).

25. For a consideration of the probable commercial motives underlying Shirley's projects, see A. S. G. Edwards, 'John Shirley, John Lydgate, and the Motives of Compilation', *Studies in the Age of Chaucer* 38 (2016): 245–54. This essay forms part of a cluster of essays that shed new light on Shirley's undertakings, with contributions by Megan Cook and Elizabeta Strakhov, Kathryn Veeman, Julia Boffey, Kara Doyle, Stephanie Downes, and R. D. Perry: 'Colloquium: John Shirley's Cambridge, Trinity College, MS R. 3.20 and the Culture of the Anthology in Late Medieval England', *Studies in the Age of Chaucer* 38 (2016): 241–308. For more on Shirley's life and career, see Margaret Connolly, *John Shirley: Book Production and the Noble Household in Fifteenth-Century England* (Aldershot, UK: Ashgate, 1998).

26. See R. D. Perry's fascinating discussion of Shirley's construction in his headnotes of 'virtual coteries' constituted from 'mutually supportive' 'imaginary and real networks' of authors, patrons, and readers in 'The Earl of Suffolk's French Poems and Shirley's Virtual Coteries', *Studies in the Age of Chaucer* 38 (2016): 299–308 (quote at p. 308).

27. Richard D. Altick, *Lives and Letters: A History of Literary Biography in England and America* (New York: Knopf, 1965), pp. 3–4.

28. Bede, *Ecclesiastical History*, p. 567.

29. *The Ecclesiastical History of Orderic Vitalis*, 6 vols., ed. and trans. Marjorie Chibnall (Oxford: Clarendon Press, 1968–80), Vol. 6: pp. 551–7.

30. William of Malmesbury, *Gesta Regum Anglorum*, Vol. 1: p. 151.

31. William of Malmesbury, *Gesta Regum Anglorum*, Vol. 1: p. 541.

32. On Petrarch's autobiographical writings, see Nicholas Mann, 'From Laurel to Fig: Petrarch and the Structures of the Self', *Proceedings of the British Academy* 105 (2000): 17–49. Mann writes, 'The whole body of texts that Petrarch has left behind…together constitutes a unique and fascinating autobiographical project' (p. 42).

33. For an overview of Petrarch's career, see Thomas G. Bergin, *Petrarch* (New York: Twayne, 1970); Morris Bishop, *Petrarch and His World* (Bloomington, IN: Indiana University Press, 1963); and Nicholas Mann, *Petrarch* (Oxford: Oxford University Press, 1984).

34. Francesco Petrarch, *Petrarch: The First Modern Scholar and Man of Letters*, ed. and trans. James Harvey Robinson (New York: G. P. Putnam, 1898), pp. 59–76, quote at p. 69.

35. Petrarch, *First Modern Scholar*, ed. and trans. Robinson, p. 64.

36. For more on this important work and its context, see Hans Baron, *Petrarch's Secretum: Its Making and Its Meaning* (Cambridge, MA: Medieval Academy of America, 1985).

37. Studies of Boethius's influence in the Middle Ages include John Marenbon, *Boethius* (Oxford: Oxford University Press, 2003) and Margaret T. Gibson, *Boethius: His Life, Thought, and Influence* (Oxford: Blackwell, 1981).

38. Augustine, *Confessions*, ed. and trans. R. S. Pine-Coffin (New York: Penguin, 1961), p. 170.

39. Francesco Petrarch, *The Secret*, trans. Carol E. Quillen (Boston, MA: Bedford/St. Martin's, 2003), p. 47. I am using this translation for all subsequent quotations and parenthetical references. Hans Baron claims that 'Petrarch's alleged intention to write for himself' is 'more than a rhetorical artifice' in *Petrarch's Secretum*, pp. 185-214 (quote at p. 195).

40. Discussions of Boethius's influence on Christine include Glynnis M. Cropp, 'Boèce et Christine de Pizan', *Le Moyen Âge* 87 (1981): 387-417, and Benjamin Semple, 'The Consolation of a Woman Writer: Christine de Pizan's Use of Boethius in *L'Avision-Christine*', in *Women, the Book, and the Worldly: Selected Proceedings of the St. Hilda's Conference, 1993*, ed. Lesley Smith and Jane H. M. Taylor, Vol. 2 (Cambridge, UK: D. S. Brewer, 1995), pp. 39-48.

41. For an overview of Christine's life and career, see Charity Cannon Willard's classic biography, *Christine de Pizan: Her Life and Works* (New York: Persea, 1984). For a more recent reassessment, see Françoise Autrand, *Christine de Pizan: Une femme en politique* (Paris: Fayard, 2009) and Suzanne Roux, *Christine de Pizan: Femme de tête, dame de cœur* (Paris: Payot, 2006). See also Leslie Altman, 'Christine de Pisan: First Professional Woman of Letters', in *Female Scholars: A Tradition of Learned Women before 1800*, ed. J. R. Brink (Montreal: Eden, 1980), pp. 7-23.

42. For quotations and page references, I use *The Vision of Christine de Pizan*, trans. Glenda McLeod and Charity Cannon Willard (Woodbridge, Suffolk: D. S. Brewer, 2005). Glenda McLeod's 'Interpretive Essay' (pp. 135-58) discusses the overall themes and structures of the *Vision*. Studies of the *Vision* as autobiography include Jean-Philippe Breaulieu, '*L'Avision Christine* ou la tentation autobiographique', *Littératures* 18 (1998): 15-30; Liliane Dulac and Christine Reno, 'The *Livre de ladvision Cristine*', in *Christine de Pizan: A Casebook*, ed. Barbara K. Altmann and Deborah L. McGrady (New York: Rutledge, 2003), pp. 199-214; and Mary L. Skemp, 'Autobiography and Authority in *Lavision-Christine*', *Le Moyen français* 35 (1996): 17-31.

43. The original French reads: 'Et non obstant que a l'usaige des philosophes fust nulle l'espargne de la pecune et avoir de mon dit pere—laquelle chose, sauve sa reverence, je ne repute cure de leur maisnage, souffraiteux après eulx puet ester a cause de leur prodigalité—toutesvoie, non obstant la liberalité de ses coustumes, la pourveance du bon roy ne laissoit a l'ostel de son amé deffaillir nulle chose neccessaire', *Le Livre de l'Advision Cristine* (Paris: Champion, 2001), p. 97.

44. Discussions of Christine's (much disputed) feminism include Rosalind Brown-Grant, *Christine de Pizan and the Moral Defence of Women: Reading Beyond Gender* (Cambridge, UK: Cambridge University Press, 1999); Mary Anne Case, 'Christine de Pizan and the Authority of Experience', in *Christine de Pizan and the Categories of Difference*, ed. Marilynn Desmond (Minneapolis, MN: University of Minnesota Press, 1998), pp. 71-87; Sheila Delany, '"Mothers To Think Back Through": Who Are They? The Ambiguous Example of Christine de Pizan', in *Medieval Texts and Contemporary Readers*, ed. Laurie Finke and

Martin Schichtman (Ithaca, NY: Cornell University Press, 1987), pp. 312–38; Christine Reno, 'Christine de Pizan: At Best a Contradictory Figure?' in *Politics, Gender and Genre: The Political Thought of Christine de Pizan*, ed. Margaret Brabant (Boulder, CO: Westview, 1992), pp. 171–91; and Joan Kelly, 'Early Feminist Theory and the *Querelle des Femmes* 1400–1789', *Signs* 8 (1982): 4–28.

45. Thomas L. Reed, *Middle English Debate Poetry and the Aesthetics of Irresolution* (Columbia, MO: University of Missouri Press, 1990).

46. A number of these autobiographical prologues can be found in *The Idea of the Vernacular: An Anthology of Middle English Literary Theory, 1280–1520*, ed. Jocelyn Wogan-Browne, Nicholas Watson, Andrew Taylor, and Ruth Evans (University Park, PA: Pennsylvania State University Press, 1999).

47. For a translation of Paris's 'Christine', see *Chaste Passions: Medieval English Virgin Martyr Legends*, ed. and trans. Karen A. Winstead (Ithaca, NY: Cornell University Press, 2000), pp. 61–9. For the original Middle English text, see the edition by Sherry L. Reames in her *Middle English Legends of Women Saints* (Kalamazoo, MI: Medieval Institute Publications, 2003), available online at http://d.lib.rochester.edu/teams/text/reames-middle-english-legends-of-women-saints-life-of-st-christina. For more on Paris, see Gordon Hall Gerould, 'The Legend of St. Christina by William Paris', *Modern Language Notes* 29 (1914): 129–33, and Mary-Ann Stouck, 'A Poet in the Household of the Beauchamp Earls of Warwick, c. 1393–1427', *Warwickshire History* 9 (1994): 113–17. On how Paris's circumstances might have inspired his choice of Christine as a subject and his treatment of her story, see Karen A. Winstead, *Virgin Martyrs: Legends of Sainthood in Late Medieval England* (Ithaca, NY: Cornell University Press, 1997), pp. 103–4.

48. Both versions of Julian's vision can be found in *The Writings of Julian of Norwich*, ed. Nicholas Watson and Jacqueline Jenkins (University Park, PA: Pennsylvania State University Press, 2006). On Julian's writing as autobiography, see Mary G. Mason, 'The Other Voice: Autobiographies of Women Writers', in *Autobiography: Essays Theoretical and Critical*, ed. James Olney (Princeton, NJ: Princeton University Press, 1980), pp. 207–35, and Christopher Abbott, *Julian of Norwich: Autobiography and Theology* (Woodbridge, Suffolk: D. S. Brewer, 1999).

49. See the 'postscript' to Garnier of Pont-Sainte-Maxence, *Garnier's Becket*, trans. Janet Shirley (London: Phillimore, 1975), p. 164. For more on Garnier's *Becket*, see Chapter One, pp. 28–31.

50. William of Malmesbury, *Gesta Regum Anglorum*, Vol. 1: p. 9. Subsequent quotes in this paragraph are also on p. 9.

51. For discussions of Bokenham and his patrons, see Gail Gibson, 'Saint Anne and the Religion of Childbed: Some East Anglian Texts and Talismans', in *Interpreting Cultural Symbols: Saint Anne in Late Medieval Society*, ed. Kathleen Ashley and Pamela Sheingorn (Athens, GA: University of Georgia Press, 1990), pp. 95–110; Sheila Delany, *Impolitic Bodies: Poetry, Saints, and Society in Fifteenth-Century England* (Oxford: Oxford University Press, 1998); and Simon Horobin, 'Politics, Patronage, and Piety in the Work of Osbern Bokenham', *Speculum* 82 (2007): 932–49.

52. Osbern Bokenham, *A Legend of Holy Women*, trans. Delany, p. 5. I am using Delany's translation for all subsequent quotations and page references.

53. Though Bokenham deleted his autobiographical prologues and epilogues, references within the legends to his visits to saints' shrines remain, as Simon Horobin discusses in 'Politics, Patronage, and Piety', pp. 938-40.

54. On the debt to Chaucer of what he terms Bokenham's 'autographic' passages, see A. C. Spearing, *Medieval Autographies: The 'I' of the Text* (Notre Dame, IN: University of Notre Dame Press, 2012), pp. 209-56. For Spearing, Chaucer is 'clearly the champion medieval prologuizer' (p. 39).

55. Much of the documentation is conveniently collected for us in the 650 pages of M. M. Crow and C. C. Olson's *Chaucer Life Records* (Oxford: Oxford University Press, 1966). Chaucer biographies based on these records (and, of course, a reading of his works) include Derek Pearsall, *The Life of Geoffrey Chaucer: A Critical Biography* (Oxford: Blackwell, 1992); Paul Strohm, *Chaucer's Tale: 1386 and the Road to Canterbury* (New York: Viking, 2014); and, more speculatively, Donald R. Howard, *Chaucer: His Life, His Works, His World* (New York: Dutton, 1987).

56. Pearsall, *The Life of Geoffrey Chaucer*, pp. 135-8; Christopher Cannon, '*Raptus* in the Chaumpaigne Release and a Newly Discovered Document Concerning the Life of Geoffrey Chaucer', *Speculum* 68 (1993): 74-94. For an overview of the controversy and a discussion of critics' intense investment in whether Chaucer was or was not a rapist, see Susan S. Morrison, 'The Use of Biography in Medieval Literary Criticism: The Case of Geoffrey Chaucer and Cecily Chaumpaigne', *Chaucer Review* 34 (1999): 69-86.

57. On Chaucer's strategies for engaging in social and political issues, see Paul Strohm, *Social Chaucer* (Cambridge, MA: Harvard University Press, 1989).

58. For a discussion of approaches to Chaucer's narrative voice and a corrective to the tendency to transform that voice into 'a full-blown fallible narrator', see A. C. Spearing, *Textual Subjectivity: The Encoding of Subjectivity in Medieval Narratives and Lyrics* (Oxford: Oxford University Press, 2005), especially pp. 69-136, quote at p. 69. Spearing revisits the issue of Chaucer's 'I' in *Medieval Autographies*.

59. The tale's strength is in its awfulness. Helen Cooper calls it 'a brilliant parody of everything that can go wrong with' the tail-rhyme romances that were popular in his day, at once 'doggerel that writes Chaucer out of the competition and a technical masterpiece'. See *Oxford Guides to Chaucer: The Canterbury Tales* (Oxford: Oxford University Press, 1989), pp. 301, 308.

60. On the social context for Chaucer's *Book of the Duchess*, see Michael Foster, 'On Dating the Duchess: The Personal and Social Context of *Book of the Duchess*', *Review of English Studies* 59 (2008): 185-96, and *Oxford Guides to Chaucer: The Shorter Poems*, ed. Alastair J. Minnis, with V. J. Scattergood and J. J. Smith (Oxford: Clarendon Press, 1995), pp. 73-160.

61. Geoffrey Chaucer, *The Riverside Chaucer*, ed. Larry D. Benson, 3rd ed. (Boston, MA: Houghton Mifflin, 1987), p. 661.

62. For a fascinating discussion of domestic violence in the *Wife of Bath's Prologue*, see Elaine Tuttle Hansen, '"Of his love daungerous to me": Liberation, Subversion, and Domestic Violence in *The Wife of Bath's Prologue and Tale*', in *The Wife of Bath*, ed. Peter G. Beidler (Boston, MA: Bedford/St. Martin's, 1996), pp. 273-89.

63. Hansen raises this question in '"Of his love"'.

64. See, for example, Strohm, *Social Chaucer*.

65. On the pitfalls of attributing Chaucer's first-person addresses to a fallible narrator, see Spearing, *Textual Subjectivity*.

66. For a useful survey of the controversy over the 'Retraction', see Peter Travis, 'Deconstructing Chaucer's Retraction', *Exemplaria* 3 (1991): 135-58.

67. John Metham, *Amoryus and Cleopes*, ed. Stephen F. Page (Kalamazoo, MI: Medieval Institute Publications, 1999), ll. 57-70.

68. On Hoccleve's vocal (and self-serving) admiration for Chaucer, see David R. Carlson, 'Thomas Hoccleve and the Chaucer Portrait', *Huntington Library Quarterly* 54 (1991): 283-300.

69. On the resemblance of Hoccleve's persona to Chaucer's, see D. C. Greetham, 'Self-Referential Artifacts: Hoccleve's Persona as a Literary Device', *Modern Philology* 86 (1989): 242-51. For a provocative discussion of Hoccleve's departure from the Chaucerian model, see Sarah Tolmie, 'The Professional Thomas Hoccleve', *Studies in the Age of Chaucer* 29 (2007): 341-73.

70. For a Middle English edition, see *Hoccleve's Works: The Minor Poems*, ed. Frederick J. Furnivall and I. Gollancz, revised by Jerome Mitchell and A. I. Doyle, Early English Text Society ES 61 and 73 (London: Oxford University Press, 1970), pp. 25-39. On Hoccleve's writing as autobiographical, see John Burrow, 'Autobiographical Poetry in the Middle Ages: The Case of Thomas Hoccleve', *Proceedings of the British Academy* 68 (1982): 389-412, and Stephen Medcalf, 'Inner and Outer', in *The Later Middle Ages*, ed. Stephen Medcalf (New York: Holmes and Meier, 1981), pp. 108-71. On the hybridity of the *Male Regle*, see Craig E. Bertolet, 'Social Corrections: Hoccleve's *La Male Regle* and Textual Identity', *Papers in Language and Literature* 51 (2015): 269-98.

71. For a succinct study of Hoccleve's career as an author and a bureaucrat, see John A. Burrow, *Thomas Hoccleve* (Aldershot, UK: Ashgate, 1994). See also Ethan Knapp, *The Bureaucratic Muse: Thomas Hoccleve and the Literature of Late Medieval England* (University Park, PA: Pennsylvania State University Press, 2001); John Bowers, 'Thomas Hoccleve and the Politics of Tradition', *Chaucer Review* 36.4 (2002): 352-69; and Tolmie, 'The Professional Thomas Hoccleve'.

72. On Hoccleve's 'ingenuous' deployment of conventions associated with the penitential lyric and the parodic qualities of his *Male Regle*, see Eva M. Thornley, 'The Middle English Penitential Lyric and Hoccleve's Autobiographical Poetry', *Neuphilologische Mitteilungen* 68 (1967): 295-321, quote at p. 321.

73. On the chronology of Hoccleve's begging poems, see Burrow, *Thomas Hoccleve*, pp. 12-13. Begging figures so prominently in Hoccleve's poetry that Robert J. Meyer-Lee has dubbed him the 'beggar laureate' of the Lancastrian court in *Poets and Power from Chaucer to Wyatt* (Cambridge, UK: Cambridge University Press, 2007), p. 88.

74. 'Balade to my Lord the Chancellor' and 'Balade...a Sire Henri Sommer, Chaunceller de leschequer', Hoccleve, *Hoccleve's Works*, pp. 58, 64-6.

75. 'Item au Roy', Hoccleve, *Hoccleve's Works*, p. 62.

76. 'Balade to my Maister Carpenter', Hoccleve, *Hoccleve's Works*, pp. 63-4.

77. On this important literary genre, see Judith Ferster, *Fictions of Advice: The Literature and Politics of Counsel in Late Medieval England* (Philadelphia, PA: University of Pennsylvania Press, 1996). For a discussion of money as an 'imaginative vehicle' in Hoccleve's poetry, see Robert J. Meyer-Lee, 'Hoccleve and the Apprehension of Money', *Exemplaria* 13.1 (2001):

173-214 (quote at p. 183). For Meyer-Lee, the *Regiment of Princes* is 'a thematically more capacious and emotionally more urgent version of *La Male Regle*'; where the *Male Regle* is 'a petition masquerading as penitence', the *Regiment* is 'a petition masquerading as advice' (pp. 194, 200). For an extended study of the *Regiment*, see Nicholas Perkins, *Hoccleve's Regiment of Princes: Counsel and Constraint* (Cambridge, UK: D. S. Brewer, 2001).

78. On Middle English debate poetry, see the study of Reed, cited in Note 45 of this chapter.

79. For some of the varied views of the autobiographical prologue's relation to the mirror for princes, see Greetham, 'Self-Referential Artifacts'; Derek Pearsall, 'Hoccleve's *Regement of Princes*: The Poetics of Royal Self-Representation', *Speculum* 69 (1994): 386-410; and James Simpson, 'Nobody's Man: Thomas Hoccleve's *Regement of Princes*', in *London and Europe in the Later Middle Ages*, ed. Julia Boffey and Pamela King (London: Centre for Medieval and Renaissance Studies, Queen Mary and Westfield College, 1995), pp. 149-80.

80. I discuss this contest of wills at greater length in '"I am al other to yow than yee weene": Hoccleve, Women, and the *Series*', *Philological Quarterly* 72 (1999): 143-55.

81. Derek Pearsall, *Old and Middle English Poetry* (London: Routledge, 1977), p. 237.

82. David Watt, 'Compilation and Contemplation: Beholding Thomas Hoccleve's *Series* in Oxford, Bodleian Library, MS Selden Supra 53', *Journal of the Early Book Society* 14 (2011): 1-39 (quote at p. 1).

83. Christina von Nolcken, '"O, why ne had y lerned for to die?": *Lerne for to Dye* and the Author's Death in Thomas Hoccleve's *Series*', *Essays in Medieval Studies* 10 (1993): 27-51.

84. John Burrow, 'Hoccleve's *Series*: Experience and Books', in *Fifteenth-Century Studies: Recent Essays*, ed. Robert F. Yeager (Hamden, CT: Archon Books, 1984), pp. 259-74.

85. Matthew Boyd Goldie, 'Psychosomatic Illness and Identity in London, 1416-1421: Hoccleve's Complaint and Dialogue with a Friend', *Exemplaria* 11 (1999): 23-52 (quote at p. 23).

86. Marion Turner, 'Illness Narratives in the Later Middle Ages: Arderne, Chaucer, and Hoccleve', *Journal of Medieval and Early Modern Studies* 46 (2016): 61-87 (quotes at pp. 69 and 72).

87. Sebastian James Langdell, '"What world is this? How vndirstande am I?" A Reappraisal of Poetic Authority in Thomas Hoccleve's *Series*', *Medium Ævum* 78 (2009): 281-99 (quote at p. 284).

88. Greetham, 'Self-Referential Artifacts'.

89. Rory G. Critten, '"Her heed they caste awry": The Transmission and Reception of Thomas Hoccleve's Personal Poetry', *Review of English Studies*, n.s., 64 (2012): 386-409.

90. Critten, 'Transmission and Reception'.

91. Critten, 'Transmission and Reception', p. 390.

92. M. C. Seymour, 'The Manuscripts of Hoccleve's *Regiment of Princes*', *Transactions of the Edinburgh Bibliographical Society* 4 (1974): 255-97.

93. Seymour, 'Manuscripts', p. 255. According to Seymour, only one of the manuscripts omitted the dialogue 'perhaps by design' (p. 280).

94. On wills as a genre of autobiography and on their conventions, see Gail McMurray Gibson, *The Theater of Devotion: East Anglian Drama and Society in the Late Middle Ages* (Chicago: University of Chicago Press, 1989), pp. 67-104. For her discussion of Lydgate's use of testamentary conventions, see pp. 89-90. See also Julia Boffey, 'Lydgate, Henryson, and the Literary Testament', *Modern Language Quarterly* 53 (1992): 41-56.

95. For discussions of Usk's politics and writing, see Paul Strohm, 'Politics and Poetics', in *Literary Practice and Social Change in Britain, 1380-1530*, ed. Lee Patterson (Berkeley, CA: University of California Press, 1990), pp. 83-112, and Marion Turner, *Chaucerian Conflict: Languages of Antagonism in Late Fourteenth-Century London* (Oxford: Clarendon Press, 2007), pp. 93-126. Gary W. Shawver surveys Usk's life in the introduction to his edition of Usk's *Testament of Love* (Toronto: University of Toronto Press, 2002), pp. 7-24.

96. On Usk's remarkable 'Appeal', see Paul Strohm, 'The Textual Vicissitudes of Usk's "Appeal"', in *Hochon's Arrow: The Social Imagination of Fourteenth-Century Texts* (Princeton, NJ: Princeton University Press, 1992), pp. 145-57.

97. On Usk's use of Boethius, as translated by Chaucer, see David Carlson, 'Chaucer's Boethius and Thomas Usk's *Testament of Love*: Politics and Love in the Chaucerian Tradition', in *The Centre and Its Compass: Studies in Medieval Literature in Honor of John Leyerle*, ed. Robert A. Taylor, James F. Burke, Patricia J. Eberle, Ian Lancashire, and Brian Merriless (Kalamazoo, MI: Western Michigan University Press, 1993), pp. 29-70.

98. On the significance of 'Margaret', a traditional symbol of purity, see S. K. Heninger, Jr, 'The Margarite-Pearl Allegory in Thomas Usk's *Testament of Love*', *Speculum* 32 (1957): 92-8. On a possible human model for 'Margaret', see Lucy Lewis, 'The Identity of Margaret in Thomas Usk's *Testament of Love*', *Medium Ævum* 68 (1999): 63-72.

99. Strohm, 'Politics and Poetics', p. 103.

100. Strohm, 'Politics and Poetics'.

101. Thomas Usk, *The Testament of Love*, ed. R. Allen Shoaf (Kalamazoo, MI: Medieval Institute Publications, 1998), pp. 3, 7.

102. On the long-lasting consequences of Usk's association with Chaucer, see Thomas A. Prendergast, 'Chaucer's Doppelgänger: Thomas Usk and the Reformation of Chaucer', in *Rewriting Chaucer: Culture, Authority, and the Idea of the Authentic Text, 1400-1602*, ed. Thomas A. Prendergast and Barbara Kline (Columbus, OH: Ohio State University Press, 1999), pp. 258-69.

103. Meyer-Lee, *Poets and Power*, p. 38.

104. For an overview of Lydgate's life and times, see Derek Pearsall, *John Lydgate* (Charlottesville, VA: University Press of Virginia, 1970), pp. 22-48.

105. There is no translation into modern English of Lydgate's *Testament*. I am citing lines and translating from the second edition of John Lydgate, *The Minor Poems of John Lydgate*, ed. Henry Noble MacCracken, Early English Text Society ES 107 (London: Oxford University Press, 1962), pp. 329-62.

106. John A. Burrow discusses Lydgate's use of a standard 'schema' as 'a framework within which the details of individual experience could be observed and understood' in *The Ages of Man: A Study in Medieval Writing and Thought* (Oxford: Clarendon Press, 1986), pp. 32-3.

107. Ruth Nisse, '"Was it not routhe to Se?": Lydgate and the Styles of Martyrdom', in *John Lydgate: Poetry, Culture, and Lancastrian England*, ed. Larry Scanlon and James Simpson (Notre Dame, IN: University of Notre Dame Press, 2006), p. 293.

108. James Simpson, *Reform and Cultural Revolution* (Oxford: Oxford University Press, 2002), p. 456.

109. Boffey, 'Literary Testament', p. 48.

110. W. H. E. Sweet, 'Lydgate's Retraction and "his resorte to his religyoun"', in *After Arundel: Religious Writing in Fifteenth-Century England*, ed. Vincent Gillespie and Kantik Ghosh (Turnhout, Belgium: Brepols, 2011), pp. 343-59.

111. James Simpson writes that in the final section of the *Testament*, 'Christ deletes Lydgate's biography' and 'Lydgate's own life has been absorbed by Christ's', in *Reform and Cultural Revolution*, p. 456.

112. Sebastian Sobecki, 'Lydgate's Kneeling Retraction: The *Testament* as a Literary Palinode', *Chaucer Review* 49 (2015): 265-93.

113. See Boffey's discussion of these manuscripts in 'Literary Testament'.

114. Boffey, 'Literary Testament', pp. 49-50.

115. Altick, *Lives and Letters*, p. 11.

116. Spearing, *Medieval Autographies*, p. 133. On Hoccleve's 'collected works', see John Bowers, 'Hoccleve Holographs', *Fifteenth-Century Studies* 15 (1989): 27-49.

Chapter 5

1. I am using Felice Lifshitz's translation in *Medieval Hagiography: An Anthology*, ed. Thomas Head (New York: Garland Publishing, 2000, pp. 179-97. In her introduction (pp. 169-77), Lifshitz surveys the genre of the martyrology and discusses Bede's innovations.

2. For a facing page edition/translation, see Christine Rauer's *The Old English Martyrology* (Cambridge, UK: D. S. Brewer, 2013).

3. For more on patterns in the Old English martyrologist's approach to female sanctity, see the following essays in *Writing Women Saints in Anglo-Saxon England*, ed. Paul Szarmach (Toronto: University of Toronto Press, 2014): Christine Rauer, 'Female Hagiography in the *Old English Martyrology*', pp. 13-29, and Jacqueline Stodnick, 'Bodies of Land: The Place of Gender in the *Old English Martyrology*', pp. 30-52.

4. For the Old English text with facing translation into modern English, see Ælfric, *Lives of Saints*, ed. Walter W. Skeat, 2 vols., Early English Text Society OS 76, 82, 94, 114 (London: N. Trubner, 1881-1900). For a general introduction to Ælfric, his writings, and his milieu, see James R. Hurt, *Ælfric* (New York: Twayne, 1972). For an introduction to the *South English Legendary*, see *Rethinking the South English Legendaries*, ed. Heather Blurton and Jocelyn Wogan-Browne (Manchester: Manchester University Press, 2011).

5. Ælfric, *Lives of Saints*, p. 117, lines 2-8.

6. *The South English Legendary*, ed. Charlotte D'Evelyn and Anna J. Mill, 3 vols., Early English Text Society OS 235, 236, 244 (Oxford: Oxford University Press, 1956, 1959), Vol. 1: p. 16, line 1.

7. On Ælfric's ambivalence towards miracles, see Malcolm Godden, 'Ælfric's Saints' Lives and the Problem of Miracles', *Leeds Studies in English* 16 (1985): 83-101. I discuss the *South English Legendary*'s approach to sainthood, as demonstrated in its virgin martyr legends, in *Virgin Martyrs: Legends of Sainthood in Late Medieval England* (Ithaca, NY: Cornell University Press, 1997), pp. 71-8.

8. On the antiworldly ideal of saintly perfection promoted in the *Legenda aurea*, see Sherry L. Reames, *The Legenda Aurea: A Reexamination of its Paradoxical History* (Madison, WI: University of Wisconsin Press, 1985).

9. On the popularity and transmission of these works, see Blurton and Wogan-Browne, *Rethinking the South English Legendaries* and Reames, *The Legenda Aurea*.

10. For the process of revision in manuscripts of the *South English Legendary*, see Blurton and Wogan-Browne, *Rethinking the South English Legendaries*.

11. I discuss Bokenham's adaptation of Jacobus in 'Osbern Bokenham's "englische boke": Re-forming Holy Women', in *Form and Reform: Reading Across the Fifteenth Century*, ed. Shannon Gayk and Kathleen Tonry (Columbus, OH: Ohio State University Press, 2011), pp. 67–87. For other studies of Bokenham's *Golden Legend*, see Simon Horobin, 'Politics, Patronage, and Piety in the Work of Osbern Bokenham', *Speculum* 82 (2007): 932–49, and Alice Spencer, *Language, Lineage and Location in the Works of Osbern Bokenham* (Newcastle, UK: Cambridge Scholars, 2013).

12. For a basic comparison, see Mary Jeremy, 'Caxton's *Golden Legend* and Varagine's *Legenda Aurea*', *Speculum* 21 (1946): 212–21.

13. For a useful overview of this tradition, with chapters devoted to Plutarch, Boccaccio, Chaucer, and Christine de Pizan, see Glenda McLeod, *Virtue and Venom: Catalogs of Women from Antiquity to the Renaissance* (Ann Arbor, MI: University of Michigan Press, 1991).

14. Alcuin Blamires, *The Case for Women in Medieval Culture* (Oxford: Oxford Clarendon Press, 1997). For an anthology of extracts from influential tracts, see *Woman Defamed and Woman Defended: An Anthology of Medieval Texts*, ed. Alcuin Blamires (Oxford: Clarendon Press, 1992). This anthology also includes extracts from classical and patristic sources.

15. Katharina M. Wilson and Elizabeth M. Makowski, *Wykked Wyves and the Woes of Marriage: Misogamous Literature from Juvenal to Chaucer* (Albany, NY: State University of New York Press, 1990).

16. Virginia Brown, Boccaccio's English translator, calls *Famous Women* 'the first collection of biographies in Western literature devoted exclusively to women'. See Giovanni Boccaccio, *Famous Women*, ed. and trans. Virginia Brown (Cambridge, MA: Harvard University Press, 2001), p. xi. For an introduction to Boccaccio's life and writings, see Thomas G. Bergin, *Boccaccio* (New York: Viking, 1981).

17. Boccaccio, *Famous Women*, p. 17 (deception); p. 207 (wantonness); p. 405 (lasciviousness); pp. 93, 267, 443 (cunning); p. 183 (luxury); p. 287 (stinginess); p. 467 (avarice).

18. Joanna, Queen of Jerusalem and Sicily, is similarly 'generous in the manner of a king rather than of a woman' (p. 471).

19. See Pamela Benson's reading of Boccaccio in her *The Invention of the Renaissance Woman: The Challenge of Female Independence in the Literature and Thought of Italy and England* (University Park, PA: Pennsylvania State University Press, 1992), pp. 9–31; Benson considers Boccaccio's *Famous Women* 'the foundation text of Renaissance profeminism' (p. 9).

20. For a sampling of the various interpretations of the tensions and (apparent) contradictions in Boccaccio's work, see Constance Jordan, 'Boccaccio's In-Famous Women: Gender and Civic Virtue in the *De mulieribus claris*', in *Ambiguous Realities: Women in the Middle Ages and Renaissance*, ed. Carole Levin and Jeanie Watson (Detroit, MI: Wayne State University Press, 1987), pp. 25–47; Stephen Kolsky, *The Genealogy of Women: Studies in Boccaccio's De mulieribus claris* (New York: Peter Lang, 2003); and Margaret Franklin, *Boccaccio's Heroines:*

Power and Virtue in Renaissance Society (Burlington, VT: Ashgate, 2006). For Franklin, Boccaccio creates 'an impression of fragmented authorial purpose' to 'mask the overriding and essentially unitary message to which each biography contributes' (p. 2).

21. On the mixed audience that Boccaccio anticipates, see Benson, *The Invention of the Renaissance Woman*, pp. 9–18. Franklin argues that Boccaccio was principally writing for other men (*Boccaccio's Heroines*, pp. 27–9).

22. On the influence of Boccaccio's *Famous Women*, see Benson, *The Invention of the Renaissance Woman* and Stephen Kolsky, *The Ghost of Boccaccio: Writings on Famous Women in Renaissance Italy* (Turnhout, Belgium: Brepols, 2005). For Boccaccio's influence on Chaucer, see Robert R. Edwards, *Chaucer and Boccaccio: Antiquity and Modernity* (New York: Palgrave, 2002) and Carolyn P. Collette, *Rethinking Chaucer's Legend of Good Women* (York: York Medieval Press, 2014). In Chapter 2, 'Exemplary Women' (pp. 33–75), Collette also compares Chaucer's approach to writing classical women's lives with Christine de Pizan's.

23. For a provocative revisiting of the issue of Chaucer's 'sincerity', see Anne Schuurman, 'Pity and Poetics in Chaucer's *Legend of Good Women*', *PMLA* 130 (2015): 1302–17. Schuurman argues that through his tales Chaucer 'undoes the binary' between 'sincerity and fakery' (1317). See also Nicole F. McDonald, 'Chaucer's *Legend of Good Women*, Ladies at Court and the Female Reader', *Chaucer Review* 35 (2000): 22–42. McDonald reads the *Legend of Good Women* as a playful treatment of the 'woman question' that would have been enjoyed by savvy men and women at court. For more on the *Legend of Good Women* as a game, see also Florence Percival, *Chaucer's Legendary Good Women* (Cambridge, UK: Cambridge University Press, 1998), pp. 299–323.

24. For thoughtful assessments of Chaucer's appropriation of hagiographical conventions, see Janet M. Cowen, 'Chaucer's *Legend of Good Women*: Structure and Tone', *Studies in Philology* 82 (1985): 416–36; Catherine Sanok, 'Reading Hagiographically: *The Legend of Good Women* and its Feminine Audience', *Exemplaria* 13.2 (2001): 323–54; and Laura J. Getty, '"Other smale ymaad before": Chaucer as Historiographer in the *Legend of Good Women*', *Chaucer Review* 42 (2007): 48–75.

25. This debate extended back to the first decade of the twentieth century, with Harold C. Goddard, 'Chaucer's *Legend of Good Women*', *Journal of English and Germanic Philology* 7 (1908): 87–129 and 8 (1909): 47–111, and John Livingston Lowes, 'Is Chaucer's *Legend of Good Women* a Travesty?' *Journal of English and Germanic Philology* 8 (1909): 513–69. For a sampling of more recent positions, see the following monographs: Robert Worth Frank, Jr, *Chaucer and the Legend of Good Women* (Cambridge, MA: Harvard University Press, 1972); Lisa J. Kiser, *Telling Classical Tales: Chaucer and the Legend of Good Women* (Ithaca, NY: Cornell University Press, 1982); Sheila Delany, *The Naked Text: Chaucer's Legend of Good Women* (Berkeley, CA: University of California Press, 1994); Percival, *Chaucer's Legendary Good Women*; and Collette, *Rethinking Chaucer's Legend of Good Women*. See also the essays in *The Legend of Good Women: Context and Reception*, ed. Carolyn P. Collette (Cambridge, UK: D. S. Brewer, 2006). For a succinct overview, see *The Oxford Companion to Chaucer*, ed. Douglas Gray (Oxford: Oxford University Press, 2003), pp. 284–8. For a more extended review and reassessment, see Alastair J. Minnis, 'The Legend of Good Women' in *Oxford Guides to Chaucer: The Shorter Poems* (Oxford: Clarendon Press, 1995), pp. 322–454.

26. See Beverly Taylor, 'The Medieval Cleopatra: The Classical and Medieval Tradition of Chaucer's *Legend of Cleopatra*', *Journal of Medieval and Renaissance Studies* 7 (1977): 249-69, and Ruth Morse, *The Medieval Medea* (Cambridge, UK: D. S. Brewer, 1996).

27. For a provocative discussion of Chaucer's subversion of his assignment, see Getty ('Chaucer as Historiographer'), who argues that that Chaucer includes women whose stories 'do not appear to have been suitable for the prescribed "rules"' for their usefulness in conveying 'metaphors about the difficulty of writing from sources'; through his commentary on the process of writing, Chaucer subverts his assignment of praising women ('Chaucer as Historiographer', p. 56).

28. Sanok ('Reading Hagiographically') and Cowen ('Structure and Tone') emphasize that Chaucer adopts the hagiographer's *modus operandi* of selection and compression.

29. Sanok, 'Reading Hagiographically', pp. 342-3. Lowes maintains that Chaucer's choice of heroines was not 'infelicitous'; he and his contemporaries would have viewed 'Cleopatra, Medea, and the rest as stock *exempla of fidelity in love*' ('Travesty', pp. 516, 546).

30. For example, Steele Nowlin, 'The *Legend of Good Women* and the Affect of Invention', *Exemplaria* 25 (2013): 16-35. Nowlin argues that the *Legend* 'destabilizes the antifeminist literary and cultural traditions its narratives would seem to represent' (p. 18).

31. Sanok ('Reading Hagiographically') finds the *Legend of Good Women* 'radically indeterminate' (p. 345) and suggests that 'Chaucer's goal was to see how open his poem could be to two widely divergent interpretations' (p. 352). See also Cowen, who rejects as too neat the view that Chaucer 'under the guise of eulogy propounds an antifeminist thesis', but concedes, 'there can be no mistaking the suppressed antifeminist joke that runs through the work' ('Structure and Tone', p. 433).

32. For an analysis of the major themes and strategies of the *City of Ladies*, see Maureen Quilligan, *The Allegory of Female Authority: Christine de Pizan's Cité des Dames* (Ithaca, NY: Cornell University Press, 1991).

33. For all references and quotations, I am using Christine de Pizan, *The Book of the City of Ladies*, trans. Earl Jeffrey Richards (New York: Persea, 1982). For extracts from Mathéolus, see *Woman Defamed and Woman Defended*, ed. Blamires, pp. 177-97.

34. Alfred Jeanroy, 'Boccace et Christine de Pisan: le *De claris mulieribus*, principale source du *Livre de la Cité des Dames*', *Romania* 43 (1922): 93-105.

35. On Christine's appropriation of Boccaccio, see Kevin Brownlee, 'Christine de Pizan's Canonical Authors: The Special Case of Boccaccio', *Comparative Studies* 32 (1995): 244-61; Quilligan, *The Allegory of Female Authority*; and Patricia Philippy, 'Establishing Authority: Boccaccio's *De claris mulieribus* and Christine de Pizan's *Livre de la Cité des Dames*', *Romanic Review* 77 (1986): 167-93.

36. Discussions of Christine's 'feminism' include Rosalind Brown-Grant, *Christine de Pizan and the Moral Defence of Women: Reading Beyond Gender* (Cambridge, UK: Cambridge University Press, 1999); Mary Anne Case, 'Christine de Pizan and the Authority of Experience', in *Christine de Pizan and the Categories of Difference*, ed. Marilynn Desmond (Minneapolis, MN: University of Minnesota Press, 1998), pp. 71-87; Sheila Delany, '"Mothers To Think Back Through": Who Are They? The Ambiguous Example of Christine de Pizan', in *Medieval Texts and Contemporary Readers*, ed. Laurie Finke and Martin Schichtman (Ithaca, NY: Cornell University Press, 1987), pp. 312-38; Christine

Reno, 'Christine de Pizan: At Best a Contradictory Figure?' in *Politics, Gender and Genre: The Political Thought of Christine de Pizan*, ed. Margaret Brabant (Boulder, CO: Westview, 1992), pp. 171–91; and Joan Kelly, 'Early Feminist Theory and the *Querelle des Femmes*, 1400–1789', *Signs* 8 (1982): 4–28.

37. Jerome originated this anecdote in *Against Jovinian*; see *Woman Defamed and Woman Defended*, ed. Blamires, p. 73. On Xanthippe and similar shrewish wives in medieval literature, see Christine Marie Neufeld, *Xanthippe's Sisters: Orality and Femininity in the Later Middle Ages*, PhD dissertation, McGill University, 2001.

38. Gray, *Oxford Companion to Chaucer*, p. 288.

39. It seems unlikely that Christine knew the more favourable portrayal of Xanthippe in Plato's *Phaedo*, but if she did, she may have seen herself as undoing (or refusing to endorse) centuries' worth of accretion of misogynist slander around Socrates' wife.

40. Judy Chicago, *The Dinner Party: A Commemorative Volume Celebrating a Major Monument of Twentieth-Century Art* (New York: Penguin, 1996), p. 21.

41. Chicago, *The Dinner Party*, p. 21.

42. For a discussion of the date of this work and the translator's treatment of his source, see Janet M. Cowen, 'An English Reading of Boccaccio: A Selective Middle English Version of Boccaccio's *De Mulieribus Claris* in British Library MS Additional 10304', in *New Perspectives on Middle English Texts: A Festschrift for R. A. Waldron*, ed. Susan Powell and Jeremy J. Smith (Cambridge, UK: D. S. Brewer, 2000), pp. 129–40. For quotes and line references, I am using Gustav Schleich's edition, *Die Mittelenglische Umdichtung von Boccaccios De Claris Mulieribus* (Leipzig: Mayer & Müller, 1924). The translations are mine.

43. For example, he attributes to Boccaccio the opinion that women deserve special praise for their achievements because nature gave them 'weaker bodies and less stable wits' (ll. 85–98).

44. I am using the abridged translation by Louis Brewer Hall, *The Fates of Illustrious Men* (New York: Frederick Ungar, 1965), pp. 2, 242–3.

45. Its influence extended well beyond the Middle Ages, too. See Meredith Skura's fascinating discussion of how William Baldwin's 1556 adaptation, *A Mirror for Magistrates*, influenced the development of English autobiography in the sixteenth century, 'A Mirror for Magistrates and the Beginnings of English Autobiography', *English Literary Renaissance* 36 (2006): 26–56.

46. For the *Monk's Tale*, see Geoffrey Chaucer, *The Riverside Chaucer*, ed. Larry D. Benson, 3rd ed. (Boston, MA: Houghton Mifflin, 1987); the translations are mine.

47. On the deliberately bad storytelling of the *Monk's Tale*, see Jahan Ramazani, 'Chaucer's Monk: The Poetics of Abbreviation, Aggression, and Tragedy', *Chaucer Review* 27 (1993): 260–76.

48. Emily Jensen, '"Winkers" and "Janglers": Teller/Listener/Reader Response in the "Monk's Tale," the Link, and the "Nun's Priest's Tale"', *Chaucer Review* 32 (1997): 183–95 (quotes at pp. 192, 189).

49. Helen Cooper, *Oxford Guides to Chaucer: The Canterbury Tales* (Oxford: Oxford University Press, 1989), pp. 326–7.

50. Nigel Mortimer, *John Lydgate's Fall of Princes: Narrative Tragedy in its Literary and Political Contexts* (Oxford: Clarendon Press, 2005), p. 1.

51. John Lydgate, *Fall of Princes*, ed. Henry Bergen, 4 vols., Early English Text Society ES 121-4 (London: Oxford University Press, 1924-7). Line references are to Bergen's edition; the translations are mine.

52. David Wallace, 'Italy', in *A Companion to Chaucer*, ed. Peter Brown (Oxford: Blackwell, 2000), pp. 218-34. Quote at p. 277.

53. Maura Nolan, '"Now wo, now gladnesses": Ovidianism in the *Fall of Princes*', *ELH* 71 (2004): 531-58 (quote at p. 532). See also Nolan's 'Lydgate's Literary History: Chaucer, Gower, and Canacee', *Studies in the Age of Chaucer* 27 (2005): 59-92.

54. On Lydgate's construction of an argument for political agency in the *Fall of Princes*, see Paul Strohm, *Politique: Languages of Statecraft between Chaucer and Shakespeare* (Notre Dame, IN: University of Notre Dame Press, 2005). See also J. Allan Mitchell, *Ethics and Eventfulness in Middle English Literature* (New York: Palgrave Macmillan, 2009).

55. For an alternative reading of Lydgate's relationship with Humphrey, see Jennifer Summit, '"Stable in study": Lydgate's *Fall of Princes* and Duke Humphrey's Library', in *John Lydgate: Poetry, Culture, and Lancastrian England*, ed. Larry Scanlon and James Simpson (Notre Dame, IN: University of Notre Dame Press, 2006), pp. 207-31. In contrast to my reading of the poet and patron as adversaries, Summit reads the relationship as productively cooperative.

Chapter 6

1. See Andy Orchard, *A Critical Companion to Beowulf* (Cambridge, UK: D. S. Brewer, 2004). For a sampling of approaches, old and new, see the essays in *The Postmodern Beowulf*, ed. Eileen A. Joy and Mary K. Ramsey (Morgantown, WV: West Virginia University Press, 2006); Peter S. Baker, ed., *Beowulf: Basic Readings* (New York: Garland, 1995) and *Interpretations of Beowulf: A Critical Anthology*, ed. R. D. Fulk (Bloomington, IN: Indiana University Press, 1991). For a synopsis of critical currents to 1994, see Seth Lerer, '*Beowulf* and Contemporary Critical Theory', in *A Beowulf Handbook*, ed. Robert E. Bjork and John D. Niles (Lincoln, NE: University of Nebraska Press, 1997), pp. 325-39.

2. *Beowulf*'s date of composition has been much debated. For an overview of scholarly opinion, see Roy Michael Liuzza, 'On the Dating of *Beowulf*', in Baker, *Beowulf: Basic Readings*, pp. 281-306; and Robert E. Bjork and Anita Obermeier, 'Date, Provenance, Author, Audiences', in Bjork and Niles, *A Beowulf Handbook*, p. 34.

3. *Beowulf: The Critical Heritage*, ed. Andreas Haarder and T. A. Shippey (New York: Routledge, 1998), pp. 57-9.

4. I am using E. Talbot Donaldson's translation, in *Beowulf*, ed. Nicholas Howe (New York: W. W. Norton, 2001).

5. Studies of the digressions in *Beowulf* and their implications include Adrien Bonjour, *The Digressions in Beowulf* (Oxford: Blackwell, 1950) and John M. Hill, *The Narrative Pulse of Beowulf: Arrivals and Departures* (Toronto: University of Toronto Press, 2008). For an overview of scholarship on this topic, see Robert E. Bjork, 'Digressions and Episodes', in Bjork and Niles, *A Beowulf Handbook*, pp. 193-211.

6. J. R. R. Tolkien reviews and refutes this tradition in *Beowulf* scholarship in his seminal 'Beowulf: The Monsters and the Critics', *Proceedings of the British Academy* 22 (1936): 245–95, reprinted in *Beowulf: Modern Critical Interpretations*, ed. Harold Bloom (New York: Chelsea House Publishers, 1987).

7. Tolkien, 'The Monsters and the Critics' (quote at p. 28).

8. Tolkien, 'The Monsters and the Critics', p. 28.

9. Michael Lapidge, 'Beowulf and the Psychology of Terror', in *Heroic Poetry in the Anglo-Saxon Period: Studies in Honor of Jess B. Bessinger, Jr* (Kalamazoo, MI: Medieval Institute Publications, 1993), pp. 373–402 (quote at p. 374).

10. That life story would go something like this: Beowulf's mother was the only daughter of the Geatish king, Hrethel (ll. 374–5). His father was Ecgtheow, probably a Waegmunding (Beowulf identifies the Waegmundings as 'our race' in ll. 2813–14). That Ecgtheow lived a long life as a 'noble leader' well known abroad was due in no small measure to Hrothgar's friendship (ll. 262–3, 456–72). Long ago, when Hrothgar was a young king, Ecgtheow slew a man, bringing on 'the greatest of feuds'. The Geats, fearing war, dared not harbour him, so he sought refuge with the Danes. Hrothgar brokered a settlement with the dead man's kinsmen and supplied the treasure needed to keep them from retaliating. Hrothgar and Ecgtheow stayed in touch: Hrothgar knew Beowulf as a child and followed the reports of his doings (ll. 372, 375–80). From the age of seven, Beowulf lived with his maternal grandfather, King Hrethel. Beowulf recalls Hrethel fondly, claiming that he treated him like his own son, lavishing gifts on him (ll. 2423–9). During his years in Hrethel's care, he formed a fast friendship with Hrethel's youngest son, Hygelac. Beowulf's youth was not all rosy, though: 'He had long been despised, so that the sons of the Geats did not reckon him brave.… They strongly suspected that he was slack, a young man unbold' (ll. 2183–8). His reputation was not helped when he lost a widely publicized swimming contest with a certain Breca (ll. 499–581). Tragedy struck: Hrethel's son Haethcyn accidentally killed his older brother Herebeald with an arrow (ll. 2430–8). Afflicted with the double sorrow of losing his son and being unable to avenge his death, Hrethel died grieving (ll. 2436–8, 2455–66). Following his death, hostilities erupted between the Geats and the Scylfings (of northern Sweden). Haethcyn died in battle, Hygelac avenged his death, and Beowulf helped Hygelac gain and maintain power, fighting boldly and earning generous rewards (ll. 2467–505). Beowulf engaged in 'many battles' and 'dared perilous straits, clashes of war' (ll. 2347–52) until an ill-judged expedition against the Frisians cost Hygelac his life (ll. 1203–4). Following the battle, Beowulf swam back to Geatland, bearing the armour of the many he had slain. There Hygelac's widow offered him the throne, believing that her young son, Heardred, could not defend the land against the inevitable attackers (ll. 2369–72). Neither she nor anybody else could induce Beowulf to accept; instead, he mentored his fatherless cousin until he grew old enough to govern (ll. 2372–9). However, Heardred made the fatal mistake of harbouring refugees from the Scylfing king, Onela (ll. 2379–85), who retaliated by launching an attack that killed Heardred, but he then returned home, allowing Beowulf to succeed Heardred as king of the Geats (ll. 2385–90). Beowulf was not about to let his lord's slaying go unpunished, however. He supported Onela's exiled enemy Eadgils with weapons and troops, underwriting an invasion that killed Heardred's

slayer (ll. 2390-6). Having avenged Heardred's death, Beowulf governed with restraint and integrity, distributing wealth liberally among his followers (ll. 2732-6, 2860-8). Unlike Hygelac, whose rash offensive against the Frisians proved fatal, King Beowulf fought to protect rather than to conquer. Because he was widely feared, his enemies dared not attack and left him to govern peacefully for fifty years (ll. 2225-35). However, this bright interval ended in bleakness: Beowulf left no son to succeed him (ll. 2729-32); the treasure he won from the dragon in his last battle was buried with his ashes in a barrow, 'as useless to men as it was before' (ll. 3137-82); and the leaderless Geats, knowing that their enemies would soon be upon them, braced themselves for the apocalypse.

11. John Leyerle discusses the multiple tellings of this episode as an example of the poet's interlacing strategy on pp. 7-9 of 'The Interlace Structure of *Beowulf*', *University of Toronto Quarterly* 17 (1967): 1-17.

12. On the poet's historical vision, see Roberta Frank, 'The *Beowulf* Poet's Sense of History', in *The Wisdom of Poetry*, ed. Larry D. Benson and Siegfried Wenzel (Kalamazoo, MI: Medieval Institute Press, 1982), pp. 53-65.

13. Leyerle, 'The Interlace Structure of *Beowulf*'.

14. On the sexual punning in this scene, see Jane Chance, 'The Structural Unity of *Beowulf*: The Problem of Grendel's Mother', in *New Readings on Women in Old English Literature*, ed. Helen Damico and Alexandra Hennessey Olsen (Bloomington, IN: Indiana University Press, 1990), pp. 248-61. For another interpretation, less flattering to Beowulf, of the discrepancies between the narrator's and Beowulf's accounts of this encounter, see Dana M. Oswald, '"Wigge under wætere": Beowulf's Revision of the Fight with Grendel's Mother', *Exemplaria* 21 (2009): 63-82.

15. On Beowulf's peace-weaving qualities, see Robert Morey, 'Beowulf's Androgynous Heroism', *Journal of English and Germanic Philology* 95 (1996): 486-96. See also Stacy S. Klein's discussion of Beowulf's reconsideration of masculinity in *Ruling Women: Queenship and Gender in Anglo-Saxon Literature* (Notre Dame, IN: University of Notre Dame Press, 2006), pp. 118-23.

16. C. N. L. Brooke, 'Geoffrey of Monmouth as a Historian', in *Church and Government in the Middle Ages: Essays Presented to C. R. Cheney on his 70th Birthday*, ed. C. N. L. Brooke, D. E. Luscombe, G. H. Martin, and Dorothy Owen (Cambridge, UK: Cambridge University Press, 1976), pp. 77-91.

17. Brooke, 'Geoffrey of Monmouth', p. 78. In describing it thus, Brooke writes, 'there has scarcely, if ever, been a historian more mendacious than Geoffrey of Monmouth' (p. 78).

18. Brooke, 'Geoffrey of Monmouth', p. 86. Brooke notes its 'extraordinary contrast' to 'the comparatively matter-of-fact tone of the *History*'.

19. Siân Echard discusses the 'strangeness of the poem's stylistic features' and Geoffrey's use of diverse literary genres in *Arthurian Narrative and the Latin Tradition* (Cambridge, UK: Cambridge University Press, 1998), pp. 214-31 (quote at p. 230).

20. For quotations and references to both the *History of the Kings of Britain* and the *Life of Merlin*, I am using Geoffrey of Monmouth, *The History of the Kings of Britain*, ed. and trans. Michael A. Faletra (Plymouth, UK: Broadview Press, 2008). The *Life of Merlin* is translated on pp. 241-76.

21. For a different, more pessimistic, reading, see Echard, *Arthurian Narrative and the Latin Tradition*.

22. The classic study of the invention of saints from such 'evidence' is Hippolyte Delehaye, *Legends of the Saints*, trans. Donald Attwater (New York: Fordham University Press, 1962).

23. *Verse Saints' Lives Written in the French of England*, trans. Delbert W. Russell (Tempe, AZ: Arizona Center for Medieval and Renaissance Studies, 2012), p. 16 (my italics). The life of Giles was written *circa* 1170-90. Russell's translation also includes lives of George, Faith, and Mary Magdalene in the same tradition. For more on the French-language lives composed in England, see Jocelyn Wogan-Browne, *Saints' Lives and Women's Literary Culture, 1150-1300: Virginity and its Authorizations* (Oxford: Oxford University Press, 2001).

24. For a translation of this life and a discussion of Paris's appropriation of his sources, see Matthew Paris, *The Life of Saint Alban*, trans. Jocelyn Wogan-Browne and Thelma S. Fenster (Tempe, AZ: Arizona Center for Medieval and Renaissance Studies, 2010). This volume also includes a translation by Thomas O'Donnell and Margaret Lamont of William of St. Albans' *Passion of Saint Alban*, Paris's main source.

25. Matthew Paris, *The History of Saint Edward the King*, trans. Thelma S. Fenster and Jocelyn Wogan-Browne (Tempe, AZ: Arizona Center for Medieval and Renaissance Studies, 2008). For more on this life, its treatment of its sources, and its major themes, see the Introduction by Fenster and Wogan-Browne and also Paul Binski, 'Reflections on *La Estoire Seint Aedward le rei*: Hagiography and Kingship in Thirteenth-Century England', *Journal of Medieval History* 16 (1990): 333-50.

26. On the contribution of Lydgate's epic legends to the English hagiographical tradition, see Karen A. Winstead, 'Lydgate's Lives of Saints Edmund and Alban: Martyrdom and "Prudent Pollicie"', *Mediaevalia* 17 (1994): 221-41.

27. On the development of Edmund's legend, see Grant Loomis, 'The Growth of the St Edmund Legend', *Harvard Studies and Notes in Philology, Language and Literature* 14 (1932): 83-113; Dorothy Whitelock, 'Fact and Fiction in the Legend of St. Edmund', *Proceedings of the Suffolk Institute of Archaeology* 31 (1969): 217-33; and the essays in *St Edmund, King and Martyr: Changing Images of a Medieval Saint*, ed. Anthony Bale (York: York Medieval Press, 2009).

28. *The South English Legendary*, ed. Charlotte D'Evelyn and Anna J. Mill, Early English Text Society OS 236 (London: Oxford University Press, 1956), pp. 511-15.

29. For an edition of this work, see John Lydgate, *Lives of Ss Edmund and Fremund and the Extra Miracles of St Edmund*, ed. Anthony Bale and A. S. G. Edwards (Heidelberg, Germany: Universitätsverlag Winter, 2009).

30. Karen A. Winstead, *John Capgrave's Fifteenth Century* (Philadelphia, PA: University of Pennsylvania Press, 2007), pp. 118-37; Fiona Somerset, '"Hard is with seyntis for to make affray": Lydgate the "Poet-Propagandist" as Hagiographer', in *John Lydgate: Poetry, Culture, and Lancastrian England*, ed. Larry Scanlon and James Simpson (Notre Dame, IN: University of Notre Dame Press, 2006), pp. 258-78; Jennifer Sisk, 'Lydgate's Problematic Commission: A Legend of St. Edmund for Henry VI', *Journal of English and Germanic Philology* 109 (2010): 349-75; Katherine J. Lewis, 'Edmund of East Anglia, Henry VI and Ideals of Kingly Masculinity', in *Holiness and Masculinity in the Middle Ages*, ed. P. H. Cullum and Katherine J. Lewis (Cardiff: University of Wales Press, 2004), pp. 158-74; and Katherine J. Lewis, *Kingship and Masculinity in Late Medieval England* (New York: Routledge, 2013). For a facsimile, with commentary, of the manuscript prepared for Henry VI, see John Lydgate, *The Life of St Edmund, King and Martyr: John Lydgate's Illustrated Verse Life Presented to Henry VI:*

A Facsimile of British Library MS Harley 2278, introduced by A. S. G. Edwards (London: The British Library, 2004).

31. Lydgate, *Lives of Ss Edmund and Fremund*, line 1617 (my translation).

32. I first discussed the criticism of Edmund that Lydgate effects by conjoining the lives in 'Lydgate's Lives of Saints Edmund and Alban', and elaborated my argument in *John Capgrave's Fifteenth Century*. For other discussions of the politics of Lydgate's epic double life, see Somerset, '"Hard is with seyntis for to make affray"'; Sisk, 'Lydgate's Problematic Commission'; and Lewis, 'Edmund of East Anglia'.

33. For Capgrave's life and career, see Winstead, *John Capgrave's Fifteenth Century*; Peter J. Lucas, *From Author to Audience: John Capgrave and Medieval Publication* (Dublin: University College Dublin Press, 1997); M. C. Seymour, *John Capgrave* (Brookfield, VT: Ashgate, 1996); Jane C. Fredeman, 'The Life of John Capgrave, O. E. S. A. (1393-1464)', *Augustiniana* 29 (1979): 197-237; and Edmund Colledge, 'John Capgrave's Literary Vocation', *Analecta Augustiniana* 40 (1977): 187-95.

34. I develop this argument, summarized below, in *John Capgrave's Fifteenth Century*, pp. 116-61.

35. For more on her legend, see Christine Walsh, *The Cult of St Katherine of Alexandria in Early Medieval England* (Burlington, VT: Ashgate, 2007); Katherine J. Lewis, *The Cult of St Katherine of Alexandria in Late Medieval England* (Woodbridge, Suffolk: Boydell Press, 2000); and *St. Katherine of Alexandria: Texts and Contexts in Western Medieval Europe*, ed. Jacqueline Jenkins and Katherine J. Lewis (Turnhout, Belgium: Brepols, 2003).

36. For a sense of the legend's diverse renderings, see the essays in Jenkins and Lewis, *St. Katherine of Alexandria*.

37. John Foxe, *Book of Martyrs and the Acts and Monuments of the English Church*, ed. John Cumming (London: Chatto and Windus, 1875), p. 133.

38. *Decline of An Empire*, 2014, directed by Michael Redwood; Sheri Holeman, *A Stolen Tongue* (New York: Atlantic Monthly Press, 1997).

39. John Capgrave, *Life of Saint Katherine of Alexandria*, trans. Karen A. Winstead (Notre Dame, IN: University of Notre Dame Press, 2011). For the Middle English, see John Capgrave, *The Life of Saint Katherine*, ed. Karen A. Winstead (Kalamazoo, MI: Medieval Institute Publications, 1999).

40. For Capgrave's interest in character, see Karen A. Winstead, 'Piety, Politics, and Social Responsibility in Capgrave's *Life of St. Katherine*', *Medievalia et Humanistica*, n.s., 17 (1990): 59-80; Jane C. Fredeman, 'Style and Characterization in John Capgrave's *Life of St. Katherine*', *Bulletin of the John Rylands Library* 62 (1980): 346-87; and Mary-Ann Stouck, 'Chaucer and Capgrave's *Life of St. Katherine*', *American Benedictine Review* 33 (1982): 276-91. On Katherine's (mis)use of her education to evade her secular responsibilities, see my *John Capgrave's Fifteenth Century*, pp. 18-50. On Capgrave's development of Katherine's learning, see also Sarah James, '"Doctryne and Studie": Female Learning and Religious Debate in Capgrave's *Life of St. Katharine*', *Leeds Studies in English*, n.s., 36 (2005): 275-302.

41. I develop this point at length in 'John Capgrave and the Chaucer Tradition', *Chaucer Review* 30 (1996): 389-400.

42. On the Chaucerian qualities of Capgrave's *Katherine*, see my 'John Capgrave and the Chaucer Tradition' and Stouck, 'Chaucer and Capgrave's *Life of St. Katherine*'.

43. Brooke, 'Geoffrey of Monmouth', p. 83.

Bibliography

Primary Sources

Abelard, Peter and Heloise. *The Letter Collection of Peter Abelard and Heloise*. Ed. David Luscombe. Trans. Betty Radice. Oxford: Clarendon Press, 2013.

Adam of Eynsham. *The Life of St Hugh of Lincoln*. Ed. Decima L. Douie and Hugh Farmer O.S.B., 2 vols. London: Thomas Nelson and Sons, 1961, 1962.

Ælfric. *Lives of Saints*. Ed. Walter W. Skeat. 2 vols. Early English Text Society OS 76, 82, 94, 114. London: N. Trubner, 1881-1900.

Aelred of Rievaulx. *Life of St. Edward the Confessor*. Trans. Jerome Bertram. Southampton, UK: Saint Austin Press, 1990.

Aelred of Rievaulx. *Spiritual Friendship*. Ed. Marsha L. Dutton. Trans. Lawrence C. Braceland. Cistercian Fathers Series 5. Collegeville, MN: Cistercian, 2010.

Augustine. *Confessions*. Ed. and trans. R. S. Pine-Coffin. New York: Penguin, 1961.

Barber, Richard, ed. and trans. *The Life and Campaigns of the Black Prince*. Woodbridge, Suffolk: Boydell Press, 1979.

Barlow, Frank, ed. and trans. *The Life of King Edward the Confessor who Rests at Westminster*. London: Thomas Nelson and Sons, 1962.

Bede. *Ecclesiastical History of the English People*. Ed. Bertram Colgrave and R. A. B. Mynors. Oxford: Clarendon Press, 1969.

Bede. *Lives of the Abbots of Wearmouth and Jarrow*. In *The Age of Bede*. Trans. D. H. Farmer. 1965. Reprint. New York: Penguin, 1983. 185-208.

Blacman, John. *Henry the Sixth*. Ed. and trans. M. R. James. Cambridge, UK: Cambridge University Press, 1919.

Blamires, Alcuin, ed. *Woman Defamed and Woman Defended: An Anthology of Medieval Texts*. Oxford: Clarendon Press, 1992.

Boccaccio, Giovanni. *The Fates of Illustrious Men*. Trans. Louis Brewer Hall. New York: Frederick Ungar, 1965.

Boccaccio, Giovanni. *Famous Women*. Ed. and trans. Virginia Brown. Cambridge, MA: Harvard University Press, 2001.

Bokenham, Osbern. *A Legend of Holy Women*. Trans. Sheila Delany. Notre Dame, IN: University of Notre Dame Press, 1992.

Boswell, James. *The Life of Samuel Johnson*. Ed. David Womersley. New York: Penguin, 2008.

Bridget of Sweden. *Liber Celestis*. Ed. Roger Ellis. Early English Text Society OS 291. Oxford: Oxord University Press, 1987.

Brown, Jennifer N., ed. *Three Women of Liège*. Turnhout, Belgium: Brepols, 2008.

Butler-Bowdon, William. *The Book of Margery Kempe*. London: Jonathan Cape, 1936.

Byrhtferth of Ramsey. *The Lives of St Oswald and St Ecgwine*. Ed. and trans. Michael Lapidge. Oxford: Clarendon Press, 2009.

Campbell, Alistair, ed. *Encomium Emmae Reginae*. London: Royal Historical Society, 1949.

Capgrave, John. *Book of the Illustrious Henries*. Trans. Francis Charles Hingeston. London: Longman, 1858.

Capgrave, John. *Abbreuiacion of Chronicles*. Ed. Peter J. Lucas. Early English Text Society OS 285. Oxford: Oxford University Press, 1983.

Capgrave, John. *The Life of Saint Katherine*. Ed. Karen A. Winstead. Kalamazoo, MI: Medieval Institute Publications, 1999.

Capgrave, John. *Life of Saint Katherine of Alexandria*. Trans. Karen A. Winstead. Notre Dame, IN: University of Notre Dame Press, 2011.

Chadwick, Elizabeth. *The Greatest Knight*. New York: Time Warner, 2005.

Chadwick, Elizabeth. *The Scarlet Lion*. Boston, MA: Little, Brown & Co., 2006.

Chadwick, Elizabeth. *A Place Beyond Courage*. London: Sphere, 2007.

Chadwick, Elizabeth. *To Defy a King*. London: Sphere, 2010.

Chaucer, Geoffrey. *The Riverside Chaucer*. Ed. Larry D. Benson. 3rd ed. Boston, MA: Houghton Mifflin, 1987.

Chicago, Judy. *The Dinner Party: A Commemorative Volume Celebrating a Major Monument of Twentieth-Century Art*. New York: Penguin, 1996.

Childs, Wendy R., ed. and trans. *Vita Edwardi Secundi: The Life of Edward the Second*. Oxford: Clarendon Press, 2005.

Christine de Pizan. *The Book of the City of Ladies*. Trans. Earl Jeffrey Richards. New York: Persea, 1982.

Christine de Pizan. *Le Livre de l'Advision Cristine*. Ed. Christine Reno and Liliane Dulac. Paris: Champion, 2001.

Christine de Pizan. *The Vision of Christine de Pizan*. Trans. Glenda McLeod and Charity Cannon Willard. Woodbridge, Suffolk: D. S. Brewer, 2005.

Colgrave, Bertram, ed. *Two Lives of Saint Cuthbert: A Life by an Anonymous Monk of Lindisfarne and Bede's Prose Life*. Cambridge, UK: Cambridge University Press, 1940.

Colgrave, Bertram, ed. *The Earliest Life of Gregory the Great*. 1968. Reprint, New York: Cambridge University Press, 1985.

Crow, M. M. and C. C. Olson, eds. *Chaucer Life Records*. Oxford: Oxford University Press, 1966.

Cuthbert of Jarrow. 'Letter on the Death of Bede'. In Bede, *Ecclesiastical History of the English People*. Ed. B. Colgrave and R. A. B. Mynors. Oxford: Clarendon Press, 1969. 579-87.

D'Evelyn, Charlotte and Anna J. Mill. *The South English Legendary*. 3 vols. Early English Text Society OS 235, 236, 244. Oxford: Oxford University Press, 1956, 1959.

Daniel, Walter. *The Life of Ailred of Rievaulx*. Trans. Maurice Powicke. Oxford: Clarendon Press, 1950.

Deferrari, Roy J., ed. *Early Christian Biographies*. Washington, DC: The Catholic University Press of America, 1952.

Durling, Nancy Vine, trans. 'Life of St. Alexis'. In *Medieval Hagiography: An Anthology*. Ed. Thomas Head. New York: Garland Publishing, 2000. 316-40.

Eadmer. *The Life of St Anselm, Archbishop of Canterbury*. Ed. and trans. R. W. Southern. Oxford: Clarendon Press, 1962.

Economou, George, ed. *Proensa: An Anthology of Troubadour Poetry*. Selected and trans. Paul Blackburn. Berkeley, CA: University of California Press, 1978.

Egan, Margarita, trans. *The Vidas of the Troubadours*. New York: Garland, 1984.

Einhard and Notker the Stammerer. *Two Lives of Charlemagne*. Trans. Lewis Thorpe. New York: Penguin, 1969.

Felix, *Felix's Life of Saint Guthlac*. Ed. Bertram Colgrave. Cambridge, UK: Cambridge University Press, 1956.

Foreville, Raymonde and Gillian Keir, ed. and trans. *The Book of St Gilbert*. Oxford: Clarendon Press, 1987.

Foxe, John. *Book of Martyrs and the Acts and Monuments of the English Church*. Ed. John Cumming. London: Chatto and Windus, 1875.

Garnier of Pont-Sainte-Maxence. *Garnier's Becket*. Trans. Janet Shirley. London: Phillimore, 1975.

Geoffrey of Monmouth. *The History of the Kings of Britain*. Ed. and trans. Michael A. Faletra. Plymouth, UK: Broadview Press, 2008.

Glück, Robert. *Margery Kempe*. New York: High Risk Books/Serpent's Tail, 1994.

Gregory of Tours. *Life of the Fathers*. Trans. Edward James. Liverpool: Liverpool University Press, 1986.

Guibert of Nogent. *Monodies and On the Relics of Saints*. Trans. Joseph McAlhany and Jay Rubenstein. New York: Penguin, 2011.

Head, Thomas, ed. *Medieval Hagiography: An Anthology*. New York: Garland, 2000.

Henry of Huntingdon. *Historia Anglorum: The History of the English People*. Ed. and trans. Diana Greenway. Oxford: Oxford University Press, 1996.

Hoccleve, Thomas. *Hoccleve's Works: The Minor Poems*. Ed. Frederick J. Furnivall and I. Gollancz. Revised by Jerome Mitchell and A. I. Doyle. Early English Text Society ES 61, 73. London: Oxford University Press, 1970.

Holden, A. J., ed. *The History of William Marshal*. Trans. S. Gregory. 3 vols. Anglo-Norman Text Society, Occasional Publications Series, Volumes 4–6. London: Anglo-Norman Text Society, 2002, 2004, 2006.

Holeman, Sheri. *A Stolen Tongue*. New York: Atlantic Monthly Press, 1997.

Hollis, Stephanie, ed. *Writing the Wilton Women: Goscelin's Legend of Edith and Liber confortatorius*. Turnhout, Belgium: Brepols, 2004.

Howe, Nicholas, ed. *Beowulf*. Trans. E. Talbot Donaldson. New York: W. W. Norton, 2001.

Jacobus de Voragine. *The Golden Legend*. Trans. William Granger Ryan. 2 vols. Princeton, NJ: Princeton University Press, 1993.

Jocelin of Brakelond. *Chronicle of the Abbey of Bury St Edmunds*. Trans. Diana Greenway and Jane Sayers. Oxford: Oxford University Press, 1989.

John of Caulibus. *Meditations on the Life of Christ*. Trans. Francis X. Taney, Anne Miller, and C. Mary Stallings-Taney. Asheville, NC: Pegasus Press, 2000.

Johnson, Samuel. *Samuel Johnson: The Major Works*. Ed. Donald Greene. Oxford: Oxford University Press, 2009.

Julian of Norwich. *The Writings of Julian of Norwich*. Ed. Nicholas Watson and Jacqueline Jenkins. University Park, PA: Pennsylvania State University Press, 2006.

Kempe, Margery. *The Book of Margery Kempe*. Ed. Sanford Brown Meech with a prefatory note by Hope Emily Allen and Notes and Appendices by Sanford Brown Meech and Hope Emily Allen. Early English Text Society OS 212. Oxford: Oxford University Press, 1940.

Kempe, Margery. *The Book of Margery Kempe*. Ed. and trans. Lynn Staley. New York and London: W. W. Norton, 2001.

Keynes, Simon and Michael Lapidge, ed. and trans. *Alfred the Great: Asser's Life of King Alfred and Other Contemporary Sources*. New York: Penguin, 1983.

Lacy, Norris J. and James J. Wilhelm, ed. *The Romance of Arthur*. 3rd ed. New York: Routledge, 2013.

Love, Rosalind C., ed. *The Hagiography of the Female Saints of Ely*. Oxford: Clarendon Press, 2004.

Lydgate, John. *Fall of Princes*. Ed. Henry Bergen. 4 vols. Early English Text Society ES 121-4. London: Oxford University Press, 1924-7.

Lydgate, John. *The Minor Poems of John Lydgate*. Ed. Henry Noble MacCracken. Early English Text Society ES 107. 2nd ed. London: Oxford University Press, 1962.

Lydgate, John. *The Life of St Edmund, King and Martyr: John Lydgate's Illustrated Verse Life Presented to Henry VI: A Facsimile of British Library MS Harley 2278*. Introduced by A. S. G. Edwards. London: The British Library, 2004.

Lydgate, John. *Lives of Ss Edmund and Fremund and the Extra Miracles of St Edmund*. Ed. Anthony Bale and A. S. G. Edwards. Heidelberg, Germany: Universitätsverlag Winter, 2009.

Malory, Thomas. *Le Morte Darthur*. Ed. Stephen H. A. Shepherd. New York: Norton, 2004.

Metham, John. *Amoryus and Cleopes*. Ed. Stephen F. Page. Kalamazoo, MI: Medieval Institute Publications, 1999.

Meyer, Paul, ed. *L'Histoire de Guillaume le Maréchal, comte de Striguil et de Pembroke*. 3 vols. Paris: Librairie Renouard, H. Laurens, successeur, 1891-1901.

Mulder-Bakker, Anneke B., ed. *Mary of Oignies: Mother of Salvation*. Turnhout, Belgium: Brepols, 2006.

Mulder-Bakker, Anneke B., ed. *Living Saints of the Thirteenth Century*. Turnhout, Belgium: Brepols, 2011.

Muserillo, Herbert, ed. and trans. *Acts of the Christian Martyrs*. Oxford: Clarendon Press, 1972.

Noble, Thomas F. X. and Thomas Head, eds. *Soldiers of Christ: Saints and Saints' Lives from Late Antiquity and the Early Middle Ages*. University Park, PA: Pennsylvania State University Press, 1995.

Orderic Vitalis. *The Ecclesiastical History of Orderic Vitalis*. Ed. and trans. Marjorie Chibnall. 6 vols. Oxford: Clarendon Press, 1968-1980.

Otter, Monica, trans. *The Book of Encouragement and Consolation [Liber Confortatorius]: The Letter of Goscelin to the Recluse Eva*. Woodbridge, Suffolk: Boydell and Brewer, 2004.

Paris, Matthew. *Life of St Edmund*. Trans. C. H. Lawrence. Stroud, Gloucestershire: Sutton Publishing, 1997.

Paris, Matthew. *The History of Saint Edward the King*. Trans. Thelma S. Fenster and Jocelyn Wogan-Browne. Tempe, AZ: Arizona Center for Medieval and Renaissance Studies, 2008.

Paris, Matthew. *The Life of Saint Alban*. Trans. Jocelyn Wogan-Browne and Thelma S. Fenster. Tempe, AZ: Arizona Center for Medieval and Renaissance Studies, 2010.

Petrarch, Francesco, *Petrarch: The First Modern Scholar and Man of Letters*. Ed. and trans. James Harvey Robinson. New York: G. P. Putnam, 1898.

Petrarch, Francesco. *The Secret*. Trans. Carol E. Quillen. Boston, MA: Bedford/St. Martin's, 2003.

Rauer, Christine, ed. and trans. *The Old English Martyrology*. Cambridge, UK: D. S. Brewer, 2013.

Reames, Sherry L. *Middle English Legends of Women Saints*. Kalamazoo, MI: Medieval Institute Publications, 2003.

Redwood, Michael, dir. *Decline of an Empire*. 2014.

Russell, Delbert W., trans. *Verse Saints' Lives Written in the French of England*. Tempe, AZ: Arizona Center for Medieval and Renaissance Studies, 2012.

Schleich, Gustav. *Die Mittelenglische Umdichtung von Boccaccios De Claris Mulieribus*. Leipzig: Mayer & Müller, 1924.

Schroeder, Mark. *The Book of Margery Kempe*. Amazon Digital Services, 2012.

Silvas, Anna, ed. and trans. *Jutta and Hildegard: The Biographical Sources*. Turnhout, Belgium: Brepols, 1998.

Skinner, John, trans. *The Book of Margery Kempe*, New York: Doubleday, 1998.

Staunton, Michael, ed. and trans. *The Lives of Thomas Becket*. Manchester: Manchester University Press, 2001.

Stephen of Ripon, *The Life of Bishop Wilfrid by Eddius Stephanus*. Ed. Bertram Colgrave. 1927. Reprint, Cambridge, UK: Cambridge University Press, 1985.

Stevenson, Joseph, trans. 'The Life of the Venerable Beda by an Unknown Author of Great Antiquity'. In *The Historical Works of the Venerable Bede*. London, 1853. xxxix–xlviii.

Swanton, Michael, trans. *Three Lives of the Last Englishmen*. New York: Garland, 1984.

Swanton, Michael, trans. *The Anglo-Saxon Chronicle*. New York: Routledge, 1998.

Symeon of Durham, *Libellus de Exordio atque procursu istius, hoc est Dunhelmensis ecclesie: Tract on the Origins and Progress of this the Church of Durham*. Ed. and trans. David Rollason. Oxford: Clarendon Press, 2000.

Talbot, C. H., ed. and trans. *The Anglo-Saxon Missionaries in Germany: Being the Lives of SS. Willibrord, Boniface, Leoba and Lebuin together with the Hodoepericon of St. Willibald and a selection from the correspondence of St. Boniface*. New York: Sheed and Ward, 1954.

Talbot, C. H., ed. and trans. *The Life of Christina of Markyate: A Twelfth Century Recluse*. Oxford: Clarendon Press, 1959.

Taylor, Frank and John S. Roskell, ed. and trans. *Gesta Henrici Quinti: The Deeds of Henry the Fifth*. Oxford: Clarendon Press, 1975.

Thomas of Cantimpré. *The Collected Saints' Lives*. Ed. Barbara Newman. Trans. Barbara Newman and Margot H. King. Turnhout, Belgium: Brepols, 2008.

Triggs, Tony D., trans. *The Autobiography of the Madwoman of God: The Book of Margery Kempe*. Tunbridge Wells, Kent: Burns & Oates, 1995.

Usk, Thomas. *The Testament of Love*. Ed. R. Allen Shoaf. Kalamazoo, MI: Medieval Institute Publications, 1998.

Usk, Thomas. *Testament of Love*. Ed. Gary W. Shawver. Toronto: University of Toronto Press, 2002.

Vitry, James. 'The Life of Mary of Oignies by James of Vitry'. Trans. Margot H. King. In *Mary of Oignies: Mother of Salvation*. Ed. Anneke B. Mulder-Bakker. Turnhout, Belgium: Brepols, 2006. 39–50.

Wace and Layamon. *Arthurian Chronicles*. Trans. Eugene Mason. Toronto: University of Toronto Press, 1996.

William VII. *The Poetry of William VII, Count of Poitiers, IX Duke of Aquitaine*. Ed. and trans. Gerald A. Bond. New York: Garland, 1982.

William of Malmesbury. *Gesta Regum Anglorum: The History of the English Kings*. Ed. and trans. R. A. B. Mynors, completed by R. M. Thomson and M. Winterbottom. 2 vols. Oxford: Clarendon Press, 1998.

William of Malmesbury. *Historia Novella: The Contemporary History*. Ed. Edmund King. Trans. K. R. Potter. Oxford: Clarendon Press, 1998.

William of Malmesbury. *Saints' Lives*. Ed. and trans. M. Winterbottom and R. M. Thomson. Oxford: Clarendon Press, 2002.

William of Malmesbury. *Gesta Pontificum Anglorum: The History of the English Bishops*. Ed. and trans. M. Winterbottom. Oxford: Clarendon Press, 2007.

William of Poitiers, *The Gesta Guillelmi of William of Poitiers*. Ed. R. H. C. Davis and Marjorie Chibnall. Oxford: Clarendon Press, 1998.

Winstead, Karen A., ed. and trans. *Chaste Passions: Medieval English Virgin Martyr Legends*. Ithaca, NY: Cornell University Press, 2000.

Wogan-Browne, Jocelyn, Nicholas Watson, Andrew Taylor, and Ruth Evans, eds. *The Idea of the Vernacular: An Anthology of Middle English Literary Theory, 1280-1520*. University Park, PA: Pennsylvania State University Press, 1999.

Wulfstan of Winchester, *The Life of St Æthelwold*. Ed. and trans. Michael Lapidge and Michael Winterbottom. Oxford: Clarendon Press, 1991.

Secondary Sources

Abbott, Christopher. *Julian of Norwich: Autobiography and Theology*. Woodbridge, Suffolk: D. S. Brewer, 1999.

Abels, Richard. *Alfred the Great: War, Kingship and Culture in Anglo-Saxon England*. London and New York: Longman, 1998.

Albu, Emily. *The Normans and their Histories: Propaganda, Myth and Subversion*. Woodbridge, Suffolk: Boydell Press, 2001.

Altick, Richard. *Lives and Letters: A History of Literary Biography in England and America*. New York: Knopf, 1965.

Altman, Leslie. 'Christine de Pisan: First Professional Woman of Letters'. In *Female Scholars: A Tradition of Learned Women before 1800*. Ed. J. R. Brink. Montreal: Eden, 1980. 7-23.

Arnold, John H. and Katherine J. Lewis, eds. *A Companion to The Book of Margery Kempe*. Cambridge, UK: D. S. Brewer, 2004.

Asbridge, Thomas. *The Greatest Knight: The Remarkable Life of William Marshal, the Power Behind Five English Thrones*. New York: Ecco, 2014.

Ashley, Kathleen M. 'Accounts of Lives'. In *A Companion to Medieval English Literature and Culture, c. 1350-c. 1500*. Ed. Peter Brown. Malden, MA: Blackwell, 2007. 437-53.

Atkinson, Clarissa. *Mystic and Pilgrim: The Book and the World of Margery Kempe*. Ithaca, NY: Cornell University Press, 1983.

Autrand, Françoise. *Christine de Pizan: Une femme en politique*. Paris: Fayard, 2009.

Baker, Peter S., ed. Beowulf: *Basic Readings*. New York: Garland, 1995.

Bale, Anthony. *St Edmund, King and Martyr: Changing Images of a Medieval Saint*. York: York Medieval Press, 2009.

Barber, Richard and Juliet Barker. *Tournaments*. Woodbridge, Suffolk: Boydell Press, 1989.

Barlow, Frank. 'Goscelin of St Bertin'. Appendix C of *The Life of King Edward who Rests at Westminster attributed to a monk of St Bertin*. Ed. Frank Barlow. London: Thomas Nelson and Sons, 1962. 91-111.

Baron, Hans. *Petrarch's Secretum: Its Making and Its Meaning*. Cambridge, MA: Medieval Academy of America, 1985.

Barron, W. R. J., ed. *The Arthur of the English: The Arthurian Legend in Medieval English Life and Literature*. Cardiff: University of Wales Press, 2001.

Bartlett, Anne Clark. 'Holy Women in the British Isles: A Survey'. In *Medieval Holy Women in the Christian Tradition c.1100-c.1500*. Ed. Alastair Minnis and Rosalynn Voaden. Turnhout, Belgium: Brepols, 2010. 165-93.

Bartlett, Robert. *England under the Norman and Angevin Kings, 1075-1225*. Oxford: Oxford University Press, 2000.

Bates, David. 'The Conqueror's Earliest Historians and the Writing of his Biography'. In *Writing Medieval Biography: Essays in Honour of Frank Barlow*. Ed. David Bates, Julia Crick, and Sarah Hamilton. Woodbridge, Suffolk: Boydell Press, 2006. 129-41.

Bates, David, Julia Crick, and Sarah Hamilton, eds. *Writing Medieval Biography: Essays in Honour of Frank Barlow*. Woodbridge, Suffolk: Boydell Press, 2006.

Bell, Rudolph M. *Holy Anorexia*. Chicago: University of Chicago Press, 1985.

Benson, Pamela Joseph. *The Invention of the Renaissance Woman: The Challenge of Female Independence in the Literature and Thought of Italy and England*. University Park, PA: Pennsylvania State University Press, 1992.

Benton, John F. 'The Personality of Guibert of Nogent'. *Psychoanalytic Review* 57 (1970): 563-86.

Bequette, John P. 'Aelred of Rievaulx's *Life of Saint Edward, King and Confessor*: A Saintly King and the Salvation of the English People'. *Cistercian Studies Quarterly* 43 (2008): 17-40.

Bergin, Thomas G. *Petrarch*. New York: Twayne, 1970.

Bergin, Thomas G. *Boccaccio*. New York: Viking, 1981.

Berschin, Walter. '*Opus deliberatum ac perfectum*: Why Did the Venerable Bede Write a Second Prose Life of St Cuthbert?' In *St Cuthbert: His Cult and His Community to AD 1200*. Ed. Gerald Bonner, David Rollason, and Clare Stancliffe. Woodbridge, Suffolk: Boydell Press, 1989. 95-102.

Bertolet, Craig E. 'Social Corrections: Hoccleve's *La Male Regle* and Textual Identity'. *Papers in Language and Literature* 51 (2015): 269-98.

Binski, Paul. 'Reflections on *La Estoire Seint Aedward le rei*: Hagiography and Kingship in Thirteenth-Century England'. *Journal of Medieval History* 16 (1990): 333-50.

Bishop, Morris. *Petrarch and His World*. Bloomington, IN: Indiana University Press, 1963.

Bjork, Robert E. 'Digressions and Episodes'. In *A Beowulf Handbook*. Ed. Robert E. Bjork and John D. Niles. Lincoln, NE: University of Nebraska Press, 1997. 193-211.

Bjork, Robert E. and John D. Niles, eds. *A Beowulf Handbook*. Lincoln, NE: University of Nebraska Press, 1997.

Bjork, Robert E. and Anita Obermeier. 'Date, Provenance, Author, Audiences'. In *A Beowulf Handbook*. Ed. Robert E. Bjork and John D. Niles. Lincoln, NE: University of Nebraska Press, 1997. 13-34.

Blamires, Alcuin. *The Case for Women in Medieval Culture*. Oxford: Clarendon Press, 1997.

Blurton, Heather. 'Guibert of Nogent and the Subject of History'. *Exemplaria* 15 (2003): 111-31.

Blurton, Heather and Jocelyn Wogan-Browne, eds. *Rethinking the South English Legendaries.* Manchester: Manchester University Press, 2011.

Boffey, Julia. 'Lydgate, Henryson, and the Literary Testament'. *Modern Language Quarterly* 53 (1992): 41–56.

Boffey, Julia. 'Middle English Lives'. In *The Cambridge History of Medieval English Literature*. Ed. David Wallace. Cambridge, UK: Cambridge University Press, 1999. 610–34.

Bolton, Brenda. 'Thirteenth-Century Religious Women: Further Reflections on the Low Countries "Special Case"'. In *New Trends in Feminine Spirituality*. Ed. Juliette Dor, Lesley Johnson, and Jocelyn Wogan-Browne. Turnhout, Belgium: Brepols, 1999. 129–57.

Bonjour, Adrien. *The Digressions in Beowulf.* Oxford: Blackwell, 1950.

Bonner, Gerald, David Rollason, and Clare Stancliffe, eds. *St Cuthbert: His Cult and His Community to AD 1200.* Woodbridge, Suffolk: Boydell, 1989.

Bowers, John. 'Hoccleve Holographs'. *Fifteenth-Century Studies* 15 (1989): 27–49.

Bowers, John. 'Thomas Hoccleve and the Politics of Tradition'. *Chaucer Review* 36.4 (2002): 352–69.

Breaulieu, Jean-Philippe. 'L'Avision Christine ou la tentation autobiographique'. *Littératures* 18 (1998): 15–30.

Breeze, Andrew. 'Arthur in Early Saints' Lives'. In *The Arthur of Medieval Latin Literature: The Development and Dissemination of the Arthurian Legend in Medieval Latin*. Ed. Siân Echard. Cardiff: University of Wales Press, 2011. 23–44.

Brett, Martin. 'John of Worcester and his Contemporaries'. In *The Writing of History in the Middle Ages: Essays Presented to Richard William Southern*. Ed. R. H. C. Davis and J. M. Wallace-Hadrill. Oxford: Clarendon Press, 1981. 101–26.

Brooke, C. N. L. 'Geoffrey of Monmouth as a Historian'. In *Church and Government in the Middle Ages: Essays Presented to C. R. Cheney on his 70th Birthday*. Ed. C. N. L. Brooke, D. E. Luscombe, G. H. Martin, and Dorothy Owen. Cambridge, UK: Cambridge University Press, 1976. 77–91.

Brown, George Hardin. *A Companion to Bede.* Anglo-Saxon Studies 12. Woodbridge, Suffolk: Boydell Press, 2009.

Brown-Grant, Rosalind. *Christine de Pizan and the Moral Defence of Women: Reading Beyond Gender.* Cambridge, UK: Cambridge University Press, 1999.

Brownlee, Kevin. 'Christine de Pizan's Canonical Authors: The Special Case of Boccaccio'. *Comparative Studies* 32 (1995): 244–61.

Burrow, John A. 'Autobiographical Poetry in the Middle Ages: The Case of Thomas Hoccleve'. *Proceedings of the British Academy* 68 (1982): 389–412.

Burrow, John A. 'Hoccleve's *Series*: Experience and Books'. In *Fifteenth-Century Studies: Recent Essays*. Ed. Robert F. Yeager. Hamden, CT: Archon Books, 1984. 259–74.

Burrow, John A. *The Ages of Man: A Study in Medieval Writing and Thought.* Oxford: Clarendon Press, 1986.

Burrow, John A. *Thomas Hoccleve.* Authors of the Middle Ages 4: English Writers of the Late Middle Ages. Aldershot, UK: Ashgate, 1994.

Bynum, Caroline Walker. *Holy Feast and Holy Fast: The Religious Significance of Food to Medieval Women.* Berkeley, CA: University of California Press, 1987.

Cannon, Christopher. '*Raptus* in the Chaumpaigne Release and a Newly Discovered Document Concerning the Life of Geoffrey Chaucer'. *Speculum* 68 (1993): 74-94.

Carlson, David. 'Thomas Hoccleve and the Chaucer Portrait'. *Huntington Library Quarterly* 54 (1991): 283-300.

Carlson, David. 'Chaucer's Boethius and Thomas Usk's *Testament of Love*: Politics and Love in the Chaucerian Tradition'. In *The Centre and Its Compass: Studies in Medieval Literature in Honor of John Leyerle*. Ed. Robert A. Taylor, James F. Burke, Patricia J. Eberle, Ian Lancashire, and Brian Merriless. Kalamazoo, MI: Western Michigan University Press, 1993. 29-70.

Case, Mary Anne. 'Christine de Pizan and the Authority of Experience'. In *Christine de Pizan and the Categories of Difference*. Ed. Marilynn Desmond. Minneapolis, MN: University of Minnesota Press, 1998. 71-87.

Chance, Jane. 'The Structural Unity of *Beowulf*: The Problem of Grendel's Mother'. In *New Readings on Women in Old English Literature*. Ed. Helen Damico and Alexandra Hennessey Olsen. Bloomington, IN: Indiana University Press, 1990. 248-61.

Clanchy, M. T. *Abelard: A Medieval Life*. Oxford: Blackwell, 1997.

Coakley, John W. *Women, Men and Spiritual Power: Female Saints and Their Male Collaborators*. New York: Columbia University Press, 2006.

Cockshut, A. O. J. *Truth to Life: The Art of Biography in the Nineteenth Century*. London: Collins, 1974.

Colledge, Edmund. 'John Capgrave's Literary Vocation'. *Analecta Augustiniana* 40 (1977): 187-95.

Collette, Carolyn P. ed. *The Legend of Good Women: Context and Reception*. Cambridge, UK: Brewer, 2006.

Collette, Carolyn P. *Rethinking Chaucer's Legend of Good Women*. York: York Medieval Press, 2014.

Collins, Roger. *Charlemagne*. Toronto: University of Toronto Press, 1998.

Connolly, Margaret. *John Shirley: Book Production and the Noble Household in Fifteenth-Century England*. Aldershot, UK: Ashgate, 1998.

Constable, Giles. 'Aelred of Rievaulx and the Nun of Watton: An Episode in the Early History of the Gilbertine Order'. In *Medieval Women*. Ed. Derek Baker. Oxford: Blackwell, 1981. 205-26.

Cook, Megan, *et multi*. 'Colloquium: John Shirley's Cambridge, Trinity College, MS R. 3.20 and the Culture of the Anthology in Late Medieval England'. *Studies in the Age of Chaucer* 38 (2016): 241-308.

Cooper, Helen. *Oxford Guides to Chaucer: The Canterbury Tales*. Oxford: Oxford University Press, 1989.

Cooper, Helen. *The English Romance in Time: Transforming Motifs from Geoffrey of Monmouth to the Death of Shakespeare*. Oxford: Oxford University Press, 2004.

Cowen, Janet M. 'Chaucer's *Legend of Good Women*: Structure and Tone'. *Studies in Philology* 82 (1985): 416-36.

Cowen, Janet M. 'An English Reading of Boccaccio: A Selective Middle English Version of Boccaccio's *De Mulieribus Claris* in British Library MS Additional 10304'. In *New Perspectives on Middle English Texts: A Festschrift for R. A. Waldron*. Ed. Susan Powell and Jeremy J. Smith. Cambridge, UK: D. S. Brewer, 2000. 129-40.

Critten, Rory G. '"Her heed they caste awry": The Transmission and Reception of Thomas Hoccleve's Personal Poetry'. *Review of English Studies*, n.s., 64 (2012): 386-409.

Cropp, Glynnis M. 'Boèce et Christine de Pizan'. *Le Moyen Âge* 87 (1981): 387-417.

Crouch, David. *William Marshal: Knighthood, War and Chivalry, 1147-1219.* London: Longman, 2002.

Crouch, David. 'Writing a Biography in the Thirteenth Century: The Construction and Composition of the "History of William Marshal"'. In *Writing Medieval Biography: Essays in Honour of Frank Barlow.* Ed. David Bates, Julia Crick, and Sarah Hamilton. Woodbridge, Suffolk: Boydell Press, 2006. 221-35.

Curley, Michael J. *Geoffrey of Monmouth.* New York: Twayne, 1994.

Dailey, Alice. *The English Martyr: From Reformation to Revolution.* Notre Dame, IN: University of Notre Dame Press, 2012.

Delany, Sheila. '"Mothers To Think Back Through": Who Are They? The Ambiguous Example of Christine de Pizan'. In *Medieval Texts and Contemporary Readers.* Ed. Laurie Finke and Martin Schichtman. Ithaca, NY: Cornell University Press, 1987. 312-28.

Delany, Sheila. *The Naked Text: Chaucer's Legend of Good Women.* Berkeley, CA: University of California Press, 1994.

Delany, Sheila. *Impolitic Bodies: Poetry, Saints, and Society in Fifteenth-Century England.* Oxford: Oxford University Press, 1998.

Delehaye, Hippolyte. *Legends of the Saints.* Trans. Donald Attwater. New York: Fordham University Press, 1962.

Dinshaw, Carolyn. *How Soon is Now? Medieval Texts, Amateur Readers, and the Queerness of Time.* Durham, NC: Duke University Press, 2012.

Dor, Juliette, Lesley Johnson, and Jocelyn Wogan-Browne, eds. *New Trends in Feminine Spirituality: The Holy Women of Liège and Their Impact.* Turnhout, Belgium: Brepols, 1999.

Duby, Georges. *William Marshal: The Flower of Chivalry.* Trans. Richard Howard. New York: Pantheon, 1986.

Dulac, Liliane and Christine Reno. 'The *Livre de ladvision Cristine*'. In *Christine de Pizan: A Casebook.* Ed. Barbara K. Altmann and Deborah L. McGrady. New York: Rutledge, 2003. 199-214.

Eakin, Paul John. *How Our Lives Become Stories: Making Selves.* Ithaca, NY: Cornell University Press, 1999.

Echard, Siân. *Arthurian Narrative and the Latin Tradition.* Cambridge, UK: Cambridge University Press, 1998.

Echard, Siân, ed. *The Arthur of Medieval Latin Literature: The Development and Dissemination of the Arthurian Legend in Medieval Latin.* Cardiff: University of Wales Press, 2011.

Edwards, A. S. G. 'John Shirley, John Lydgate, and the Motives of Compilation'. *Studies in the Age of Chaucer* 38 (2016): 245-54.

Edwards, Robert R. *Chaucer and Boccaccio: Antiquity and Modernity.* New York: Palgrave, 2002.

Elkins, Sharon K. *Holy Women of Twelfth-Century England.* Chapel Hill, NC: University of North Carolina Press, 1988.

Fanous, Samuel. 'Christina of Markyate and the Double Crown'. In *Christina of Markyate: A Twelfth-Century Holy Woman.* Ed. Samuel Fanous and Henrietta Leyser. London: Routledge, 2005. 53-78.

Fanous, Samuel and Henrietta Leyser, eds. *Christina of Markyate: A Twelfth-Century Holy Woman.* London: Routledge, 2005.

Fenton, Kirsten A. *Gender, Nation and Conquest in the Works of William of Malmesbury.* Woodbridge, Suffolk: Boydell and Brewer, 2008.

Ferster, Judith. *Fictions of Advice: The Literature and Politics of Counsel in Late Medieval England.* Philadelphia, PA: University of Pennsylvania Press, 1996.

Finke, Laurie A. and Martin Shichtman. *King Arthur and the Myth of History.* Gainesville, FL: University Press of Florida, 2004.

Flint, Valerie I. J. 'The *Historia Regum Britanniae* of Geoffrey of Monmouth: Parody and Its Purpose. A Suggestion'. *Speculum* 54 (1979): 447-68.

Foot, Sarah. 'Finding the Meaning in Form: Narrative in Annals and Chronicles'. In *Writing Medieval History*. Ed. Nancy Partner. London: Hodder Education, 2005. 88-108.

Foster, Allyson. 'A *Shorte Treatyse of Contemplacyon: The Book of Margery Kempe* in its Early Print Contexts'. In *A Companion to The Book of Margery Kempe*. Ed. John H. Arnold and Katherine J. Lewis. Cambridge, UK: D. S. Brewer, 2004. 95-112.

Foster, Michael. 'On Dating the Duchess: The Personal and Social Context of *Book of the Duchess*'. *Review of English Studies* 59 (2008): 185-96.

Frank, Robert Worth, Jr. *Chaucer and the Legend of Good Women.* Cambridge, MA: Harvard University Press, 1972.

Frank, Roberta. 'The *Beowulf* Poet's Sense of History'. In *The Wisdom of Poetry*. Ed. Larry D. Benson and Siegfried Wenzel. Kalamazoo, MI: Medieval Institute Press, 1982. 53-65.

Franklin, Margaret. *Boccaccio's Heroines: Power and Virtue in Renaissance Society.* Burlington, VT: Ashgate, 2006.

Fredeman, Jane C. 'The Life of John Capgrave, O. E. S. A. (1393-1464)'. *Augustiniana* 29 (1979): 197-237.

Fredeman, Jane C. 'Style and Characterization in John Capgrave's *Life of St. Katherine*'. *Bulletin of the John Rylands Library* 62 (1980): 346-87.

Friesen, Bill. 'The *Opus Geminatum* and Anglo-Saxon Literature'. *Neophilologus* 95 (2011): 123-44.

Fuchs, Miriam and Craig Howes, eds. *Teaching Life Writing Texts.* New York: The Modern Language Association of America, 2008.

Fulk, R. D., ed. *Interpretations of* Beowulf: *A Critical Anthology.* Bloomington, IN: Indiana University Press, 1991.

Geddes, Jane. 'The St Albans Psalter: The Abbot and the Anchoress'. In *Christina of Markyate: A Twelfth-Century Holy Woman*. Ed. Samuel Fanous and Henrietta Leyser. London: Routledge, 2005. 197-216.

Geddes, Jane, ed. *The St Albans Psalter: A Book for Christina of Markyate.* London: British Library, 2005.

Georgianna, Linda. '"In Any Corner of Heaven": Heloise's Critique of Monastic Life'. In *Listening to Heloise: The Voice of a Twelfth-Century Woman*. Ed. Bonnie Wheeler. New York: St. Martin's Press, 2000. 187-216.

Gerould, Gordon Hall. 'The Legend of St. Christina by William Paris'. *Modern Language Notes* 29 (1914): 129-33.

Gerrard, Daniel. 'Jocelin of Brakelond and the Power of Abbot Samson'. *Journal of Medieval History* 40 (2014): 1-23.

Getty, Laura J. '"Other smale ymaad before": Chaucer as Historiographer in the *Legend of Good Women*'. *Chaucer Review* 42 (2007): 48-75.

Gibson, Gail McMurray. *The Theater of Devotion: East Anglian Drama and Society in the Late Middle Ages.* Chicago: University of Chicago Press, 1989.

Gibson, Gail McMurray. 'Saint Anne and the Religion of Childbed: Some East Anglian Texts and Talismans'. In *Interpreting Cultural Symbols: Saint Anne in Late Medieval Society*. Ed. Kathleen Ashley and Pamela Sheingorn. Athens, GA: University of Georgia Press, 1990, 95–110.

Gibson, Margaret T. *Boethius: His Life, Thought, and Influence*. Oxford: Blackwell, 1981.

Given-Wilson, Chris. *Chronicles: The Writing of History in Medieval England*. London: Hambledon, 2004.

Goddard, Harold C. 'Chaucer's *Legend of Good Women*'. *Journal of English and Germanic Philology* 7 (1908): 87–129 and 8 (1909): 47–111.

Godden, Malcolm. 'Ælfric's Saints' Lives and the Problem of Miracles'. *Leeds Studies in English* 16 (1985): 83–101.

Goldie, Matthew Boyd. 'Psychosomatic Illness and Identity in London, 1416–1421: Hoccleve's Complaint and Dialogue with a Friend'. *Exemplaria* 11 (1999): 23–52.

Golding, Brian. *Gilbert of Sempringham and the Gilbertine Order, c. 1130–c. 1300*. Oxford: Clarendon Press, 1995.

Gransden, Antonia. 'Realistic Observation in Twelfth-Century England'. *Speculum* 47 (1972): 29–51.

Gransden, Antonia. *Historical Writing in England, c. 550–c. 1307*. Ithaca, NY: Cornell University Press, 1974.

Gransden, Antonia. 'Bede's Reputation as an Historian in Medieval England'. *Journal of Ecclesiastical History* 32 (1981): 397–425.

Gransden, Antonia. *Historical Writing in England, c. 1307 to the Early Sixteenth Century*. Ithaca, NY: Cornell University Press, 1982.

Gransden, Antonia. *A History of Bury St Edmunds, 1182–1256: Samson of Tottington to Edmund of Walpole*. Woodbridge, Suffolk: Boydell and Brewer, 2007.

Gray, Douglas, ed. *The Oxford Companion to Chaucer*. Oxford: Oxford University Press, 2003.

Greetham, D. C. 'Self-Referential Artifacts: Hoccleve's Persona as a Literary Device'. *Modern Philology* 86 (1989): 242–51.

Haarder, Andreas and T. A. Shippey, eds. *Beowulf: The Critical Heritage*. New York: Routledge, 1998.

Haney, Kristine. *The St. Albans Psalter: An Anglo-Norman Song of Faith*. New York: Peter Lang, 2002.

Hanning, Robert W. *The Vision of History in Britain from Gildas to Geoffrey of Monmouth*. New York: Columbia University Press, 1966.

Hansen, Elaine Tuttle. '"Of his love daungerous to me": Liberation, Subversion, and Domestic Violence in *The Wife of Bath's Prologue and Tale*'. In *The Wife of Bath*. Ed. Peter G. Beidler. Boston, MA: Bedford/St. Martin's, 1996. 273–89.

Hayward, Rebecca. 'Spiritual Friendship and Gender Difference in the *Liber confortatorius*'. In *Writing the Wilton Women: Goscelin's Legend of Edith and Liber confortatorius*. Ed. Stephanie Hollis. Turnhout, Belgium: Brepols, 2004. 341–53.

Hayward, Rebecca and Stephanie Hollis. 'The Female Reader in the *Liber confortatorius*'. In *Writing the Wilton Women: Goscelin's Legend of Edith and Liber confortatorius*. Ed. Stephanie Hollis. Turnhout, Belgium: Brepols, 2004. 385–99.

Head, Thomas. *Hagiography and the Cult of the Saints: The Diocese of Orléans, 800–1200*. Cambridge, UK: Cambridge University Press, 2005.

Head, Thomas. 'Hagiography', *The ORB: On-line Reference Book for Medieval Studies* (http://the-orb.arlima.net/encyclop/religion/hagiography/hagindex.html, accessed 28 August 2017).

Heffernan, Thomas J. *Sacred Biography: Saints and Their Biographers in the Middle Ages*. New York: Oxford University Press, 1988.

Heninger, S. K., Jr. 'The Margarite-Pearl Allegory in Thomas Usk's *Testament of Love*'. *Speculum* 32 (1957): 92-8.

Hill, John M. *The Narrative Pulse of Beowulf: Arrivals and Departures*. Toronto: University of Toronto Press, 2008.

Hill, Joyce. 'Carolingian Perspectives on the Authority of Bede'. In *Innovation and Tradition in the Writings of the Venerable Bede*. Ed. Scott DeGregorio. Morgantown, WV: West Virginia University Press, 2006. 227-49.

Hirsh, John C. *Hope Emily Allen: Medieval Scholarship and Feminism*. Norman, OK: Pilgrim Books, 1988.

Holbrook, Sue Ellen. 'Margery Kempe and Wynkyn de Worde'. In *The Medieval Mystical Tradition in England: Exeter Symposium IV*. Ed. Marion Glasscoe. Cambridge, UK: D. S. Brewer, 1987. 27-46.

Hollis, Stephanie. 'Goscelin's Writings and the Wilton Women'. In *Writing the Wilton Women: Goscelin's Legend of Edith and Liber confortatorius*. Ed. Stephanie Hollis. Turnhout, Belgium: Brepols, 2004. 217-44.

Hollis, Stephanie. 'Edith as Contemplative and Bride of Christ'. In *Writing the Wilton Women: Goscelin's Legend of Edith and Liber confortatorius*. Ed. Stephanie Hollis. Turnhout, Belgium: Brepols, 2004. 281-306.

Horobin, Simon. 'Politics, Patronage, and Piety in the Work of Osbern Bokenham'. *Speculum* 82 (2007): 932-49.

Howard, Donald R. *Chaucer: His Life, His Works, His World*. New York: Dutton, 1987.

Hunt, Tony. 'The *Life* of St Alexis, 475-1125'. In *Christina of Markyate : A Twelfth-Century Holy Woman*. Ed. Samuel Fanous and Henrietta Leyser. London: Routledge, 2005. 217-28.

Hurt, James R. *Ælfric*. Twayne's English Authors Series 131. New York: Twayne, 1972.

Hutton, Ronald. 'The Early Arthur: History and Myth'. In *The Cambridge Companion to the Arthurian Legend*. Ed. Elizabeth Archibald and Ad Putter. Cambridge, UK: Cambridge University Press, 2009. 21-35.

Innes, Matthew. 'The Classical Tradition in the Carolingian Renaissance: Ninth-Century Encounters with Suetonius'. *International Journal of the Classical Tradition* 3 (1997): 265-82.

James, Sarah. ' "Doctryne and Studie": Female Learning and Religious Debate in Capgrave's *Life of St. Katharine*'. *Leeds Studies in English*, n.s., 36 (2005): 275-302.

Jarman, Thomas L. *William Marshal: First Earl of Pembroke and Regent of England*. Oxford: Blackwell, 1930.

Jeanroy, Alfred. 'Boccace et Christine de Pisan: le *De claris mulieribus*, principale source du *Livre de la Cité des Dames*'. *Romania* 43 (1922): 93-105.

Jenkins, Jacqueline and Katherine J. Lewis, eds. *St. Katherine of Alexandria: Texts and Contexts in Western Medieval Europe*. Turnhout, Belgium: Brepols, 2003.

Jensen, Emily. ' "Winkers" and "Janglers": Teller/Listener/Reader Response in the "Monk's Tale," the Link, and the "Nun's Priest's Tale" '. *Chaucer Review* 32 (1997): 183-95.

Jeremy, Mary. 'Caxton's *Golden Legend* and Varagine's *Legenda Aurea*'. *Speculum* 21 (1946): 212-21.

Jolly, Margaretta. 'Biography and Autobiography'. In *Oxford Bibliographies: British and Irish Literature* (http://www.oxfordbibliographies.com). Last modified 20 September 2012.

Jordan, Constance. 'Boccaccio's In-Famous Women: Gender and Civic Virtue in the *De mulieribus claris*'. In *Ambiguous Realities: Women in the Middle Ages and Renaissance*. Ed. Carole Levin and Jeanie Watson. Detroit, MI: Wayne State University Press, 1987. 25-47.

Joy, Eileen A. and Mary K. Ramsey, eds. *The Postmodern Beowulf*. Morgantown, WV: West Virginia University Press, 2006.

Keeler, Laura. *Geoffrey of Monmouth and the Late Latin Chroniclers, 1300-1500*. Berkeley, CA: University of California Press, 1946.

Keene, Catherine. *Saint Margaret, Queen of the Scots: A Life in Perspective*. New York: Palgrave Macmillan, 2013.

Kelly, Joan. 'Early Feminist Theory and the *Querelle des Femmes*, 1400-1789'. *Signs* 8 (1982): 4-28.

Kiser, Lisa J. *Telling Classical Tales: Chaucer and the Legend of Good Women*. Ithaca, NY: Cornell University Press, 1982.

Klein, Stacy S. *Ruling Women: Queenship and Gender in Anglo-Saxon Literature*. Notre Dame, IN: University of Notre Dame Press, 2006.

Knapp, Ethan. *The Bureaucratic Muse: Thomas Hoccleve and the Literature of Late Medieval England*. University Park, PA: Pennsylvania State University Press, 2001.

Kolsky, Stephen. *The Genealogy of Women: Studies in Boccaccio's De mulieribus claris*. New York: Peter Lang, 2003.

Kolsky, Stephen. *The Ghost of Boccaccio: Writings on Famous Women in Renaissance Italy*. Turnhout, Belgium: Brepols, 2005.

Koopmans, Rachel. 'The Conclusion of Christina of Markyate's *Vita*'. *Journal of Ecclesiastical History* 51 (2000): 663-98.

Koopmans, Rachel. 'Dining at Markyate with Lady Christina'. In *Christina of Markyate: A Twelfth-Century Holy Woman*. Ed. Samuel Fanous and Henrietta Leyser. London: Routledge, 2005. 143-59.

Laistner, M. L. W. *A Hand-List of Bede Manuscripts*. Ithaca, NY: Cornell University Press, 1943.

Langdell, Sebastian James. '"What world is this? How vndirstande am I?" A Reappraisal of Poetic Authority in Thomas Hoccleve's *Series*'. *Medium Ævum* 78 (2009): 281-99.

Lapidge, Michael. 'The Saintly Life in Anglo-Saxon England'. In *The Cambridge Companion to Old English Literature*. Ed. Malcolm Godden and Michael Lapidge. Cambridge, UK: Cambridge University Press, 1991. 251-72.

Lapidge, Michael. 'Beowulf and the Psychology of Terror'. In *Heroic Poetry in the Anglo-Saxon Period: Studies in Honor of Jess B. Bessinger, Jr*. Kalamazoo, MI: Medieval Institute Publications, 1993. 373-402.

Lapidge, Michael. *Anglo-Latin Literature, 600-899*. London: Hambledon Press, 1996.

Leckie, R. W., Jr. *The Passage of Dominion: Geoffrey of Monmouth and the Periodization of Insular History in the Twelfth Century*. Toronto: University of Toronto Press, 1981.

Leclerq, Jean. *The Love of Learning and the Desire for God: A Study of Monastic Culture*. Trans. Catharine Misrahi. New York: Fordham University Press, 1961.

Lee, Hermione. *Biography: A Very Short Introduction*. Oxford: Oxford University Press, 2009.

Lejeune, Philippe. *On Autobiography*. Trans. Paul John Eakin and Katherine Leary. Minneapolis, MN: University of Minnesota Press, 1989.

Lerer, Seth. '*Beowulf* and Contemporary Critical Theory'. In *A Beowulf Handbook*. Ed. Robert E. Bjork and John D. Niles. Lincoln, NE: University of Nebraska Press, 1997. 325-39.

Lewis, Gertrud Jaron. *By Women, for Women, about Women: The Sister-Books of Fourteenth-Century Germany*. Toronto: Pontifical Institute of Mediaeval Studies, 1996.

Lewis, Katherine J. *The Cult of St Katherine of Alexandria in Late Medieval England*. Woodbridge, Suffolk: Boydell Press, 2000.

Lewis, Katherine J. 'Edmund of East Anglia, Henry VI and Ideals of Kingly Masculinity'. In *Holiness and Masculinity in the Middle Ages*. Ed. P. H. Cullum and K. J. Lewis. Cardiff: University of Wales Press, 2004. 158-74.

Lewis, Katherine J. 'Margery Kempe and Saint Making in Later Medieval England'. In *A Companion to the Book of Margery Kempe*. Ed. John H. Arnold and Katherine J. Lewis. Woodbridge, Suffolk: D. S. Brewer, 2004. 195-215.

Lewis, Katherine J. *Kingship and Masculinity in Late Medieval England*. New York: Routledge, 2013.

Lewis, Lucy. 'The Identity of Margaret in Thomas Usk's *Testament of Love*'. *Medium Ævum* 68 (1999): 63-72.

Leyerle, John. 'The Interlace Structure of *Beowulf*'. *University of Toronto Quarterly* 17 (1967): 1-17.

Liuzza, Roy Michael. 'On the Dating of *Beowulf*'. In *Beowulf: Basic Readings*. Ed. Peter S. Baker. New York: Garland, 1995. 281-306.

Lloyd-Morgan, Ceridwen. 'The Celtic Tradition'. In *The Arthur of the English: The Arthurian Legend in Medieval English Life and Literature*. Ed. W. R. J. Barron. Cardiff: University of Wales Press, 2001. 1-9.

Loomis, Grant. 'The Growth of the St Edmund Legend'. *Harvard Studies and Notes in Philology, Language and Literature* 14 (1932): 83-113.

Lovatt, Roger. 'John Blacman: Biographer of Henry VI'. In *The Writing of History in the Middle Ages: Essays Presented to Richard William Southern*. Ed. R. H. C. Davis and J. M. Wallace-Hadrill. Oxford: Clarendon Press, 1981. 415-44.

Lovatt, Roger. 'A Collector of Apocryphal Anecdotes: John Blacman Revisited'. In *Property and Politics: Essays in Later Medieval English History*. Ed. Tony Pollard. New York: St. Martin's Press, 1984. 172-97.

Lowes, John Livingston. 'Is Chaucer's *Legend of Good Women* a Travesty?' *Journal of English and Germanic Philology* 8 (1909): 513-69.

Lucas, Peter J. *From Author to Audience: John Capgrave and Medieval Publication*. Dublin: University College Dublin Press, 1997.

McDonald, Nicole F. 'Chaucer's *Legend of Good Women*, Ladies at Court and the Female Reader'. *Chaucer Review* 35 (2000): 22-42.

McGuire, Brian Patrick. 'The Collapse of a Monastic Friendship: The Case of Jocelin and Samson of Bury'. *Journal of Medieval History* 4 (1978): 369-97.

McGuire, Brian Patrick. *Friendship & Community: The Monastic Experience, 350-1250*. Kalamazoo, MI: Cistercian Publications, 1988.

McLaughlin, Mary M. 'Abelard as Autobiographer: The Motives and Meaning of His "Story of Calamities"'. *Speculum* 42 (1967): 463-88.

McLeod, Glenda. *Virtue and Venom: Catalogs of Women from Antiquity to the Renaissance.* Ann Arbor, MI: University of Michigan Press, 1991.

Mann, Nicholas. *Petrarch.* Oxford: Oxford University Press, 1984.

Mann, Nicholas. 'From Laurel to Fig: Petrarch and the Structures of the Self'. *Proceedings of the British Academy* 105 (2000): 17–49.

Marenbon, John. *Boethius.* Oxford: Oxford University Press, 2003.

Mason, Mary G. 'The Other Voice: Autobiographies of Women Writers'. In *Autobiography: Essays Theoretical and Critical.* Ed. James Olney. Princeton, NJ: Princeton University Press, 1980. 207–35.

Matthew, Donald. 'The Incongruities of the St Albans Psalter'. *Journal of Medieval History* 34 (2008): 396–416.

Matthews, Stephen. 'The Content and Construction of the Vita Haroldi'. In *King Harold II and the Bayeux Tapestry.* Ed. Gale R. Owen-Crocker. Woodbridge, Suffolk: Boydell & Brewer, 2005. 65–73.

Medcalf, Stephen. 'Inner and Outer'. In *The Later Middle Ages.* Ed. Stephen Medcalf, 108–71. New York: Holmes and Meier, 1981.

Meyer-Lee, Robert J. 'Hoccleve and the Apprehension of Money'. *Exemplaria* 13.1 (2001): 173–214.

Meyer-Lee, Robert J. *Poets and Power from Chaucer to Wyatt.* Cambridge, UK: Cambridge University Press, 2007.

Minnis, Alastair J. 'The Legend of Good Women'. In *Oxford Guides to Chaucer: The Shorter Poems.* Ed. Alastair J. Minnis, with V. J. Scattergood and J. J. Smith. Oxford: Clarendon Press, 1995. 322–454.

Minnis, Alastair J., with V. J. Scattergood and J. J. Smith, eds. *Oxford Guides to Chaucer: The Shorter Poems.* Oxford: Clarendon Press, 1995.

Minnis, Alastair and Rosalynn Voaden, eds. *Medieval Holy Women in the Christian Tradition, c.1100–c.1500.* Turnhout, Belgium: Brepols, 2010.

Misch, Georg. *Geschichte der Autobiographie.* Leipzig: G. B. Teubner, 1959.

Mitchell, J. Allan. *Ethics and Eventfulness in Middle English Literature.* New York: Palgrave Macmillan, 2009.

Mitchell, Marea. *The Book of Margery Kempe: Scholarship, Community, and Criticism.* New York: Peter Lang, 2005.

Moore, R. I. 'Ranulf Flambard and Christina of Markyate'. In *Christina of Markyate: A Twelfth-Century Holy Woman.* Ed. Samuel Fanous and Henrietta Leyser. London: Routledge, 2005. 138–59.

Morey, Robert. 'Beowulf's Androgynous Heroism'. *Journal of English and Germanic Philology* 95 (1996): 486–96.

Morrison, Susan S. 'The Use of Biography in Medieval Literary Criticism: The Case of Geoffrey Chaucer and Cecily Chaumpaigne'. *Chaucer Review* 34 (1999): 69–86.

Morse, Ruth. *The Medieval Medea.* Cambridge, UK: D. S. Brewer, 1996.

Mortimer, Nigel. *John Lydgate's Fall of Princes: Narrative Tragedy in its Literary and Political Contexts.* Oxford: Clarendon Press, 2005.

Mulder-Bakker, Anneke B. *Lives of the Anchoresses: The Rise of the Urban Recluse in Medieval Europe.* Trans. Myra Heerspink Scholz. Philadelphia, PA: University of Pennsylvania Press, 2005.

Nelson, Janet L. 'Did Charlemagne have a Private Life?' In *Writing Medieval Biography: Essays in Honour of Frank Barlow.* Ed. David Bates, Julia Crick, and Sarah Hamilton. Woodbridge, Suffolk: Boydell Press, 2006. 15–28.

Neufeld, Christine Marie. *Xanthippe's Sisters: Orality and Femininity in the Later Middle Ages*. PhD dissertation, McGill University, 2001.

Newman, Barbara. *From Virile Woman to Woman Christ*. Philadelphia, PA: University of Pennsylvania Press, 1995.

Newman, Barbara. 'Authority, Authenticity, and the Repression of Heloise'. In *From Virile Woman to Woman Christ*. Philadelphia, PA: University of Pennsylvania Press, 1995. 46-75.

Newman, Barbara. 'Three-Part Invention: The *Vita S. Hildegardis* and Mystical Hagiography'. In *Hildegard of Bingen: The Context of her Thought and Art*. Ed. Charles Burnett and Peter Dronke. London: Warburg Institute, 1998. 189-210.

Newman, Barbara, ed. *Voice of the Living Light: Hildegard of Bingen and Her World*. Berkeley, CA: University of California Press, 1998.

Newman, Barbara. 'Sibyl of the Rhine: Hildegard's Life and Times'. In *Voice of the Living Light: Hildegard of Bingen and Her World*. Ed. Barbara Newman. Berkeley, CA: University of California Press, 1998. 1-29.

Nisse, Ruth. '"Was it not routhe to Se?": Lydgate and the Styles of Martyrdom'. In *John Lydgate: Poetry, Culture, and Lancastrian England*. Ed. Larry Scanlon and James Simpson. Notre Dame, IN: University of Notre Dame Press, 2006. 279-98.

Nolan, Maura. '"Now wo, now gladnesses": Ovidianism in the *Fall of Princes*'. ELH 71 (2004): 531-58.

Nolan, Maura. 'Lydgate's Literary History: Chaucer, Gower, and Canacee'. *Studies in the Age of Chaucer* 27 (2005): 59-92.

Nowlin, Steele. 'The *Legend of Good Women* and the Affect of Invention'. *Exemplaria* 25 (2013): 16-35.

Olson, Linda and Kathryn Kerby-Fulton. *Voices in Dialogue: Reading Women in the Middle Ages*. Notre Dame, IN: University of Notre Dame Press, 2005.

Orchard, Andy. *A Critical Companion to Beowulf*. Cambridge, UK: D. S. Brewer, 2004.

Oswald, Dana M. '"Wigge under wætere": Beowulf's Revision of the Fight with Grendel's Mother'. *Exemplaria* 21 (2009): 63-82.

Owen-Crocker, Gale R., ed. *King Harold II and the Bayeux Tapestry*. Woodbridge, Suffolk: Boydell & Brewer, 2005.

Painter, Sidney. *William Marshal: Knight-errant, Baron, and Regent of England*. Baltimore, MD: Johns Hopkins University Press, 1933.

Parkes, Malcolm B. 'The Scriptorium of Wearmouth-Jarrow'. In *Scribes, Scripts, and Readers: Studies in the Communication, Presentation, and Dissemination of Medieval Texts*. London: Hambledon, 1991.

Partner, Nancy. *Serious Entertainments: The Writing of History in Twelfth-Century England*. Chicago: University of Chicago Press, 1977.

Partner, Nancy. 'Reading the Book of Margery Kempe'. *Exemplaria* 3 (1991): 29-66.

Partner, Nancy. 'The Family Romance of Guibert of Nogent: His Story/Her Story'. In *Medieval Mothering*. Ed. Bonnie Wheeler and John Carmi Parsons. New York: Garland, 1996. 357-77.

Partner, Nancy, ed. *Writing Medieval History*. London: Hodder Education, 2005.

Pearsall, Derek. *John Lydgate*. Charlottesville, VA: University Press of Virginia, 1970.

Pearsall, Derek. *Old and Middle English Poetry*. London: Routledge, 1977.

Pearsall, Derek. *The Life of Geoffrey Chaucer: A Critical Biography*. Oxford: Blackwell, 1992.

Pearsall, Derek. 'Hoccleve's *Regement of Princes*: The Poetics of Royal Self-Representation'. *Speculum* 69.2 (1994): 386–410.

Pearsall, Derek. *Arthurian Romance: A Short Introduction*. Oxford: Blackwell, 2003.

Percival, Florence. *Chaucer's Legendary Good Women*. Cambridge, UK: Cambridge University Press, 1998.

Perkins, Nicholas. *Hoccleve's Regiment of Princes: Counsel and Constraint*. Cambridge, UK: D. S. Brewer, 2001.

Perry, R. D. 'The Earl of Suffolk's French Poems and Shirley's Virtual Coteries'. *Studies in the Age of Chaucer* 38 (2016): 299–308.

Pfaff, Richard W. 'Bede among the Fathers? The Evidence from Liturgical Commemoration'. *Studia Patristica* 28 (1993): 225–9.

Philippy, Patricia. 'Establishing Authority: Boccaccio's *De claris mulieribus* and Christine de Pizan's *Livre de la Cité des Dames*'. *Romanic Review* 77 (1986): 167–93.

Poe, Elizabeth W. 'The *Vidas* and *Razos*'. In *A Handbook of the Troubadours*. Ed. F. R. P. Akehurst and Judith M. Davis. Berkeley, CA: University of California Press, 1995. 185–97.

Powell, Morgan. 'Making the Psalter of Christina of Markyate (The St. Albans Psalter)'. *Viator* 36 (2005): 293–336.

Prendergast, Thomas A. 'Chaucer's Doppelgänger: Thomas Usk and the Reformation of Chaucer'. In *Rewriting Chaucer: Culture, Authority, and the Idea of the Authentic Text, 1400–1602*. Ed. Thomas A. Prendergast and Barbara Kline. Columbus, OH: Ohio State University Press, 1999. 258–69.

Quilligan, Maureen. *The Allegory of Female Authority: A Commentary on Christine De Pizan's Livre de la Cité des Dames*. Ithaca, NY: Cornell University Press, 1991.

Ramazani, Jahan. 'Chaucer's Monk: The Poetics of Abbreviation, Aggression, and Tragedy'. *Chaucer Review* 27 (1993): 260–76.

Rand, E. K. 'On the History of the *De vita Caesarum* of Suetonius in the Early Middle Ages'. *Harvard Studies in Classical Philology* 37 (1926): 1–48.

Rauer, Christine. 'Female Hagiography in the *Old English Martyrology*'. In *Writing Women Saints in Anglo-Saxon England*. Ed. Paul Szarmach. Toronto: University of Toronto Press, 2014. 13–29.

Raven, Jesse R. *William the Marshal: The Last Great Feudal Baron*. London: P. Owen, 1962.

Reames, Sherry L. *The Legenda Aurea: A Reexamination of its Paradoxical History*. Madison, WI: University of Wisconsin Press, 1985.

Reed, Thomas L. *Middle English Debate Poetry and the Aesthetics of Irresolution*. Columbia, MO: University of Missouri Press, 1990.

Reno, Christine. 'Christine de Pizan: At Best a Contradictory Figure?' In *Politics, Gender and Genre: The Political Thought of Christine de Pizan*. Ed. Margaret Brabant. Boulder, CO: Westview, 1992. 171–91.

Reuter, Timothy, ed. *Alfred the Great: Papers from the Eleventh-Centenary Conferences*. Aldershot, UK, and Burlington, VT: Ashgate, 2003.

Riddy, Felicity. 'Text and Self in *The Book of Margery Kempe*'. In *Voices in Dialogue: Reading Women in the Middle Ages*. Ed. Linda Olson and Kathryn Kerby-Fulton. Notre Dame, IN: University of Notre Dame Press, 2005. 435–53.

Riddy, Felicity. 'Afterwords'. In *Voices in Dialogue: Reading Women in the Middle Ages*. Ed. Linda Olson and Kathryn Kerby-Fulton. Notre Dame, IN: University of Notre Dame Press, 2005. 454-7.

Rider, Jeff. 'Arthur and the Saints'. In *King Arthur through the Ages*. Ed. Valerie M. Lagorio and Mildred Leake Day. New York: Garland, 1990.

Ridyard, Susan J. *The Royal Saints of Anglo-Saxon England: A Study of West Saxon and East Anglian Cults*. Cambridge, UK: Cambridge University Press, 1988.

Roux, Suzanne. *Christine de Pizan: Femme de tête, dame de cœur*. Paris: Payot, 2006.

Rubenstein, Jay. *Guibert of Nogent: Portrait of a Medieval Mind*. New York: Routledge, 2002.

Rubenstein, Jay. 'Biography and Autobiography in the Middle Ages'. In *Writing Medieval History*. Ed. Nancy Partner. London: Hodder Arnold, 2005. 22-41.

Salih, Sarah. *Versions of Virginity in Late Medieval England*. Woodbridge, Suffolk: D. S. Brewer, 2001.

Salih, Sarah. 'Staging Conversion: The Digby Saint Plays and *The Book of Margery Kempe*'. In *Gender and Holiness: Men, Women and Saints in Late Medieval Europe*. Ed. Samantha J. E. Riches and Sarah Salih. London: Routledge, 2002. 121-34.

Sanok, Catherine. 'Reading Hagiographically: *The Legend of Good Women* and its Feminine Audience'. *Exemplaria* 13.2 (2001): 323-54.

Scanlon, Larry and James Simpson, eds. *John Lydgate: Poetry, Culture, and Lancastrian England*. Notre Dame, IN: University of Notre Dame Press, 2006.

Schuurman, Anne. 'Pity and Poetics in Chaucer's *Legend of Good Women*'. *PMLA* 130 (2015): 1302-17.

Semple, Benjamin. 'The Consolation of a Woman Writer: Christine de Pizan's Use of Boethius in *L'Avision-Christine*'. In *Women, the Book and the Worldly: Selected Proceedings of the St. Hilda's Conference, 1993*. Ed. Lesley Smith and Jane H. M. Taylor. Vol. 2. Cambridge, UK: D. S. Brewer, 1995. 39-48.

Seymour, M. C. 'The Manuscripts of Hoccleve's *Regiment of Princes*'. *Transactions of the Edinburgh Bibliographical Society* 4 (1974): 255-97.

Seymour, M. C. *John Capgrave*. Brookfield, VT: Ashgate, 1996.

Simpson, James. 'Nobody's Man: Thomas Hoccleve's *Regement of Princes*'. In *London and Europe in the Later Middle Ages*. Ed. Julia Boffey and Pamela King. Westfield Publications in Medieval Studies 9. London: Centre for Medieval and Renaissance Studies, Queen Mary and Westfield College, 1995. 149-80.

Simpson, James. *Reform and Cultural Revolution*. Oxford: Oxford University Press, 2002.

Sisk, Jennifer. 'Lydgate's Problematic Commission: A Legend of St. Edmund for Henry VI'. *Journal of English and Germanic Philology* 109 (2010): 349-75.

Skemp, Mary L. 'Autobiography and Authority in *Lavision-Christine*'. *Le Moyen français* 35 (1996): 17-31.

Skura, Meredith. 'A *Mirror for Magistrates* and the Beginnings of English Autobiography'. *English Literary Renaissance* 36 (2006): 26-56.

Sobecki, Sebastian. 'Lydgate's Kneeling Retraction: The *Testament* as a Literary Palinode'. *Chaucer Review* 49 (2015): 265-93.

Sobecki, Sebastian. '"The wryting of this tretys": Margery Kempe's Son and the Authorship of Her Book'. *Studies in the Age of Chaucer* 37 (2015): 257-83.

Somerset, Fiona. '"Hard is with seyntis for to make affray": Lydgate the "Poet-Propagandist" as Hagiographer'. In *John Lydgate: Poetry, Culture, and Lancastrian England*. Ed. Larry Scanlon and James Simpson. Notre Dame, IN: University of Notre Dame Press, 2006. 258-78.

Southern, R. W. *Saint Anselm: A Portrait in a Landscape*. Cambridge, UK: Cambridge University Press, 1990.

Spearing, A. C. *Textual Subjectivity: The Encoding of Subjectivity in Medieval Narratives and Lyrics*. Oxford: Oxford University Press, 2005.

Spearing, A. C. *Medieval Autographies: The 'I' of the Text*. Notre Dame, IN: University of Notre Dame Press, 2012.

Spencer, Alice. *Language, Lineage and Location in the Works of Osbern Bokenham*. Newcastle, UK: Cambridge Scholars, 2013.

Squire, Aelred. *Aelred of Rievaulx: A Study*. Kalamazoo, MI: Cistercian, 1981.

Stafford, Pauline. 'The Portrayal of Royal Women in England, Mid-Tenth to Mid-Twelfth Centuries'. In *Medieval Queenship*. Ed. John Carmi Parsons. New York: St. Martin's Press, 1993. 143-67.

Staley, Lynn. *Margery Kempe's Dissenting Fictions*. University Park, PA: Pennsylvania State University Press, 1994.

Stanbury, Sarah and Raguin, Virginia. *Mapping Margery Kempe: A Guide to Late Medieval Material and Spritual Life*. (http://college.holycross.edu/projects/kempe/, accessed 15 September 2017).

Staples, Kathryn Kelsey and Ruth Mazo Karras. 'Christina's Tempting: Sexual Desire and Women's Sanctity'. In *Christina of Markyate: A Twelfth-Century Holy Woman*. Ed. Samuel Fanous and Henrietta Leyser. London: Routledge, 2005. 184-96.

Stauffer, Donald. *English Biography Before 1700*. Cambridge, MA: Harvard University Press, 1930.

Stodnick, Jacqueline. 'Bodies of Land: The Place of Gender in the *Old English Martyrology*'. In *Writing Women Saints in Anglo-Saxon England*. Ed. Paul Szarmach. Toronto: University of Toronto Press, 2014. 30-52.

Stouck, Mary-Ann. 'Chaucer and Capgrave's *Life of St. Katherine*'. *American Benedictine Review* 33 (1982): 276-91.

Stouck, Mary-Ann. 'A Poet in the Household of the Beauchamp Earls of Warwick, c. 1393-1427'. *Warwickshire History* 9 (1994): 113-17.

Strohm, Paul. *Social Chaucer*. Cambridge, MA: Harvard University Press, 1989.

Strohm, Paul. 'Politics and Poetics'. In *Literary Practice and Social Change in Britain, 1380-1530*. Ed. Lee Patterson. Berkeley, CA: University of California Press, 1990. 83-112.

Strohm, Paul. 'The Textual Vicissitudes of Usk's "Appeal"'. In *Hochon's Arrow: The Social Imagination of Fourteenth-Century Texts*. Princeton, NJ: Princeton University Press, 1992. 145-57.

Strohm, Paul. *Politique: Languages of Statecraft between Chaucer and Shakespeare*. Notre Dame, IN: University of Notre Dame Press, 2005.

Strohm, Paul. *Chaucer's Tale: 1386 and the Road to Canterbury*. New York: Viking, 2014.

Summit, Jennifer. '"Stable in study": Lydgate's *Fall of Princes* and Duke Humphrey's Library'. In *John Lydgate: Poetry, Culture, and Lancastrian England*. Ed. Larry Scanlon and James Simpson. Notre Dame, IN: University of Notre Dame Press, 2006. 207-31.

Sweet, W. H. E. 'Lydgate's Retraction and "his resorte to his religyoun"'. In *After Arundel: Religious Writing in Fifteenth-Century England*. Ed. Vincent Gillespie and Kantik Ghosh. Turnhout, Belgium: Brepols, 2011. 343-59.

Szarmach, Paul, ed. *Writing Women Saints in Anglo-Saxon England*. Toronto: University of Toronto Press, 2014.

Tanner, Norman P. *The Church in Late Medieval Norwich, 1370-1532*. Toronto: Pontifical Institute of Medieval Studies, 1984.

Taylor, Beverly. 'The Medieval Cleopatra: The Classical and Medieval Tradition of Chaucer's *Legend of Cleopatra*'. *Journal of Medieval and Renaissance Studies* 7 (1977): 249-69.

Thornley, Eva M. 'The Middle English Penitential Lyric and Hoccleve's Autobiographical Poetry'. *Neuphilologische Mitteilungen* 68 (1967): 295-321.

Tolhurst, Fiona. *Geoffrey of Monmouth and the Feminist Origin of the Arthurian Legend*. New York: Palgrave, 2012.

Tolkien, J. R. R. '*Beowulf*: The Monsters and the Critics'. *Proceedings of the British Academy* 22 (1936): 245-95. Reprinted in *Beowulf: Modern Critical Interpretations*. Ed. Harold Bloom. New York: Chelsea House Publishers, 1987. 5-31.

Tolmie, Sarah. 'The Professional Thomas Hoccleve'. *Studies in the Age of Chaucer* 29 (2007): 341-73.

Travis, Peter. 'Deconstructing Chaucer's Retraction'. *Exemplaria* 3 (1991): 135-58.

Turner, Marion. *Chaucerian Conflict: Languages of Antagonism in Late Fourteenth-Century London*. Oxford: Clarendon Press, 2007.

Turner, Marion. 'Illness Narratives in the Later Middle Ages: Arderne, Chaucer, and Hoccleve'. *Journal of Medieval and Early Modern Studies* 46 (2016): 61-87.

Van Houts, Elisabeth. 'The Flemish Contribution to Biographical Writing in England in the Eleventh Century'. In *Writing Medieval Biography: Essays in Honour of Frank Barlow*. Ed. David Bates, Julia Crick, and Sarah Hamilton. Woodbridge, Suffolk: Boydell Press, 2006. 111-27.

van't Spijker, Ineke. 'Saints and Despair: Twelfth-Century Hagiography as "Intimate Biography"'. In *The Invention of Holiness*. Ed. Anneke B. Mulder-Bakker. London: Routledge, 2002. 185-205.

Vauchez, André. *Sainthood in the Later Middle Ages*. Trans. Jean Birrell. Cambridge, UK: Cambridge University Press, 1997.

Vincent, Nicholas. 'The Strange Case of the Missing Biographies: The Lives of the Plantagenet Kings of England, 1154-1272'. In *Writing Medieval Biography: Essays in Honour of Frank Barlow*. Ed. David Bates, Julia Crick, and Sarah Hamilton. Woodbridge, Suffolk: Boydell Press, 2006. 237-57.

Von Nolcken, Christina. '"O, why ne had y lerned for to die?": *Lerne for to Dye* and the Author's Death in Thomas Hoccleve's *Series*'. *Essays in Medieval Studies* 10 (1993): 27-51.

Wallace, David. 'Italy'. In *A Companion to Chaucer*. Ed. Peter Brown. Oxford: Blackwell, 2000. 218-34.

Walsh, Christine. *The Cult of St Katherine of Alexandria in Early Medieval England*. Burlington, VT: Ashgate, 2007.

Warren, Ann K. *Anchorites and Their Patrons in Medieval England*. Berkeley, CA: University of California Press, 1985.

Watson, Nicholas. 'Julian of Norwich'. In *Medieval Women's Writing*. Ed. Carolyn Dinshaw and David Wallace. Cambridge, UK: Cambridge University Press, 2003. 210-21.

Watson, Nicholas. 'The Making of *The Book of Margery Kempe*'. In *Voices in Dialogue: Reading Women in the Middle Ages*. Ed. Linda Olson and Kathryn Kerby-Fulton. Notre Dame, IN: University of Notre Dame Press, 2005. 395-434.

Watt, David. 'Compilation and Contemplation: Beholding Thomas Hoccleve's *Series* in Oxford, Bodleian Library, MS Selden Supra 53'. *Journal of the Early Book Society* 14 (2011): 1-39.

Weiler, Björn. 'William of Malmesbury on Kingship'. *History* 90 (2005): 3-22.

Whatley, E. Gordon, *et multi.* 'Acta Sanctorum'. In *Sources of Anglo-Saxon Literary Culture, Volume 1: Abbo of Fleury, Abbo of Saint-Germain-des-Prés, and Acta Sanctorum.* Ed. Frederick M. Biggs, Thomas Hill, Paul Szarmach, and E. Gordon Whatley. Kalamazoo, MI: Medieval Institute Publications, 2001. 22-486.

Wheeler, Bonnie, ed. *Listening to Heloise: The Voice of a Twelfth-Century Woman.* New York: St. Martin's Press, 2000.

Whitelock, Dorothy. 'Fact and Fiction in the Legend of St. Edmund'. *Proceedings of the Suffolk Institute of Archaeology* 31 (1969): 217-33.

Willard, Charity Cannon. *Christine de Pizan: Her Life and Works.* New York: Persea, 1984.

Wilson, Katharina M. and Elizabeth M. Makowski. *Wykked Wyves and the Woes of Marriage: Misogamous Literature from Juvenal to Chaucer.* Albany, NY: State University of New York Press, 1990.

Windeatt, Barry. 'Introduction: Reading and Re-reading *The Book of Margery Kempe*'. In *A Companion to The Book of Margery Kempe.* Ed. John H. Arnold and Katherine J. Lewis. Cambridge, UK: D. S. Brewer, 2004. 1-16.

Winstead, Karen A. 'Piety, Politics, and Social Responsibility in Capgrave's *Life of St. Katherine*'. *Medievalia et Humanistica*, n.s., 17 (1990): 59-80.

Winstead, Karen A. 'Lydgate's Lives of Saints Edmund and Alban: Martyrdom and "Prudent Pollicie"'. *Mediaevalia* 17 (1994): 221-41.

Winstead, Karen A. 'John Capgrave and the Chaucer Tradition'. *Chaucer Review* 30 (1996): 389-400.

Winstead, Karen A. *Virgin Martyrs: Legends of Sainthood in Late Medieval England.* Ithaca, NY: Cornell University Press, 1997.

Winstead, Karen A. '"I am al other to yow than yee weene": Hoccleve, Women, and the *Series*'. *Philological Quarterly* 72 (1999): 143-55.

Winstead, Karen A. *John Capgrave's Fifteenth Century.* Philadelphia, PA: University of Pennsylvania Press, 2007.

Winstead, Karen A. 'Osbern Bokenham's "englische boke": Re-forming Holy Women'. In *Form and Reform: Reading Across the Fifteenth Century.* Ed. Shannon Gayk and Kathleen Tonry. Columbus, OH: Ohio State University Press, 2011. 67-87.

Wogan-Browne, Jocelyn. *Saints' Lives and Women's Literary Culture, 1150-1300: Virginity and its Authorizations.* Oxford: Oxford University Press, 2001.

Yohe, Katherine TePas. 'Aelred's Recrafting of the Life of Edward the Confessor'. *Cistercian Studies Quarterly* 38 (2003): 177-89.

Yorke, Barbara. '"Carriers of the Truth": Writing the Biographies of Anglo-Saxon Female Saints'. In *Writing Medieval Biography: Essays in Honour of Frank Barlow.* Ed. David Bates, Julia Crick, and Sarah Hamilton. Woodbridge, Suffolk: Boydell Press, 2006. 49-60.

Zumthor, Paul. 'Autobiography in the Middle Ages?' *Genre* 6 (1973): 29-48.

Index